THE GOVERNMENT OF PRINCE EDWARD ISLAND

CANADIAN GOVERNMENT SERIES

R. MacG. Dawson, *Editor*

1. DEMOCRATIC GOVERNMENT AND POLITICS
   By J. A. CORRY

2. THE GOVERNMENT OF CANADA
   By R. MACGREGOR DAWSON

3. CONSTITUTIONAL AMENDMENT IN CANADA
   By PAUL GÉRIN-LAJOIE

4. THE CANADIAN HOUSE OF COMMONS: REPRESENTATION
   By NORMAN WARD

5. THE GOVERNMENT OF PRINCE EDWARD ISLAND
   By FRANK MACKINNON

THE GOVERNMENT OF
PRINCE EDWARD ISLAND

BY

FRANK MacKINNON
M.A., Ph.D., LL.D.
*Principal, Prince of Wales College
Charlottetown*

TORONTO
UNIVERSITY OF TORONTO PRESS
1951

Copyright, Canada, 1951
University of Toronto Press
Printed in Canada
London: Geoffrey Cumberlege
Oxford University Press

TO MY WIFE

FOREWORD

THIS IS the first book ever written about the government of a province of Canada. It is hoped that the Canadian Government Series will eventually include a similar study for each of the ten provinces.

One of the shocking facts about Canadian politics is that even such major political units as the provinces rarely know what one another is doing and, it might be added, seem to care less. Few provinces, if any, have a complete file of the other provinces' publications, and no effort has been made (such as a scheme of automatic interchanges) to obtain constant as opposed to sporadic information on all phases of provincial activity. Even the provincial legislative libraries have been lukewarm in their efforts to secure material of this kind, despite the fact that a very large portion of it deals with problems which are common to all provinces.

The Government of Prince Edward Island and similar volumes should make a notable contribution along these lines by informing other parts of Canada how a particular province conducts its government. It is not uncharitable to assume that this book will also add greatly to the knowledge which the people of Prince Edward Island have of their own political history and institutions. For a large part of the material has been rescued from the obscurity of the archives, and a substantial amount is derived from such intangible and elusive sources as the usages of the province and the habits of mind of its inhabitants.

Prince Edward Island is, of course, by far the smallest of the Canadian provinces both in area and in population, but in terms of constitutional interest it is well up near the top. Things have been done there—and are still being done—which make the hair of constitutional authorities stand on end, while in some respects (such as the written records of Cabinet meetings) the Island government has taken the lead and anticipated developments which have later occurred in other much more august bodies. But despite a certain awkwardness in trying to apply rules of cabinet government to a small population operating over a very limited area and despite occasional lapses from strict constitutional perfection, Prince Edward Island has furnished a most interesting example of the practical working out of the ideas of democratic government within the general traditions of the British people.

R. MacGregor Dawson

PREFACE

THE GOVERNMENT of Prince Edward Island illustrates the operation of an elaborate constitution in a small place. The same system which functions in the large and populous parts of the British Commonwealth has developed in a tiny and isolated province which boasts few economic advantages and a population of only 90,000 people, and has resulted in an unusual example of local democracy. The turbulent political history of the Island in the early years and the nature of her institutions of government have resulted, not only from the normal growth of the parliamentary system, but also from the difficult process of adjusting that system to the local environment. The purpose of this book is to outline the development of the Island's public affairs in the colonial period and to describe the political institutions and the characteristics of provincial government and politics. It is appropriate that the book should appear on the one hundredth anniversary of the granting of responsible government to the province.

The scarcity of secondary material on Prince Edward Island history and the complete absence of any description of provincial politics has required several years of research on official documents, journals, and contemporary newspapers, and many discussions with local public men. I must acknowledge with grateful thanks the kindness which I have received from those who have given me material and information.

Miss Nora Storey and her staff in the manuscript room of the Public Archives of Canada, Mr. F. A. Hardy and his assistants in the Library of Parliament at Ottawa, and Miss Jean Gill of the Charlottetown Public Library have always been most generous in placing their facilities and material at my disposal. I am also indebted to numerous Prince Edward Island public officials for their patience and courtesy in supplying government documents and answering the endless questions which I have asked them. Professor Alexander Brady of the University of Toronto and Dr. Eugene Forsey of Ottawa have read the manuscript and made many useful suggestions. The editorial staff of the University of Toronto Press have been most helpful and efficient during the preparation of the book for the printers. The Social Science Research Council of Canada has assisted financially the publication of this work, and the author, along with others in the social sciences, owes much to the Council's interest and encouragement.

It is a particular pleasure to acknowledge the guidance of Professor Robert MacGregor Dawson of the University of Toronto. Dr. Dawson has carefully read and re-read every chapter of the book, and his expert advice and frank criticism have been generous, stimulating, and immensely valuable.

Above all I am indebted to my wife who for years has tolerated a houseful of papers and books and has given me constant encouragement in my work. To her this book is affectionately dedicated.

F. M.

CONTENTS

FOREWORD. *By* R. MACGREGOR DAWSON vii

PREFACE ix

PART I. COLONIAL GOVERNMENT

I   Early Government 3

II   Colonial Institutions 21

III   Responsible Government 61

IV   Constitutional Adjustment, 1851-1873 86

V   The Land Question 105

VI   Confederation 120

PART II. PROVINCIAL GOVERNMENT

VII   The Lieutenant-Governor 143

VIII   The Cabinet 168

IX   The Administration 195

X   The Legislature 210

XI   Political Parties 242

XII   The Judiciary 259

XIII   Local Government 274

XIV   The Province and the Dominion 287

CONTENTS

APPENDICES

A   Commission to Governor Walter Patterson, August 4, 1769 . 319

B   Instructions to Governor Walter Patterson, August 4, 1769 . 327

C   Sections of the British North America Act Affecting the Government of Prince Edward Island 344

D   Documents Respecting the Entrance of Prince Edward Island into Confederation 353

E   The Lieutenant-Governors of Prince Edward Island from 1769 to Confederation 362

F   The Lieutenant-Governors of Prince Edward Island since Confederation 363

G   The Premiers of Prince Edward Island from the Granting of Responsible Government to Confederation 364

H   The Premiers of Prince Edward Island since Confederation . 365

BIBLIOGRAPHY 367

INDEX 373

PART I

COLONIAL GOVERNMENT

CHAPTER I

EARLY GOVERNMENT

THE TURMOIL of Prince Edward Island's early political history is in striking contrast to the size of the province. That local administration flourished at all was a miracle; that it developed slowly and painfully was inevitable under the series of unfortunate circumstances which plagued the Island for more than a century. Government, consequently, was often a farce in colonial times, and the resulting anomalies left their mark upon all the political institutions. The early difficulties were not without advantages, however, for what was gained by many mistakes and severe lessons was later treasured, and it became manifest in profound respect for local self-government, however limited in extent and influence the latter might be. The chief reason for the inauspicious beginning was that government started too early and on too ambitious a scale. When the British type of constitution was assigned to the Island the environment was not prepared to receive it.

"History passed it by," said Stephen Leacock of Prince Edward Island in its earliest years.[1] Île Saint-Jean, as the French called it, was of slight significance in the colonial rivalry of France and England. Neither knew what to do with it; nor were they concerned with its fate so long as it did not become a source of embarrassment. It was too small and isolated to be significant, and yet too strategically situated in the Gulf of St. Lawrence to be ignored. Until 1713 it played an obscure role as a fisheries concession to certain French colonial enterprisers; after that date it was a forlorn outpost for Louisbourg which treated it with a neglect commensurate with the indifference of the home government in Paris. The few French settlers who crossed to the Island from Acadia suffered famine and plague during a series of unsuccessful attempts to establish settlements. The colony fell to the British in 1745, to the French again in 1748, and finally to the British a decade later. When French rule came to an end, most of the Acadians moved away or were deported. The two or three hundred who remained had not had

[1]Stephen Leacock, *Canada* (Montreal, 1941), p. 90.

sufficient opportunity to develop the essential factors of a community—a stable population, a culture, industries, and communications. When the British assumed control after the Treaty of Paris of 1763 there was no established tradition, either French or British, upon which to build a government.[1] The Imperial authorities, lacking a policy, temporized by annexing the colony to Nova Scotia. The apparent value of the fisheries nevertheless suggested immediate investigation, and the Island was the first part of the territory in North America to be surveyed by Captain Samuel Holland, the King's Surveyor, in 1764.

The British Government was quite determined on one point: the Island was not sufficiently important to justify any drain on His Majesty's Treasury. A scheme was therefore sought which would pass over the administration to someone who would assume both the responsibility and the expense. One proposal was that of the Earl of Egmont, then First Lord of the Admiralty. He petitioned the King for a grant of the whole Island, and suggested that it be granted to "Peers, great Commoners, eminent merchants, and other Gentlemen of Distinction," and organized on a feudal basis with hundreds, manors, and freeholds complete with courts baron and lords of the manor.[2] This and other similar schemes were rejected on the ground that feudalism along these lines would be impractical. Instead, the Government adopted a plan which called for a survey of the Island and its division into counties, parishes, and townships, and the distribution of grants of land directly and separately to persons deserving the patronage of the Crown. An essential part of the arrangement was that it should provide the Treasury with a substantial revenue from quit rents.[3] After His Majesty had approved this apparently simple and remunerative proposal, the Island was surveyed and divided into sixty-seven lots. All but two of these were distributed among petitioners who claimed the King's favour, in a way which indicated

---

[1]See D. C. Harvey, *The French Régime in Prince Edward Island* (New Haven, 1926).
[2]Memorial of John, Earl of Egmont to the King, Public Archives of Canada, Colonial Office Records (P.E.I.), A series, vol. 1, p. 1.
[3]Report of the Board of Trade, March 23, 1764, *ibid.*, p. 67.

that concern for the welfare of the colony was as small as the grantees' limited knowledge of their new lands.¹

The first government of St. John's Island was the result of a misunderstanding. When the new grants were made, the Imperial authorities determined to entrust Lord William Campbell, the Governor of Nova Scotia, with the task of making some temporary arrangements for settlement until the proprietors were able to assume the development of their holdings. Campbell, however, was on leave of absence, and the instructions were sent to his Lieutenant-Governor, Michael Francklin. Lord Hillsborough, the Colonial Secretary, in a confusing despatch, ordered Francklin to report on "the necessary establishment . . . taking care in the meantime to make such temporary Regulations" as would provide new settlers with "a full and complete participation of those benefits enjoyed by His Majesty's other subjects in the Continental Parts of Nova Scotia."² Francklin evidently misinterpreted the despatch and thought that he was expected to establish a new government on St. John's. Despite the objections of "some of the clearest headed members of the Council" he rushed "with too great zeal" into his misguided task.³ He sent to the Island a naval officer, a provost marshal, a registrar of deeds, and a clerk of the Crown, as well as a surveyor to prepare town sites and erect necessary buildings and a judge to establish a court of common pleas and supervise settlement. Charlottetown was selected as the capital, a choice originally recommended by Captain Holland because "as this side of the Island cannot have a fishery it may probably be thought expedient to indulge it with some particular privileges."⁴ This small establishment was designed by Francklin as primarily a commission of development rather than a government, for the opening up of the wilderness presented a more complicated task than the rule of a few scattered inhabitants.⁵

¹See also chapter v, *infra.*
²Hillsborough to Francklin, Feb. 26, 1768, Public Archives of Canada, Colonial Office Records (N.S.), A series, vol. 81, p. 135.
³Campbell to Hillsborough, Nov. 18, 1768, *ibid.*, A 84, p. 3.
⁴Duncan Campbell, *History of Prince Edward Island* (Charlottetown, 1875), p. 7.
⁵Francklin to Hillsborough, May 21, 1768, P.A.C. (N.S.), A 82, p. 59; May 26, 1768, *ibid.*, pp. 67-83; July 31, 1768, *ibid.*, A 83, p. 791.

When Hillsborough learned of Francklin's efforts he lost no time in advising the erring Lieutenant-Governor that the new establishment was "highly disapproved by the King" and was the result of "a total and entire misapprehension" of His Majesty's instructions. Francklin should merely have reported "his opinion what Establishments may be necessary in the future" and meanwhile confined himself to making necessary regulations. "His Majesty was so far from adopting any such Plan as that pursued by Mr. Francklin," wrote Hillsborough, "that it was in contemplation by what means a new Government could be so formed as that the expense should be entirely borne by the Grantees." The home Government even threatened to refuse payment of the expenses incurred by Francklin, and only forgave him after considering his "mistaken zeal for His Majesty's service" and the apologies of Governor Campbell.[1] The result of this unhappy mistake was the recall of the Island's officials to Halifax. A new plan for the administration of the colony was then considered.

Early in 1768 the fortunate recipients of grants of land on the Island proposed to the King that the colony be separated from Nova Scotia and given a government of its own. They stated:

That this Island must, if properly encouraged, become a place of great Trade, and of very considerable advantage both to Great Britain and the Colonies, as well from its convenient situation with regard to the Fisheries, and the fertility of the Soil, so well adapted to the production of Corn and Hemp, Masts and other Naval Stores, as from the Excellence of its Bays and Harbours. That notwithstanding these great natural Advantages the settlement of this Island will be very much retarded by its dependence on the Government of Nova Scotia, as no legal Decisions can be obtained nor any matters of Property determined without a tedious and expensive voyage to Halifax (where the Superior Courts of Judicature and all the Publick offices of Government are held) which during the Winter Months is impracticable on account of the Ice; this must unavoidably be attended with great Detriment both to the Trader and Planter. That many industrious and able Settlers are deterred by these considerations from bringing their Families and Property to a Place so circumstanced.

[1] Hillsborough to Campbell, Sept. 12, 1768, *ibid.*, p. 127.

That these inconveniences would be effectively remedied, and the settlement rendered speedy and certain if it should please Your Majesty to form this Island into a separate Government.[1]

His Majesty's advisers discussed this proposal with the proprietors and agreed to it provided "the expense attending the execution of the measures recommended might be defrayed without any additional Burthen upon this Kingdom."[2] The cost of the proposed separate government was to be met by quit rent payments for a period of ten years, that is, "until the Island should be in a state to provide for its own Establishment." A regulation of ominous portent provided "that in case the amount of them [the quit rents] should fall short of the intended Establishment, either by a failure of consent in any number of the Proprietors to the alteration now proposed in the conditions of their Grants, or hereafter by any other accident or defect whatever, the Salaries and Allowances to the Officers should be diminished in Proportion and no demand whatever brought either upon Parliament or upon the Treasury to make good such Deficiency."[3] It was expected that this arrangement would "not only facilitate the Settlement of this Island" but also secure "a very considerable Quit Rent, which will after a short period revert into Your Majesty's Treasury."[4] The King approved the plan on June 28, 1769.

Although the Island was to suffer great inconveniences from this arrangement, it nevertheless owed its independence and separate government to the proprietors. Perhaps they thought it would be more likely to prosper under its own administration. They may have noted that in previous cases of joint governorships, the weaker colony was generally neglected,[5] or considered that their own rights and privileges as landlords would be safer under a separate government than under one administered from Halifax. In any event their motives combined effectively with the Imperial Government's lack of interest in promoting change.

[1]Order-in-Council, June 28, 1769, P.A.C. (P.E.I.), A 1, p. 93.
[2]*Ibid.*, p. 95.   [3]*Ibid.*, p. 98.
[4]*Ibid.*, p. 99.
[5]Examples are discussed in A. B. Keith, *Constitutional History of the First British Empire* (Oxford, 1930), p. 189.

The attitude of the home Government is explained in part by circumstances in North America at the time. It was the crucial period between the end of the Seven Years' War and the American Revolution. The British public faced the war weariness and doubts which followed the first conflict, and its view of colonial affairs was easily clouded by these circumstances. Economy was needed, and the colonies were expected to bear part of the load. The plan for taxation in the colonies which could contribute was accompanied by the demand for frugality in those less favourably situated. Excessive governmental economy in St. John's Island thus went hand in hand with demands for taxes from the colonies to the south. Moreover, the restlessness which was to result in the American Revolution had its effect in other colonies as well. Home officials wanted stability in the colonies, and in testing times it might be needed in the new acquisition in the Gulf of St. Lawrence, only recently taken over from France. A few months after the Island's proprietors received their grants in 1767, Governor Carleton of Quebec had written home to the effect that the French seigniorial system in that province had "established Subordination . . . which preserved the internal Harmony . . . and secured Obedience to the Supreme Seat of Government from a very distant Province."[1] Hillsborough, the Colonial Secretary, held the same opinion.[2] It was not entirely strange, therefore, that the Colonial Office should have readily entertained at this time the petitions and proposals of the proprietors of St. John's. The rejection of freehold tenure for the Island can thus be ascribed in part to conditions and trends only remotely concerning the colony itself.

Proprietorships elsewhere had not, however, been particularly encouraging as precedents for the establishing of leasehold tenure on St. John's. In the "proprietary" type of colony (as distinct from the "royal" type which boasted direct control from the Crown) the dominant motif was feudalism, or what E. B. Greene called "the association of rights in the soil with rights of government."[3]

[1]Carleton to Shelbourne, Dec. 24, 1767, A. Shortt and A. G. Doughty, eds., *Documents Relating to the Constitutional History of Canada, 1759-1791* (Ottawa, 1918), vol. I, p. 289.
[2]*Ibid.*, p. 553.
[3]E. B. Greene, *The Provincial Governor* (New York, 1907), p. 9.

It was distinguished by the grant of a certain portion of the King's prerogative powers to one proprietor or a group of proprietors. The Governor, for example, was appointed by the proprietor, although generally such an appointment required royal approval, whereas in the royal type the Governor was appointed and instructed directly by the King. The weaknesses of the proprietary colonies lay in the fact that landlordism and administration went hand in hand. The proprietors identified their own affairs with the public interest, but more often than not the two clashed. The payment of the quit rent, for example, was frequently allowed to lapse, although its enforcement was obviously necessary for good government. With assemblies eager to replenish the public purse, the proprietors had to fight legislation designed to enforce quit rent payment. To complicate matters the Governor, who was the head of the administration, was sometimes a proprietor himself, or, failing that, the proprietors' agent, and, as such, he generally found himself among the contestants in a dispute between colonists and proprietor and reminded of his duty to both. Still more serious was the feeling, frequently prevalent in such systems, that the community welfare was being subordinated to the private fortunes of a few individuals, a situation by no means favourable to colonial development. "The proprietorships," wrote one authority, "were the weakest and on the whole the least satisfactory of the three forms of colonial government."[1]

The Order-in-Council of 1769 which authorized the establishment of a new government on Prince Edward Island indicated that since the colony was "almost wholly unsettled, and void of inhabitants," all it would need at the beginning in the way of institutions of government was a Governor, Council, and Supreme Court. Later, as conditions permitted, an Assembly would be added which would raise "such a permanent Revenue by proper Duties or Taxes as may amount to all the expenses of Government upon some certain Estimate." The order provided the sum of £1,470 annually to pay the expenses of the proposed establishment, which sum (as stated above) was to be defrayed by the quit rent for the

[1]H. L. Osgood, *American Colonies in the 18th Century*, quoted in Chester Martin, *Empire and Commonwealth* (Oxford, 1929), p. 17.

first ten years and afterwards by the colony itself. This modest provision was deemed sufficient for such a primitive colony even though the British authorities were depending on someone else to pay the bills. The personnel of this government was to consist of a Governor, Chief Justice, Secretary and Registrar, Attorney-General, Clerk of the Crown and Coroner, Provost Marshal, and Agent and Receiver of Quit Rents.[1]

The source of authority for the new constitution was the royal prerogative which enabled the King to establish governments in the colonies without any action by Parliament. His Majesty's initial commands with respect to the structure and details of government were contained in the Commission and Instructions which were issued to the first Governor and which formed the cornerstones of the constitution.

The Commission of Walter Patterson, the first Governor, appointed him Captain-General and Governor-in-Chief of St. John's and revoked the Commission of the Governor of Nova Scotia in so far as it affected the Island.[2] It set forth the powers attached to his office including those which enabled him to appoint a Council, summon an Assembly, and constitute courts, and provided for the devolution of government in case of His Excellency's death or absence from the colony. Detailed orders with respect to the exercise of the powers conferred by the Commission were provided in the accompanying Instructions. This document contained a set of rules by which the colony was to be governed, the annual estimates, regulations for the Council and the Assembly, certain instructions from the Bishop of London concerning the ecclesiastical policy of the Church of England, and other miscellaneous provisions.

"This the King's Commission," wrote Thomas Pownal, an early Governor of Massachusetts, "becomes the known, established constitution of that province which hath been established on it, and whose laws, courts, and whole frame of legislature and judi-

[1] Order-in-Council, June 28, 1769, P.A.C. (P.E.I.), A 1, p. 100.
[2] Patterson's Commission and Instructions are found in Public Archives of Canada, Commissions and Instructions (P.E.I.), 1766-1839, M series, vol. 593. They are reproduced here in Appendices A and B.

cature are founded on it: It is the charter of that province."¹ Walter Patterson's Commission was exactly that, and as His Majesty attached his signature on August 4, 1769, the British form of constitutional government was inaugurated on St. John's Island. It was obvious from the first that this experiment would be interesting and, at times, complicated. The small colony had only 271 inhabitants of whom 203 were non-British;² its natural resources were undeveloped; and its contacts with the outside world were few and uncertain. Yet all the trappings of government were provided, Governor, Lieutenant-Governor, Council, and Supreme Court, with an Assembly to be created in the immediate future.

Conditions on St. John's determined that the new government should have a very simple beginning. Governor Patterson took the oath of office in London on August 4, 1769, but the advanced season prevented him from proceeding to his post until the following spring. Upon his arrival he found that his first duty was to build a house "in such a manner as I hope will keep out a little of the approaching cold."³ Little could be done by way of administration because of the primitive state of the colony. The Chief Justice put in an appearance, but hastily returned to Halifax for the winter, "as he had neglected to lay in Provisions for himself and Family during the Summer; they must otherwise have been starved."⁴ Patterson hoped fervently that the Lieutenant-Governor would not come that year from England; "I dread the consequences if they do, as there is not a house for to put their Heads into, and if they do not bring Provisions to serve them until next June, they must absolutely starve, for there is not one loaf of Bread, nor Flower [sic] to make one, to be bought on the Island."⁵ These difficulties were similar to those encountered in the adjoining colonies. Colonel Philipps, an early Governor of Nova Scotia, had referred to his own administration as "hitherto no more than a Mock Government—Its authority haveing never yet extended

---

[1] Quoted by Greene, *The Provincial Governor*, p. 95.
[2] *P.E.I. House of Assembly Debates*, 1864, p. 33.
[3] Patterson to Hillsborough, Oct. 24, 1770, P.A.C. (P.E.I.), A 1, p. 156.
[4] *Ibid.*   [5] *Ibid.*

beyond cannon reach of this Fort."¹ Governor Patterson could not even boast a fort. Nevertheless he was optimistic. "I really think this Island," he wrote the Colonial Secretary, "if well nursed in its present infant state, may be made as usefull to Great Britain, and as plentyful within itself as any country of its size in North America; but to bring it to that, we will require Your Lordship's countenance and influence to procure some assistance for us, from our Mother Country."²

Patterson's optimism was severely tested during the first years of his administration. There were neither roads nor public buildings, labour was not available to build them, and the Governor faced the discouraging task of commencing public works without funds. He appealed to the Secretary of State, and, after months of correspondence, succeeded in obtaining a parliamentary grant of £1,500 for a church, court-house, and jail. Hillsborough encouraged him in his plans for such works "considering yourself at full Liberty in every respect but the Expense, which must be kept within the sum allowed, as any exceeding will consequently . . . be made good out of your own private fortune."³ This assistance, however, was not enough. No adequate provision had been made for the payment of the quit rents which were to meet the expenses of government, and the proprietors showed no inclination to pay without being pressed. Meanwhile, Patterson and his small group of officials received no salaries for more than five years. "Deprived by their Station of the advantages of a Peasant," complained the Governor, "they are obliged to support the appearances of gentlemen, without the means."⁴ The Chief Justice spent four years of hardship without remuneration, and finally died of gout and starvation;⁵ the Attorney-General was harassed by his many creditors in England;⁶ and petitions from embarrassed officials at Charlottetown arrived steadily at the Colonial Office. It was small

[1] Quoted in Martin, *Empire and Commonwealth*, p. 57.
[2] Patterson to Hillsborough, Oct. 24, 1770, P.A.C. (P.E.I.), A 1, p. 155.
[3] Hillsborough to Patterson, Dec. 4, 1771, *ibid.*, p. 276. See also Hillsborough to Patterson, March 6, 1771, *ibid.*, p. 192; Patterson to Hillsborough, Oct. 25, 1770, *ibid.*, p. 168.
[4] Patterson to Dartmouth, May 20, 1773, *ibid.*, A 2, p. 106.
[5] Patterson to Dartmouth, May 21, 1774, *ibid.*, p. 230.
[6] Michael Swan to Dartmouth, undated, 1772, *ibid.*, p. 86.

wonder that the Lieutenant-Governor postponed his departure from his home in Ireland, and the first Church of England clergyman resigned his charge rather than embark for the colony.[1]

Despite these difficulties the government made some progress. Upon his arrival Patterson called a meeting of some of the principal inhabitants of the Island, had his Commission read, and took and administered the necessary oaths. He forthwith appointed a Council which consisted of only seven members because he could not find enough suitable citizens to make up the complement of twelve provided by the Instructions. His Excellency and the Council, which included all the public officers in the colony, made the necessary policies and regulations for the administration of the Island in the period 1770-3. But this was government in name only, for there was much doubt as to whether the Governor and the Council could enact legislation without an Assembly.

The establishment of an Assembly was, the Instructions indicated, "a consideration that cannot be too early taken up, and ought to be maturely weighed; for until this object is attainable the most important interests of the inhabitants will necessarily remain without that advantage and protection which can only arise out of the vigour and activity of a complete constitution." The Governor was therefore instructed to study the possibilities of representative government in the light of local conditions and experience with assemblies in other colonies. But Patterson considered that the physical conditions of the Island, particularly with regard to communications, were so backward that a popular house was impracticable. The Colonial Secretary informed him, however, that regulations made by the existing government had no validity.[2] Other factors, meanwhile, were also making a meeting of an Assembly imperative. The question of revenue had dogged the administration from the beginning, and the chief financial difficulty was the enforcement of quit rents. The home Government was of the opinion that payments could never be enforced unless there

[1] Dartmouth to the Rev. Mr. Caulfield, Nov. 26, 1773, *ibid.,* p. 168; Caulfield to DesBrisay, April 12, 1774, *ibid.,* p. 202.
[2] Hillsborough to Patterson, Aug. 7, 1772, *ibid.,* p. 69; Dartmouth to Patterson, Nov. 4, 1772, *ibid.,* p. 76.

was an Assembly to pass the necessary legislation and that there would be less likelihood of demands on the Treasury for funds if the colony had an Assembly to look after the public purse.[1] The proprietors for their part admitted that the colony suffered distress from arrears in quit rents, but held that payments could not be enforced without an Assembly and that no meeting could be convened without adequate communications.[2] Yet such communications depended on funds, and the latter on the calling of an Assembly. In 1773, therefore, Patterson and the Council decided to take the decisive step, and the first Assembly was summoned for July 7 of that year.[3]

The Commission had given the Governor and the Council the power to constitute as many courts of justice as they thought "fit and necessary for the hearing and determining of all causes, as well criminal as civil, according to law and equity," and to appoint judges and other necessary officials; while the Instructions ordered the Governor to see that the colonists obtained "that privilege and protection which the British constitution allows them in all parts of our dominions" and to ensure that "justice be administered in the most speedy and effectual way." To this end a Supreme Court of judicature was established by the King on September 24, 1770, and His Majesty appointed John Duport, a former Nova Scotia judge, Chief Justice "during our Will and Pleasure" and "with full power and lawful authority to hear, try, and determine all Pleas whatever, Civil, Criminal, and Mixed; according to the Laws, Statutes, and Customs of our Kingdom of England, and the Laws and usages of our said Island of Saint John not being repugnant thereto, and Executions of all Judgments of the said Court to award; and to make such Rules and orders in this said Court as may be found convenient and useful, and as near as may be agreeable to the Rules and Order of our Court of King's Bench, Com-

---

[1] Dartmouth to Patterson, Dec. 1, 1773, *ibid.*, p. 169; also copy of memorandum from Dartmouth Papers, *ibid.*, p. 175.
[2] Petition of Samuel Smith on behalf of the proprietors to Dartmouth, Dec. 30, 1772, *ibid.*, p. 82.
[3] The first Assembly confirmed the proceedings made under the ordinances of the Governor and Council prior to its establishment (13 Geo. III, c. 1), and also the past proceedings of the Supreme Court (13 Geo. III, c. 2).

mon Pleas, and Exchequer in England."¹ Appeals on writs of error were allowed from the Supreme Court to the Governor-in-Council when the amount concerned exceeded £300 sterling, and appeals from the Governor-in-Council to the King-in-Council were permitted when the amount concerned was more than £500 sterling.²

The establishment of the Council, the Assembly, and the Supreme Court was followed by a period of confusion as the three bodies and the Governor sought a degree of prestige and authority which their limited experience and primitive surroundings were as yet unable to command. These early administrators were obviously inexperienced. "The government being new," wrote Patterson, "there is not one precedent to direct me. I have not an officer about me, who was ever before in the civil line; they, therefore, know but little of forms, and I am sorry to say my own experience is not great, nor have I ought to recommend me, save industry and a strong desire of doing right."³ Administration consequently became more and more difficult until the Colonial Office became convinced that "it is now too plain that those who solicited the establishment of Government . . . were greatly deceived in their expectations."⁴

Isolation added to this confusion. Colonial officials were required to conform to the general pattern of Imperial politics, and their activities were subjected to the scrutiny of the Colonial Office. The time consumed by the passage of official despatches back and forth across the Atlantic led to delay and uncertainty. Patterson's impatience was reflected in his periodic requests for leave of absence to go to London. "I would be of more service to the Island by spending a little time among the Proprietors at home, than I can possibly be of in the same space by remaining here."⁵ This attitude, common enough among Governors who felt that half

¹Commission to John Duport as Chief Justice, dated Sept. 24, 1770, P.A.C. (P.E.I.), A 1, p. 157.
²See John Stewart, *An Account of Prince Edward Island* (London, 1806), p. 285.
³Patterson to Germain, June 9, 1781, P.A.C. (P.E.I.), A 4, p. 194.
⁴Germain to Callbeck, April 1, 1776, *ibid.*, A 3, p. 126.
⁵Patterson to Dartmouth, Sept. 2, 1774, *ibid.*, A 2, p. 249.

the difficulty of colonial administration was keeping the Imperial authorities informed of distant problems, was a particular obsession with Patterson who considered that the opinions and attitudes of the proprietors carried more weight in London than those of the colonists.[1]

The tiny government had scarcely commenced when it disintegrated in the period 1775-85. The Governor went to England in 1775 on a year's leave of absence which lasted for five years. The American Revolution was in progress and shortly after his departure a group of Americans raided Charlottetown and kidnapped Philipps Callbeck, the Attorney-General, who was then administering the government, and kept him from his post until 1776. Chief Justice Duport died in January, 1776; the Provost Marshal and Collector of Revenue was away for four years; the Lieutenant-Governor, who had been appointed in 1769, had not yet arrived; and the Council and the Assembly were not functioning because of absenteeism and lack of salaries.[2]

Patterson in London and Callbeck on the Island vainly sought adequate financial aid from the British Government in their distress. The Imperial officials were by then convinced that a mistake had been made in setting up a separate government, and were "positively of opinion that the Government could not continue long on that footing."[3] Moreover they lost no opportunity of reminding local officials of the original arrangement whereby no demands were to be made on His Majesty's Treasury for the civil establishment of the Island. Patterson considered that the home authorities were being unduly stubborn. He stressed the defenceless state of the colony, the lack of attention on the part of the proprietors,

---

[1] Governor Carleton at Quebec had expressed similar views with respect to his province, and felt that he could accomplish more "by a Residence of a few months in London than of so many years in this Country." Carleton to Secretary of State, March 15, 1769; Shortt and Doughty, *Documents Relating to the Constitutional History of Canada, 1759-1791*, vol. I, p. 392.

[2] John Budd (Clerk of the Crown and Coroner) to Dartmouth, Nov. 25, 1775, P.A.C. (P.E.I.), A 3, p. 36; Callbeck to Dartmouth, Jan. 5, 1776, *ibid.*, p. 52, and Jan. 15, 1776, *ibid.*, p. 67; Stewart to Dartmouth, Dec. 8, 1775, *ibid.*, p. 38; Wright to Dartmouth, Dec. 15, 1775, *ibid.*, p. 40. See also Helen Jean Champion, "The Disorganization of the Government of Prince Edward Island during the American Revolutionary War," *Canadian Historical Review*, March, 1939, p. 37.

[3] Patterson to Dartmouth, undated, 1776, P.A.C. (P.E.I.), A 3, p. 102.

and, above all, the absence of funds and salaries. "After all," he said, "I cannot oblige a man to do his duty vigorously, who depends on Hope alone for the maintenance of his Family. . . . All this tends to make such a shadow of me in the Eyes of the People, that, I hope it will not be laid to my charge if the public business is not carried on with that vigour which is necessary for the good of His Majesty's Service, and the benefit of the country."[1]

The troubles of the tiny government were accentuated by an unusual amount of personal rivalry. The Governor's relations with the Lieutenant-Governor, Council, Assembly, and Chief Justice deteriorated rapidly after 1780 and the resulting controversies, which will be discussed in detail in the following chapter, did more than anything else to emphasize the need for reform. The Governor's alleged interference with the militia, manipulation of land grants, high-handed tactics with various officials, and lack of sympathy with the proprietors were the subject of numerous petitions for recall. The rivalry of cliques and compacts in the Council and the Assembly virtually stopped the effectiveness of those institutions, and the Supreme Court ceased to function with the suspension of the Chief Justice after a spectacular feud with Patterson. Administration ended in complete deadlock in 1784.

The patience of the Secretary of State had by this time become exhausted. For a small colony the Island had provided an ample share of problems at a time when the Imperial authorities were concerned with the aftermath of the American Revolution and the movement of the Loyalists to the remaining parts of British North America. It was now the intention of His Majesty's Government "to make arrangements of some magnitude for the better government of his remaining Possessions in North America."[2] As part of the general plan Nova Scotia was to be divided into two separate colonies, one of which became New Brunswick, and the unruly Island was to be re-annexed to the administration at Halifax. Although the government of St. John's was small, the mother country could scarcely permit its disputes to remain un-

[1]Patterson to Lord North, Nov. 15, 1783, *ibid.*, A 5, pp. 111-13.
[2]Copy of a letter (unsigned) from Whitehall to Patterson, dated June 8, 1784, *ibid.*, p. 172.

checked in an already troubled British America. To Patterson went the announcement from Whitehall:

> I think it proper to acquaint you, that as a part of the arrangement, His Majesty has, upon considering that the conditions upon which the Island of St. John was originally separated from that Province, have not been fulfilled, and that the Civil Establishment still continues a Burthen upon this country, thought fit to declare His Royal Intention of reducing the Island to a Lieutenant-Government, with a suitable Civil Establishment, and re-annex it to the Eastern part of Nova Scotia, permitting it notwithstanding to enjoy its present constitution, and remain under its own Jurisdiction.[1]

Patterson lodged an ineffective protest. He did not like being subordinated to Governor Parr of Nova Scotia who was his junior in the colonial service, and thought that his position would be "lessened in the eyes of the people" unless his personal rank as Governor could be maintained.[2] He was also very suspicious of Nova Scotia. "The whole province of Nova Scotia are its enemies from principle. They know its superiority in point of natural advantages, and fear being robbed of their Inhabitants, for which reason, they say every ill they can invent of the Island."[3]

In 1784 John Parr was given his Commission as Captain-General and Governor-in-Chief of the Province of Nova Scotia and the Islands of St. John and Cape Breton. The old Island constitution of 1769 was nevertheless retained and the structure of government was unimpaired except that the office of Governor was joined to that of Nova Scotia. Parr's Commission provided that all "powers, authorities, and Directions" in so far as they concerned the Island were to be enjoyed by the Governor only when he was "actually upon the spot," and that at all other times they were to be exercised by the Island's Lieutenant-Governor.[4] Patterson's Commission as Lieutenant-Governor merely revoked his

---
[1]*Ibid.*
[2]John Patterson (on behalf of Walter Patterson) to Lord Sydney, July 16, 1784, *ibid.*, A 6, p. 1.
[3]Patterson to Sydney, Dec. 2, 1784, *ibid.*, p. 119.
[4]Commission to John Parr, Public Archives of Canada, Nova Scotia Commissions, 1766-1807, M series, vol. 588. See also Sydney to Patterson, Sept. 27, 1784, P.A.C. (P.E.I.), A 6, p. 38.

first one and that of the old Lieutenant-Governor, and gave him his new appointment "with such powers and authorities according to such directions as are or shall be expressed in our commission and instructions" to John Parr.[1]

Yet another shift in status occurred two years later when the Island was placed under a new chief. In 1786 Lord Dorchester (the former Guy Carleton) was appointed Governor-in-Chief of all the British North American provinces save Newfoundland as a result of a policy of consolidating British interests in America by bringing the colonies together under a common executive. The Island now had a Governor-in-Chief at Quebec in addition to a Lieutenant-Governor in Charlottetown, and her connection with Nova Scotia was severed once more. Under the new arrangement she kept her own administration, but along with her neighbours she came under the general supervision of Lord Dorchester. Before the change Parr's powers were to have been significant only in the improbable event of his visiting the Island, but Lord Dorchester was now to keep a close watch on local affairs and receive regular reports on the state of the colony from the Lieutenant-Governor. He was empowered to proceed to the Island and take over command whenever he deemed such action expedient.[2] Like the preceding change, however, this one was also to have little effect upon the actual administration of the Island except in so far as the presence of a higher authority would check to a certain degree the rivalry between the colony's political institutions.

During these constitutional changes some consideration was given to the name of the colony. The Indians had called it *Abegweit*,[3] the French renamed it Île Saint-Jean, and the English had been content with a translation of the latter. But St. John's was often confused with St. John's in Newfoundland and Saint John in New Brunswick, and the local Assembly sought a more distinctive name. Governor Patterson suggested New Ireland,

---

[1] Commission to Walter Patterson as Lieutenant-Governor, P.A.C., Commissions and Instructions (P.E.I.), 1766-1839, M 593.
[2] Draft of Particular Instructions to Carleton, Shortt and Doughty, *Documents Relating to the Constitutional History of Canada, 1759-1791*, vol. II, pp. 813-14.
[3] This word can be translated "cradled on the waves."

which, with respect to the land question at least, might have been most appropriate, and the Colonial Office favoured New Guernsey or New Anglesea, but none of these was acceptable.[1] The Duke of Kent, father of Queen Victoria, had displayed a passing interest in the defences at Charlottetown, and his royal notice was accordingly honoured by the adoption in 1798 of "Prince Edward Island" as the future designation of the colony.[2]

[1] Germain to Patterson, Feb. 28, 1781, P.A.C. (P.E.I.), A 4, p. 165.
[2] The Assembly passed the necessary act in 1798 and the name was confirmed by His Majesty in Council on Feb. 1, 1799 (39 Geo. III (P.E.I.), c. 1). See Fanning to Portland, Nov. 27, 1798, P.A.C. (P.E.I.), A 14, p. 247; The King to Fanning, Feb. 5, 1799, *ibid.*, A 15, p. 4; *ibid.*, p. 51.

CHAPTER II

COLONIAL INSTITUTIONS

THE LIEUTENANT-GOVERNOR

THE GOVERNORSHIP of the Island was, by and large, a thankless post in the colonial period. Virtually all the incumbents were discontented during their terms and the citizens almost always had some complaint to lodge against Government House. This dissatisfaction was primarily due to the fact that the Island's constitution put the Governor in a most unsatisfactory position, which combined the functions of dignitary, administrator, diplomat, and even hotel keeper. "Thus play I in one person many people, and none contented," lamented Richard II. His Excellency at Charlottetown could with much truth have spoken likewise.[1]

Patterson's Commission and Instructions of 1769 set forth the powers of his office. They were substantially those of a Governor in any British colony. He was to take and administer the necessary oaths, call a Council, and summon a general Assembly "so soon as the situation and circumstances of our Island under your government will admit thereof and . . . in such manner as you in your discretion shall judge most proper or according to such further powers, instructions and authorities as shall be at any time hereafter granted and appointed you." The Governor was then empowered by and with the consent of the Council and the Assembly to make laws for the Island, which laws were not to be repugnant to the laws of England, and were to be sent to London within three months of their passage for approbation or disallowance. His Excellency was to enjoy a negative voice in the passage of legislation, and to him was assigned the power to adjourn, prorogue, and dissolve the Assembly at his own discretion. He was authorized to establish, with the advice of the Council, courts of judicature, and to appoint the necessary judges, justices of the peace, sheriffs, and other officers of justice. Upon him was conferred the prerogative of mercy or power of pardoning criminals, which, except in cases

[1] A list of the Governors of Prince Edward Island in the colonial period will be found in Appendix E.

of treason or murder where the King alone could grant reprieve, was limited only by his discretion.

The Governor was also to keep the Great Seal of the colony, fill ecclesiastical vacancies, raise fortifications, muster arms and men and lead them in military operations as the occasion required, and to take certain steps for the observance of the law of Admiralty, but not to institute proceedings thereunder. Public money could only be issued upon the Governor's warrant with the advice and consent of the Council, and it was to be spent for the support of government only. The granting of undisposed public lands was to be in his hands, as was the establishment of markets, ports, and other conveniences of commerce. All these powers and the post itself were to be held by Patterson during the "will and pleasure" of the King. The Commission also provided for the devolution of government, in case of the death or absence of the Governor, upon the Lieutenant-Governor, or, if there were none at the time, upon the eldest Councillor then resident in the colony.[1]

As the first chapter has indicated, the governorship of the Island had a tempestuous beginning with the incumbency of Walter Patterson, whose failure could be attributed chiefly to a combination of administrative difficulties and personal deficiencies, and the office was reduced to a lieutenant-governorship in 1784. The constitution was too elaborate for such a small colony, and friction between the Governor and his colleagues was almost inevitable in the scramble for the limited power and influence afforded by local politics. Patterson took himself too seriously and became overbearing in his treatment of those who worked with him. He did a fair job in establishing the Council, Assembly, and Supreme Court, but when they began to function he revealed a singular lack of diplomacy in his relations with them. The office of Governor was much abused and it remained unpopular during Patterson's term. Moreover, when there were both a Governor and

[1]The Administrator was to exercise these powers in the same manner as the Governor himself save that important provisions were included in the Instructions prohibiting the Chief Justice from taking over the administration, and providing that the eldest Councillor, when Administrator, was to pass only essential measures and should not dissolve the Assembly or remove or suspend any official without the consent of at least seven Councillors.

a Lieutenant-Governor at Charlottetown, the latter office, which was a sinecure, was held by Thomas DesBrisay. This official was an incompetent trouble-maker who appeared to miss no opportunity to embarrass Patterson, his colleagues, and the Colonial Secretary, and who avoided dismissal from office only by virtue of the fact that twelve children depended on him for support.

The Governor's struggle with the Assembly over the raising of money illustrates these difficulties. The Assembly was dissolved by the Governor on January 14, 1784, to meet again after an election in March. In the interval Patterson planned, with the Council's consent, to increase the revenue by imposing a tax to which he knew the Assembly would be opposed. "Apprehending ... a strong opposition to this measure," the Governor secretly proceeded with his plans and during the election "took every step which I judged consistent with my situation, to procure the most respectable assembly our little community would afford."[1] This invasion of the Assembly's power of the purse met with a natural response, and opposition arose under the leadership of John Stewart, the son of Chief Justice Peter Stewart. John Stewart campaigned against the Governor personally and against the imposition of a general tax. He was supported by a slate of candidates pledged to oppose both Governor and tax, and his group succeeded in winning two-thirds of the seats in the Assembly. Moreover, the Chief Justice supported his son and acted during the campaign as counsel for some of the candidates.

When the Assembly met on March 6, John Stewart was chosen Speaker. The House discussed its grievances against the Governor for nineteen days and then adjourned without consulting His Excellency. When it met again after two or three adjournments for lack of a quorum, Patterson issued a proclamation declaring that the Assembly had dissolved itself. The members had no alternative but to disperse, but not before they hung a notice in a public place accusing the Governor of appropriating land and moneys to his own use, encouraging arbitrary proceedings in the sale of for-

[1]Patterson to North, April 15, 1784, Public Archives of Canada, Colonial Office Records (P.E.I.), A series, vol. 5, p. 137.

feited lands, spreading "the principles of infidelity and irreligion thro' the Colony," browbeating the Council and thereby bringing it into contempt, interfering in elections, and generally being an obstacle to colonial development. They met again later and urged the populace to join them in seeking redress from the King. Nor were constitutional principles alone involved. The weary Secretary of State for the Colonies, Lord Sydney, was informed by the Chief Justice that the Governor had succeeded in winning the intimate affections of Mrs. Stewart, the Chief Justice's wife and the stepmother of the Speaker of the Assembly, with the result that her husband dismissed her from his home and Patterson had to send her to Canada. While the Governor denied the story, it resulted in a spectacular family row the details of which made a great scandal in the colony and, no doubt, provided interesting reading for the clerks at the Colonial Office.[1] The results of all this conflict were more petitions for recall, Patterson's suspension of Chief Justice Stewart and the halt in the administration of justice which followed it, and complete deadlock between the Governor and the Legislature.[2]

If His Excellency's dignity was ruffled by his experiences in Charlottetown, it was lost completely in his ignominious departure. The Secretary of State ordered an investigation of affairs on the Island and the unfortunate Patterson was ordered home to account for his difficulties.[3] He was advised by Lord Sydney that General Edmund Fanning, the former Lieutenant-Governor of Nova Scotia, was to take charge "during your absence," and "upon his arrival you will deliver to him such Papers and Documents in your charge as may be necessary to enable him to carry on the public service."[4] At the same time the Colonial Secretary wrote to Fanning instructing him to proceed to Charlottetown at once and make "such arrangements with the said Lieutenant-Governor previous to his departure as may be necessary for your carrying on the Public

[1] Chief Justice Stewart to Lord Sydney, June 2, 1784, *ibid.*, p. 161; Patterson to Sydney, Dec. 12, 1784, *ibid.*, A 6, p. 165.
[2] Address from Committee of the House of Representatives to Lord Sydney, *ibid.*, p. 135.
[3] Colonial Office Memorandum, dated Oct. 26, 1785, *ibid.*, A 7, p. 89.
[4] Sydney to Patterson, June 30, 1786, *ibid.*, A 8, p. 184.

COLONIAL INSTITUTIONS

business of the Island."[1] With Fanning's arrival the Island entered upon one of the most complicated political issues of its history.

Fanning stepped ashore on November 4, 1786, complete with his Commission as Lieutenant-Governor. Patterson refused, however, to give up the reins of office until he was prepared to leave the Island, and that, he told Fanning and Lord Sydney, would not be until the following spring. His view was that Fanning could not act except in his absence, although Fanning's Commission read that he was appointed "in the room of Walter Paterson."[2] Neither would withdraw until His Majesty's pleasure should be further signified. Thus during the winter of 1786-7, the Island, which was scarcely large enough for one Lieutenant-Governor, experienced an extraordinary combination of two.[3] Public men were compelled to make a choice as to which they would recognize, and Island officials lined up in two opposing camps and supported their favourites by petitions, public meetings, and letters to the Colonial Office. The Chief Justice and the Speaker of the Assembly naturally supported Fanning against their old enemy. Although he kept the Colonial Office and Governor-General Lord Dorchester informed, Fanning made no public utterance until April, 1787. He then issued a proclamation publishing his Commission, announced his assumption of office, and formed a Council. Patterson thereupon published a counter-proclamation.[4] On May 3 Fanning dissolved the Assembly by proclamation, and two days later Patterson prorogued it by proclamation until June 4.[5] This conflict lasted until May when Patterson's dismissal arrived from London. Even the Colonial Secretary appears to have been in some doubt as to which was the rightful office holder, for in despatches to Fanning and Patterson, each dated April 5, 1787, Lord Sydney addressed them both as Lieutenant-Governor![6]

[1]Sydney to Fanning, June 30, 1786, *ibid.*, p. 186.
[2]Commission to Edmund Fanning, Public Archives of Canada, Commissions and Instructions (P.E.I.), 1766-1839, M series, vol. 593, at p. 69.
[3]Patterson to Sydney, Nov. 5, 1786, P.A.C. (P.E.I.), A 8, p. 220; Patterson to Fanning, Nov. 7, 1786, *ibid.*, p. 224; Fanning to Sydney, Nov. 8, 1786, *ibid.*, p. 230.
[4]Executive Council Minute Books, Legislative Building, Charlottetown, vol. I, p. 101.
[5]Fanning to Sydney, May 10, 1787, P.A.C. (P.E.I.), A 9, p. 50; Nov. 9, 1786, *ibid.*, A 8, p. 234. [6]*Ibid.*, A 9, pp. 42, 44.

This disruption in the governorship was reflected in the other branches of the government. The Assembly did not know whether it was prorogued or dissolved and its members simply stayed home. The Supreme Court could not function after the break between the Chief Justice and Patterson. Disaffection was also serious in the Council. When Fanning took over, those who had supported his predecessor resigned, and, in addition, the militia, which was now showing signs of restlessness, influenced two military members of the Council to vacate their seats because, said one of them, "my brother officers have informed me that they considered my being in Council, in the present situation of affairs, as improper. Two of them object to my keeping company with the gentlemen of whom it is composed."[1] When Lord Dorchester learned of these difficulties, he ordered the punishment of the militia and, in decided terms, encouraged Fanning to strengthen the executive authority by liberal use of the power of suspension on those "who have withdrawn themselves from their duty."[2] The civilian dissenters thereupon returned to Council after promising to support Fanning. This action was the only significant intervention of the Governor-General in Island affairs in the period before responsible government.[3]

Aside from the political confusion created by so novel an exhibition, the issue raised the question of what gave constitutional power to a Governor. The Commission was the instrument which apparently conferred that power on a new incumbent, particularly since it revoked the power previously given to the old. "The authority of the governor," says Greene, "ceased on the arrival of his successor and the publication of the latter's commission."[4] Yet even after Fanning had arrived and published his

[1] Quoted in Fanning to Sydney, May 10, 1787, *ibid.*, p. 50.
[2] Dorchester, whose mediation had been requested by Fanning, was furious that the King's orders should be slighted by military men. He gave Fanning an order to dismiss the commandant of the militia and promised to remove the whole company at the first opportunity. "These gentlemen did not, I hope, mean to recommend themselves for Preferment by caballing against His Majesty's Lieutenant Governor." Dorchester to Fanning, June 14, 1787, *ibid.*, p. 73.
[3] For detailed correspondence between Fanning and those who resigned from the Council, see Executive Council Minute Books, Legislative Building, Charlottetown, vol. I, pp. 110-27.
[4] E. B. Greene, *The Provincial Governor* (New York, 1907), p. 50.

Commission, Patterson considered he could retain office so long as he refused to give up the Great Seal and public documents of the colony. The Colonial Office itself did not attempt to settle the question, for, while on the one hand it condemned Patterson for disobedience of the King's orders,[1] the Under Secretary of State also advised Fanning privately that he was wrong in pressing his claim "whilst Patterson held the Government."[2] In other words, it would appear that the holding of His Majesty's Commission was not in itself sufficient authority for a Governor to take office; he had also to obtain the Seal and public papers from his predecessor.[3]

The Governor's judicial duties often caused almost as much discord as his executive ones. His Excellency was the Chancellor of the colony and as such presided over the Court of Chancery. This function developed from the ancient right of petition to the King praying for relief from the rigours of the common law. In England the office of the Chancellor, a dignified functionary in the royal household who originally reviewed such petitions for the King, developed into the Court of Chancery, and chancery and common law courts emerged side by side and dealt with their respective cases on two sets of principles. A similar development took place in the colonies where the Governors originally sat as Chancellors. In Prince Edward Island the early Governors generally acted in this capacity with the advice of the Chief Justice and the Attorney-General, and were assisted by a Master who was sometimes the Attorney-General but often another member of Council

[1] Sydney to Patterson, April 5, 1787, P.A.C. (P.E.I.), A 9, p. 42.
[2] Nepean to Fanning, Sept. 22, 1787, *ibid.*, p. 104.
[3] The Patterson-Fanning issue was not unique, for at almost the same time a similar incident occurred in Cape Breton. Governor DesBarres of that colony had been called home to answer charges which had been laid against him after a series of disputes between him and other officers of government and after certain irregularities with respect to his accounts. When his successor William Macarmick arrived at Sydney, he found that DesBarres had not left, and he "was induced from motives of Delicacy" to remain on board ship and postpone the publication of his Commission until DesBarres had quitted the capital. When DesBarres did leave, he did not transfer all the public documents to Macarmick and the latter had to send for copies to Lord Dorchester at Quebec. Macarmick to Sydney, Oct. 19, 1787, Public Archives of Canada, Colonial Office Records (Cape Breton), A series, vol. 4, p. 109. The difficulties associated with the transfer of documents were ended in all colonies in 1822 when Lord Bathurst gave instructions that henceforth such papers were to be handed from Governor to Governor and not removed from the colony.

without legal training. The Chancellor heard some original proceedings himself and also appeals from the Master.

When quarrelsome Governors suspended the Chief Justice, the Supreme Court ceased to function, and many of its cases consequently came before the Court of Chancery. Indeed the two courts were rival tribunals during the long feud between Governor J. F. W. DesBarres and Chief Justice Caesar Colclough after 1807.[1] When Governor C. D. Smith presided in Chancery from 1813 to 1824 he named his son-in-law as Master, and the two were accused of oppressive and illegal conduct in depriving litigants of proper hearings and in exacting unauthorized fees. When seven citizens protested to the King and their petition was printed in a local newspaper, the publisher was hailed before the Chancellor for "publishing a contemptuous libel" against the court, and the seven were remanded in custody for several days without a hearing, despite a protest from the Attorney-General. "I compassionate your youth and inexperience," said the Chancellor in an extraordinary admonition of the publisher. "Did I not do so I would lay you by the heels long enough for you to remember it. But I caution you when you publish anything again keep clear, sir, of a chancellor, beware sir, I say, of a chancellor."[2] The issue raised so much controversy that Judge Brenton Halliburton of the Supreme Court of Nova Scotia was sent to investigate by Governor Sir James Kempt of that colony at the request of the Colonial Secretary. Halliburton reported that he could find no illegal proceedings, but clearly indicated that the Chancellor and his son-in-law had gone as far as they could under the law.[3] The real consequences of the dispute were felt not merely in the Court of Chancery, but also in the Council and the Assembly where the Governor's critics attacked him savagely.

The Governor was not only the head of the local government, but he was also the connecting link between it and London. After

[1]See P.A.C. (P.E.I.), A 25.
[2]Attorney-General William Johnston to Lord Bathurst, undated, 1823, *ibid.*, A 39-2, p. 533. The petition of the seven citizens is in *ibid.*, p. 545. See also Proceedings of the Court of Chancery, *The Register,* Oct. 27, 1823, *ibid.,* p. 567.
[3]Halliburton to Sir James Kempt, May 22, 1824, *ibid.,* A 41-2, p. 651.

1831, all resolutions of the Council and the Assembly, together with addresses to the Sovereign, were sent to His Excellency for transmission overseas, and all Imperial despatches returned through the same channel. In the colony's early years much inconvenience was experienced from the sending of memorials and petitions to the Colonial Office by subordinate officials and private citizens without the Governor having an opportunity to make his comments; there was a consequent delay in action and reply until they were sent back to the colony for His Excellency's opinions. Lord Goderich ruled in 1831 that henceforth all such representations were to be sent through the Governor, or direct to the Colonial Office only if a copy were sent to Government House in order that the Governor's views should be available for the home authorities.[1] Although this liaison was convenient from the standpoint of administration, it was often irritating to the colonists, especially to the Assembly on occasions of controversy with His Excellency. Yet the rule was stressed even when the Speaker of the Assembly went to London in 1839 to lay the House's complaints before Lord John Russell. The Colonial Secretary refused to see him on the grounds that "the subjects to which your letters refer could not be properly discussed between his Lordship and a delegate from the House of Assembly of Prince Edward Island, even in written or oral communications, and that the views of Her Majesty's Government respecting them will be communicated to the Lieutenant-Governor through the regular channel of official correspondence with that officer."[2]

The office of Lieutenant-Governor and its influence on constitutional development were marked to a great degree by the personal attributes of the incumbents. The Island's administration was led by an interesting variety of Governors from the able to the mediocre to the completely inept. The manner in which they were chosen made such a consequence almost inevitable.

The appointments of Governors to the Island were affected by the usual factors which controlled the filling of offices in the

[1]Goderich to Administrator, May 2, 1831, *ibid.*, G 7, p. 111.
[2]James Stephen to William Cooper, Sept. 20, 1839, *P.E.I. House of Assembly Journals*, 1840, Appendix B, p. 12.

colonies, and few of these factors were in any way related to administrative ability. Personal influence with the Colonial Office, either through direct acquaintance with the Colonial Secretary or through the efforts of a patron, was the most common prerequisite for obtaining the position. Military service would often secure promotion to Government House although it did not necessarily indicate an aptitude for administration. Some Governors were men of experience, such as Fanning, who had been Lieutenant-Governor of Nova Scotia; others, such as Smith, had little previous training and revealed the lack while at Charlottetown. At least one, J. F. W. DesBarres, had been sent to the Island after an unsatisfactory administration elsewhere, while few, Sir John Harvey and Colonel John Ready excepted, were to attain any prominence after leaving it.

That the governorship got off to a bad start on the Island was thus in good measure the fault of the Colonial Office, for the calibre of its first appointees was not comparable to the task they had to perform. Three of the first four were incompetent at a time when the new colony required a strong and capable hand to guide it to maturity. Patterson, who established the government, had no experience which would indicate that he could deal with men or institutions. DesBarres, who was sent out in 1805, was over eighty when he arrived and over ninety when he retired. After DesBarres left the government in a state of chaos, and the need for a statesman was apparent, the administration was entrusted to C. Douglas Smith who had nothing to recommend him for the office save family connections, and who proved to be the worst Governor in the history of the province.[1] These men headed the Island's government for thirty-five of its formative years, and their combined efforts did much to weaken both the office they held and the administration which depended upon them for leadership. In later years, when the constitutional crisis which accompanied the struggle for responsible government might have been mitigated by wisdom, the stubborn and quarrelsome Henry Vere Huntley was Governor

[1]Smith received his appointment through the influence of his brother Sir Sydney Smith with Lord Bathurst and the Prince Regent; C. D. Smith to Peel, July 20, 1812, P.A.C. (P.E.I.), A 25, p. 99.

and his mistakes prolonged and added bitterness to the issue. The Colonial Office was constantly impatient with the difficulties of government on the Island, but it was never disposed to apply one of the most obvious remedies, the elimination of the incompetents whom it appointed.[1]

Some of the Governors, however, were comparatively satisfactory. Edmund Fanning spent twenty hard years in a prolonged encounter with primitive conditions, rival factions, and interfering proprietors, and received a public expression of thanks from local officials and a pension on his retirement. The completion of John Ready's six years in 1824 was accompanied by numerous petitions for an extension of his term; the eminent Sir John Harvey left an excellent reputation behind him when he went to the New Brunswick governorship in 1837 after but a year on the Island; Sir Charles Fitzroy and his wife added lustre to the office by their leadership in governmental and other circles in Charlottetown from 1837 to 1841; and although George Dundas did not shrink from stretching his powers during the Confederation era, his zeal for the public service was widely appreciated.[2]

The early Governors were appointed during pleasure, a fact which resulted in a sixteen-year tenure for Patterson, twenty years for Fanning, nine for DesBarres, and eleven for Smith, all of which periods were too long for their holders. A shorter tenure was substituted in 1830 when the Secretary of State in a circular despatch advised colonial Governors that in future their appointments would be for six years except in special cases.[2] Thereafter petitions were sometimes sent him for extensions of terms for certain Governors;

---

[1] The same was true of other officials. Most offices of government in the colony were subject to the manœuvres of office seekers and their patrons. An example was a petition from Lady Lucy Stuart to the Colonial Office requesting the office of Solicitor-General of the Island for one William Ronhell, who, though she did not know him, was a friend of "respectable and most worthy" friends of hers on the Island. Lady Lucy Stuart to Peel, May 10, 1812, *ibid.*, p. 90. Another was the appointment of one McDonald to be commandant of the militia in Kings County, P.E.I., "provided the exercise of that command should not be permitted to interfere with the discharge of his duties as Paymaster of the 30th Regiment now stationed in Bermuda." Fitzroy Somerset to James Stephen, Dec. 26, 1838, *ibid.*, A 56-1, p. 2. Many such cases are recorded in the Colonial Office Records.

[2] Ready to Murray, June 7, 1830, P.A.C. (P.E.I.), A 47, p. 145.

but the Colonial Office did not favour them, for as Lord Grey indicated, the six-year term had been adopted because "it prevents officers holding the highest authority in the Colony from becoming involved in the disputes of local parties, which it is frequently difficult for a Governor to avoid if allowed to remain for a longer period than six years in the same Colony."[1] This policy was subsequently to become a convention on the Island, for George Dundas was the only Governor in the entire history of the Island to be given a second term.[2]

Many of the difficulties of the governorship resulted from conditions in the colony itself. In the first years the maintenance of viceregal dignity in a glorified log cabin amid inexperience and poverty, and in what Fanning called "perpetual banishment" from home and friends, was hardly conducive to His Excellency's satisfaction. It was not until official and social life had developed in the capital that the dignity of the office became manifest and the Governor could boast of the physical comforts and decorative trappings associated with the King's representative. The importance of the office was further limited by the size and isolation of the colony. Politics on the Island in the early years were never on such a grand scale as to provide momentous issues of imperial or international import, but were more often in the nature of a sideshow which reflected in miniature the events in the main tent. The Governor did not—indeed he could not—preside over this circle with viceregal detachment, rather he was inescapably a part of it. He knew most of the prominent local citizens and he was associated with many of their disputes, political and social. His every action was open to the public gaze and his opinions and attitudes subject to close scrutiny. A Governor could hardly remain in office for long under such circumstances without raising some opposition or at least losing some of the public interest in himself and his family. He was too close to the peculiar characteristics of his surroundings to enjoy the enchantment lent by distance.

[1] Grey to Huntley, Aug. 12, 1847, *ibid.*, G 17, p. 143.
[2] Dundas held office for eleven years. He was reappointed in 1865 because he was opposed to Confederation and the anti-confederates had successfully petitioned the Colonial Secretary for his reappointment.

The local representative of the King was not above the common feeling of being underpaid for his services. Successive Governors complained of low salaries and heavy expenses, and of the expenditure of large amounts of their own private fortunes to keep themselves in decent existence.[1] Early Governors, moreover, were generally absent from England for many years and were thus unable to attend personally to their business affairs at home. Consequently they usually had to hire London agents to do this for them. Since many of the Governor's functions were of a social nature, his efforts were frequently judged by the amount of expenditure. Sir John Harvey indicated the political significance of the salary question when he reported to the Colonial Secretary that "it has not been possible to represent the King in this Island, in respect to those Hospitable attentions which the Principal Inhabitants (as well as the Legislative Bodies) in every 'Separate' Government, expect occasionally to receive, and which are so useful, and in my view so necessary, not only for the purpose of keeping up that reciprocal good feeling which should exist between the Governor and the government, but with the object of elevating the Tone of Society, in such Colonies, to a point approaching as nearly as possible to the Standard of European manners."[2] The dignity of the office, the demands of official entertainment, the expenses of the large government house which was built in 1834, the necessity of entertaining visiting strangers, and at the same time the inability to engage in private business made "elevating the Tone of Society" an expensive task.

The smallness of the salary resulted at first from dependence upon the quit rents, and later from Parliament's reluctance to grant an increase and the local Assembly's refusal to provide an expense account. The complaints of the Governors fell upon unsympathetic ears. "No man thinks his income enough," wrote Colonial Secretary Sir George Grey, "to enable him to live as expensively in his

---

[1] Patterson's salary was £1,000 a year; that of Fanning was £500, while DesBarres received £800. They, along with certain other officials, also received small fees for issuing deeds, writs, permits, and licences and performing other such duties. See 16 Geo. III (P.E.I.), c. 1.
[2] Harvey to Glenelg, Jan. 22, 1837, P.A.C. (P.E.I.), A 45-1, p. 7.

Govt., as he wishes, and the hopelessness of an increase is the only cure."[1] The whole question was appropriately summed up by a sympathetic Colonial Office clerk who added to Grey's note his own opinion: "It may be said that this argues merely a want of moral courage in refusing unreasonable demands or in declining to entertain their guests with the frugality which would be commensurate with the resources of the host," but "it would demand much more than an average degree of moral courage to decline the expensive duty which the expectations of society impose upon a Governor. . . . New Governors cannot indeed risk the unpopularity of such a refusal without seriously endangering the success of their administration." Despite these financial difficulties, however, there was no lack of applicants for the post when it became vacant.

THE COUNCIL

The constitution of the colony provided a Council of twelve members to "advise and assist" the Governor in his administration. The members were to be chosen from among the "principal inhabitants and proprietors of land" and to be invested with "all the powers, privileges and authority usually exercised and enjoyed by the members of our Councils in our other American colonies."

The Council was granted certain specified powers in addition to the more general ones of giving advice and assistance. Its advice and consent were necessary for the summoning of assemblies, for the passage of bills, the establishing of courts of judicature, the building of fortifications and harbours, the expenditure of public money, and the disposal of public lands. The Governor presided at Council meetings. The eldest Councillor (as already stated) was named Administrator in case of the death or absence of the Governor. Councillors, with the exception of *ex-officio* members (the Chief Justice and the Bishop of Nova Scotia), were appointed by the King upon the recommendation of the Governor and they held office during pleasure. The Governor could appoint new Coun-

[1]Comment on despatch from Fitzroy to Glenelg, Jan. 26, 1838, *ibid.*, A 55-1, p. 57.

cillors, subject to royal confirmation, if the number resident in the colony dropped below seven, a necessary provision for a small shifting population. The Governor could suspend or remove a member but only for "good and sufficient cause" and provided a majority of Council gave its assent after investigation and a hearing. A report of the suspension had then to be sent to the Colonial Secretary. If a Governor wished to suspend a Councillor for reasons "not fit to be communicated to the Council" he could do so provided he sent a detailed report to London. Councillors could not be absent from the colony for more than six months without the Governor's leave, or for more than a year without permission from the King. Members could not "wilfully absent themselves when duly summoned" to meetings of Council "without a just and lawful cause" upon pain of suspension.

During the early years of the colony the Councillors advised and assisted the Governor as individuals rather than as a group. This was particularly true when, during Patterson's term, the Governor quarrelled with several members and could turn to only a few friends for assistance. Moreover, the amount of business was scarcely sufficient to require frequent meetings of the full Council. There were five public officers in Patterson's Council, and each of these directed his main efforts to physical improvements in the colony; indeed there was little else for them to do during the first years. Other Councillors, who did not hold official positions, were even more preoccupied with farm and family, and rarely took the trouble to journey to the capital on public business. Consequently the Council seldom met, and for four years the Governor relied mainly on his officials for such little administrative assistance as he required.[1] The Council's activities, however, increased gradually as the public business grew in volume and importance and as the relations between the Governor and his advisers became less difficult.

[1] According to its minute books the Council apparently met formally only seven times in its first four years; there were six meetings in 1770, one in 1771, and none in 1772 and 1773. See Executive Council Minute Books, Legislative Building, Charlottetown.

When the first Assembly was summoned in 1773, the Council became the upper house of the Legislature. Thenceforth it was known as the "Executive Council" in its advisory capacity and the "Legislative Council" when it acted as a branch of the Legislature. The same personnel served in both until 1784. The Legislative Council was no more impressive than the Executive Council, for it was little else but a small committee of five or six under the chairmanship of the Chief Justice instead of the Governor, although it gravely followed the forms and procedure of a "house." For the first fifty years, or until the development of a reasonably effective Legislature, the Legislative Council was of little significance in the government of the Island.

With a view to making the Executive Council a more effective advisory body, the home Government in 1784 reduced the number of members in it from twelve to nine of which a quorum was five. The number in the Legislative Council remained at twelve. Even then the Governor could not find enough competent men who lived sufficiently near the capital to make up a quorum.[1] If a member went on a visit to the mainland or to England his seat was vacant for many months. In the spring of 1805, for instance, Fanning could not hold a meeting of the Executive Council, for of the nine members, two were ill, two were out of the colony, and two lived away from the town and could not attend.[2] On one occasion the Solicitor-General was absent nearly two years practising law in England;[3] on another a prominent member could not be present because of "indisposition and pecuniary embarrassment."[4] When the Bishop of Nova Scotia was an *ex-officio* member, one chair was always vacant. Since appointments were in effect for life, there were usually one or two aged and infirm members who could contribute little to the proceedings and a few members whose inefficiency belied the wisdom of permanent tenure.

The Governors devised various means of remedying these weaknesses. Some did not even bother to call the Executive Coun-

[1] Fanning to Grenville, July 15, 1790, P.A.C. (P.E.I.), A 11, p. 44.
[2] Fanning to Camden, May 12, 1805, *ibid.*, A 19, p. 66.
[3] Ready to Sir G. Murray, Aug. 28, 1828, *ibid.*, A 45, p. 349.
[4] Young to Stanley, re the Hon. Fade Goff, Jan. 5, 1834, *ibid.*, A 51, p. 29.

cil when the available membership was low, and either administered the government by themselves or with the assistance of individual Councillors. Some filled vacancies with members of the militia who, being stationed near Charlottetown, were always on hand.[1] Governor Young tried the unconstitutional experiment of increasing the number to ten members because he knew they would not all turn up, a plan which drew some questioning comments from the Colonial Office.[2] The one extra member appointed was retained for two years until a vacancy occurred; but this device was not tried again.

As in other colonies family connections provided easy access to positions in the two Councils. Some Governors, notably Smith and DesBarres, appointed sons and other relations at every opportunity. Smith advised Lord Bathurst of the importance of the patronage which would "conduce to my political weight as a Patron here" and afford "the means of creating a degree of requisite influence" which otherwise he could not enjoy.[3] Four members of Fanning's Council and the Clerk were closely connected by marriage.[4] Chief Justice Stewart's son and daughter married a daughter and son of Thomas DesBrisay, a member of Council; William Townsend, Collector of Customs, was a son-in-law of the Chief Justice; Thomas Wright, Surveyor-General, was a brother-in-law of the wife of the Speaker of the Assembly, John Stewart, who in turn was a son of the Chief Justice; Charles Stewart, the Clerk of the Executive Council, was also Registrar of Chancery, Coroner, and Receiver of Inland Revenue and was a son of the Chief Justice and brother of John Stewart; Robert Gray was Assistant Judge of the Supreme Court, Provincial Treasurer, and private secretary to the Lieutenant-Governor. One of the Assembly's chief complaints even as late as the 1840's was that practically all members of the Councils

[1] Fanning to John King, Under Secretary of State, June 10, 1801, *ibid.*, A 16, p. 14.
[2] Young to Stanley, Jan. 5, 1834, *ibid.*, A 51, p. 29; May 16, 1834, *ibid.*, p. 207; Stanley to Young, April 5, 1834, *ibid.*, p. 207.
[3] Smith to Bathurst, June 15, 1815, Public Archives of Canada (P.E.I.), Lieutenant-Governor's Letterbook, 1813-17, p. 201; Oct. 14, 1817, *ibid.*, 1817-20, p. 31.
[4] P.A.C. (P.E.I.), A 17-2, p. 299.

were related.¹ Personal relationships and family disputes inevitably became a vital element in both the composition and the work of the Councils. Some families held seats so long that they felt they held a perpetual interest in them. The DesBrisays and the Stewarts, for example, had a long-standing feud which began in part over a quarrel between Thomas DesBrisay and Chief Justice Stewart as to which had precedence as senior member.² Lord Bathurst finally took measures to counteract the "inconvenience of making a particular office hereditary in a family" and the evil was finally checked. Nevertheless, by 1842, the office of Surveyor-General had been held by a member of the Wright family for three generations, a situation which Lord Stanley regarded as objectionable in "a Colony so limited as Prince Edward Island in its opportunities of affording public employment."³

This family clique or "compact" controlled the administrative and judicial posts as well. Such officials as the Surveyor-General, Town Major, Provost Marshal, Attorney-General, Colonial Treasurer, and Collector of Import Duties were generally in the Executive Council, and it was not uncommon for an individual to hold four or five such posts. Even the Chief Justice and assistant judges of the Supreme Court were members of both Councils until 1839. For many years, therefore, the compact included executive, legislative, judicial, and administrative officers. In earlier times this combination was promoted and even made necessary by the lack of competent personnel in a small colony; but at a later period it provoked the most violent criticism from the constitutional reformers.

---

¹On April 23, 1841, a committee of the whole Assembly on the state of the colony examined the family connections of the members of the Executive Council which consisted of: (1) George Wright, father-in-law to the prothonotary who was a brother-in-law of (2) Robert Hodgson, the Attorney-General, who was a cousin of (3) John Brecken, who was a brother-in-law of (4) T. H. Haviland, Colonial Secretary, who was a brother-in-law of (5) James Peake; (6) Donald Macdonald, a brother-in-law of Haviland and of Brecken and a cousin of (7) J. S. Macdonald who was connected with Messrs. Brecken, Peake, and Haviland; (8) Joseph Pope, a relation of George Wright, and (9) Ambrose Lane, a brother-in-law of Robert Hodgson. A study of the Legislative Council revealed similar family connections. See *Assembly Journals*, 1841, p. 151.
²DesBrisay to Lord Hobart, Oct. 30, 1801, P.A.C. (P.E.I.), A 16, p. 38.
³Stanley to Hunter, July 16, 1842, *ibid.*, G 14, p. 129.

COLONIAL INSTITUTIONS 39

The deficiencies of the members of the compact earned them much criticism. Governor Ready advised that the Councils be thoroughly overhauled so as to leave out "obnoxious individuals" who are of "no weight, property, or respectability in the country," for "without a material change in our Council, it is in vain to expect any improvement" in the government.[1] Chief Justice Colclough frequently requested to be relieved of his duty as President of the Legislative Council which, he said, was "three times as much trouble" as his judicial duties and made him "very much harrassed and distressed."[2] Even Lord Selkirk, who visited the Island in 1803, noted that "very improper people are allowed to remain in Council" which was expected to work with a Governor "of no superabundant head," a senior Councillor who was a "very improper" person, and a Chief Justice who was "not deficient in the national qualification of enhancing his own importance."[3]

The Executive Council, with all its weaknesses and dissension, could, nevertheless, boast some degree of unity. The ideas of cooperation, solidarity, and secrecy, so necessary in cabinet government of later years, developed early on the Island, and both the Colonial Office and the Council itself had many opportunities for emphasizing them. When, for instance, Attorney-General Joseph Aplin resigned in 1798 after a scathing denunciation of public life on the Island, his colleagues, the Governor, and the Colonial Office joined in extolling the principles of executive solidarity and secrecy, and the offender was recalled to England to explain his conduct.[4] A similar view was taken of John Wentworth's extraordinary experience in the Council as one of two Attorneys-General, and he too was removed from the colony after a few months.[5] Moreover

[1]Ready to Huskisson, May 20, 1828, *ibid.*, A 45, p. 103; May 27, 1828, *ibid.*, p. 205.
[2]Colclough to Cooke, April 12, 1808, *ibid.*, A 22, p. 140; Aug. 14, 1809, *ibid.*, A 23, p. 187.
[3]Selkirk Diary, Aug. 11, 1803, Public Archives of Canada, Selkirk Papers, vol. 74, p. 79.
[4]Executive Council Minute Books, Legislative Building, Charlottetown, Feb. 6, 1798, vol. I, pp. 357-62; also Whitehall to Fanning (unsigned), July 27, 1798, P.A.C. (P.E.I.), A 14, p. 187.
[5]Wentworth was sent out as Attorney-General by the British Government in 1800. He had scarcely assumed his duties when the Colonial Secretary, by mistake, also appointed Peter McGowan, a local official, to the post. Neither would resign and both appeared before the Supreme Court which was forced

there were so many disputes between the Council and the other institutions of government that solidarity became the Council's surest protection against attack.

Although the benefits of solidarity and secrecy in the Executive Council were recognized, its members had no corporate responsibility. Responsibility was borne by the Governor alone, and the Councillors were his advisers and not his colleagues. When Sir Henry Huntley attempted to excuse some of his actions on the ground that the Council had agreed with him, the Colonial Secretary quickly made his constitutional position clear: "The office of Governor has not been placed in Commission, nor have the Executive Councillors been constituted the colleagues of the Lieutenant-Governor. They are your official advisers and nothing more . . . and I cannot admit that you are exempt from the responsibility attaching to any measure, if otherwise indefensible, from the circumstance of their having councelled or concurred in it."[1]

Because of its many weaknesses the clique which composed the Executive and Legislative Councils was singularly inefficient either as an institution of government or as a group of supposed leaders of the community. Since the Executive Council was expected to assist the Governor, its faults threw a greater burden upon him and encouraged the weak man, such as DesBarres, to be ineffective, and the autocratic one, such as Smith, to abuse his power. The group, moreover, became a constant obstacle in the legislative process, as the Assembly developed into an effective popular chamber. The fault did not lie entirely in the Councils, however, nor can it be said that all the members were inefficient. Unwise and quarrelsome Governors fostered similar characteristics in the Councils. The isolated community, low salaries, and lack of promotion bred lethargy and inexperience among officials. Despite these circumstances some Councillors were able and public-spirited citizens who

to decide which was Attorney-General. McGowan was recognized and Wentworth forthwith did all he could to embarrass McGowan, the Supreme Court, and the Government generally. Fanning to Portland, Sept. 23, 1800, *ibid.,* A 15, p. 130.
[1]Grey to Huntley, Sept. 16, 1846, *ibid.,* G 16, p. 551.

COLONIAL INSTITUTIONS 41

devoted long years and much labour to the welfare of the Island. But they were exceptions to the prevailing mediocrity of the early years which emphasized so clearly the need for reform.

THE ASSEMBLY

The beginning of the Legislative Assembly of Prince Edward Island was no less humble than that of the other institutions of government. Governor Patterson found it so difficult to gather a group of Councillors about him, that he doubted if the colony could provide enough qualified citizens to make an effective Legislature. "I am obliged," he wrote the Colonial Secretary in 1773, "to limit the number for the present to Eighteen Members, as I wish to have those who are to be chosen, as respectable as possible, and I know there are about so many, who will make a very tolerable appearance."[1]

The first Assembly was elected on a wide franchise. No qualification was demanded of candidates or voters except residence and Protestantism, because the greatest need was to give all of the limited number of freeholders the opportunity to select the best possible representatives. Although the Governor's Instructions had suggested that the existing division of the Island into counties, townships, and parishes would be useful in determining constituencies for members of the Assembly, it was decided that, in view of the unequal distribution of population, voting would be at large for the whole slate of candidates. The campaign and the election were very informal and were accompanied by much drinking and fighting, yet eighteen stout pioneers were returned to join the Governor and the Council in the administration of public affairs. The *début* of this House was picturesque, for, after a quorum of members was rounded up from their agricultural pursuits, it met in a tavern and, no doubt, mixed business with pleasure. The town constable, who acted as Sergeant-at-Arms and doorkeeper, left his opinion of the proceedings for posterity by remarking aloud that "this is a damned queer parliament," which frank judgment is

[1]Patterson to Dartmouth, Feb. 17, 1773, *ibid.*, A 2, pp. 91-2.

reputed to have cost him the displeasure of the House and a five shilling fine.¹

While Patterson apologized to the Colonial Secretary for the shortcomings of the new House, Lord Dartmouth assured the Governor that it had given him "great satisfaction" to note that "a method of constituting a complete Legislature for the Island" had been found which would "lay the foundation of its future welfare and Prosperity. . . . With regard to the form and manner of selecting the new Assembly, it must, like everything of the same nature adopted only on a Plan of Experiment, be in many respects imperfect; but I have the satisfaction to say that it appears to me, in the general view of it, not liable to any very material objection."² Dartmouth reminded the Governor to bring the quit rent problem before the Assembly, inasmuch as the Imperial Treasury would not be "burthened with any expense whatever for the civil establishments."

It was inevitable that this first Assembly should be neither impressive nor efficient. The choice of candidates had been limited, and those who were elected could scarcely be said to bring with them a "public opinion" from remote settlements where there were virtually no communications and where interest in politics was subordinated to the work of making a living. The outposts were far from the capital, and, since the demands of pioneer life did not cease for the session, it was difficult to get a quorum, and adjournments were frequent from lack of attendance.³ Indeed the first Assembly had scarcely met when Patterson and the Council decided to dissolve it and call an election in the hope of obtaining a better one after the arrival "of many respectable people who purpose coming to the Island this summer."⁴ Legislation was limited in general to local community regulations such as the use of the com-

---

¹J. E. B. McCready, quoted in Charlottetown *Guardian*, Nov. 19, 1946.
²Dartmouth to Patterson, Dec. 1, 1773, P.A.C. (P.E.I.), A 2, p. 169.
³See Patterson to Germain, July 30, 1780, *ibid.*, A 4, p. 84. Compulsion was planned in 1774 when an act was passed "to prevent the non-attendance of Representatives to serve in General Assembly," which measure was deemed foreign to parliamentary usage by the home authorities in that it threatened the independence of members, subjected them to the penalties of justices of the peace, and made a magistrate of the Speaker. Richard Jackson to Board of Trade, Nov. 13, 1775, *ibid.*, A 3, p. 29.
⁴Patterson to Dartmouth, July 15, 1773, *ibid.*, A 2, p. 122.

mon, the maintenance of animals, and the building of fences. The Assembly, moreover, had no money to spend and little prospect of finding any save by shaking the pockets of absentee proprietors.

The financial position of the colony made urgent the improvement of the House. The Legislature had to pass the necessary measures to enforce the payment of quit rents and thereby create public funds. It had also to wield the taxing power to provide for the civil establishment after the quit rents reverted to His Majesty's Treasury and the colony was left to fend for itself. The Governor and the Colonial Office were therefore anxious to increase the prestige and authority of the Assembly, and the House itself soon became aware of the stimulus offered by the power of the purse.

Despite these good intentions, however, the Assembly was, for the first half-century of government, the Cinderella of the administration which found itself tolerated when needed and its power confined by the other branches. One obstacle to its prestige was its control by the Governor. His Excellency could call it when he saw fit, for the grant from Parliament made an annual session unnecessary. The Governor's friends in the Council, moreover, frequently opposed the Assembly because of the latter's criticism of the family compact. Furthermore, improvement in the Assembly's position had to await the development of the colony and of public interest in politics without which representative government was basically immature. When improvement did come, it was manifested in the Assembly's insistence on the dignity and prestige associated with parliamentary privilege.

Many privileges of the House of Commons in England had been won against the arbitrary power of early monarchs, and they find classic expression in the demand in the Speaker's petition at the opening of Parliament for freedom from arrest and from molestation, freedom of speech, access to the King, and the placing of a "favourable construction" on the actions of the House. In other words, the respect of the Crown for the position and powers of the Commons was sought and won as a necessary feature of the development of representative government. Moreover, the mother of parliaments had for generations established its right to protect and control its members, regulate its proceedings, and enforce its authority. Similar privileges were claimed in the British colonial legislatures, and early colonial constitutions implied their transfer overseas. But new undeveloped legislatures did not actually enjoy immediately the privileges which the parent House had taken centuries to acquire, for they were forced to establish themselves first and convince the Governors of their rights. "It is probable," writes one authority, "that among all the activities of the assembly and all phases of its development, nothing did more to emphasize its importance, to give wide-spread publicity to its claims of power, or to foster in the respective colonies a sense of political independence, than the manifold demonstrations of the authority of the house that can be summed up under the term parliamentary privilege."[1]

The Assembly of Prince Edward Island, like the legislatures of the mother country and of other colonies, had to fight for an effective position in the government and win its prestige and dignity after a long struggle for the recognition of parliamentary privilege. The traditional demands of the Speaker's petition were regularly presented to the Governor who in return granted "all their [the members'] privileges in as full a manner as they have been at any time granted or allowed by any former Governor of this Island," or, if he were more definite, "all their privileges conformably to ancient usage, the laws of the land, and Her Majesty's Instructions." Such assurances, however, were just so many words to some early Governors who considered the Assembly too immature to deserve them, and indeed the House was at first too weak to enforce its demands. The administration of Governor Smith, however, provided issues which prompted the Assembly to fight for the recognition of its privileges. Smith made many solemn pronouncements on the rights of the House, but actually he rarely placed a favourable construction on its actions, and, indeed, did all he could to show his disrespect in a manner reminiscent of King Charles I.

Smith "hazarded the experiment of convening the General Assembly" during his first year of office in 1813, but, since his enemies were so active in the House, he "found it expedient sud-

[1]Mary P. Clarke, *Parliamentary Privilege in the American Colonies* (New Haven and London, 1943), p. 269.

denly to surprize them by a Prorogation."[1] His Excellency then determined to do without the services of the Assembly for a time because he could not be assured of "a sufficient number of respectable and well disposed persons even offering themselves as candidates at an election."[2] His aim was to dominate the House by showing that he could get along without it.[3] He thereupon strengthened the Executive Council by filling up its vacant seats and proceeded to govern without the popular house from May, 1813 to July, 1817. When J. B. Palmer, Smith's chief opponent in the House, left the Island for a few months in 1817, Smith permitted the Assembly to meet, but, finding it no less stubborn, he abruptly dissolved it and called a general election. The new House lasted one session until it too was dissolved. The Assembly elected in 1820 proved no more amenable, and the Governor dispensed with its services for the remaining four years of his term, and relied for funds on the grant from the British Parliament and duties on and licences for the import and sale of spirituous liquors.[4]

The memorable session of 1818 revealed the nature of the tension between Smith and the Assembly. In its address to the Governor at the beginning of the session, the House regretted that His Excellency had not assented to a roads bill which had been passed the previous year. Although couched in formal and polite terms, this reference was in reality an expression of the Assembly's resentment at the Governor's obstructing legislation which had received the approval of both houses of the Legislature. This Smith called an "unconstitutional animadversion as well as unparliamentary retrospect."[5] He refused to accept the address, while the Assembly declined to amend it and returned it to him the second time. Smith refused again because the question involved "a constitutional principle of the first importance and therefore a point that cannot possibly be conceded."[6] "I saw who I had to deal

[1]Smith to Bathurst, Jan. 15, 1814, P.A.C. (P.E.I.), A 28, p. 1.
[2]Smith to Bathurst, Sept. 17, 1814, P.A.C. (P.E.I.), Lieutenant-Governor's Letterbook, 1813-17, p. 79.
[3]Smith to Bathurst, March 23, 1815, *ibid.*, p. 99; Feb. 27, 1816, *ibid.*, p. 188.
[4]These funds are discussed *infra*, pp. 67-9.
[5]P.A.C. (P.E.I.), *Assembly Journals*, 1818-19, p. 24, a note in Smith's own handwriting.
[6]Assembly Proceedings, 1818-19, P.A.C. (P.E.I.), A 34, pp. 94-6.

with," he wrote Lord Bathurst, "and that the session would be one series of Insults if I did not stand firm."¹ The Assembly answered the Governor by renewing discussions on the vetoed measure and making barbed references to His Excellency's stubbornness.

Charlottetown was then treated to a legislative circus. On December 15, 1818 Smith requested the Assembly to adjourn for three weeks, but the House ignored his order. Then, records the *Journal,* the Governor's private secretary and son-in-law, J. E. Carmichael, appeared at the bar and announced: "Mr. Speaker, if you sit in that Chair one minute longer as Speaker this house will be dissolved." "By whose authority?" asked the Speaker. "The Lieutenant-Governor's," was the reply. The Speaker requested the order in writing. "I will not," said Carmichael, "it is enough for you that you have received it." "And," reports the *Journal,* "he then retired in a contemptuous manner." The Speaker was ordered by the House to issue a warrant against the intruder. Just then the Governor arrived and sent for the Speaker, and, in the words of the House's subsequent address to the King, "holding up his watch to him said he would allow the house three minutes before the expiration of which if they did not adjourn it should be dissolved, thereby exhibiting a degree of illegal violence and unconstitutional conduct of which we believe there is no other example." The House adjourned. To complete the sitting, Henry Smith, the Governor's son, put his fist through the windows of the legislative chamber and was promptly committed to jail by the House.² As James Stephen of the Colonial Office subsequently remarked in his official report on the matter, "it would of course be superfluous to make any comment on such a narrative as this."³

Both parties to the dispute recognized that the main questions were crucial: was the Assembly entitled to respectful treatment from the Governor; and did it have the right to criticize the Government without being considered disloyal? The Assembly

---

¹P.A.C. (P.E.I.), *Assembly Journals,* 1818-19, p. 39, a note in Smith's handwriting.
²*Assembly Journals,* 1818, P.A.C. (P.E.I.), A 39-2, pp. 611-32; see Address of the House of Assembly to the King, Nov. 15, 1823, *ibid.,* p. 755.
³Stephen to Under Secretary of State, March 29, 1824, P.A.C. (P.E.I.), A 41-2, pp. 845, 879.

asserted that it could "remonstrate or complain to His Excellency the Lieutenant-Governor of any public acts of his Government," and at the same time such complaint could be "loyal, respectful, and constitutional." After all, said its members, the Governor was "the most regular and constitutional channel through which their wants or grievances can reach the throne."[1] Smith's view of the Assembly's rights was quite different. "I was actuated by very pure constitutional motives. It was, and is a fixed principle in my mind, according to the British Constitution, that no Branch of the Legislature can animadvert upon the conduct of any other, nor any two branches upon the third, otherwise, the branch so liable to be animadverted upon, would become inferior and subordinate."[2] In other words, the Assembly, although it was expected to provide funds for administration, was not to criticize or question the Government, even on the expenditure of these funds.

The Colonial Office, after much investigation, denounced the Governor's views. The law officer of the Crown in his report indicated that Smith had been wrong, that the Assembly's "animadversion" had not been unconstitutional, and that even if the address of the Assembly had condemned the Governor's conduct, he should have received it, since its terms were "temperate and respectful."[3] Aside from the constitutionality of Smith's action, its wisdom was doubtful, and as Lord Bathurst wrote, could "with difficulty be reconciled with that discretion and moderation which is essential in any communication with the House of Assembly . . . while it has effectually and I fear for some time diverted the attention of the House from every subject of useful deliberation."[4] Bathurst's fears were well grounded, for the Assembly determined to continue its opposition to arbitrary power, while the Governor, in a professed effort to prevent "intemperance and violence" and "resolutions of the greatest and most offensive impropriety," declined to summon the House again.[5] To stem the tide of criticism

[1] *Assembly Journals*, Nov. 6, 1818, P.A.C. (P.E.I.), A 39-2, p. 632.
[2] Smith to Under Secretary of State, April 29, 1825, P.A.C. (P.E.I.), A 41-2, p. 785.
[3] James Stephen to Under Secretary of State, March 29, 1824, *ibid.*, p. 845 at p. 879.
[4] Bathurst to Smith, Nov. 30, 1819, *ibid.*, G 5, p. 93.
[5] Smith to Bathurst, June 9, 1824, *ibid.*, A 40, p. 187.

which resulted, Smith dismissed a number of public officials, including the High Sheriff, for encouraging public protest. Nor was he at peace with his Council, for he also suspended several of its members, including the Attorney-General, for agreeing with the Assembly. The break-down in administration which followed resulted in a general condemnation of Smith and culminated in his recall by the home Government.[1]

The new Governor, John Ready, had scarcely arrived when he summoned a new Assembly. The House met for two sessions during his first year of office, and from 1825 held regular annual meetings. The Assembly had won a victory by revealing that the Governor could not manage the administration effectively without it, and that its right of criticism must be respected. The controversy with Smith forced it to defend its privileges and status and thereby enhanced its position as a recognized Legislature.

Access to the Governor and favourable construction on its activities were only two of the important privileges which the Assembly had to establish. Clarification of the rights of the House to protect and control its members, regulate its proceedings, and enforce its authority was a necessary manifestation of its development as an effective part of the Legislature and of its rising influence in government. Privileges in these categories had long been recognized in the British Parliament where members had insisted on freedom from arrest (save in indictable offences) during the session and for periods of forty days before and after the session, freedom of speech during debate, power to discipline members and non-members who gave insult or injury to the House or its members, the right to determine disputed elections, the right to receive petitions, and other privileges of a similar character.[2] Many colonial assemblies took these privileges very seriously during the periods of self-consciousness before their authority was firmly established, and often the power to enforce rules and punish offenders was wielded with arbitrary severity.

[1]Bathurst to Smith, April 10, 1824, *ibid.*, G 5, p. 255.
[2]See Clarke, *Parliamentary Privilege in the American Colonies;* A. Beauchesne, *Parliamentary Rules and Forms* (Ottawa, 1943), pp. 79-86 and xxvi-xl; R. MacGregor Dawson, *The Government of Canada* (Toronto, 1947), pp. 397-404.

COLONIAL INSTITUTIONS

The Assembly of Prince Edward Island was no exception, although it was at first only a glorified committee of eighteen persons representing a few hundred citizens. Governors could sneer at what Sir Henry Huntley called "homespun experience," but the jail awaited those more humbly situated who by word or deed reflected upon the decorum of the House. Many sessions saw non-members before the bar receiving the admonition of the Speaker for various offences from "contemptuous conduct in beating the floor of the Assembly Room"[1] to "throwing a copper coin from the gallery during the proceedings."[2] Members were frequently humiliated on the House's order for unbecoming conduct such as the use of "indecorous, unparliamentary, and improper language" in debate,[3] disrespectful conduct toward fellow members when outside the House,[4] and even "illegal and oppressive conduct" in the courts.[5] Much excitement was caused by a prominent member who was expelled in 1840 for being seen "on more than one occasion, in a state of inebriety in the streets and public market place, and even on the floor of the House, to the great scandal and disgrace of himself and this House, of which he is a member."[6] If the accused did not express what the House termed "the utmost contrition for his offence" he was committed to the custody of the Sergeant-at-Arms until the required apology was made. Even the Governor's advisers were not exempt. The Treasurer was expelled from the House in 1830 for mismanaging public funds;[7] the Queen's Printer was committed to custody along with the Leader of the Opposition in 1853 for being absent without leave;[8] and in 1858 another Minister was imprisoned for describing the majority of the House as corrupt and refusing to apologize on being brought to the bar.[9]

Molestation was not tolerated, and severe punishment was meted out to anyone who committed assault against a member.[10] The traditional freedom from arrest was always asserted, and in 1845, when one of the members was imprisoned for debt, the House

---

[1] *Assembly Journals*, 1828, p. 4.
[2] *Ibid.*, 1847, p. 25.
[3] *Ibid.*, 1827, p. 25.
[4] *Ibid.*, 1832, p. 6.
[5] *Ibid.*, 1825, p. 5.
[6] *Ibid.*, 1840, pp. 64-5.
[7] *Ibid.*, 1830, p. 12.
[8] *Ibid.*, 1853, pp. 77-8.
[9] *Ibid.*, 1858, pp. 52-3.
[10] The most interesting illustration of molestation was the Jenkins case, *ibid.*, 1863, pp. 10-32; *infra*, p. 232.

resolved that even if members are arrested during recess they ought to be liberated when the House is convened.[1] This privilege applied to House officials as well. On one occasion when the Clerk Assistant was summoned before a debt court, the House instructed him not to obey the summons;[2] and on another an offender was imprisoned for taking an action against the High Sheriff when the latter was carrying out an order of the House.[3]

The right to determine contested elections was important in the days when bribery and intimidation were common accompaniments of electoral contests. The receipt of election returns by the House was a mere formality in most cases, but when disputed elections were brought forward through petitions from aggrieved parties, the Committee on Elections, a Committee of the Whole, heard witnesses and reported to the House itself which thereupon made a decision.[4] Actually contested elections were never numerous, for irregularities were so common on both sides of most contests that few candidates could safely challenge the results.

One of the most prominent forms of privilege was the right of petition which had everywhere enhanced the prestige of legislatures in their relations with constituents. In virtually every session the Island Assembly received and dealt with scores of petitions from individuals and groups seeking such things as relief for the poor and aged, pensions for retired servants or their widows, assistance for public works, patronage for fairs and exhibitions, and support for campaigns against alleged social and economic evils such as the land question and the liquor traffic. These petitions took up much of the time of the House, which received them and heard supporting witnesses in Committee of the Whole on Petitions, for members could not avoid championing the causes of constituents and powerful interest groups. Clergymen, for example, appeared regularly for many years to exhort the House on the evils of intemperance or to express opinions on the school question. The Assembly took this function seriously and required petitioners to approach the House with respect or suffer humiliation at the bar.[5] The right of petition

[1]*Ibid.*, 1845, p. 24.   [2]*Ibid.*, 1852, p. 11.   [3]*Ibid.*, 1825, p. 19.
[4]See *ibid.*, 1847, Appendix I, concerning Belfast election of 1846.
[5]On one occasion the House expressed its disapproval of an offensive petition by ordering that it be thrown under the table. *Ibid.*, 1825, p. 23.

did much to keep the House in close contact with the people, and, in some connections, particularly the land question, strengthened its reputation as the champion of popular rights.[1]

The election of members to the Assembly was subject to trial and error during its first fifty years, for the choice of legislative personnel among a small, scattered, and isolated population was extremely difficult. Although preoccupation with pioneering pursuits at first slowed the development of public interest in politics, the rivalries of a small community which frequently made vital crusades out of ordinary issues encouraged colonial Islanders to take their politics very seriously. Most observers, including all the Governors, noted the continuous storm in a teacup that marked the colony's public affairs. The conflict of personalities, together with the prevailing issues of land, religion, and responsible government, joined to complicate the franchise and to encourage the growth of party spirit.

The franchise was wide, but representation was often unfair. Until 1838 four members were elected at large for each of the three counties and two from each of the three county towns. The town of Princetown was for some years under this arrangement a rotten borough consisting of three houses and being represented by two members. In an extraordinary election in 1803 Robert Hodgson was chosen a member from three different constituencies on the same day, in one of which he received a unanimous vote! He took one seat and left the other two vacant.[2] "Housekeepers," lessees of land in possession, and proprietors, if they were Protestant, could vote for county members, while urban "housekeepers" and proprietors of town or pasture lots, if they were Protestant, could also vote for the town members. The same qualifications applied to the candidates.[3] Thus both voters and candidates were either proprietors or tenants, a classification which to some extent facilitated the drawing of party lines at elections and in the House. Although

---

[1]Greater publicity was given to the Assembly's proceedings after 1847, in which year the House permitted special accommodation for the press. *Ibid.*, 1847, p. 19.

[2]Hodgson to Mills (Colonial Office), June 21, 1803, P.A.C. (P.E.I.), A 18-2, p. 274.

[3]See also John Stewart, *An Account of Prince Edward Island* (London, 1806), pp. 267 ff.

the absentee proprietors were not popular on the Island, there were always a few local proprietors in the Assembly as well as a number of agents for the absentees.

General elections sometimes took place throughout the colony on the same day, but more often they were spread out over a longer period. Fanning usually held them on one day, but the proprietors preferred them on several days, which plan, said Fanning, had "a tendency to procure a representation of Property and Influence, more than a Representation of the People or Inhabitants," because "men of influence and property might go from one town and county to another" and thus spread their efforts over a wide area.[1] For seventy-five years this method increased and prolonged the excitement at election time, and the one-day system was not adopted until 1848. The election at large of the county members took place at one county poll. This arrangement led to much disturbance during elections, for extreme groups could concentrate their efforts in one place where, as Attorney-General Hodgson indicated, "as generally happens the most violent and outrageous succeed in intimidating the more moderate and better disposed portions of the community."[2] The fact that voting was open and oral also encouraged such intimidation.

The number of members in the Assembly remained at the original eighteen for over sixty years. This was more than sufficient until the growth of communications, towns, and commerce had progressed sufficiently to warrant an increase. An Election Act of 1838 increased the number of members to twenty-four[3] and another of 1856 raised it to thirty.[4] The constituency system was changed by the first of these acts. Each county was divided into three districts, each of which returned two members; the three county towns retained their two members apiece.[5] The population of the Island trebled in the twenty-five years before 1856, and, as

---

[1]Fanning to Privy Council, April 7, 1792, P.A.C. (P.E.I.), A 12, p. 57.
[2]Report of Attorney-General, March 10, 1838, *ibid.*, A 55-1, p. 143. See also *Assembly Journals*, 1832, pp. 6, 7 and Appendix.
[3]1 Vic., c. 9.
[4]19 Vic., c. 21.
[5]An unsuccessful attempt was made to give Charlottetown the right to elect three members. *Assembly Journals*, 1838, p. 61.

a result, in that year three more county districts were created, each returning two members.¹ The total membership was therefore now thirty. At the same time the boundaries of the constituencies were adjusted slightly in an attempt to secure equality of representation. From this point the franchise and the structure of the Assembly remained unchanged as a whole until after Confederation.

Other reforms accompanied alterations in the electoral machinery. For thirty years the term of the Legislature was indefinite and its length depended entirely on the will of the Governor. The average term for the first seven Assemblies was approximately four and one-half years, and these terms varied from one to twelve years. In 1806 the term of the Assembly was fixed by statute at seven years,² but in 1833 it was reduced to four years,³ subject in both instances to earlier dissolution at the pleasure of the Governor and to the ancient practice which terminated Parliament upon the death of a sovereign. The shorter term, in the words of the Assembly, was designed to "strengthen the confidence of the Public in the popular branch of the legislature, and also prove conducive to the purity of that body were the sense of the people agreeably to ancient usage more frequently appealed to."⁴ An act of 1834 ended the old system by which the Assembly was dissolved and a new one elected upon the demise of the Crown.⁵ Four years earlier, following similar legislation in the mother country in 1829, all political disabilities upon Roman Catholics were repealed, so that adherents of that faith could thenceforth vote, be elected to the Assembly, and hold civil and military office.⁶

THE BEGINNING OF PARTIES

Party politics developed early on the Island and thrived on personal and group rivalry and the issues of land reform and responsible government. The politics of the Patterson and Fanning

¹19 Vic., c. 21; *Assembly Journals,* 1856, p. 91.
²47 Geo. III, c. 3.
³4 Wm. IV, c. 15.
⁴Report of Attorney-General Hodgson, April 27, 1833, P.A.C. (P.E.I.), A 50, p. 159.
⁵*Assembly Journals,* 1834, p. 42.
⁶11 Geo. IV, c. 7; *Assembly Journals,* 1830, p. 5.

administrations had been stimulated by the animosities of clique feuds and family rivalry, but it was not until the DesBarres régime that the first organized political party appeared. The growth of this party was provoked by land abuses and the blunderings of Governors DesBarres and Smith. The aged DesBarres befriended one J. B. Palmer who was able, by holding a number of offices himself and controlling others through his friends, to wield substantial power in the colony. He was a leader of the "Club of Loyal Electors," whose members Chief Justice C. J. Colclough called "Jacobins," and which was organized as a political party for the purpose of opposing the proprietors and gaining control of the Assembly at election time. Through Palmer and the Governor it soon controlled the Council. A number of American Loyalists were among the moving spirits of the organization.

This body was regarded with hostility and alarm in many quarters. "Democracy is making such rapid strides here," said Chief Justice Colclough in 1812, "that without some man of firmness and sense is sent or the Island annexed to Nova Scotia I really trouble for its safety should there be a war with America." Governor DesBarres, who cordially disliked the Chief Justice, and who appeared to have only a vague knowledge of Palmer's activities, instructed Attorney-General Charles Stewart to make an official report on the "Loyal Electors." The resulting document, written in 1811, is an interesting observation on the novelty of parties and their effect upon colonial government.[1]

Stewart called the organization "a self-created permanent political body—organized after the manner of corporations and associated for the purpose of controlling the representation of the people in the House of Assembly, as well as the appointment of public officers." The main club functioned at Charlottetown and established branches throughout the Island. It held numerous meetings at various points to rally supporters and promote discussion of public questions, particularly the land issue. "This same society," said the Attorney-General, "have had the temerity of more than insinu-

[1]Charles Stewart to DesBarres, Oct. 18, 1811, P.A.C. (P.E.I.), A 25, p. 247.

ating that they could procure a dissolution of the General Assembly of the Island, whenever it suited their views." They professed loyalty to the King, yet their avowed object was to "obtain possession of the whole power of the Government, Legislative, Judicial and Executive." Stewart then concluded "that any self-created society or body of men with such principles and objects . . . is highly illegal and unconstitutional and ought not to be endured in any Government blessed with the benefits and privileges of the British Constitution and therefore ought to be discountenanced and suppressed."

The "Loyal Electors" stirred up much public interest in politics, but lost their patronage after DesBarres retired. Governor Smith would not tolerate such a body and forced it to operate in secret. "The Club," he reported in 1815, "though it has not dared to act openly since my arrival has nevertheless been constantly and secretly at work watching every opportunity for mischief."[1] Smith hounded Palmer and his friends at every opportunity, while they in turn supported the Governor's numerous enemies in the many violent disputes of his term. They even included the judiciary in their activities; they assisted DesBarres in his opposition to Chief Justice Colclough, and later helped Chief Justice Thomas Tremlett in his feud with Smith. At this stage party politics reverted to its original basis of personal rivalry and intrigue, and for a time thrived on the conflict of factions in the Councils and the Assembly.

As the following chapter will indicate, it was the struggle for responsible government that gave the main stimulus to political parties on the Island, and it was the development of effective political parties that made responsible government possible. In the process personal altercation and feuds between cliques were replaced by constitutional principles as the stimuli for party politics. The Liberals and Conservatives of the Island were then able to join their counterparts in other provinces in the great movement which was to end in the overthrow of the old colonial system. This new phase was not to rest on constitutional reform alone, for Island politics and party alignments were also to be affected by the land

[1] Smith to Goulburn, April 24, 1815, *ibid.*, A 29, p. 105.

issue and the religious struggles resulting from the school question. Truly, as Bacon says, "if there be fuel prepared, it is hard to tell whence the spark shall come that shall set it on fire." Prince Edward Island politics never lacked sparks.

The Judiciary

When His Majesty enjoined Governor Patterson to see that justice was speedily and effectively administered on the Island, he set a task which was virtually impossible to fulfil for over half a century. The judiciary was affected by the same forces which disturbed the other public institutions—the backward community, incompetent personnel, and official rivalry—and, in consequence, the Supreme Court had to undergo a long period of adjustment before it could obtain the dignity and detachment which were necessary for the dispensing of justice.

The early judges were unfortunate in their personal qualifications and in their mode of life in the colony. After the first Chief Justice died from the strain of three years without a decent home, salary, or court-house, there was no one to take his place. The only lawyer in the colony was the Attorney-General who could not act as a judge, and the powers of the Chief Justice were consequently granted to a commission of three citizens who presided over the Court for several months without the benefit of legal training.[1] After Peter Stewart was appointed Chief Justice he had to support a wife and ten children with a small and irregular salary and an inadequate, broken-down house.[2] Thomas Cockram, who was appointed in 1801, remained only six months and considered himself fortunate when transferred to Upper Canada. His successor, Robert Thorpe, had an unhappy and stormy four years on the Island bench, and when he too was appointed to Upper Canada he advised the Under Secretary of State that "the worst people in the world are at Prince Edward Island. . . . I blessed you for sending me away."[3] Chief Justice C. J. Colclough was suspended from

[1]Patterson to Dartmouth, May 21, 1774, *ibid.*, A 2, p. 230.
[2]Stewart to Board of Trade, Oct. 30, 1781, *ibid.*, A 4, p. 252; Stewart to Germain, July 10, 1779, *ibid.*, p. 26.
[3]Quoted in A. B. Warburton, *History of Prince Edward Island* (Saint John, 1923), p. 428.

COLONIAL INSTITUTIONS 57

office after he had disagreed with practically every other official in the colony. His successor, Thomas Tremlett, who had never been trained in the law, had had a stormy career as Chief Justice of Newfoundland which was matched by an even worse ten years on the Island. Chief Justice Archibald, who was appointed in 1824, lived and practised law in Nova Scotia and performed his judicial duties on the Island in the summer only. It was not until Chief Justice Jarvis arrived in 1828 that the Supreme Court settled down to a quiet routine under a satisfactory chief. The background, temperament, and attitudes of these men were the main factors in the early weakness of the Court.[1]

The amount of legal business during the early years of the colony did not encourage improvement in the judiciary. The practice of law was almost negligible. Even as late as 1809 there were only six persons with legal training besides the Chief Justice, and, said Governor DesBarres in 1810, "the profits of the profession of Law will not maintain a Gentleman."[2] There were no county courts, and all litigation was handled by the Supreme Court. The Court sat in Charlottetown only and it was difficult for distant residents to avail themselves of its services.[3] There was at first no jail in which to imprison offenders and the carrying out of sentences frequently had to be suspended because of this lack. On one occasion the Court sentenced a soldier to death for robbery, but the Provost Marshal refused to hang him because of the possibility of reprisals from the militia, although the Governor himself was ready to assist in the execution. The accused was subsequently set free because there was nothing else to do with him.[4]

[1]For similar difficulties in the early courts of other colonies see Martin Wight, *The Development of the Legislative Council, 1606-1945* (London, 1946), Appendix 5, p. 166; also W. R. Riddell, "Notes on the Pre-Revolutionary Judiciary in English Colonies," *Canadian Bar Review*, 1933, pp. 376-7.
[2]DesBarres to Liverpool, July 3, P.A.C. (P.E.I.), A 24, p. 11.
[3]One observer quaintly indicated the situation in an anonymous letter to a local newspaper: "If I reside in East Point or Cape North and have an account of five pounds against my neighbor I must send and generally speaking come to Charlottetown before I can compel him to pay me. If I am poor it would be madness for me to attempt to defend an appeal in Charlottetown because my gain would be a certain loss. If I go to Charlottetown I am led into dissipation there and return home with an aching head, and empty pocket, and a half-starved horse." Quoted in John A. Mathieson, "Bench and Bar," in *Past and Present in Prince Edward Island*, ed. D. A. MacKinnon and A. B. Warburton (Charlottetown, 1905), p. 134.
[4]Patterson to Germain, Jan. 25, 1782, P.A.C. (P.E.I.), A 5, p. 2.

Another major weakness of the judiciary was the absorption of the Chief Justice in other governmental duties. Not only was he a member of the Executive Council and President of the Legislative Council, but he was also a confidential adviser to both the Governor and the Colonial Office. Governor Ready considered this advisory function more important than His Lordship's duties on the bench.[1] Chief Justice Duport was told that "it would not be unacceptable" for him to write the Colonial Secretary from time to time and advise him confidentially of conditions on the Island, and Duport and many of his successors regularly followed this practice.[2] This close association with politics and administration often brought the Chief Justice into sharp disagreement with the Governor or the Assembly or both, and His Lordship was generally deeply involved in the personal and clique rivalry of the early years. Peter Stewart provides the best example, for he and his immediate descendants were in constant trouble with both local officials and the Colonial Office. Chief Justice Tremlett was the enemy of both the Assembly, which repeatedly demanded his removal, and the Governor who called him "my greatest hindrance in the government of the colony. . . . I never can feel safe with him in my council."[3] Judicial independence was impossible under these circumstances, and the Chief Justice's political adventures seriously affected his position as a judge. Moreover, since His Lordship was appointed directly by the Crown during pleasure, his tenure was constantly jeopardized by petitions from his enemies to the King seeking his removal from office.

The position of Chief Justice S. G. W. Archibald illustrates clearly the judicial situation in the 1820's. A distinguished lawyer and Speaker of the Assembly in Nova Scotia, Archibald became the Island's chief judge in 1824 upon the understanding that he would reside in Halifax and carry on his practice and political life there, and hold court in Charlottetown during the summer.[4] Although it was generally agreed that Archibald was an able judge, the

[1] Ready to Goderich, July 24, 1827, *ibid.*, A 44, p. 137.
[2] Duport to Hillsborough, April 23, 1771, *ibid.*, A 1, p. 195.
[3] Smith to Bathurst, July 8, 1815, P.A.C. (P.E.I.), Lieutenant-Governor's Letterbook, 1813-17, p. 128.
[4] *Assembly Journals*, 1825, p. 29.

Assembly complained that his absence during most of the year delayed the legal process and deprived the colony of a vital member of the Council and adviser to the Governor; and it regarded with "feelings of deep mortification, that High Officer of the Colony practising as an Attorney in the Courts of Nova Scotia."[1] Archibald himself considered that his absence was an asset rather than a disadvantage under the peculiar circumstances of the colony, for he emphasized how necessary it was that the Chief Justice should "be independent of all popular and party feeling; and also how difficult it would be to procure a person to reside constantly in a small government, and with a small salary, likely to have, and maintain, such a character." His usefulness as a judge, he thought, was much like that of a circuit judge in England who was not involved in local politics.[2] Archibald's view that a combination of absenteeism and judicial independence was preferable to the unsatisfactory mixture of justice and politics which had prevailed on the Island pointed to the fundamental weakness of the court system and the urgent need for reform.

The office of Assistant Judge of the Supreme Court was of very limited usefulness in the early years. At first there were two unpaid assistant judges, usually laymen, who held several other posts along with their seats on the bench. They were often members of both Councils, and, like their chief, they took part in political controversies. When the Chief Justice was ill or absent from the colony, these non-professional men were the only judges available, a fact which raised much protest from the bar.[3] After the appointment in 1848 of a salaried assistant judge to replace the two laymen some inconvenience resulted from the fact that the two judges had to agree or there could be no decision.[4] Finally in 1859 the Assembly agreed with considerable reluctance to establish a third judgeship.[5] These additional appointments were agreed to, not so

[1]*Assembly Journals*, 1828, p. 17. Governor Ready voiced similar protests; Ready to Goderich, July 24, 1827, P.A.C. (P.E.I.), A 44, p. 137.
[2]Archibald to Ready, May 8, 1827, *ibid.*, A 45, p. 135.
[3]Jarvis to Fitzroy, March 19, 1841, *Assembly Journals*, 1841, Appendix N; *ibid.*, 1837, p. 73; *P.E.I. House of Assembly Debates*, 1869, p. 28.
[4]For a discussion of this two-man court see *P.E.I. Legislative Council Debates*, 1869, p. 21.
[5]*Assembly Debates*, 1868, pp. 198-202; *Assembly Journals*, 1869, pp. 98 and 110-15.

much to strengthen the Supreme Court, as to postpone the establishment of courts of inferior jurisdiction.

The position of the judiciary improved with constitutional reform and colonial development. When the Executive and Legislative Councils were separated in 1838[1] the Chief Justice was thenceforth excluded from both Councils, while the assistant judges were taken out of the Executive Council. "The King thinks it right," wrote Lord Glenelg, "that neither the Chief Justice nor any other judges should be present at any of the proceedings of the council in its Executive capacity . . . all the judges including the Chief Justice should be entirely withdrawn from all Political discussions."[2] The assistant judges were removed from the Legislative Council when their posts became permanent and salaried. Although it took time for local officials to regard the judges as detached from politics, reform came with the rapid advance of business and industry on the Island which stimulated the legal profession and increased the importance of the Court. Improvement was particularly evident from 1835 when, after court-houses and jails were built in the county towns, the Court went on circuit and thereby carried its services into the different parts of the colony.

[1]*Infra*, p. 65.
[2]Glenelg to Sir Colin Campbell, April 30, 1837, P.A.C. (P.E.I.), G 10, p. 60.

CHAPTER III

RESPONSIBLE GOVERNMENT

THE NATURE and growth of political institutions in Prince Edward Island, as in the other British American colonies, were but one aspect of their constitutional history. The adjustment of the relations among these bodies in an effort to reach an effective division of governmental power accompanied this growth and its chief manifestation was the movement toward responsible government. The struggle occurred in the relations between the Assembly on the one hand and the Governor and Executive and Legislative Councils on the other. Under the old colonial system the Assembly was kept in the background as much as possible, and it had to challenge the other institutions, separately and collectively, before it could take its place at the centre of rather than outside the government.

The fight for responsible government was closely identified in the early years with the activities of the "Loyal Electors." This group resented the inferior position of the Assembly and the subordination of the colony's affairs to the interests of the landed proprietors. Its members set about remedying the situation through party activity which they recognized as the most effective instrument for combatting the combined forces of Governor, Councils, and proprietors. This challenge alarmed the cliques and compacts in public affairs and the struggle for power began.

The reformers provoked several issues for the contest by using the improved status of the Assembly as a means of seeking more power. Although the assistance of the House was necessary in legislation, particularly in finance, and its right of discussion and criticism had survived the struggle with Governor Smith, there was still a wide gap between the Assembly and the executive. Whereas in England the King was advised by persons who held seats in Parliament and were responsible to the House of Commons, the colonial Governor was assisted by appointed Councillors who comprised the major part of the upper house and who were not members of the Assembly or responsible to it. The Executive Council's membership and policies were frequently unacceptable to the representatives of the people whose business it was conducting, while the actions of the Legislative Council were often obstacles to the measures sponsored by the popular house. After impressing the Governor with the need for the presence and opinions of the Assembly, the reformers turned their attention to the personnel and powers of the group which advised him.

The separation of the Executive and Legislative Councils was an important feature of the movement to close the gap between the Assembly and the executive. This distinction between the two bodies, which was made in the Canadas in 1791, in New Brunswick in 1832, and in Nova Scotia in 1837, came at last to Prince Edward Island in 1839. The Island's experience was therefore rendered somewhat easier by events in the neighbouring colonies since the change was a natural adjustment in the broad movement for reform throughout British America. In all colonies the general pattern was the same. The councils, which combined executive and legislative and sometimes judicial functions, were composed of life members who were inherently conservative in status and opposed to reform elements in the assemblies. To weaken their hold on power by separating them into distinct executive and legislative bodies and by securing places on the executive councils for some members of the popular chamber, was a vital part of the tactics of the reform parties in their quest for responsibility of power.[1]

Encouraged by the New Brunswick reform of 1832, the Island Assembly in 1834 petitioned the King for a separate Legislative Council, "distinct from that of the Executive, to be composed of gentlemen possessing a knowledge of the wants and resources of the Colony, and who hold no situation or office of emolument at the pleasure of the Crown."[2] The Colonial Office thought that "in the present state of society in P. E. I." such a move would be "impolitic," although if it could be shown that there were "a sufficient number of Persons fit for the duty of Legislative Councillors," the request would be considered.[3] As for the exclusion from a Legis-

[1] See also Martin Wight, *The Development of the Legislative Council, 1606-1945* (London, 1946), p. 127; Paul Knaplund, *The British Empire, 1815-1939* (New York, 1941), pp. 78-9.
[2] *P.E.I. House of Assembly Journals*, 1834, p. 87.
[3] Colonial Office notes on Young to Stanley, April 2, 1834, Public Archives of Canada, Colonial Office Records (P.E.I.), A series, vol. 51, p. 171.

lative Council of persons holding official situations, that was something "which His Majesty's Government would deem most objectionable in principle."[1] The Assembly voted a number of resolutions and petitions during these years which emphasized that the inclusion of executive officials in the upper house was an invasion of the privileges and independence of the Legislature and contrary to the principles of representative government, but its efforts in this direction met with little success.

When Nova Scotia received a separate Legislative Council in 1837 the Island Assembly tried once more.[2] At the same time Sir John Harvey, a wise and broad-minded Governor, advised Lord Glenelg confidentially of what he called "the anomalous and defective composition of the Legislative Council." He described the proceedings of the Councils in some detail. The Councillors met as a legislative chamber with the Chief Justice in the chair; then the Governor took the chair to give the assent to bills which had been passed; thereupon His Excellency left the room for a few minutes while the Chief Justice adjourned the House, and then returned to take the chair again to preside over the executive, and all this with a group of eight people! Since seven of the eight held offices of emolument, all were residents of Charlottetown with only a slight knowledge of the wants of rural inhabitants. Some members, moreover, were proprietors' agents who did not possess the public confidence. Harvey thought that a sufficient number of qualified persons could be found with which to form a Legislative Council and he recommended the granting of three seats in the Executive Council to members of the Assembly.[3]

---

[1]Spring Rice to Young, July 31, 1834, *Assembly Journals*, 1835, p. 19. Not all the Colonial Secretaries agreed with Spring Rice. In 1832 Lord Ripon said that the Legislative Council "should principally consist of Gentlemen independent of and unconnected with the Executive Government." Quoted in Glenelg to Sir. A. Campbell, Aug. 31, 1836, *Assembly Journals,* 1837, pp. 8-11. Lord Glenelg, in a despatch to the Lieutenant-Governor of New Brunswick, recognized "the importance of securing the independence of the Legislative Council . . . the introduction into it of too large a number of persons holding places of emolument under the Executive Government, would tend to detract from its weight as an independent branch of the Colonial Legislature." *Ibid.*
[2]*Ibid.,* 1838, p. 72.
[3]Harvey to Glenelg, March 11, 1837, P.A.C. (P.E.I.), A 54-1, p. 156.

The Colonial Office, however, was still cautious. Lord Glenelg told Governor Campbell of Nova Scotia that the results of the separation of the councils in the Canadas and in New Brunswick "had not been such as to exclude any serious doubts respecting its real usefulness,"[1] and that, although he had agreed to the change in Nova Scotia with a "peculiar pleasure" in view of the advice of its respected Assembly, he was not so sure that the situation on the Island warranted a similar policy.[2] A new Governor, Sir Charles Fitzroy, who was about to embark for the Island, was then instructed to study the issue and make a report.

In a "private and confidential" despatch Fitzroy agreed with Harvey that the existing system was objectionable. Although he admitted the existence of a family compact in the old Councils, he doubted whether there were enough competent individuals who could be appointed without arousing local jealousies and friction.[3] By the spring of 1838 Fitzroy had been in Charlottetown long enough to appreciate the local problems, and he urged the separation of the Councils and the appointment of some members of the Assembly to the Executive Council.[4] To this Glenelg agreed, but action was postponed in view of Lord Durham's contemplated recommendation for the abolition of the legislative councils in all the colonies. When Durham decided differently, the necessary change was authorized upon the urging of Governor Fitzroy.[5]

It was provided in the Instructions to Sir John Colborne, who succeeded Lord Durham as Governor-in-Chief, that henceforth in Prince Edward Island there were to be "two distinct and separate Councils to be respectively called the Legislative Council and the Executive Council," the former to consist of not more than twelve and the latter nine members. The old provisions for tenure during pleasure and removal for "good and sufficient cause" were retained,

---

[1] Glenelg to Sir Colin Campbell, April 30, 1837, *ibid.*, G 10, p. 48.
[2] See also Chester Martin, *Empire and Commonwealth* (Oxford, 1929), pp. 173-4.
[3] Fitzroy to Glenelg, Sept. 15, 1837, P.A.C. (P.E.I.), A 54-1, p. 321.
[4] Fitzroy to Glenelg, March 10, 1838, *ibid.*, A 55-1, p. 122.
[5] Fitzroy to Glenelg, Sept. 5, 1838, *ibid.*, A 55-2, p. 527; Oct. 16, 1838, *ibid.*, p. 621.

and the Governor was to permit the members "freedom of debate and vote in all affairs of public concern."[1] Glenelg instructed Fitzroy to "select those who from their character, their attainments and their standing in Society appear to you most likely to command the public respect and confidence, and you will so govern your selections as to ensure as much as possible the presence in your Councils of Members from all parts of the Island and representing its principal interests."[2] An important innovation was the exclusion of the Bishop of Nova Scotia and the Chief Justice from both Councils. The latter's place as presiding officer of the Legislative Council was taken by the Assistant Judge of the Supreme Court who held the posts of Treasurer and Provost Marshal as well.

The change was formally announced by Fitzroy in a proclamation dated March 4, 1839.[3] Meanwhile the disadvantages of appointed Councils were becoming apparent to the Assembly, and in February it attempted to have the change postponed in the hope that it would then be able to secure a measure that would make the Legislative Council elective.[4] Fitzroy advised that the original plans had been carried too far for any change to be embodied in them and thus postponed a controversial point for posterity to settle.[5]

Six of the nine new Executive Councillors had been in the old Councils. Five of the old members and one of the new held one or more public offices as well. In the new Legislative Council were four members of the new Executive Council, which four had also been in both the old Councils. Of the twelve five held office under the Crown. To impress the Assembly Fitzroy elevated two of its members to the Executive Council, and the Speaker and another

[1] Instructions to Sir John Colborne as Governor of Prince Edward Island, "or in his absence to Our Lieutenant-Governor," dated Dec. 13, 1838, Public Archives of Canada, Commissions and Instructions (P.E.I.), 1766-1839, M series, vol. 593, p. 259.
[2] Glenelg to Fitzroy, May 4, 1838, *ibid.*, A 57, p. 76.
[3] *Assembly Journals*, 1839, 2nd session, p. 1.
[4] *Ibid.*, 1st session, p. 68.
[5] *Ibid.*, p. 73. It is significant to note that William Cooper, who led the demand for an elective Legislative Council and annoyed the Governor by his conduct in so doing, was elected Speaker of the Assembly in 1839. Further demands for reform were thus assured.

member to the upper house. He also appointed representatives of the "agricultural and mercantile interests" to both bodies.[1]

This separation of the Councils made further inroads on the old executive oligarchy and improved the position of the Assembly. Although the family compact had not been removed, its personnel was sufficiently dispersed to weaken its hold on power. The Assembly could now boast of representation on the Executive Council as well as of having some of its former members in the upper house, and there were seats in both bodies for representatives of districts and interests outside Charlottetown. Yet this was not responsible government. The members of the Assembly who were appointed to the Executive Council were not necessarily persons of whom the Assembly approved, and, since their appointments were virtually permanent, there was no assurance that they would continue to represent the prevailing views of the popular house.

The reformers not only advocated the inclusion of a few members of the Assembly in the Executive Council, but they also urged that public approval should be obtained by prospective Councillors before assuming office. The Assembly consequently passed a bill in 1835 which provided that no member of the House could accept an office of emolument under the Crown, unless he resigned his seat and was re-elected, and that no member could enter into a contract for the performance of any public work or become security for a contractor who undertakes a public work without vacating his seat.[2]

There was much dispute for some years, however, as to whether this principle should apply only to members who took seats in the executive with emolument attached, or to all Councillors whether they were paid or not. From 1839 to 1847 there were three cases of members of the Assembly (one of them the Speaker) accepting seats in the Executive Council without remuneration and without vacating their seats in the popular house. The point was settled by the Assembly in 1848. James Warburton had been appointed to the Executive Council, but Governor Campbell did not consider that

[1] Fitzroy to Glenelg, March 4, 1839, P.A.C. (P.E.I.), A 58, p. 22; see also *ibid.*, pp. 3 and 259-60.
[2] 5 Wm. IV, c. 1. A similar provision was included in an election act of 1836, 6 Wm. IV, c. 24.

his seat in the Assembly was thereby vacated, and refused upon the advice of the law officers to issue a writ for a by-election. The Assembly maintained that it alone was competent to declare whether or not a seat had been vacated, but the Governor refused to act. The matter was then referred to the Colonial Secretary who advised Campbell that the Assembly's wishes should be respected.[1] Although Grey recognized the Assembly's right of deciding the matter, he did not agree with the House's reasoning and thought it was going too far. "The opinion that a seat in the Executive Council is an office of emolument," he wrote to Campbell, "appears to be not only entirely new, but also without substantial foundation," for "a Member of the House of Commons does not vacate his seat by being sworn into the Privy Council, unless he at the same time accepts some office of emolument." The Assembly thought differently and won its point, although it was by no means unanimous and only sustained its decision by a vote of 12 to 10.[2] This case finally established the need for popular approval of participation in the executive by members of the Assembly. The principle of executive solidarity required their loyalty to the Council,[3] while that of popular re-election assured some degree of responsibility to the Assembly, the party, and the people.

A major factor in the struggle between the Assembly and the executive was the principle of popular control of public funds which had been of vital importance in the development of parliamentary government in every part of the Empire. The fact that the Island had little to spend in comparison with the other colonies did not lessen the desire of her reformers to control it. The resulting tur-

---

[1] "As the House was acting strictly within its proper jurisdiction," said Grey, "its decisions cannot be questioned, unless it should appear to be unsupported by public opinion, in which case, your proper course will be, to dissolve the present Assembly, and call a new one. This is the only remedy which the Constitution provides against an abuse of its powers by the representative branch of the Legislature." Grey to Campbell, March 27, 1848, P.A.C. (P.E.I.), G 18, p. 147.

[2] *Assembly Journals,* 1848, pp. 6-7; 16, 25, 37-8; *ibid.,* 1847, pp. 80-1; Grey to Campbell, March 27, 1848, *ibid.,* 1848, Appendix O; Grey to Campbell, Sept. 22, 1848, P.A.C. (P.E.I.), G 18, p. 341.

[3] Grey had stressed to Campbell that Executive Councillors "must distinctly understand that they are not at liberty, as Members of the Legislature, to oppose any of the measures of Government, and at the same time retain their offices." Grey to Campbell, Jan. 1, 1849, *ibid.,* G 19, p. 1.

moil, arising out of the constitutional principle rather than the amount involved, added a vigour to the fight for responsible government which surprised even the Island's neighbours who faced the same demand for reform. Governor Kempt of Nova Scotia thought that these Island "squabbles" would "have a bad effect both in this province and in New Brunswick," while Speaker Archibald in Halifax was "desirous the example should never gain ground among us."[1] "The whole Revenue about which the Council and Assembly are at Open War," noted Kempt, "does not amount to 2000 pounds a year!!! . . . It is really too bad." The issue was manifested in the Assembly's struggle with the executive and the Colonial Office over the disposal of the revenues of the Crown and with the Legislative Council over appropriations.

The revenue of the Island in this period came from two sources: (1) the annual grant from the British Parliament amounting to approximately £3,000 which was used to pay the salaries and expenses connected with the offices of government; and (2) local revenue levied by the Assembly in the form of (a) duties on and licences for the import and retail of spirituous liquors, which amounted annually to approximately £1,000,[2] and (b) an assessment on land which yielded a similar amount.[3] The total revenue was sufficient to meet the modest needs of the small government, but political events complicated both the collection and the disposal of it. The Assembly had the taxing authority, while the Crown controlled the parliamentary grant, and each attempted to coerce the other with its respective fund. The Assembly provoked uncooperative Governors by voting supply for one year rather than for a longer period or by simply refusing supply, and some Governors, notably Smith, dispensed with the Assembly and relied entirely on the parliamentary grant and the liquor revenue. Moreover the proprietors were able, by lobbying at Downing Street, to encourage the royal veto on assessment acts, and the family compact represented

[1] *Cambridge History of the British Empire,* vol. VI, pp. 274-5.
[2] See 14 Geo. III, c. 5; 19 Geo. III, c. 2; 21 Geo. III, c. 7; 25 Geo. III, c. 4; and 35 Geo. III, c. 10.
[3] See also DesBarres to Liverpool, April 16, 1812, P.A.C. (P.E.I.), A 25, p. 4.

other special interests in financial matters through its influence in both the Executive and the Legislative Councils. When annual legislative sessions were instituted after the departure of Governor Smith in 1824, the Assembly, with its new appreciation of its influence, determined to bring control of the entire revenue into its own hands.

At the close of the 1825 session the Speaker of the Assembly, in offering the revenue bills for Governor Ready's assent, stated that the House was not satisfied with the way in which public funds had been spent under previous Governors, and expressed the hope that Ready would at some period be inclined to assent to an annual appropriation act which would include the permanent revenue of the Crown.[1] The response to this request, and to a similar one in 1832, came from the Colonial Office, which made it quite clear that the Crown's revenue would be appropriated solely at the discretion of His Majesty's Government until such time as the colony was in a position to raise sufficient funds to defray its expenses without assistance from Parliament.[2]

Official independence was a major consideration of both the Assembly and the Colonial Office. The reformers knew that they could control public officials from the Governor down if salaries were subject to annual appropriation. The Imperial Government, on the other hand, wished to preserve the independence of the officials by making permanent provision for their salaries.[3] The conflict was illustrated in connection with a seven-year grant made by the Island Legislature to Governor Ready for special expenses over and above the salary provided by the home Government. This grant was changed to an annual one when Governor Young took office, but His Excellency was forbidden to accept it since it was not "permanent" and it would place him in an "improper subserviency." "The fickleness of our Popular Assembly," said Young, "would be a sufficient warning to guard against placing myself at

[1]*Assembly Journals*, 1825, 1st session, p. 62, and *ibid.*, 2nd session, p. 25; Ready to Bathurst, June 21, 1825, P.A.C. (P.E.I.), A 42, p. 193.
[2]Bathurst to Ready, Oct. 26, 1825, *Assembly Journals*, 1827, p. 9; Goderich to Young, Nov. 25, 1832, *ibid.*, 1833, p. 65.
[3]Goderich to Young, Nov. 23, 1832, P.A.C. (P.E.I.), G 7, p. 223.

their mercy."[1] The House protested that this attitude "was not in accordance with that courtesy which was due the House of Assembly as a branch of the Legislature,"[2] but the Colonial Office agreed with Young and instructed him not to yield any concessions or compromise his position in any way.[3]

The Assembly, undaunted, pursued its demand into the 1840's only to be warned by Gladstone that its impatience might result in the stoppage of the annual grant altogether.[4] The issue was carried from this point to the round of bargaining which immediately preceded the winning of responsible government.

Another financial issue was a deadlock between the Assembly and the Legislative Council over appropriations. Until 1810 it had been the practice of the Assembly to send appropriations separately to the Legislative Council so that the latter could assent to, or reject, them singly as it wished. In 1825 the House sent all the appropriations to the upper house together in one revenue bill with the obvious implication that the items had to be accepted *in toto* or the entire revenue would not be forthcoming.[5] The upper chamber assented to the bill because of the lateness of the session and the inconvenience which would result from lack of funds, but, in an indignant resolution, it advised the Assembly that it would not consent in future to any such legislation unless its members could "exercise their right of deliberating separately upon every measure for which provision is to be made in the Appropriation bill."[6]

[1]Young to Goderich, April 4, 1832, *ibid.*, A 48, p. 99; *ibid.*, A 50, p. 109; *Assembly Journals*, 1832, pp. 108-9, 130.
[2]*Assembly Journals*, 1833, pp. 86, 87, 92.
[3]The Governor-in-Chief, Charles Poulett Thompson, later Lord Sydenham, visited Fitzroy in 1840. He reported to Lord John Russell that the Islanders expected too much from the Governor in the way of maintaining an expensive household, the dignities of office, and the entertainment of strangers on a pittance of £1,000 a year. He advised the Colonial Secretary to tell the Assembly that if it did not vote a suitable increase to the Governor the colony would be annexed to Nova Scotia. Thompson to Lord John Russell, July 27, 1840, Public Archives of Canada, Colonial Office Records (Lower Canada), G 12, vol. 57, p. 7. Russell was content, however, to leave the question, for he doubted "the propriety of attempting to extort it by a threat of doing that which, in itself, is not expedient." Russell to Fitzroy, Sept. 10, 1840, P.A.C. (P.E.I.), G 13, p. 25.
[4]Gladstone to Huntley, May 29, 1846, *ibid.*, G 16, p. 387; *Assembly Journals*, 1847, Appendix B.
[5]Huntley to Stanley, May 12, 1845, *ibid.*, Appendix C.
[6]Resolution of Council, Oct. 27, 1825, *ibid.*, 1825, 2nd session, p. 24.

The matter came to a head in 1827 during a debate on the raising of import duties. The Assembly anticipated obstruction from the Legislative Council and passed a resolution to the effect that the popular house had the "ancient and undisputed" right to grant supply to His Majesty and that the upper house should not make any change in the grants. The Legislative Council would not agree that the right was either ancient or undisputed, and pointed out that Patterson's Instructions had stressed that "the greatest care should be taken that no colour or pretence is given for the assumption of any powers or privileges by the said lower House of Assembly or House of Representatives which have not been allowed to Assemblies in other colonies." The Council then reminded the lower house that in the Instructions to the Governor of Nova Scotia dated 1756 it was stated that some assemblies "have taken upon them the solid framing of money bills, refusing to let the Council alter or amend the same," which practice was "very detrimental to our prerogative . . . ; it is also our further pleasure that the Council have the like power of framing money bills as the Assembly." It was also pointed out that in the neighbouring colonies the general practice was for the Assembly to submit appropriations separately to the Legislative Council and that the Island Assembly should not seek privileges which did not prevail elsewhere.[1]

Governor Ready was consulted on the question, and he sought advice from Chief Justice Archibald, the Speaker of the Nova Scotia Assembly. Archibald expressed the opinion that the Island reformers were going too far in their demands and advised that in his province and in New Brunswick the Assembly permitted the Legislative Council an important part in the passing of appropriation bills.[2] The Assembly answered this opinion by refusing "to draw the Legislature of this Island into an ignominious de-

[1] *Ibid.*, 1827, pp. 6, 41, 42.
[2] "The Assembly of Nova Scotia, of which I have the honor to be Speaker, never claimed to exercise the powers the House (of P.E.I.) have assumed; and while the Council there do not interfere with the House in originating Money Bills, the House invariably allow the Council to exercise their opinion upon every subject separately; and only such as are agreed to by both branches, in separate resolutions are inserted in the Appropriation Bill; and I think I am correct when I add that the same course is pursued in New Brunswick." Archibald to Ready, May 8, 1827, P.A.C. (P.E.I.), A 45, p. 135.

pendence on the usage of another Colony, of which it is, and hath been, quite independent"; it had rules and practices of its own, and would maintain its demands for the sole power in respect to money bills.[1]

An interesting feature of the issue was that Governor Ready sympathized with the Assembly, for he realized that not only a constitutional principle but also "much private feeling and animosity has, I fear, been mixed up in this dispute."[2] Too many relatives and friends of former Governors held official positions who did not enjoy the confidence of the Assembly, and a number of them, including a son of Governor DesBarres and a son-in-law of Governor Smith, had been dismissed for various irregularities and neglect of duties.[3] Ready was not impressed with arguments which relied on the practice in other colonies. It was quite different in Nova Scotia, he pointed out to the Colonial Secretary, where the Legislative Council included "the wealth, the talents, the respectability, and persons of weight and consequence in the Country." In the Island's upper chamber "we have no such persons, and cannot have for some time to come." He doubted whether any benefit would result from giving the existing Legislative Council the right to interfere in the appropriations. Such a right might be used for private purposes and might result in the refusal of the Assembly to vote supplies.[4]

This was a severe indictment on the part of the Governor of persons who in their executive capacity were his own advisers, an opinion which led, for the time being, to the unusual spectacle of the Governor and Assembly joining hands against the two Councils. His Excellency even considered dismissing several members of the upper house as a possible solution of the problem, but he was prevented from doing so by the Colonial Secretary.[5] Ready's

[1] *Assembly Journals,* 1827, p. 43.
[2] Ready to Bathurst, June 12, 1827, P.A.C. (P.E.I.), A 44, p. 97.
[3] See Report of the Commissioners of Customs, July 21, 1827, *ibid.,* p. 97; Ready to Huskisson, June 24, 1828, *ibid.,* A 45, p. 317; *Assembly Journals,* May 3, 1828, p. 37.
[4] Ready to Bathurst, June 12, 1827, P.A.C. (P.E.I.), A 44, p. 97.
[5] James Stephen to Under Secretary of State, Oct. 16, 1828, *ibid.,* A 45, p. 209.

fears were justified, for the deadlock between the two houses resulted in the stoppage of supply in the sessions of 1827 and 1828.[1]

The Governor guided the administration as best he could under the circumstances, spending what small moneys were at his disposal only on the most important works and leaving the competing houses to settle their own differences. "A system of mutual compromise," he told them, "appears to me the best mode for both parties to pursue."[2] The reformers shifted their attention during the next decade to the demand for the separation of the Executive and Legislative Councils, while compromise and the tact of Governors Young, Harvey, and Fitzroy kept the appropriations issue in the background.[3]

The question broke out again, however, in the 1840's when the two houses bickered constantly over the revenue, and the blundering Governor Huntley, noted for his language rather than his sagacity, entered the fray on behalf of the Legislative Council, which by now had been separated from the Executive Council. This time the Governor did all he could to convince the British Government of the respectability of the upper house and the arrogance of the lower. He wrote the Colonial Secretary that the Legislative Councillors were "men of Education, experience in the world . . . who from their Cradles had been bred up in the manly tone of a Gentleman's mind" and who had to "oppose the overbearing dominion of ignorance" of the members of the Assembly who mistook "the effect of manual labor and frugality for the working of a superior intellect."[4] The Legislative Council no doubt was duly flattered by the Governor's exalted opinion of it, but His Excellency's views only served to increase the antagonism between the two houses, and the question joined the other issues in the final move toward responsible government. The Colonial

---

[1] See also *Assembly Journals*, 1828, pp. 29-38.
[2] *Ibid.*, 1829, p. 3.
[3] See for example Young's conciliation in the threatened break-down of 1835, *ibid.*, 1835, p. 157.
[4] Huntley to Stanley, April 22, 1845, P.A.C. (P.E.I.), G 48, p. 204; *Assembly Journals*, 1846, pp. 42-3 and 90-100; Huntley to Gladstone, April 17, 1846, P.A.C. (P.E.I.), G 48, p. 284.

Office was unable to settle it by giving a definite opinion, because successive Secretaries of State disagreed on the matter. It therefore contented itself with recommending to the two houses "a temperate and conciliatory course," which suggestion, said Sir James Stephen, "avoids all difficulties by leaving them all undecided."[1]

These controversies were further complicated by the fact that the Imperial Government kept control over all legislation, financial and otherwise. It could do this through the suspending clause, the Governor's power to refuse assent or reserve bills for the King's pleasure, and the King's prerogative of disallowance.

In certain cases the Assembly was not supposed to pass legislation without a suspending clause which provided that "nothing herein contained shall be of any force or effect until His Majesty's pleasure is known," and if the royal confirmation were not signified within three years, the legislation concerned was inoperative.[2] The suspending clause was a serious limitation on the legislative powers of any colonial assembly. It was particularly burdensome on the Prince Edward Island Legislature, which by this device was frequently frustrated in its efforts to increase its meagre revenues by taxes on land and imports. The suspending clause was thus used to safeguard property rights. The Instructions provided that "no law or ordinance respecting private property be passed without a clause suspending its execution until our royal will and pleasure is known." The Assembly could therefore do nothing with respect to the land question without the constant scrutiny of the Colonial Office, and it found this limitation on its powers particularly galling when it knew that the proprietors themselves had easy access to the Secretary of State.

By his Commission the Governor enjoyed a "negative voice in the making and passing of all laws, statutes and ordinances," which enabled him to refuse his assent to legislation. Moreover,

---

[1]See Huskisson to Ready, Oct. 20, 1827, *P.E.I. House of Assembly Debates,* 1828, p. 34; Gladstone to Huntley, June 30, 1846, *Assembly Journals,* 1847, Appendix B; James Stephen to Under Secretary of State, Oct. 16, 1828, P.A.C. (P.E.I.), A 45, p. 209; Colonial Office Memorandum by "J. S.," Feb. 11, 1841, *ibid.,* A 60-1, p. 243.

[2]See Fanning to Portland, Sept. 10, 1801, *ibid.,* A 16, p. 28.

he was ordered in his Instructions to seek the King's permission before giving assent to any bills "of an unusual or extraordinary nature and importance." Actually, however, these powers were of little practical importance, for the Colonial Office encouraged the use of the suspending clause as a way of avoiding antagonism between the Governor and the Assembly which might be provoked by action of His Excellency. "When you may entertain doubts of the policy of any measure proposed," Lord Bathurst instructed Smith, "it is not necessary that you should take upon yourself the responsibility of its rejection, provided that you secure the insertion in the Bill of a suspending clause."[1] Moreover, if the Assembly anticipated the Governor's opposition to its measures, it was generally inclined to use the suspending clause as a means of seeking assent directly from the Sovereign.

The Imperial authorities also used the power of disallowance to ensure that colonial legislation would not be "repugnant to the laws of England," and a number of acts were disallowed on this score.[2] Many statutes, too, were disallowed because of defective construction or careless drafting.[3] In the young colony there were few officials who understood the fine points of drafting statutes, and it was not until a group of competent lawyers appeared in its government that this objection declined in importance. The delay and uncertainty which accompanied this supervision from London irked the Assembly and contributed substantially to the confusion associated with responsible government and the land question.[4]

[1]Bathurst to Smith, Nov. 18, 1817, *ibid.*, G 4, p. 268.
[2]See Board of Trade to the King, Nov. 24, 1775, *ibid.*, A 3, p. 35.
[3]E.g., for technical errors, Stanley to Young, May 28, 1834, *Assembly Journals*, 1835, pp. 20-1; and for "unusual carelessness" in drafting, Newcastle to Dundas, Aug. 19, 1861, *ibid.*, 1862, Appendix E.
[4]On one occasion the Colonial Secretary described what happened to colonial legislation after it reached London. "All Acts when received from the Colony," he wrote, "are transmitted to the Lord President to be laid before His Majesty in Council, and being then referred to a committee of Privy Council, reports are made from that Committee for the assistance of His Majesty in deciding upon each Act. When such reports are confirmed, an order to that effect is drawn up at the Colonial Office, and is thence conveyed to this Department for transmission to the Colony. In the course of these proceedings a considerable time may often be consumed even when the utmost activity is employed, because their progress is subject to the delays of protracted enquiry, of hearing parties objecting to the confirmation of particular laws, and of holding meetings of the Privy Council." Goderich to Young, July 4, 1832, P.A.C. (P.E.I.), G 7, p. 188.

During the general process of adjustment among institutions of government which preceded the granting of responsible government, the Island reformers watched with hope the parallel developments in other colonies. Events in Nova Scotia under the spectacular leadership of Joseph Howe and the general agitation in Upper and Lower Canada greatly overshadowed what took place in Charlottetown. To a certain extent they made reform on the Island almost inevitable. Papineau of Lower Canada had exhorted the Island Assembly to co-operate "in procuring a better Colonial system for *all*," and the reformers never lost sight of events on the mainland, and, indeed, used the example of those events to further their own ends.[1] When the various reform movements on the Island joined for a show-down with the Imperial authorities in the late 1840's the real issue was not so much the desirability of responsible government—that had already been settled—but rather whether the system which had been won in the other colonies would fit the geographic, economic, and political circumstances of a tiny island with a small population.

Responsible government implied a responsible executive which would be chosen so as to conform with the party pattern of the popularly elected house and which would change with the rise and fall of party fortunes. It required a number of available and suitable Executive Councillors, not a scarce supply of paid officials sent out from England, and the presence of alert and effective political parties, not a number of mere factions based on personal and group rivalries. It assumed also an interested public opinion and a degree of independence from the Colonial Office. The question of whether Prince Edward Island was prepared for such a government was the basis of the colony's politics after 1840.[2]

The Assembly requested the Queen in April, 1840 to grant a system of responsible government to the Island. In a formal Address it asserted that nothing could be done under existing circum-

---

[1] L. J. Papineau to Speaker of House of Assembly, P.E.I., *Assembly Journals*, 1836, pp. 114-18.

[2] A detailed account of the final stages of the responsible government movement in the colony is contained in W. Ross Livingston, "Responsible Government in Prince Edward Island," *University of Iowa Studies in the Social Sciences*, vol. IX, no. 4, 1931.

stances to settle the land question, for the proprietors and their agents had too much influence in administration. It threatened that, unless the Imperial Government did something about the land issue, "the House of Assembly must consult their constituents as to the propriety of being annexed to one of the adjacent Colonies, as the inhabitants will never agree to submit their property and political rights to the will of the proprietors and their agents." The Queen was told that the Assembly had no confidence in either the Executive or the Legislative Council. She was requested to put into effect the "principles of responsibility of public officers" expressed by the Secretary of State, Lord John Russell, and to settle the grievances "by removing some of those who are opposed to the wishes of the majority of the people, and selecting those in whom the people of this Island and their Representatives have confidence, and with whom your Petitioners could cooperate for the general good."[1]

What prompted the Assembly to action was the famous circular despatch of Lord John Russell, dated October 16, 1839, which had been sent to the colonial governors and which became one of the chief documents of the responsible government era. The Colonial Secretary had noted that public officers in the colonies who had been appointed during pleasure were in effect retained for life. This situation resulted from the fact that such officials were originally brought out from England, and that, therefore, security of tenure was a necessary feature if suitable men were to be obtained. As colonial residents became available for official positions the need for life appointments lessened. Russell thereupon instructed the governors to make it "generally known, that hereafter the tenure of Colonial officers held during Her Majesty's pleasure, will not be regarded as equivalent to a tenure during good behaviour," and that such officers will be called upon "to retire from the public service as often as any sufficient motives of public polity may suggest." This was not to apply to judicial officers or to persons exercising functions of a

[1] Address to the Queen, April 27, 1840, *Assembly Journals*, 1840, pp. 146-51.

non-political nature, but to "ministerial" officials including members of the Executive Council.¹

The despatch was received with enthusiasm by the reformers on the Island and they quoted it at every turn for the next ten years. In Nova Scotia and in the Canadas too it was regarded by reformers as the signal for responsible government. But the British Government had not intended it to make the executive responsible to the Assembly, but rather to the Governor, and through him to the Colonial Office. Sir Colin Campbell at Halifax wrote (with the subsequent approval of the Imperial authorities) that the despatch was "not intended to sanction any fundamental change of the Constitution, but merely to strengthen the hands of the Governor by enabling him more effectively to control refractory Public functionaries." This was also the interpretation of Sir Henry Huntley of Prince Edward Island. In that colony, as in Nova Scotia and the Canadas, the despatch encouraged results different from those intended. The Island's Executive Council had been made politically vulnerable, so as to increase popular control over its members; the reformers now recognized that their next step was to ensure that the Governor used his Council according to the wishes of a majority in the Assembly.²

Governor Huntley soon reminded the Assembly that reform had not yet come. The House in 1841 had requested His Excellency not to reappoint one Peter Maccallum as Sheriff, whose office was one of those specifically mentioned in the Russell despatch as being subject to change as "motives of public polity may suggest." The Governor refused to follow the Assembly's wish, and stressed that "he must continue to exercise his own discretion in a matter which concerns the Prerogative of the Crown, and for which he alone is responsible."³ A similar attack was made on the two Councils. A committee of the Assembly studied the connections and interests of the members of the Councils, found most of them related by blood or marriage, and recorded their conviction that "a family compact of such magnitude, however well

[1]Russell to Fitzroy (circular), Oct. 16, 1839, *ibid.*, Appendix M.
[2]See also Chester Martin, *Empire and Commonwealth*, pp. 186-8; 245-6.
[3]*Assembly Journals*, 1841, pp. 128, 131.

disposed in advising the Executive, will take care of themselves and their friends in the first place, and the interests of the Colony only as a secondary consideration."[1] The Governor, however, strove at first to protect these people from "the wild and destructive spirit" of the Assembly,[2] and the Colonial Secretary showed no inclination to weaken the "Prerogative of the Crown." Huntley did not wish his Councillors to bow to the lower house, and he blocked every attempt "to concentrate the whole governing power in the Assembly, where there neither is, nor do I think there can be for a long time yet, any sufficient intelligence to govern at all."[3] To the Governor there were too many "plausible paupers" in the House and not enough "men of sound judgment and integrity" because the constituents "are very carefully taught that only a 'backwoodsman' knows how to legislate for a 'backwoodsman.'"[4] Although the reform party received a substantial majority in the general elections of 1846, Huntley was able to illustrate what he meant when violence and bloodshed resulted from the Belfast election riots of that year.[5]

The fact that the Assembly turned deaf ears to His Excellency's appeal for additional salary and was "quite careless" of the "respectability about the position of the Lieutenant-Governor" prompted much of Huntley's sarcasm.[6] Another important issue was a feud between His Excellency and Joseph Pope, the Speaker of the Assembly and a member of the Executive Council. Pope had blocked a proposal to increase the Governor's salary in view of the Assembly's policy of holding out for control of the Crown revenues, a stand which put him in a difficult position in his role as one of the Governor's advisers. Moreover, he had accused Huntley of "submission to backstairs advisers" and deception and underhand proceedings in connection with his secret despatches to England. Huntley responded by dismissing Pope from the

[1] See *supra*, pp. 37-8; *Assembly Journals*, 1841, p. 151.
[2] Huntley to Stanley, Feb. 11, 1843, *ibid.*, 1844, p. 49.
[3] Huntley to Gladstone, April 22, 1846, P.A.C. (P.E.I.) G 48, p. 295.
[4] *Ibid.*
[5] See Sheriff to Colonial Secretary, March 2, 1847, *Assembly Journals*, 1847, Appendix I.
[6] Huntley to Stanley, July 15, 1844, P.A.C. (P.E.I.), G 48, p. 175; Dec. 23, 1844, *ibid.*, p. 183.

Executive Council without consulting the Council in the manner required by his Instructions, which abrupt procedure had been prompted by his knowledge that the Council would have opposed the suspension unless the Secretary of State were consulted.[1] The Assembly thereupon rallied to the support of its Speaker, resolved that Huntley's action was "an unwarranted and uncalled for exercise of power," and, by a vote of 14 to 3, expressed its want of confidence in the Governor.[2] It then reported Huntley's "continued acts of petty despotism" to the Queen and asked for his removal.[3] For two months a constant stream of documents on the issue reached London from the Assembly, from Pope, and from Huntley in a series of denunciations couched in his most picturesque language.[4]

The Colonial Office quickly put the Governor in his place. Gladstone scolded him for "sarcastic and contemptuous language" and ordered him to use in his despatches "that calm and measured tone" necessary in communications concerning the Queen's business.[5] Lord Grey, Gladstone's successor, expressed regret that Huntley had become involved in such an unseemly controversy. He should not have noticed Pope's criticism in the Assembly, nor should he have resorted to such a "highly irregular" process of suspension. Huntley was instructed to cease all proceedings against Pope, reinstate him in the Executive Council, and submit all the despatches on the subject to the Council for its examination.[6] There the matter rested temporarily, for Pope had resigned his seat in the Council.[7]

In the following year the Assembly passed a resolution by a vote of 18 to 3 to the effect that members of the Executive Council who lose the confidence of a majority in the Assembly should resign and be replaced by others having such confidence.[8] Surprisingly enough

[1] Huntley to Gladstone, April 17, 1846, *ibid.*, p. 284.
[2] *Assembly Journals*, April 7, 8, 1846, pp. 97, 99.
[3] *Ibid.*, pp. 114-16.
[4] P.A.C. (P.E.I.), G 48, G 49.
[5] Gladstone to Huntley, June 30, 1846, *ibid.*, G 16, p. 459.
[6] Grey to Huntley, Aug. 13, 1846, *ibid.*, p. 511; Sept. 16, 1846, *ibid.*, p. 551.
[7] Grey advised that a member of the Council could not say what he liked in the House about the Governor and remain in the Council; he should resign before indulging in such criticism. *Ibid.*
[8] *Assembly Journals*, 1847, p. 63.

Huntley, who in the previous year considered that the "abstruse subject of Colonial Responsible Government . . . had confounded all reasonable and practical systems of Colonial rule,"[1] now promised the Assembly his "best support." "Whatever doubt I may at one time have entertained," he said, "has been dispelled by the experience obtained from the political events which have distinguished the last twelve months in this Colony." "Unanimity of political views," he declared, should prevail between the Governor and his Executive Council, and, on the understanding that the Councillor must retain office only on his agreement with the Governor, he thought responsible government was "as requisite to the free exercise of the Constitutional authority, and beneficial influence of the Lieut. Governor himself, as . . . advantageous to the People of the Island generally."[2]

Although this declaration seems to be a direct change of heart on the part of Huntley, it was not prompted by any love for genuine responsible government or by any sympathy with the Assembly. He and the popular house were actually looking for two different things. As he told Grey, he wished to "preserve that authority which is due to the position of the representative of the Sovereign" by breaking "a small party in Charlottetown [who] have virtually ruled the Colony confining to themselves and their alliances all promotions to positions of emolument and influence."[3] In other words, he was doing nothing more than following the spirit of Lord John Russell's despatch of 1839 by increasing the responsibility of the executive *to the Governor* and thereby putting himself in a better position to deal with recalcitrant Councillors, two of whom (Joseph Pope and Edward Palmer) had resigned from the Council and had embarked for England to seek Huntley's recall. Although this was not responsible government as the reformers wished it, the Governor's attitude contributed in some measure to their bargaining power.

Meanwhile, negotiations for responsible government were being continuously carried on in the other colonies, and the Island re-

[1] Huntley to Gladstone, April 17, 1846, P.A.C. (P.E.I.), G 48, p. 284.
[2] *Assembly Journals*, 1847, p. 145.
[3] Huntley to Grey, May 9, 1847, P.A.C. (P.E.I.), G 48, p. 408.

formers were anxious to obtain any concessions which might be gained elsewhere. The Colonial Office made it clear, however, that the Island's circumstances did not warrant the automatic application to its government of principles which might be recognized in the other colonies. Gladstone warned the Assembly that there were "wide distinctions" between the colony and Canada with respect to "the fundamental rules of the constitution" and the "sources whence the charges of their respective Governments are defrayed," "a dissimilarity which Her Majesty considers as conclusive against the general inference or assumption, that either Colony is entitled to claim the benefit of any particular political usage, which it may be desirous to adopt and borrow from the other."[1] Earl Grey, although favourably disposed to the principle of responsible government, took the same view even after its achievement in the other provinces. Responsible government was "a work of time" and had been postponed in other colonies "until the gradual increase of the community in wealth, numbers and importance appeared to justify it." "Prince Edward Island is comparatively small in extent and population, and its commercial and wealthy classes confined almost to a single town," and "wanting as yet, in the external circumstances which would render the introduction of Responsible Government expedient." "Time, and the natural progress of events, can alone remove the present deficiency. . . . The time has not yet arrived for any fundamental change in the manner in which the Government of Prince Edward Island is now carried on."[2] Governor Campbell, Huntley's successor, echoed his chief's opinions and reinforced them in a series of despatches on the conditions

[1] Gladstone to Huntley, May 28, 1846, *Assembly Journals*, 1847, Appendix B. This statement was not consistent with a principle expressed twenty years before by Lord Glenelg: "In the conduct of affairs in British North America no principle is of more importance than the maintenance of one consistent and uniform course of policy in the administration of the Government of the different Provinces which comprize His Majesty's Dominions in that Quarter of the Globe. It is vain to suppose that any concession can be made to the General Assembly of any one of those Provinces, and withheld from the rest, or that on the part of the Crown any prerogative can be effectively asserted in one, unless it be maintained with equal firmness in the others." Glenelg to Lord Gosford, copy to Sir John Harvey, Sept. 30, 1836, P.A.C. (P.E.I.), G 8, p. 140.

[2] Grey to Campbell, Jan. 1, 1849, *Assembly Journals*, 1849, Appendix D; see also Grey to Huntley, Sept. 3, 1847, P.A.C. (P.E.I.), G 17, p. 167.

in the colony.¹ Campbell reported that the colony was backward and harassed by land troubles, that its material resources were few, and that there was an insufficient number of politically informed citizens to make responsible government work.

The opinions of the Governors-General confirmed the views of the Imperial authorities with respect to the Island's preparation for responsible government. Charles Poulett Thompson was singularly unimpressed with the colony and its government during his visit to Charlottetown in 1840.² Lord Elgin admitted to the Colonial Secretary that he was "too little informed with respect to men and things" on the Island, but suggested that although the colony's government was not sufficiently matured, "it would not be expedient . . . to attempt to move in any direction except toward what is termed 'Responsible Government.'"³ His doubt was sufficient, however, to confirm Grey's opinions of the Island, and the latter remained content to await "time and the natural progress of events."

The Colonial Secretary found, however, that the Island reformers did not wish to do without a boon which had been bestowed on the other colonies. Moreover they had a weapon with which to force his hands—the civil list issue. On December 14, 1848 Grey advised Governor Campbell that the British Government had borne the expenses of the Island's government since 1776, and now that the colony had developed and its revenue was greater than its expenditure, he would advise Parliament to discontinue the annual grant to the colony, except the salary of the Governor. In later despatches he advised that the new arrangement would come into effect on April 1, 1849. Henceforth the Island would have to carry its own load and its expenditures would depend solely on the discretion of the Legislature. This plan, he indicated in 1850, would not require responsible government, but he would not "advise Her Majesty to refuse this concession if it

¹*Ibid.*, G 17, 18, 19.
²Thompson (later Lord Sydenham) to Lord John Russell, July 27, 1840, P.A.C. (Lower Canada), G 12, vol. 57, p. 7.
³See Elgin to Grey, July 27, 1847, *Elgin-Grey Papers, 1846-1852*, ed. A. G. Doughty (Ottawa, 1937), vol. I, p. 60; Sept. 14, 1847, *ibid.*, p. 68; Sept. 25, 1847, *ibid.*, vol. IV, Appendix IX, p. 1375.

should appear that it is the real wish of the inhabitants of the Colony in general."¹

The Island Assembly was quick to bargain. It proposed that the Imperial authorities should grant responsible government and control of the revenues of the Crown first, and then the House would assume the civil list.² Earl Grey and Governor Campbell were prepared to agree, but in the reverse order, financial provision first, and constitutional reform afterwards.³ The Assembly stood firm, however, and in 1850 passed a Civil List Bill with a provision that it would go into effect only upon the transfer of the Crown revenues and the granting of responsible government.

Meanwhile Campbell had dissolved the Assembly because he saw "no hope that the House would consent to separate the question of Responsible Government from the settlement of the Civil List."⁴ A new Assembly was elected with a majority of 18 to 6 in favour of reform. Early in the new session the reform leader, George Coles, moved and carried a vote of want of confidence in the Executive Council,⁵ and a few days later a resolution was passed stating that since the executive showed no indication of implementing the expressed wishes of the people regarding responsible government, the House would refuse to vote supply.⁶ After a month's adjournment the House would agree only to a conditional revenue bill and was thereupon lectured by the Governor for "this premeditated neglect of your Legislative functions."⁷

The persistence of the reformers and the evident wishes of the people at last prevailed, and in January, 1851 Sir Alexander Bannerman, who succeeded to the governorship upon the death of Campbell, was instructed to implement responsible government upon the Island and surrender to the Assembly the Crown revenues

---

¹Grey to Campbell, Dec. 14, 1848, *Assembly Journals,* 1849, Appendix C; Feb. 7, 1849, *ibid.,* Appendix K; Dec. 27, 1849, *ibid.,* 1850, 1st session, Appendix A; Feb. 18, 1850, *ibid.,* Appendix E.
²*Ibid.,* 1849, March 17, pp. 45, 108-9.
³*Ibid.,* p. 50; Grey to Campbell, Dec. 27, 1849, P.A.C. (P.E.I.), G 19, p. 281; Feb. 18, 1850, *ibid.,* p. 345.
⁴Campbell to Grey, Jan. 9, 1850, *ibid.,* G 49, p. 215.
⁵*Assembly Journals,* 1850, 1st session, p. 15.
⁶*Ibid.,* p. 33.
⁷*Ibid.,* 1850, 2nd session, pp. 8-16.

in return for adequate compensation to the existing office holders. Reform, Earl Grey stressed, was not granted as a condition of a civil list bill, but, as in the case of the other colonies, "on the faith of the Crown."[1] Bannerman announced the arrangement to the Assembly at the opening of the session of 1851. A few days later, on April 24, George Coles advised the House that he had been commanded by His Excellency to form a Government which would have the confidence of the Assembly.

[1] Grey to Bannerman, Jan. 31, 1851, *ibid.*, 1851, Appendix D.

CHAPTER IV

CONSTITUTIONAL ADJUSTMENT, 1851-1873

PRINCE EDWARD ISLAND was granted self-government in 1851, but some time elapsed before the system became completely established. The two decades before the Island entered Confederation were marked by many adjustments in the various political institutions and in their new relations to one another. It took time for the Cabinet to become an efficient team, for the Governor to realize that his position had become largely decorative and formal, for the Legislative Council to resign itself to the role of a secondary chamber, and for the Assembly to become accustomed to its new responsibilities and importance.

The four Governors whose terms followed the granting of responsible government were reluctant to accept the new limitations upon their powers. Bannerman meddled in plans for settling the land question; Daly was too free with his advice and opinions; the able but critical George Dundas had several differences with his Premiers; and William Robinson injected much intrigue into the Confederation negotiations. The chief difficulty was the awkward position of an English official in the concentrated turmoil of Island politics. Some of the Governors felt that the province was too small and politically unstable for responsible government, while all excused their interference on the basis of a knowledge superior to that of local politicians.

The Governor's salary was still a major difficulty. When the civil list was transferred to the Island, the British Government agreed to retain the charge for the salary as compensation for the colony's expenses in connection with the land question. This arrangement was continued even after the other provinces had taken over the payment of such salaries. Yet the Imperial authorities expected the local Assembly to provide a supplementary allowance, which the popular house declined to do despite the complaints of the Governors. After much dispute, the British authorities advised the Island Government that it would have to assume responsibility for the salary when Dundas had completed his term.[1] Although the Assembly annually expressed deep regret at the change, it faced the new charge in 1869, and provided a sum of £1,400 sterling.[2] The Governors' salaries now depended on the good will of the Assembly, and this arrangement continued to provide the Governor, the Cabinet, and the House with a constant excuse for bickering.

The four Governors took seriously their roles of representatives of the Colonial Office by penning secret, newsy, and not always complimentary despatches on events and personalities on the Island. The Liberals were suspicious of these communications and emphasized that His Excellency should have no such secret correspondence under responsible government.[3] The Conservatives, on the other hand, recognized the "prerogative of the Crown in submitting or withholding despatches," and refused to concede that responsible government had placed the Queen's representative in the position of a "mere automaton."[4] The Colonial Office ignored the Liberal complaints and continued to direct the Governors either to reveal or to withhold the contents of despatches.

The salary and despatch questions were not serious constitutional issues, but, together with the Governors' propensity to meddle, they prompted much public criticism of the office and person of the Governor. Even at the time the Island entered Confederation the Governor was entertaining odd notions of his function as head of the government. Following the defeat of the Haythorne administration in the general election of April, 1873, Governor Robinson summoned James C. Pope, a Conservative, to form a Government and specified that the new Premier was to do his best to bring the province into Confederation on the terms then offered by the Dominion.[5] Although Pope was in favour of the Confederation terms, he declined "the honor of attempting to form

[1]For the correspondence on this subject see *P.E.I. House of Assembly Journals*, 1868, Appendix C; *ibid.*, 1869, Appendix O.
[2]32 Vic., c. 3. This was changed to $7,000 a year in 1872.
[3]*Assembly Journals*, 1861, pp. 90-6; *P.E.I. House of Assembly Debates*, May 10, 1866, pp. 122-7; *ibid.*, 1869, p. 141.
[4]*Ibid.*, 1860, p. 32; *ibid.*, 1866, pp. 122-7.
[5]This correspondence is contained in W. L. Cotton, *Chapters in Our Island Story* (Charlottetown, 1927), pp. 66-71; copies are in the Confederation Chamber of the Legislative Building in Charlottetown.

a Government pledged to your Honor to pursue any definite policy." "I trust that I may be pardoned," he said, "if I remind your Honor that the people of this Island have the right to self-government, and that as one of their representatives I can never undertake, at the instance of the representative of the Crown, to do any act calculated in the slightest degree, to abridge this right." Robinson assured Pope that he did not wish to infringe on the rights of the people, but that "the Crown should be aware of and have full reliance in, the personal views of the Minister in whom it proposes to place its chief confidence." When Pope again refused, the Governor said that he had to make sure that the views of Pope and the Legislature on union would not "be so wide apart as to be practically irreconcilable." Without such assurance he would have to summon another "whose estimate of the relative position of the Crown and its chief adviser shall better accord with my own." Such a threat to a party leader who had just received a handsome majority at the polls was singularly naïve. "As a matter of course," said Pope, "if I were to fail to acquiesce in the decision of the Legislature upon this or any other question, I would at once cease to be one of Your Honor's constitutional advisers." Robinson was forced to remove the condition, and the new Government was formed.

The changes associated with the development of responsible government were manifest, not only in the office of Lieutenant-Governor, but also in the process by which his powers devolved upon an Administrator in case of his death or absence. This was an important and interesting question in Prince Edward Island where practical conditions did not permit the successful application of the then customary procedure for the devolution of government which prevailed elsewhere in British North America, and where, consequently, the general practice of a much later day was first adopted.

Patterson's Commission named the eldest resident Councillor as Administrator, but much confusion resulted when several persons claimed seniority,[1] or when special provision had to be made

[1] E.g. during the absence of Patterson and Callbeck in 1775, Public Archives of Canada, Colonial Office Records (P.E.I.), A series, vol. 3, pp. 33-8.

for incompetent or aged eldest Councillors.[1] Early Administrators, moreover, were never sure of the limits of their powers, and their colleagues were often inclined to treat their authority lightly in view of the temporary character of their jurisdiction. Consequently an act was passed in 1836 which provided that all the powers vested in the Governor were to extend to the Administrator for the time being.[2]

By the 1830's the Imperial Government had provided that the governments of the colonies should devolve upon the senior officers commanding in the absence of the Governors, and this provision prevailed in most colonies until Confederation. The change did not suit the Island, for the senior officer commanding was usually a subaltern and only occasionally a captain, a rank which Governor Fitzroy thought was scarcely high enough for an acting Governor. Lord Glenelg appreciated this and indicated that "if timely notice be given of any approaching vacancy" the officer in command of the forces at Halifax could send a man of senior rank to Charlottetown specially for the occasion.[3] Such a plan would be impractical in case of the sudden death of a Governor, and in 1841 the senior Councillor was again given the right to act as Administrator by a special Royal Warrant to him personally.[4]

The Island procedure was unsuitable in a system of responsible government. George Coles was senior Councillor after 1851 and he

---

[1] E.g. Thomas DesBrisay in 1812, and Robert Gray in 1825; see also L. W. Labaree, *Royal Instructions to British Colonial Governors, 1670-1776* (New York, 1935), pp. 76-7.

[2] 6 Wm. IV, c. 17. For a time the Governors of the Island were involved in the devolution of government in Nova Scotia. When the two governments were placed under the Governor-General it was provided that in case of the death or absence of the Governor of Nova Scotia his powers should fall to the senior of the Governors of the Island and of Cape Breton. When Governor Parr died at Halifax in 1791, Fanning became Administrator of Nova Scotia but he never actually took over. P.A.C. (P.E.I.), A 11, pp. 246, 255; *ibid.*, A 20-1, p. 124. Later Governor DesBarres was advised that in such emergencies he should remain on the Island and not proceed to Nova Scotia unless he received royal instructions to do so. *Ibid.*, A 22, p. 3; *ibid.*, G 3, p. 112. This provision never came into effect.

[3] Fitzroy to Glenelg, July 5, 1838, *ibid.*, A 55-2, p. 482.

[4] After Fitzroy resigned in 1841, Surveyor George Wright acted without constitutional authority for some months before his warrant arrived and special legislation had to be passed to confirm his acts. 5 Vic., c. 1; P.A.C. (P.E.I.), G 14, p. 61. In the ten days between the departure of Huntley and the arrival of Campbell in 1848, the government was carried on without an Administrator. Campbell to Grey, Jan. 11, 1849, *ibid.*, G 49, p. 43.

held the King's Warrant to act as Administrator.¹ Coles, however, was the first Premier under responsible government, and, when Governor Bannerman was on a visit to Boston in 1853, Coles acted for a month as both Premier and Administrator at the same time. In such a position he could advise himself to give the royal assent or dissolve the Legislature, and in general govern as Administrator on the advice of himself as Premier!² Coles resigned his warrant in the following year upon his defeat at the polls and Bannerman recommended a similar warrant for John Holl, the new Premier. The Duke of Newcastle refused to appoint again a person who could not "escape the obvious suspicion of being actuated by party motives in the administration of the government." The Queen thereupon commissioned the Town Major, the commandant of the local battery, who was then the most available person with a tolerably high military rank, and thus brought the Island practice into line with that in the other provinces.³

The Town Major administered the government for only three days between the terms of Bannerman and Daly. The question of rank and position was raised once more, and the Administrator's Commission was again changed in 1855, this time in favour of the President of the Legislative Council.⁴ Here the matter rested until 1859 when, after Daly's departure, his powers devolved on Charles Young, then President of the upper house. Young, however, was an active and prominent Opposition politician who had just previously had a violent quarrel with the Government, and an embarrassing question arose as to the possibility of cordial and confidential relations between him and the Premier. The proceedings were made as constitutional as possible by an apology from Young to the Executive Council for certain strong language he had previously used, and a temporary truce which lasted until the new Governor arrived.⁵

¹See Bannerman to Grey, April 29, 1851, *ibid.*, G 50, p. 3.
²Newcastle to Bannerman, Aug. 19, 1853, *ibid.*, G 22, p. 267.
³Newcastle to Bannerman, April 25, 1854, *ibid.*, G 23, p. 73; Bannerman to Newcastle, May 23, 1854, *ibid.*, G 50, p. 360.
⁴Sidney Herbert, Colonial Office, to Daly, Feb. 16, 1855, *ibid.*, G 24, p. 90.
⁵Young was Surrogate and Judge of Probate as well and he had resigned his judicial post for the time being. After his term as Administrator was up,

CONSTITUTIONAL ADJUSTMENT, 1851-1873   91

After the senior Executive Councillor, the Town Major, and the President of the Legislative Council had been tried without success, the Administrator's Commission was then given in 1859 to the Chief Justice "in furtherance of that policy of removing from the chance of administering the Government those who are actually engaged in the strife of political party."[1] This was a constitutional innovation, for, since the establishment of the government, the Chief Justice had been specifically excluded from administering in the absence of the Governor. His Lordship, however, had sometimes acted on the Governor's behalf in giving royal assent to bills and proroguing the Legislature.[2] He, therefore, was the logical choice, and Sir Robert Hodgson became the first chief justice in British North America to hold the Administrator's Commission.[3]

The new Commission was in the name of the Chief Justice personally. If he died during the Governor's absence his power devolved, at first on the senior officer commanding, after 1870 on the President of the Legislative Council, and after 1872 on the Master of the Rolls, a process which thus completed the exclusion of politicians and minor military men from the administratorship.[4] For a time this arrangement had an adverse effect upon the work of the Supreme Court since it involved the occasional absence from the bench of its Chief Justice. It was provided in 1869 that "the Chief Justice of the Court of Appeal in Equity shall not be

a legal issue arose as to whether he could resume his judicial duties and displace another judge whom the Government had artfully appointed in his stead. Dundas to Newcastle, Aug. 8, 1859, *ibid.*, G 52, p. 11.
[1] Newcastle to Dundas, Sept. 24, 1859, *ibid.*, G 28, p. 267.
[2] When the Governor was unable to attend the Legislature he frequently constituted the Chief Justice or an Assistant Judge of the Supreme Court a Commission to act on his behalf; but if he were absent from the colony the Administrator assumed his powers, not the Commission.
[3] A similar change can be traced in Canada years later. The senior officer commanding was Administrator in the absence of the Governor-General until 1899 when Lord William Seymour acted in the absence of Lord Minto. The administratorship then passed to the Chief Justice of the Supreme Court of Canada, the first instance being that of Sir Henry Strong from June 9 to July 26, 1902, again in the absence of Lord Minto. Meanwhile, however, the Chief Justice occasionally acted as Deputy Governor while the Governor-General was in the country.
[4] *Assembly Journals*, 1879, Appendix C; *Assembly Debates*, 1871, p. 378; Commission to Sir Robert Hodgson, Jan. 29, 1872, P.A.C. (P.E.I.), G 41, p. 48.

disqualified from presiding over such Court of Appeal by reason of administering the Government of the Colony."[1] The Chief Justice did not try cases when Administrator except where the Court sat as a Court of Appeal.[2] This difficulty ceased after the number of judges was increased to three and a system of inferior courts was set up. Responsible government on the Island, therefore, showed that the Governor's powers could not be exercised effectively by political persons in the executive or the Legislature, and that, judicial independence notwithstanding, the only alternative was a judge.

The development of cabinet government in this period was affected by three major problems, the frequent break-down in solidarity and collective responsibility, the limitations on the powers of the Cabinet, and the difficulties of relating a comparatively large executive to a small Legislature.[3]

While solidarity and collective responsibility were of slight consequence during the terms of the early Governors, the need for them became urgent with responsible government. Yet it was exceedingly difficult, and often virtually impossible to obtain teamwork and mutual confidence under the political conditions of the fifties and sixties. The controversial issues of religion, land, and union split many Cabinets and continuity and efficiency became impossible with no less than fifteen Governments in twenty-five years. Disputes over the teaching of the Bible in public schools and the incorporation of the Orange Lodge subordinated political differences to denominational bitterness. Less intense, but almost as troublesome, were controversies over proposals for the confiscation of the landed estates. Proprietors and tenants proclaimed their rights to the land, while tenant leagues and the authorities clashed frequently as raids, skirmishes, and arrests kept many communities in constant turmoil.[4] In the Confederation era considerations of

[1] 32 Vic., c. 4.
[2] Sir Robert Hodgson was Administrator for a full year in 1869-70, and in 1874 he became Governor, not, however, without much criticism of the use of the bench for the convenience of Government House.
[3] A list of the Premiers of Prince Edward Island from the granting of responsible government to Confederation with the year of the formation of their Governments and their party allegiance will be found in Appendix G.
[4] See chapter v.

union and independence were added to the boiling pot of local politics.

These circumstances were reflected in the party structure and, in turn, in the Cabinet. Support of and opposition to responsible government were the distinguishing characteristics of the Liberals and Conservatives respectively in the early 1850's. This original classification soon gave way, however, as both parties became loose associations of interest groups temporarily united by shifting loyalties, and Governments were either unsteady coalitions or strongholds for denominational crusaders. Team-work could not thrive in such an atmosphere, and administration was weak and vacillating so long as non-political affiliations prevented any steady adherence to either party or Cabinet.

Local politicians, moreover, were often confused by their responsibilities as Ministers of the Crown. Accustomed to taking issue with the Governor and the Assembly, they found it difficult to put aside old antagonisms in favour of a close harmony with both Crown and Legislature as well as with one another. The rules and practices of cabinet government were unfamiliar, and successive issues resulted in several constitutional anomalies. Hon. Kenneth Henderson, for example, insisted on remaining in the Pope Cabinet of 1865-7 despite the wishes of his colleagues, the Governor, and the electorate, and he resigned only upon a threat of dismissal.[1] A secret "resignation" of Hon. Henry Beer from the Haythorne Government was an extraordinary disregard for Cabinet responsibility. Beer resigned on February 13, 1873, because he was opposed to sending a union delegation to Ottawa. He did not sit in the Cabinet after that date, but he and his colleagues kept the

---

[1]Henderson was a member of the Legislative Council. His seat therein became vacant in December, 1866 when he did not choose to stand for re-election to that House, and an Opposition member gained the seat. The reason he gave was that he intended to run for the Assembly in the elections of March, 1867. He was asked by the Premier to resign from the Cabinet, but he refused and insisted on attending all Cabinet meetings although no hints were spared that he was not wanted. Finally Premier Pope requested the Governor to dismiss Henderson. Dundas then asked the Minister to submit his resignation and thereby relieve His Excellency from having to resort to a dismissal. Henderson thereupon resigned. This is a unique instance of a Governor and a Cabinet combining to force the resignation of a recalcitrant Minister. P.A.C. (P.E.I.), G 53, p. 275.

matter from both the Governor and the public until after the resignation of the whole Government a few weeks later.¹ In 1871 Hon. Benjamin Davies remained in office thirty-six hours after the resignation of Premier Haythorne and the rest of the Cabinet, spoke for the "Government" in the House, and was recognized as a one-man administration by both parties.² On another occasion a member of the House was elected Speaker and appointed to a seat in the Cabinet on the same day, and retained both places for a week.³ An unexpected result of rapidly changing Cabinets was the large number of "Honourables" in the small province after Executive Councillors were given their titles for life in 1852. The system was changed again in 1863 and from that date to Confederation life titles were conferred only with the Queen's permission.⁴

Two limitations upon Cabinet powers added to the difficulties. The Imperial authorities emphasized that responsible government did not extend to political relations with foreign countries or to attempted settlement of the land question through infringing on property rights.

The local Government had to be reminded from time to time that its external affairs were the responsibility of the Colonial and Foreign Offices, for in the 1850's the Island was inclined to facilitate friendly relations with the United States on its own initiative. "There is no Colony in North America," wrote Bannerman in 1853, "where a stronger disposition has prevailed in the government and people ... for cultivating and promoting free and friendly intercourse with the United States."⁵ The Colonial Office was aware of this disposition and reminded the Islanders to refrain from inflicting "minor colonial matters" upon the relations between the mother country and the United States.⁶ In 1861 the Island

¹*Assembly Debates*, 1873, p. 32.   ²*Ibid.*, 1871, pp. 49-51.
³Hon. John Yeo, *Assembly Journals*, 1871, p. 3.
⁴Newcastle to Dundas, April 4, 1863, P.A.C. (P.E.I.), G 32, p. 114; Packington to Bannerman, Dec. 23, 1852, *ibid.*, G 21, p. 365. Until 1862 all Cabinet appointments had been subject to confirmation by the Queen. In that year such confirmation was discontinued as unsuited to responsible government. Newcastle to Dundas, Jan. 18, 1862, *ibid.*, G 31, p. 17.
⁵Bannerman to Packington, Nov. 8, 1852, *Assembly Journals*, 1853, Appendix E.   ⁶*Ibid.*

CONSTITUTIONAL ADJUSTMENT, 1851-1873 95

Assembly passed a resolution expressing "sorrow and regret" that the Civil War had broken out in the United States and sent it to Washington. Governor Dundas, the British Minister at Washington, and the Colonial and Foreign Secretaries at Downing Street criticized the Island Government because "the function of communicating with Foreign Powers is confined to Her Majesty's Government on behalf of the whole Empire."[1]

Another issue resulted in 1869 from a visit of General Benjamin Butler and a Committee of Congress to Charlottetown to discuss a plan for reciprocal free trade between the Island and the United States. The local Government received and entertained the visitors despite the objections of the Governor who made it a point to be absent in Halifax during the visit after warning his advisers that "a Colonial Government has not any authority whatever to enter into any arrangement with a foreign power, or with the representatives of a Legislative body of a foreign country."[2] The Colonial Office agreed with him and was "clearly of opinion that your Government exceeded their proper authority, in thus treating with the Committee of Congress."[3] Dundas was subjected to much criticism in the Assembly for obstructing his Government and slighting the delegation of Americans.[4]

A more serious limitation on the Cabinet was its lack of power to interfere with property rights. Indeed it was constantly frustrated by the fact that it was powerless to settle the colony's main problem, the land question. Many reformers had counted on responsible government to free them from proprietary influence, but the Imperial Government soon discouraged such hope. "The Lieutenant-Governor and Legislature of Prince Edward Island must remember," warned Sir George Grey in 1855, "that, although Responsible Government has been established in that Island, Responsible Government exists also in Great Britain; and Her

[1]P.A.C. (P.E.I.), G 30, pp. 311, 321, 333.
[2]Dundas to Council, Aug. 27, 1868, *Assembly Journals*, 1869, Appendix D.
[3]*Assembly Debates*, 1869, p. 224; see also P.A.C. (P.E.I.), G 37, p. 384; ibid., G 38, p. 65.
[4]Premier Hensley nevertheless attempted to protect the Governor by remarking that "in this house there is perfect freedom to make any remarks we like, but, as a general rule, it is better to make as little allusion as possible to the Representative of Royalty." *Assembly Debates*, 1869, p. 141.

Majesty's Government cannot take upon themselves the responsibility of advising the Crown to give its assent to Colonial Acts which are at variance with the principles of justice and invade those rights of property which are the foundation of social organization."[1] More than any other single factor, save denominational controversy, this limitation, which will be discussed in the following chapter, hampered the development of the Cabinet and restricted its effectiveness.

The most intricate problem which followed responsible government was the adjustment of the Executive Council to a small Assembly and an appointed Legislative Council. The reformers still insisted on the Cabinet being responsible to the Assembly, but a number of difficulties limited the application of this principle. There were only twenty-four members in the Assembly before 1856 and thirty after that date, and nine members in the Cabinet, so that if the Government had a bare majority in the Assembly and had few or no followers in the upper chamber, most of its supporters in the House would be Ministers. In other words, the Cabinet was too big for the Assembly, and its influence there, said Edward Palmer when Leader of the Opposition, had "an improper effect upon the independence of the legislature."[2] The Premier, moreover, had a limited number of persons from whom to select his colleagues. It was often difficult, too, for Ministers to find seats in the Assembly. They were therefore frequently appointed to vacancies in the Legislative Council and thus they endeavoured "to conform outwardly to the letter while sacrificing the true principle of responsibility to the people."[3]

It was the Liberal view that all heads of departments, salaried or otherwise, who were members of the Cabinet should also hold seats in the Legislature. Coles formed his first Government upon this theory and selected the nine members from the two Houses. He might have made the selection easier by reducing the size of the Cabinet by statute, but he carried on the original number which had been retained by custom and statute since 1784.

[1] Grey to Daly, Nov. 17, 1855, P.A.C. (P.E.I.), G 24, p. 331.
[2] Palmer to Daly, April 7, 1859, *ibid.*, G 51, p. 299.
[3] *Ibid.*, p. 302.

The Liberal plan soon showed its weaknesses. The election of 1854 gave the Liberals seventeen out of the twenty-four seats in the Assembly. Coles had wished to select all his Ministers from that House, but he had a restricted panel of only seventeen persons from whom to choose nine Ministers. His task became still more difficult when, within a two-year period 1857-9, five of his colleagues were defeated upon their seeking seats in the Assembly and he was unable to find a seat for the Attorney-General. His only alternative was to appoint salaried officers to the upper chamber and thereby incur the charge that he had in effect removed them from responsibility to the electors.[1] The difficulty increased when the election of July, 1858 returned a Government majority of only two, which was reduced to one when a member refused to take the oath and stalemate resulted from failure to elect a Speaker. It proved impossible to select a Cabinet of nine and a Speaker from only twelve available members, and after two days the Assembly was dissolved.

The Conservatives, on the other hand, advocated an arrangement whereby no department head, salaried or otherwise, should hold a seat in either House of the Legislature. This would make the Assembly independent of the executive, prevent the loading of the appointed upper house with members of the executive who could not secure seats in the popular chamber, and forbid the use of places in the Legislature as mere stepping stones to salaried offices. This, protested the Liberals, was an attempt "to introduce ingredients of Government from the United States into the constitution of this Her Majesty's Colony."[2] Governors Bannerman and Daly and the Secretary of State for the Colonies opposed the Conservative view and criticized tendencies to exclude the executive from the Legislature.[3]

The Conservatives had a chance to test their theory when they won the general election of 1859, for Palmer took office on the understanding that he could try it out. The new Cabinet was com-

[1]*Assembly Journals*, 1859, pp. 101-3.
[2]*Ibid.*, pp. 84-5; see also *Biographical Sketch of the Honourable Edward Whelan*, ed. Peter McCourt (Charlottetown, 1888), pp. 63-70.
[3]*Assembly Journals*, 1854, p. 8; P.A.C. (P.E.I.), G 32, p. 80; G 51, p. 297.

posed entirely of Ministers without Portfolio who served unpaid and who sat in the Assembly, while department heads were civil servants. The experiment was a failure. The Ministers had to be department heads in fact, if not in theory, if they were to control the administration effectively. It proved impossible to keep Ministers out of the Legislative Council, for the Government found itself hampered by the Liberal upper house in which it had only two supporters, and the Premier himself had to take a seat there in an attempt to make it more co-operative.[1] Few Ministers could afford to work unpaid, and after a year and a half in office Palmer himself found he could no longer serve without remuneration, and he placed his resignation in the hands of the Governor. No one else would take the premiership under the circumstances, and the Government therefore agreed to provide remuneration for its leader.[2] This departure from the theory was soon followed by others, and a paid Attorney-General and Colonial Secretary once more appeared in the Cabinet. By the election of 1864, therefore, the Conservatives had reverted to the old practice, which, observed the Colonial Office with approval, "is supported by general experience and usage in other places."[3]

The fundamental problem of relating a nine-man Ministry to a small Assembly and an appointed Legislative Council still remained. Associated with it was a prevailing inefficiency in the civil service. The tenure of Ministers depended on the uncertainties of politics and changes were frequent. They took their own appointees into their departments, and when they resigned the departmental officers went out also. The result was a constant upheaval which the Governor and the Colonial Secretary thought was responsible government carried to excess.[4]

Though nothing was done at this time to make the civil servants independent of politics, some improvement resulted during the Coles administration from the removal of a few of the lesser salaried officers from the Cabinet as well as from the Legislature.

[1] *Assembly Journals*, 1859, pp. 101-3; Dundas to Newcastle, Jan. 20, 1860, P.A.C. (P.E.I.), G 52, p. 70.
[2] Dundas to Newcastle, Dec. 10, 1860, *ibid.*, p. 163.
[3] Newcastle to Dundas, Feb. 25, 1863, *ibid.*, G 32, p. 80.
[4] *Assembly Journals*, 1855, p. 35; P.A.C. (P.E.I.), G 29, p. 115.

Such functionaries as the Registrar of Deeds, the Controller of Navigation Laws, and the Queen's Printer, all of whom held Cabinet rank in the Coles Government of 1851, were gradually removed from the Cabinet to the civil service. This arrangement proved a satisfactory compromise. Palmer went too far in attempting to deprive all Ministers of remuneration, for he found that such important officials as the Premier, the Attorney-General, and the Colonial Secretary, who devoted much of their time to their posts, could not serve without salary, and he had to return to the practice of permitting these officials to accept emolument and run by-elections, while other Ministers served unpaid. After filling the executive and the Legislature with paid office holders, Coles had found numerous by-elections inconvenient at a time of political uncertainty, and he too had to compromise by limiting the number of salaried Ministers to the Premier, the Attorney-General, and the Colonial Secretary. By the 1860's, then, it was the general practice of both parties to exclude all paid office holders from the Legislature and the Cabinet with the exception of the three senior Ministers. All nine Governments which held office from 1863 to 1873, save that of Haythorne, conformed to this practice.[1]

The place in a system of responsible government of a Legislative Council of life appointees was an important issue in the decade after 1851. Could it, its critics asked, be made effectively responsive to the wishes of the people with whom it had no contact through the electoral process, and could it, as a relatively stable body, co-operate with the changing personnel of the executive and the Assembly? Was an appointed, as distinct from an elective, chamber to be defended, as Edward Whelan defended it, as an instrument of responsible government; or was it what T. Heath Haviland called "the old ladies' end of the building"?[2] Actually "responsibility" was only a convenient battlecry; the real

[1]The Haythorne Government of 1872 contained no salaried officers because of a narrow majority in the Assembly. This was the controversial "warming-pan" Ministry, so called because the places of the Attorney-General and Colonial Secretary were filled by persons who were not members of either the Cabinet or the Legislature and who were nicknamed "warming-pans" because of their temporary character. *Assembly Debates,* 1872, 2nd session, pp. 7, 218.
[2]*Ibid.,* April 25, 1872, 2nd session, p. 28.

factor was the position of the Legislative Council in relation to a constantly shifting balance of power.

One of the principal political movements of the 1850's aimed at making the Legislative Council elective. A somewhat unusual but significant fact in this development was that the defenders of the upper house were the reformers who had sought to make government responsible to the people, while the opponents who clamoured to remove it from its privileged and protected position were the Conservatives. The Liberals were in power almost continuously from 1851 to 1859, and their supporters held most of the seats in the upper house. Unlike their counterparts in the Province of Canada, they did not seek to make it a popular body. The President of the Legislative Council was a prominent party leader who was a useful assistant in office and an effective critic in opposition.[1] Accordingly the Holl Government, which held office for a few months in 1854, found itself blocked by the Legislative Council. It thereupon led an active campaign against the Council,[2] and attacked particularly the Liberal practice of appointing salaried Ministers to the upper house when they could not be elected to the Assembly.[3]

Premier Coles, on the other hand, contended that the Council was a "check upon crude and hasty legislation on the part of this House."[4] Responsible government, said Edward Whelan, the Liberal reformer, "would in my opinion cease to exist the moment you made the upper branch of the Legislature subject to popular control the same as ours. . . . It might often be that members of the Council, fresh from their elections, and animated by party feelings, may come into direct collision with the House of As-

---

[1] The presidency of the Legislative Council was changed in 1853 from the senior member to a nominee of the Cabinet. Governor Bannerman wanted to select the President himself, but the Colonial Secretary considered that the appointment should be the responsibility of the Government of the day. Newcastle to Bannerman, Feb. 23, 1853, P.A.C. (P.E.I.), G 22, p. 39. Until the Legislative Council became elective the presidency was a permanent post, so that, when party fortunes changed at the polls, a new Government would find itself hampered by a hostile upper house under the permanent leadership of a prominent Opposition politician.

[2] See Edward Palmer in *Assembly Debates*, 1855, p. 82.

[3] *Assembly Journals*, 1853, p. 78; *ibid.*, 1855, p. 113; *ibid.*, 1856, p. 127.

[4] *Assembly Debates*, 1855, p. 83.

sembly."[1] Yet, as the Opposition pointed out, Coles and Whelan could well preach responsible government while they controlled the majority in the upper house.

The Conservatives turned their attention to reforming the Legislative Council when they entered upon an eight-year term of office in 1859. Among alternative methods of doing it was that of increasing the number of members, a common proposal in the history of second chamber reform. The Colonial Secretary had warned some years before, however, that this method was to be used only as a last resort and "not . . . with a view to changing the character of the majority, except under circumstances of clear and obvious necessity." An "anticipation that public business will be impeded" by the Legislative Council would not be a sufficient reason unless "that body be found obstructing pertinaciously the progress of public business, and the passing of laws which public opinion demands."[2]

But in 1859 the Liberals had such a firm hold on the Council and the Conservative Government was so emphatic on the need for the elective principle, that the Imperial authorities recognized the existence of a "clear and obvious necessity" and instructed the Governor to increase the number of Legislative Councillors from twelve to seventeen.[3] This arrangement helped to ease the strain on the Conservatives, for it converted a Liberal majority in the upper house of 10 to 2 to one of 10 to 7. It was obvious that this change was motivated by hard political facts and not by sanctimonious pronouncements on responsibility.

The Conservative majority in the Assembly was nevertheless not satisfied with the change. In 1859 the House passed a bill to make the Legislative Council elective, and sent a copy to the Queen with an address praying that the Governor be given power to reconstruct the upper house so as to bring it into agreement with the Assembly on the salaried officers question. This direct approach was considered necessary since there was no hope of the Legislative Council agreeing to the bill of its own volition.

[1] *Ibid.*, p. 81.
[2] Grey to Harvey, Nov. 3, 1846, P.A.C. (P.E.I.), G 18, p. 245.
[3] *Assembly Journals*, 1859, p. 132.

The Colonial Secretary refused to advise Her Majesty's intervention, for, he said, "to give such authority would be in point of fact to coerce an independent division of the Legislature."[1]

By 1861 death and the power of appointment had given the Conservatives the support of a majority in the Legislative Council. They were thus able to secure the passage through both houses of a second bill which provided for an elected upper chamber of thirteen members, four from each county and one from Charlottetown and Royalty. There were to be two districts in each county, each district returning two members for a term of four years; the one district in the capital was to return one member for eight years. Half the chamber was to be elected every four years, and, to inaugurate this arrangement, half of the first Council was elected for eight years. Councillors were to be male British subjects, thirty years of age or over, and residents of the province of at least five years' standing; they were to be eligible for re-election. There was no property qualification for candidates. The voters for this house had to be males, over twenty-one years of age, and have freehold or leasehold property to the value of £100 currency.[2] The same laws with respect to the administration of elections that prevailed for the Assembly were applied to the Legislative Council. A significant section provided that "the Crown shall have no

---

[1] Newcastle to Dundas, Sept. 1, 1859, P.A.C. (P.E.I.), G 28, p. 231; *Assembly Journals*, 1859, p. 97. An institution which had a certain limited effectiveness in facilitating the business of the two houses was the "Committee on Good Correspondence" set up each session "to keep up a good correspondence between the two Houses of the Legislature, and to report their proceedings from time to time." See, for example, *Assembly Journals*, 1838, pp. 7, 10. Its membership in the 1830's was 4 from the lower house and 2 from the upper; in the 1840's the proportion was 5 and 3; in the 1850's and thereafter usually 6 and 3 respectively. In times of difficulty between the two houses, each would appoint a special committee, and the two committees would meet to discuss the problem together, for example inspection of public accounts and deadlock over bills. Then each committee would report back to its respective house. For a decision to be reached, the two houses would have to agree, and not the joint committee alone. In some cases a house would instruct its committee merely to hear the proposal of the committee of the other without making a reply thereto. On the whole this machinery was most ineffective in cases of deadlock, although it was of limited value in the exchange of ideas and suggestions between the two houses. If the Government controlled the majority in the upper house it was superfluous; if not, it was largely ineffective against inter-party rivalry.

[2] This provision was amended two years later to exclude aliens. 27 Vic., c. 15.

power to dissolve the Legislative Council when elected under this Act."¹

The provisions of this statute had been suggested by the Colonial Secretary, the Duke of Newcastle, whose views were fully stated in a despatch to the Governor.

> In a popular Assembly the numbers, and the practical energy, and . . . the immediate desires of the community find a ready expression. . . . an Upper Chamber is generally intended to represent not only the settled principles and what on a large scale is called the traditional policy of the country; but also to a certain extent, its property, experience and education. . . . In order to make a Council what it ought to be, the property qualification should be applied not to the candidate but to the voter. Speaking broadly, a well chosen constituency will choose a good representative, and any limitation upon its choice can only operate by occasionally preventing them [the voters] from choosing the best. An ill-chosen constituency, on the contrary, will tend to choose an indifferent representative. . . . In Prince Edward Island I would enforce a tolerably high property qualification in the case of the electors, but of the candidates [*sic*] I would only require that he should be a British subject, resident in the Colony, and 30 years of age.²

"The constitutional position and functions of the Council," indicated the Speech from the Throne in 1863, "remain exactly what they were: its deliberations will be strengthened by a consciousness of popular support, while its construction is such as to reflect the settled wishes, rather than the transitory impulses of the People."³ After the Queen's assent was given, the act came into force on December 2, 1862 by proclamation of the Governor. The Legislative Council thereafter became more responsive to public opinion, but the question of its share in legislative prestige and power had still to be settled after the province entered Confederation.⁴

¹25 Vic., c. 18.
²Newcastle to Dundas, Feb. 4, 1862, *Assembly Journals*, 1862, Appendix G.
³*Ibid.*, 1863, p. 8.
⁴Some members of the Assembly wanted to give the Crown the power of dissolving the Legislative Council if it rejected a measure sent up by the Assembly in two successive sessions where such measure was tested by a dissolution of the Assembly between these two sessions. This proposal was rejected in the Assembly by a vote of 19 to 4. *Assembly Debates*, 1861, p. 54.

The influence of the Legislative Council in the Cabinet nevertheless continued to decline as the Assembly became the main arena of party politics. Successive Governments found it convenient to maintain their effective strength in the lower house rather than in the upper. Even the Premiers who sat in the upper house found it difficult to lead the Legislature from there; and the House leader in the Assembly either overshadowed his chief or was hampered by his position as deputy. When Premier Edward Palmer sat in the Legislative Council, Colonel J. H. Gray as House leader found it difficult being the "other leader."[1] Following the general election of 1863, Gray assumed the premiership while Palmer served under him, because "it was, amongst other things, deemed expedient that the leader of the Government should be in the House of Assembly."[2] Premier R. P. Haythorne, who led the Government from the upper chamber in 1869 and again in 1871, had to rely on others to lead the Assembly. This divided leadership proved again very unsatisfactory, and Haythorne was the last Premier to sit in the Legislative Council.

The Legislative Council's lack of influence in the Cabinet was but a reflection of a waning prestige as a legislative body. Even election could not redeem it, and although it lasted for another thirty years, its importance gradually receded. Yet property interests were sufficiently strong to maintain their foothold in the Legislature through the property franchise in the Legislative Council; while the unsteady party fortunes which resulted from the issues of religion, land, and union kept alive the feeling that a second chamber was necessary as a check upon irresponsible politics.

[1]*Ibid.*, 1862, p. 29.
[2]Dundas to Newcastle, March 14, 1863, P.A.C. (P.E.I.), G 52, p. 396.

CHAPTER V

THE LAND QUESTION

THE DEVELOPMENT of Prince Edward Island was retarded for many decades by the land question which was a major theme of every chapter in the Island's history. Lord Durham was not far wrong when he wrote that the colony's "past and present disorders are but the sad result of that fatal error which stifled its prosperity in the very cradle of its existence, by giving up the whole Island to a handful of distant proprietors."[1] The land question, wrote Joseph Howe, "was unexampled, perhaps, for length and virulence in the history of colonization."[2] It hampered political and economic development and was a constant worry to everyone concerned with the administration.

When the original grants were made in 1767 certain conditions were laid down which indicated that the proprietors were expected to take their responsibilities seriously. These conditions included the payment of quit rents; reservation of areas for public, religious, and educational purposes, and for fisheries and mining; the settlement, on townships, by the grantees, of "European foreign Protestants" and persons with two years' residence in British America, in the proportion of one to every two hundred acres within a period of ten years; and the settlement of one-third of the land within four years upon pain of forfeiture. The proprietors accepted the grants on these terms. When they won the establishment of the Island as a separate government free from the influence of Nova Scotia, they thereupon increased their responsibilities.

Government had scarcely begun when it became obvious that the proprietors were in no hurry to live up to their promises. Not only did the lack of a steady quit rent fund threaten to result in a break-down in administration,[3] but the absence of initiative on the part of most landowners retarded or prevented settlement and delayed the economic development of the colony. Thirty years after

[1]*Lord Durham's Report on the Affairs of British North America*, ed. Sir C. P. Lucas (Oxford, 1912), vol. II, p. 198.
[2]J. A. Roy, *Joseph Howe* (Toronto, 1935), p. 222.
[3]*Supra*, pp. 12-14.

the grants were made, one-half the Island contained a total population of 216 persons, and in only twenty-six of the sixty-seven lots had the conditions of settlement been fulfilled.[1] From then on a constant stream of petitions, addresses to the Queen, despatches, commission reports, and delegations to London complained that the proprietors had not kept faith, and that the colony was suffering as a result from lack of funds, settlers, and economic development. As one Colonial Secretary said a century later, "The lottery . . . afforded a curious picture of the Colonial Administration of the day . . . the consequence was that property which was lightly won was lightly treated."[2]

The tenants, the proprietors, the Government, and the Imperial authorities were all affected by the land problem, and responsibility for finding a solution was tossed from one to another for a hundred years. At a later date the Dominion Government too became involved, and the issue became a controversial problem of Dominion-provincial relations.

The settler who took up land on the Island as a tenant rather than an owner soon complained that the advantages of his efforts were being reaped, not by himself, but by the proprietor. He had to pay rent, and as he worked and raised the value of his holdings the purchase price became too high for his thin purse. If he held his land on a long lease his descendants could never be sure of a clear title; if on a short lease, he and his family were at the mercy of the landlord, who could, if he wished, raise the rent, or sell the land to someone else. For those who remained under such conditions, there was an obstacle to that incentive so necessary in a pioneering community. For others who might have become settlers the long-term prospects were not inviting. As one Secretary of State admitted, "when land could be so easily acquired on free-hold tenure in the neighbouring British Provinces, and in the United

---

[1] Of the lots, 23 contained no settlers in 1797, 12 contained 216, 6 contained 300, and only 26 were "settled agreeably to the terms of the grants." "Report of the Commissioners Appointed by the Queen to Inquire into the Differences Prevailing in Prince Edward Island Relative to the Rights of Landowners and Tenants," 1861, p. 2. This report is reproduced in full in *P.E.I. House of Assembly Journals*, 1862, Appendix O, and is one of the best outlines of the land question.

[2] Lord Carnarvon in the House of Lords, July 26, 1875, *ibid.*, 1876, Appendix E.

THE LAND QUESTION

States of America, but few settlers would consent to become tenants in Prince Edward Island, or having done so, would continue to remain there."[1]

The tenant, moreover, could never understand why the proprietor should be permitted to retain the land. He himself was on the spot, built his house and barns, tilled the soil, and brought up his family to be citizens of a new land—and he paid rent besides. The proprietor, in many cases, had never seen the colony, took no interest in it except for the rents, and exercised his rights by virtue of an obscure bargain of 1767 in which neither the settlers nor the colony itself had had a part. Why, the tenants could ask, should Sir Samuel Cunard own 212,000 acres or about one-seventh of the whole Island, and why should the Government of the province have to pay £53,000 to buy the Cunard estate in 1866?[2] They considered their rent a burden placed upon them by the original grantors, and they were never satisfied to pay money which would go out of the colony. They thought it most unfair that they should have to fulfil their obligations when the absentee proprietors failed to assume theirs. They demanded remedies from the home Government: the confiscation of the estates of neglectful proprietors, or the opportunity to purchase the land at a reasonable price.

The dissatisfaction of the tenants increased with their political consciousness, and they formed "tenant leagues" in attempts to force their opinions upon the Government, to oppose the collection of rents, or to seek a compromise with the proprietors. Their efforts were generally conducted within the bounds of the law through party activity, petitions, or delegations, but bitterness occasionally led the tenants to mob violence and resistance to authority.[3] "The

[1] Glenelg to Harvey, Aug. 10, 1836, Public Archives of Canada, Colonial Office Records (P.E.I.), A series, vol. 53, p. 187.

[2] Dundas to Cardwell, July 14, 1866, *Assembly Journals,* 1867, Appendix H.

[3] In the 1860's tenant leagues were formed throughout the Island to encourage the withholding of rent payments until the proprietors should agree to sell their lands. Seizures of tenants' properties by sheriffs were resisted and riots broke out. "Immediately a Sheriff's officer is observed to enter a settlement," wrote the Administrator in 1865, "tin trumpets are blown in all directions, many of the inhabitants assemble, surround the officers, blow trumpets in their faces and insult and defy them." Disorder became so widespread on one occasion that the Administrator sent to Halifax for a detachment of troops. See *ibid.,* 1866, Appendix G.

amount of money and time wasted in public controversy," reported the investigation commission in 1861, "no man can estimate; and the extent to which a vicious system of colonization has entered into the daily life of this people, and embittered their industrial and social relations, it is painful to contemplate and record."[1]

There was something to be said, however, for the much-abused proprietors. Whatever the weakness of the original policy of granting the lands, the grantees possessed a full legal title. They sold their properties or passed them on to their descendants, and as succeeding generations claimed the estates, it became increasingly obvious that the owners could not be forcibly dispossessed merely to remedy a mistaken policy which had benefited their predecessors. In other words, once the King had sanctioned the original grants, the laws of property had to be respected. Yet the grants had been bestowed with certain conditions and it was clear that in many instances these conditions had not been fulfilled. For this the proprietors gave many reasons. The Island was small, isolated, and undeveloped, and the expenses of a programme of settlement were great. Some grantees had devoted much time and money to their holdings and had encouraged large numbers of settlers to take up land, only to find that the settlers became dissatisfied with conditions on the estates and moved to other estates, or to other colonies where they could live as freeholders. The tenant, from the very poverty of his existence, could not pay rent to the proprietor, who, in turn, received inadequate returns for his capital outlay. Moreover, when land taxes were levied, an additional burden was placed upon already unproductive property. For these reasons, the proprietors argued, they could not fulfil the conditions of the grants. From time to time, therefore, the estates would become liable to forfeiture, but, through influence with the Colonial Office, the proprietors were usually able to secure confirmation of their holdings and to thwart any efforts at escheat. Regardless of the wisdom of such a policy, it was quite legal, and it left their titles unharmed. Successive Secretaries of State and Lieutenant-Governors stressed the legal rights of the proprietors. "Whatever

[1]"Report of the Commissioners," 1861, p. 18, in *ibid.*, 1862, Appendix O.

character may properly attach to the circumstances connected with the original grants," wrote the Colonial Secretary in 1855, "they could not with justice be used to defeat the rights of the present owners who have acquired their property by Inheritance, by Family settlements or for valuable consideration . . . the rights of the proprietors could not be sacrificed without manifest injustice."[1]

To the criticism that they should have sold their holdings to the tenants at a fair price, the proprietors replied that they had expended a substantial capital outlay, had a large backlog of unpaid rents coming to them, and could scarcely be expected to hand over their long-standing rights at bargain prices. Moreover, it was pointed out from time to time that all proprietors did not deserve the prevailing criticism. Some had fulfilled the terms of settlement and a number had sold much of their land to the tenants by mutual arrangement. Nor were all of the proprietors absentees; a few lived on the Island and contributed in many ways to the political and economic life of the colony.[2]

Some proprietors admitted that a mistake had been made in establishing the Island as a separate government and pointed out that under existing circumstances they had to bear a disproportionate share of the taxation necessary for a relatively expensive form of administration.[3] One proprietor shifted the blame for many of the difficulties of the colony from the land question to "its being a separate government." "Had the Colony never been separated from Nova Scotia," he wrote, "there is little reason to doubt that it would have been in a much more flourishing condition than it is at present."[4] This argument conveniently omitted the fact that it was the proprietors who, in the first instance, petitioned for a separate government.

The administration of government was affected at every point by some aspect of the land question. The Governors were obstructed

---

[1] Labouchere to Daly, Dec. 21, 1855, P.A.C. (P.E.I.), G 24, p. 358.
[2] See also two memorials on behalf of the proprietors: P.A.C. (P.E.I.), A 19, p. 128; A 54-2, p. 532.
[3] See Sir Samuel Cunard to Newcastle, Nov. 14, 1862, *P.E.I. House of Assembly Debates*, 1863, Appendix C.
[4] *Remarks upon That Portion of the Earl of Durham's Report Relating to Prince Edward Island*, by A Proprietor (London, 1839), p. 5.

continually by the proprietors and were often obliged to defend themselves from accusations made to the home Government by proprietors and their agents. Fanning and his Council, for example, proposed an act for escheating lands where the owners had not paid quit rents, and were promptly charged as criminals wielding a "despotick power" and deserving recall. The Colonial Secretary investigated, the Island Government was forced to incur the expense of sending representatives to London to defend itself against the charges, and a long series of disheartening accusations and defences followed. A special committee of the Privy Council examined the case and dismissed the charges as groundless, while a footnote to its report deplored "the most malicious and wicked plot on the part of the complainants, and their emissaries, to ruin the Defendants, that was ever devised by the malignity of mankind." Such proceedings hampered the government of the colony and discouraged its officials; they were a long way from London and they were never sure who was undermining their labours by backstairs influence at Downing Street.[1] It was significant, Governor Fitzroy reported, that one of the proprietors wrote to Sir Aretus Young to congratulate him on his appointment to the governorship and at the same time advised His Excellency of the number of Governors he "had been instrumental in getting removed, and trusting that Sir Aretus's measures would be satisfactory to that body of the Proprietors of which he formed a part!"[2] Fitzroy fared no better, for he became involved in much controversy with the proprietors after he had sought to act as mediator between the contending parties.

Governors Fitzroy and Harvey attempted to help matters by sending circular letters to the proprietors suggesting that the latter grant long leases, make allowances to the tenants for improvements, take payment in agricultural products, and remit arrears of rent.[3] Harvey remained only a few months on the Island and Fitzroy received the full blast of the proprietors' reply. "I deny the right,"

[1]See P.A.C. (P.E.I.), A 11, pp. 100, 109, 119, 136, 146; *ibid.*, A 12, pp. 1, 122; *ibid.*, A 13, p. 29.
[2]Fitzroy to Glenelg, Nov. 29, 1837, *ibid.*, A 54-2, p. 432.
[3]Harvey to Proprietors, Feb. 15, 1837, *ibid.*, A 54-1, p. 138; Fitzroy to Proprietors, Oct. 3, 1837, *ibid.*, p. 380.

wrote Lord Selkirk, the son of the original owner of the Selkirk estates, to the Colonial Secretary, "and I more than doubt the policy, or expediency, of the Governor of a Colony interfering with the management of private property in the manner adopted by Sir Charles A. Fitzroy."[1] From then on Fitzroy knew no peace. Beset on all sides by proprietors and their agents, he reported to Glenelg within a few months of his arrival that his sympathies were with the tenants. He warned the Colonial Secretary of the dangers involved in the lobbying of the proprietors at the Colonial Office, and in the prevailing idea among the landowners that "the Lieutenant-Governor is placed here solely to watch over their peculiar interests; without any reference to the general welfare of the Inhabitants." Such a situation, he said, would prevent local officials from performing their duties with either satisfaction or efficiency.[2] For many months the Colonial Office passed the accusations back and forth between Fitzroy and the proprietors, until finally Imperial officials realized that the dispute served no better purpose than to weaken the local Government and lower the influence of the Governor.[3]

Nevertheless the sentiments which Fitzroy expressed in private despatches to the Colonial Secretary could hardly be revealed by the Governor in public. He warned the Assembly that the "deluded Tenantry" should cease their agitation for escheat, since offences against "the execution of the Laws . . . the peace of the Colony or . . . the rights of property . . . will most assuredly be visited with the utmost severity of the Law." Nor should they be "led away by specious, but deceptive hopes and expectations."[4]

Other Governors, however, were more zealous in guarding the rights of proprietors during constitutional reform. One of the reasons for Campbell's opposition to the introduction of responsible government had been that the power thereby secured to the local administration might lead to the confiscation of the estates. After 1851 Bannerman added that "those who think so seem to forget . . . the Lieutenant-Governor" who can "interfere and pre-

---

[1] A. Colvile, on behalf of Lord Serkirk, to Glenelg, Dec. 6, 1837, *ibid.*, A 54-2, p. 595.
[2] Fitzroy to Glenelg, Nov. 29, 1837, *ibid.*, p. 427; May 24, 1838, *ibid.*, A 55-2, p. 436.
[3] See *ibid.*, A 55-1.   [4] *Assembly Journals*, 1838, p. 125.

vent" any such action.[1] Daly also indicated that "my constant endeavours have been directed to upholding the rights of property."[2]

The Governor, therefore, occupied a difficult position between the Imperial Government and the proprietors on the one hand and the Island Government and tenant interests on the other. Whatever stand he took, one side would undermine his prestige and authority: the proprietors by applying pressure at the Colonial Office if he did not display sufficient interest in defending the rights of property, or the tenants by disturbing the peace or securing the passage of escheat bills in the colonial Legislature if he were not sympathetic with them. After responsible government was established his task was no less delicate, for he was expected to be the guardian of property regardless of the advice of his Ministers.

The old Council, too, was beset by the land issue. If, like Fanning's Council, it did not contain a sufficient number of proprietors or their agents it was looked upon with suspicion in England; if it contained too many such elements, as it did in the 1840's, the reformers branded it as reactionary. The problem added to the already sufficient number of issues between the Council and the Assembly. After the Executive and Legislative Councils were separated, the upper house was looked upon as the preserve of the propertied interests to whose convenience its composition and franchise were adjusted. This characteristic, which was by no means uncommon in the rest of the Empire, was accentuated in the Island Legislature by the prevailing interest in land and its ownership.[3]

When the old Executive Council developed into a responsible Cabinet, the associations of certain Ministers with the propertied interests were often incompatible with their responsibilities to their colleagues and the public. The Palmers and the Popes were proprietors, and they incurred some suspicion with respect to their dealings with other proprietors or to the sale of their lands to the Crown while they held office. The strain was obvious in the Davies

[1]Bannerman to Grey, April 2, 1851, P.A.C. (P.E.I.), G 49, p. 320.
[2]Daly to Labouchere, *ibid.*, G 51, p. 73.
[3]See also *supra,* p. 103.

coalition Government of 1876-9, when a proprietor's agent who was a member of the Cabinet opposed his own Government's land purchase bill and fought it in the courts while retaining his portfolio.[1] For years after the granting of responsible government the Cabinet suffered a sense of frustration from its inability to pursue a definite policy with respect to the land question. Each party made extravagant promises of reform at election time, but once in power it could do little against the combined forces of the Governor, the Colonial Office, and the proprietors. "I can now truly say," wrote Colonel J. H. Gray in 1865, "after a considerable experience as a member of this Government for six years, that I sincerely believe that the Acts of this Legislature weigh no more than a feather in the scales, compared with the influence possessed by a few private individuals of whose second-hand intermeddling we have lately had a pretty fair specimen."[2] The resulting difficulties contributed in large measure to the instability of administration which was manifest in the frequent changes of Government. After a number of measures had been refused royal assent through the efforts of the proprietors in London, the Cabinet warned the Governor that it resented this intrusion and obstruction of its efforts by "a Body unknown to the Constitution, and consisting of parties, for the most part, who, though unable to command attention in the local Legislature, nevertheless seek to counteract its decisions at the Colonial Office."[3] The Colonial Secretary's reply that responsible government did not apply to the settlement of the land question only increased the dissatisfaction of the executive.[4]

The theme of the events which the land issue provoked in the Assembly was sounded in 1837 by William Cooper, a member of the House and the leader of the escheat party, when he emphasized that "it requires a degree of public excitement" to impress His Majesty's Ministers with the seriousness of the question.[5] Cooper, once a proprietors' agent, and now an active crusader against "the oppression of the Colonists by a faction," organized public protest

[1]*Infra,* pp. 187-8. [2]*Assembly Debates,* 1865, p. 46.
[3]Minute of Executive Council, Aug. 27, 1855, *Assembly Journals,* 1855, Appendix E.
[4]*Supra,* pp. 95-6.
[5]Cooper to T. H. Haviland, Jan. 24, 1837, P.A.C. (P.E.I.), A 54-1, p. 52.

meetings during the 1830's to encourage tenants to "withhold rent and their property from the Landlords until the Government interfered" in order to force a settlement of the question once and for all. Sir John Harvey branded the actions of Cooper's friends "as highly unconstitutional, if not actually treasonable," although he did not wish to prosecute them and so to "afford them a triumph, to elevate them into the position of Martyrs in the cause of the People." His successor, Fitzroy, who opposed the proprietors but supported the law, deprived Cooper of some small appointments and of his commission as a captain in the militia. The Colonial Secretary's attitude to the actions of Cooper and the tenants was that "it would be impossible for His Majesty's Government to interfere, otherwise than as a mediator between them and their landlords."[1] When Fitzroy complained to the House, the anti-escheat party committed Cooper and two of his colleagues to the custody of the Sergeant-at-Arms for two sessions because they had refused to apologize for their activities.[2] Lord Glenelg thereupon advised that "His Majesty has perceived with peculiar satisfaction the prompt determination evinced by the House of Assembly to vindicate and maintain the rights of Individuals and the prerogatives of the Crown."[3]

This treatment of Cooper and his supporters did exactly what Harvey had feared, for they were elevated "into the position of Martyrs in the cause of the People." In the general election of 1838 Cooper's party secured an overwhelming majority in the Assembly, and Cooper himself was raised to the speakership. Fitzroy found this a bitter pill, but warned the Colonial Office that popular agitation was rising and that the "more respectable portion of the community" could do nothing "as long as the influence of the Proprietors at home was sufficiently powerful to frustrate any measure, however equitable, which interfered with their own immediate interests." In a pathetic despatch he revealed his awkward position and pled with the Secretary of State to decide future

[1] See the proceedings of the Hay River meeting of Dec. 20, 1836, in *Royal Gazette*, Jan. 10, 1837, *ibid.*, p. 16, and correspondence pertaining thereto in *ibid.*, pp. 10, 41, 44, 52, 63, 64, 90, 215, 361.
[2] *Assembly Journals*, 1837, 1st session, p. 35.
[3] Glenelg to Administrator, May 1, 1837, *ibid.*, 1839, 1st session, p. 43.

measures on their merits without "interference of parties who have hitherto considered that the interests of this Colony should be subservient to their private views."[1] Lord John Russell coldly comforted Fitzroy with the suggestion that he might consider the expediency of dissolving the House if it persisted in its present tactics.[2] Here the question of a solution rested in stalemate while the escheat issue was joined with the struggle for responsible government. It provided excellent political capital for the more radical reformers who promised the confiscation of the estates and freehold tenure when self-government was achieved.

The first Cabinet under responsible government in 1855 made it clear to the Governor and the Colonial Office that its new status gave it the right to seek freedom from the proprietors. Two bills were passed in April of that year which were designed to force the issue.[3] The Cabinet anticipated the opposition of the proprietors, and passed an appropriate minute which indicated that "the people of this Island had reason to expect, that when Her Majesty graciously accorded them what is commonly termed Responsible Government, this secret and baneful influence would be discarded, and the discussion of Island affairs no longer take place through the oratory of malcontents assembled in Downing Street, but in the Colonial Legislature."[4] In an address to the Queen the House took the same view and described the interference and memorials of the proprietors as "untenable, frivolous, and in part highly offensive to the Legislature and people of this Island and derogatory to their honor and independence."[5] The Colonial Secretary refused to advise royal assent to the bills on the ground that one was "oppressive class legislation" and the other "a measure of undisguised spoliation," although he did wish "to allow the fullest possible scope to the principle of local independence in Legis-

[1]Fitzroy to Normanby, May 7, 1839, P.A.C. (P.E.I.), A 58, p. 123.
[2]Russell to Fitzroy, Sept. 17, 1839, *ibid.*, p. 145.
[3]"An Act to impose a Rate or Duty on the Rent Rolls of the Proprietors of certain Township Lands . . . in order to defray the expenses of any Armed Force which may be required . . . and for the further encouragement of Education"; and "An Act to secure compensation to tenants . . . and thereby to promote the improvement of the soil."
[4]Minute of Executive Council, Aug. 27, 1855, *Assembly Journals*, 1855, Appendix E.
[5]*Ibid.*, 1856, pp. 123-5.

lative matters"![1] This decision was made even less agreeable to the Assembly by the knowledge that the proprietors had been consulted beforehand.

For session after session such exchanges were among the chief features of the relations between the Assembly and the Colonial Office. The results were bad in every way, for the Imperial Government was as anxious to defend property rights as the Assembly was to exert its independence. The resulting dissatisfaction on both sides added to the difficulties associated with the adjustment of relations among the Island's political institutions at times when the Island could ill afford the luxury of additional constitutional issues.

The Imperial Government deserved little credit for its handling of the land question, except perhaps from the proprietors who benefited from its mistakes. The impression left on the colonists was that British aloofness was based on a lack of interest in the Island and a determination not to relieve the colony from the absentee proprietor system. Every effort on the part of successive Island Governments was blocked in London. Although agents for the colony were appointed from time to time to look after its interests in England, their efforts proved largely ineffective against the influence of the landowners. The documents of the period reveal the constant and discouraging feeling of neglect which this cool, casual carelessness of the mother country caused in the colony. The policy of the home Government never changed through the decades. It would not consent to compulsory interference with the rights of the proprietors, and insisted that any remedy for the land question would have to proceed from an arrangement between the tenants and the proprietors. The wisdom of this policy was hardly commensurate with its consistency, for it was obvious that many of the tenants and proprietors would never come to an arrangement in the absence of outside pressure.

Successive Secretaries of State did not lack expert advice and warning. Able Governors like Sir John Harvey and Sir Charles Fitzroy kept them well informed. Lord Durham's report contained one of the best analyses by an independent observer:

[1]Grey to Daly, Nov. 17, 1855, P.A.C. (P.E.I.), G 24, p. 331; *Assembly Journals,* 1856, Appendix E.

One of the most remarkable instances of evils resulting from profuse grants of land is to be found in Prince Edward's Island. Nearly the whole of the island (about 1,400,000 acres) was alienated in one day, in very large grants, chiefly to absentees, and upon conditions which have been wholly disregarded. The extreme improvidence which dictated these grants is obvious; the neglect of the government as to enforcing the conditions of the grants, in spite of the constant efforts of the people and the legislature to force upon its attention the evils under which they laboured, is not less so. The great bulk of the island is still possessed by absentees, who hold it as a sort of reversionary interest, which requires no present attention, but may become valuable some day or other through the growing wants of the inhabitants. But in the meantime, the inhabitants are subjected to the greatest inconvenience, nay, to the most serious injury from the state of property in land. The absentee proprietors neither improve the land, nor will let others improve it. They retain the land, and keep it in a state of wilderness. . . .

Had its natural advantages been turned to proper account, it might at this time have been the granary of the British Colonies. . . . Of nearly 1,400,000 acres contained in the island, only 10,000 are said to be unfit for the plough. Only 100,000 are now under cultivation. No one can mistake the cause of this lamentable waste of the means of national wealth. It is the possession of almost the whole soil of the island by absentee proprietors, who would neither promote nor permit its cultivation, combined with the defective government which first caused and has since perpetuated the evil.[1]

Yet Durham's remarks, which should have stirred even the most lethargic government to action, were rendered ineffective by proprietors, one of whom labelled them as the "illiberal, unjust, and unfounded" opinions of the "ex-Dictator of Canada."[2] The Colonial Secretaries should not have needed Durham's observations to guide them, when they had those of one of the ablest of their own officers, Sir James Stephen, which were made about the same time, and which were similar to those of Durham.[3] Sir George

---

[1] *Lord Durham's Report*, ed. Lucas, vol. II, pp. 198, 241-2. See also the *Minutes of Evidence* of the General Commission of Inquiry for Crown Lands and Emigration which was appointed by Lord Durham (Quebec: Queen's Printer, 1839), section on Prince Edward Island.
[2] *Remarks upon That Portion of the Earl of Durham's Report Relating to Prince Edward Island*, p. 5.
[3] Memorandum by "J. S.," Dec. 12, 1837, P.A.C. (P.E.I.), A 54-2, p. 702; Jan. 30, 1838, *ibid.*, A 55-1, p. 89.

Grey's reply to Stephen was typical: "It is undesirable to make too much of this Escheat excitement."[1] Three years later Lord John Russell dismissed the issue as "a fruitless and irritating contest," an attitude which Lord Stanley interpreted as meaning that "both parties were too unreasonable."[2]

The Colonial Office consented, however, to the appointment of an investigation commission in 1860 after the Assembly had requested that such a body be set up to study the land question thoroughly and make recommendations for a solution. The proprietors agreed to the proposal after stipulating that the decision of the commission should be made "effective." The Colonial Secretary thereupon stressed that the tenants would have to accept the decision as binding and that the Island Legislature should agree to pass such measures as would embody the recommendations made. The House agreed on behalf of the tenants and the commission was appointed on these conditions.

The Commissioners[3] wrote a unanimous report which was distinctly unfavourable to the proprietors and which placed a large share of the blame for the unsatisfactory situation upon the Imperial Government. They recommended "two simple principles": to give the tenant "the right to purchase the land on which he lives" and "to give the landlord and tenant the security of a fair valuation of the land in case of difference."[4] The commission expressed "the hope that if their suggestions are adopted, enfranchised and disenthralled from the poisoned garments that enfold her, Prince Edward Island will yet become, what she ought to be, the Barbadoes of the St. Lawrence."[5]

The Assembly, highly pleased by the results of the investigation, passed two acts to give effect to the recommendations; but the proprietors objected to being bound by the commission which, they said, exceeded its authority. The Duke of Newcastle, who had

[1] *Ibid.*
[2] Russell to Fitzroy, June 25, 1841, *Assembly Journals,* 1842, Appendix B; see also *ibid.,* Appendix L.
[3] J. W. Ritchie and Joseph Howe, representing the proprietors and tenants respectively, and John Hamilton Gray of New Brunswick, the Chairman nominated by the Queen.
[4] "Report of the Commissioners," 1861, in *Assembly Journals,* 1862, Appendix O.
[5] See also *Assembly Journals,* 1875, Appendix E.

been careful to bind the tenants and the Assembly, thereupon advised the Governor that the award was not binding on the proprietors, that it was merely "an expression of opinion" and that the proprietors had only agreed that the commission should inquire and decide![1] Again Her Majesty's unofficial advisers in London had won over her constitutional advisers in Charlottetown. An outstanding sentence of the commission's report was thereby confirmed: "It is apparent . . . that the proprietors, down to the present hour, have been treated by the Crown with an excessive indulgence, which warrants the exercise of the prerogative in the application of remedial measures, after a century's experience of a vicious system." This rebuff resulted in the land controversies of the 1860's at public gatherings, at the polls, and in the Legislature. Troops were called in from Nova Scotia to quell the disturbances. Even at this point the Colonial Secretary was unimpressed, and warned the Island's Government that it would have to pay the expenses of the troops, which suggestion drew the frank reply that the Island would do no such thing, for since "Imperial error" had caused the trouble, Imperial funds could bear the costs.[2]

The emergence of the Confederation issue gave the Imperial Government an opportunity to avoid action once more in the hope that new political developments might supply a remedy. "Having regard to the evident uncertainty whether the Colony of Prince Edward Island will or will not soon unite itself to the Dominion of Canada," wrote Lord Granville in 1869, "I am not prepared to enter on the consideration of a question with which, if such union were to ensue, the Imperial Government would probably cease to concern itself, the Land Question therefore should, in my opinion, be left as far as possible for the decision of those who, under the altered circumstances of the Colony, would have to carry into execution any measures connected with it."[3] The land question was thus displaced by the Confederation issue, although the respite was only temporary and the struggle threatened to break out again at the first convenient moment.

[1]*Assembly Debates,* 1863, pp. 27-30; *Assembly Journals,* 1864, Appendix W.
[2]*Ibid.,* 1866, Appendix G.
[3]Granville to Administrator, March 13, 1869, *ibid.,* 1869, Appendix S.

CHAPTER VI

CONFEDERATION

Two DECADES of responsible government in the British North American colonies culminated in federal union. Many forces encouraged it: political deadlock in the Province of Canada, dreams of a commercial empire on the St. Lawrence, fear of the consequences of American continental expansion, and ambitions for the opening of the West. Half a continent was available to the five British colonies if they could seize the opportunity of forming a nation from sea to sea. Few of these forces were felt to any extent in Prince Edward Island, however, and the small colony held aloof from the union movement as long as she could, until political and economic currents drew her into the main stream. The position of the Island in the Confederation negotiations and the circumstances which preceded her entry illustrate in large measure the characteristics of her institutions of government and of her politics, and provide a background for her place in Dominion-provincial relations.

Prince Edward Island's associations with her neighbours during the colonial period were determined by her desire to retain the independent government which she had enjoyed so long. Consequently the small colony was always suspicious of any suggestion of union or annexation and she helped to maintain the isolation which hampered her social, economic, and political intercourse with Nova Scotia and New Brunswick. This outlook, which had been apparent as early as the separation from Nova Scotia in 1769,[1] was also evident on all subsequent occasions when union was suggested. Thus local politicians vigorously protested the brief re-annexation of 1784-6,[2] sympathized with Cape Breton after the latter's absorption by Nova Scotia in 1820, and expressed much resentment when distinguished outsiders, such as the Duke of Kent and the Earl of Durham, recommended that the Island be united to Nova Scotia.[3] The fear of union was so widespread in 1832 that

[1]*Supra*, p. 6.   [2]*Supra*, p. 18.
[3]*Lord Durham's Report on the Affairs of British North America*, ed. Sir C. P. Lucas (Oxford, 1912), vol. II, pp. 320-1; see also Lord Sydenham, *supra*, pp. 70, n. 3; 83, n. 2.

CONFEDERATION 121

the Colonial Secretary instructed the Governor "to make it known, in the most public manner, that no such plan has ever been under the contemplation of His Majesty's Government."[1]

This desire for independence greatly affected the Island's commercial and political relations with other colonies. In the 1820's she found it difficult to co-operate with her neighbours on problems of navigation.[2] Self-sufficiency in agriculture made her unresponsive to proposals for intercolonial free trade.[3] In 1845 her Governor refused an offer of union from the Magdalene Islands.[4] The same attitude was evident in the unsuccessful attempts of Island adherents of the Church of England to obtain a bishop of their own and thereby be removed from the jurisdiction of the Bishop of Nova Scotia. The Roman Catholics were equally insistent upon their right to be independent of the Bishop of Quebec and to have a separate diocese with a Scotch or Irish rather than a French bishop.[6] The Islanders repeatedly emphasized that they preferred to manage their own affairs rather than trust them to the ministrations of distant and possibly uninterested authorities. This policy of exclusiveness determined the Island's attitude to Confederation.

During the interprovincial negotiations which immediately preceded Confederation the Island was as usual unresponsive. In 1859 the Governor-General, Sir Edmund Head, sent to Charlottetown a

[1]Goderich to Young, Jan. 31, 1833, *P.E.I. House of Assembly Journals,* 1833, p. 121.
[2]*Ibid.,* 1825, p. 23; *ibid.,* 1829, pp. 10, 16.
[3]W. M. Whitelaw, *The Maritimes and Canada before Confederation* (Toronto, 1934), pp. 86-7.
[4]In 1783 Governor Patterson had recommended unsuccessfully the annexation of the Magdalenes, then a part of Lower Canada. Patterson to North, July 18, 1783, Public Archives of Canada, Colonial Office Records (P.E.I.), A series, vol. 5, p. 91. In 1798 the Magdalenes were granted to Admiral Sir Isaac Coffin as proprietor. Sir Isaac's nephew, John T. Coffin, inherited the proprietary rights in 1839, and after six years of difficulty he petitioned for annexation to Prince Edward Island. Charlottetown was much nearer than Montreal, and consequently a more accessible seat of government. The Colonial Office consulted Governor Huntley who recommended against the proposal because he felt that it would be difficult for the Magdalenes to contribute to the expenses of government and that the administration of law and justice from a distance would not be practicable. John T. Coffin to the Queen, undated, 1845, *ibid.,* G 16, p. 37; Huntley to Stanley, May 15, 1845, *ibid.,* A 48, p. 224.
[5]Bishop of Nova Scotia to Sir William Molesworth, Oct. 25, 1855, *ibid.,* G 24, p. 319; Stanley to Huntley, Feb. 14, 1832, *ibid.,* G 14, p. 33.
[6]Thomas Aubin (Foreign Office) to Cardinal Lambruschini (Papal Secretary of State), Oct. 2, 1837, *ibid.,* A 54-2, p. 478.

report of his Executive Council suggesting consultation among the colonies on the subject of reciprocal free trade with one another. Governor Dundas replied that the Island could not enter into any such arrangement.[1] Lord Monck forwarded a similar feeler in 1862, but again the Island Government refused to negotiate.[2] The following year further proposals for discussions among delegates to be chosen by the provinces to consider federal union were received from Nova Scotia and London, but the Island was still unimpressed. When the Assembly debated the question, the Speaker exhorted the members to recall Cape Breton and not sell their birthright for a mess of pottage. The House thereupon criticized the principle of union in detail, and only agreed to consider proposals after the party leaders assured it that "a consultation of delegates could be of no disadvantage."[3]

In 1864 Governor Doyle of Nova Scotia wrote to the Governors of the other Maritime colonies advising that his Government was about to submit a resolution to the Legislature authorizing the appointment of delegates for a conference on Maritime union with representatives from the other colonies, and he suggested that New Brunswick and Prince Edward Island follow suit.[4] The subject was received most unfavourably in the Island Legislature. Premier Gray, who was somewhat friendly to the idea of a federation of all the provinces, did not favour Maritime union unless, he said, Nova Scotia and New Brunswick were to be annexed to Prince Edward Island![5] "The Tilleys and Tuppers," said the Speaker of the House, "would fain have a wider field for the exercise of their talents and the extension of their sway, but it is our duty to protect the rights of those whose representatives we are, and what public man will not hesitate ere he votes that our institutions shall become nonentities?"[6] The members agreed, nevertheless, to appoint delegates "for the purpose of discussing the expediency of a Union," since "common courtesy" prevented them from refusing.[7]

[1]*Assembly Journals*, 1859, Appendix T.
[2]*Ibid.*, 1862, Appendix F; *P.E.I. House of Assembly Debates*, 1862, p. 110.
[3]*Assembly Journals*, 1863, pp. 62, 142, and Appendix I.
[4]Doyle to Dundas, Feb. 8, 1864, *ibid.*, 1864, Appendix A.
[5]*Assembly Debates*, 1864, p. 32.   [6]*Ibid.*, pp. 37-8.
[7]*Assembly Journals*, 1864, Appendices A and I.

The three provinces agreed that Charlottetown should be the place of meeting, and it was arranged that the conference should open on September 1, 1864. The Canadian Government meanwhile requested the privilege of sending a delegation to the conference to ascertain whether the proposed union could be extended to include all the provinces. This request was granted and a delegation of seven Canadian statesmen headed by John A. Macdonald came to Charlottetown to join in the discussions as unofficial observers.[1] The people of the Island, nevertheless, showed little interest in the conference. No official welcome was given the Nova Scotia delegates on their arrival, while the Canadians were greeted only by W. H. Pope who, in a rowboat, met their ship "with all the dignity he could." The delegates had to remain aboard ship since they could find no accommodation in Charlottetown which was full of visitors, attracted, not by the conference, but by a circus which was then in town.[2]

There is no official report of the proceedings at the Charlottetown Conference, and the participants later disagreed in their interpretations of what had been decided, but, from the meagre information available, it is apparent that the discussions produced three definite results. First, Maritime union was virtually shelved in the process of welcoming the Canadians and hearing their proposals for a union of all the provinces. After some discussions among the Maritime delegates it became obvious that Prince Edward Island would not join with her immediate neighbours, except perhaps if the Maritime capital were located at Charlottetown, and there was little point in pursuing the matter at that stage when so attractive an alternative was proposed.[3] In the second place, the discussions resulted in a unanimous opinion that the larger scheme was feasible and that a further conference should be held at Quebec to examine it in detail. The delegates even went so far as to agree provisionally on certain principles which should be incorporated in

---

[1] For details of the events leading up to the Charlottetown Conference, see Whitelaw, *The Maritimes and Canada before Confederation*, pp. 185-221; also *Assembly Journals*, 1865, Appendix E.
[2] Whitelaw, *The Maritimes and Canada before Confederation*, p. 220.
[3] *Ibid.*, pp. 223-4; Edward Whelan, *The Union of the British Provinces* (Gardenvale, Que., 1927), p. 5.

the larger plan, e.g., representation by population in the lower house, and by region in the upper house, of the central legislature.[1] The third, and in some ways the most important, achievement of the conference was the exchange of goodwill and opinion among the delegates. The leading statesmen of the provinces had had little opportunity of getting to know one another, and both the formal discussions and the social activities at Charlottetown did much to facilitate the personal relationships so necessary for future negotiations.

The delegates toured the Maritimes after leaving Charlottetown and then proceeded to Quebec. The Island representatives joined the party and belied their hostility to union by sharing wholeheartedly in the festivities *en route*. The second conference met in October and drew up a series of resolutions on which the proposed union was to be based. These Quebec Resolutions were then sent for approval to the Governments of the provinces concerned.

The Resolutions were formally passed by the Canadian Legislature, but the response was originally negative in all four of the Maritime provinces. The plan was voted down in New Brunswick, and in Prince Edward Island, while in Nova Scotia and in Newfoundland it was kept temporarily in the background. By 1866, after constant manipulation on the part of union advocates, the political situation had changed sufficiently to permit the Governments of Nova Scotia and New Brunswick to push resolutions through their Legislatures authorizing delegates to discuss the question with the Imperial Government. Representatives from Canada and these two Maritime provinces then met at the Westminster Palace Hotel conference in London. Here were completed the details of the British North America Act, which became the basis of Confederation on July 1, 1867.

The refusal of Prince Edward Island to join the Confederation was not unexpected in view of the fairly constant attitude of her public men before 1864. In fact there is no evidence that the Canadians or the other Maritimers were greatly worried whether she

[1]R. G. Trotter, *Canadian Federation* (Toronto, 1924), pp. 97-8. See also Senate of Canada, *Report on the British North America Act* (Ottawa, 1939), Annex 4, pp. 32-6.

joined them at that stage or not. During the conferences and the festivities which accompanied them, delegates frequently spoke of "wooing" the Island and teased her representatives about her size and significance. At a banquet in Charlottetown, a Nova Scotian delegate humorously said that the conference adjourned to Halifax "lest Nova Scotia and New Brunswick should, without further notice, become annexed to Prince Edward Island."[1] "Now don't you be too boastful about your little island," warned D'Arcy McGee, "don't let us hear so much about it, or we will send down a little tug boat and draw you up into one of our lakes, where we will leave you to take care of yourselves."[2] The Island delegates admitted frequently that theirs was a very small province, but a province nevertheless, with a government and with interests all its own, and they made it clear that they were getting along quite well and would require adequate assurances before they would enter a union with much larger provinces. Prince Edward Island "could contribute its mite," said Premier Gray, "it could be to the other provinces what Rhode Island was to the other states of the American Union."[3] A member of the Island Assembly told the delegates that the province would "willingly yield up the little paraphernalia of a very little government for the more respectable and powerful status of being part of confederated British North America," but, said he, "what is required is to convince the people that their real and substantial interests will be advanced by the change."[4]

The Island people objected to union for both political and economic reasons.[5] They wanted to enjoy their political independence after the recent acquisition of responsible government, and they feared that their local institutions might become insignificant in the Confederation. "In this House," said George Coles to the Assembly, "scarcely anything would be left us to do but to legislate about dog taxes and the running at large of swine."[6] More-

[1]Adams G. Archibald, reported in Whelan, *The Union of the British Provinces*, p. 11.
[2]*Ibid.*, p. 195.   [3]*Ibid.*, p. 81.   [4]F. D. Brecken, *ibid.*, p. 17.
[5]Detailed discussion on the union question is contained in *Assembly Debates*, 1865.
[6]*Ibid.*, p. 68.

over, previous experience with the administration of the proprietors and Imperial authorities in London had taught them to be suspicious of a distant government which might not have a sympathetic understanding of local problems. It was also pointed out that the Canadians were unable to settle their own difficulties, let alone those of others, and this judgment appeared to be confirmed after the first Dominion Day by the loud protests from Nova Scotia.

The economic objections arose from the fact that Prince Edward Island had previously had no commercial contacts with Canada. The chief industries of the Island were agriculture and fishing, the products of which were consumed at home or exported to the United States, the West Indies, and Europe in exchange for needed imports. Local public men pointed out that under union the Island would be included in the Canadian tariff structure which would prevent her from importing from former customers and thereby force her to buy for cash from Canada which took nothing from her in return. It was predicted that other countries would cease to buy from her under such an arrangement and that her trade position would consequently be ruined. A situation of this kind would be disastrous for a province which had no prospects of being a manufacturing centre or a producer of something which the other provinces did not have in abundance. Moreover the Island was cut off from the continental arteries of trade, and she would therefore have to compete with other localities which were more strategically situated with respect to the chief markets.

The opponents of union could not see that there would be any substantial returns from the federal taxation to which they would be subjected. Little would be needed by way of federal public works on the Island, but its people would be expected to contribute to the expensive network of railways and canals in the other provinces for which they would have little use, and to defence projects for which they could not see the need since they were then on cordial terms with the Americans.

The absence of any special financial arrangements to offset these disadvantages[1] convinced the local Legislature that it should

[1]J. A. Maxwell, *Federal Subsidies to the Provincial Governments in Canada* (Cambridge, Mass., 1937), p. 13; A. A. Macdonald, "Notes on the Quebec Conference," ed. A. G. Doughty, *Canadian Historical Review*, March, 1920, p. 45.

decline to join a union which, it thought, "would prove politically, commercially, and financially disastrous to the rights and interests of the people."[1]

Although the arguments against union prevailed in 1867, a few political leaders pointed out that the Island was not large and influential enough to remain an independent country on the doorstep of a united Canada. "Are we going to stand alone," asked John H. Gray, "to become the resort of smugglers and a nest of hornets in the sides of the Confederation?"[2] The answer of the unionists was that the province would be better off as a part of a large nation than as, what one of them called it, an "isolated sand bank in the Gulf of St. Lawrence,"[3] and some even suggested annexation to the United States as a possible solution if Canada would not agree to suitable terms.[4]

It appears, however, that this argument was prompted by the need for finding solutions for local difficulties rather than by any liking for union. Local politics were stirred by religious animosities and controversies over land. Catholics and Protestants were disputing the questions of separate schools, Bible reading in the schools, and the incorporation of the Orange Lodge, and much bitterness prevailed as a result.[5] The tenants and the proprietors were as usual disputing their rights to the land. Some public men therefore looked to Confederation as a means of overshadowing local matters by larger national issues in such a way as to diminish the prevailing bitterness. But this argument was not sufficiently strong to balance the disadvantages of union, and the people as a whole seemed to agree with the Speaker of the Assembly that it was better "to bear the ills we had than fly to those we know not of."[6]

[1]*Assembly Debates,* 1865, p. 44. It was on this occasion that the celebrated controversy occurred in the Legislature between J. C. Pope, the Premier, and his brother, W. H. Pope, the local Colonial Secretary. When the Premier, who was opposed to union, was about to rise to move the House into committee on the union issue, his colleague rose before the Premier had a chance to speak and submitted a series of resolutions in favour of union. They fought over the issue in Cabinet and in the House for more than a year before W. H. Pope finally resigned. The Opposition leaders were similarly divided. *Assembly Journals,* 1865, p. 45; *Assembly Debates,* 1865, pp. 39 ff.
[2]*Ibid.,* 1866, p. 196.   [3]*Ibid.,* 1870, p. 21.
[4]*Ibid.,* 1865, pp. 46, 49; *ibid.,* 1866, p. 106.
[5]See, for example, the dispute between W. H. Pope, the Colonial Secretary, and Rev. Angus Macdonald, the Rector of St. Dunstan's College. P.A.C. (P.E.I.), G 52, pp. 318-23; also *ibid.,* G 32, p. 83.
[6]*Assembly Debates,* 1870, p. 31.

The new Dominion, however, could not remain indifferent to the decision of the Island. Small though she was, she might prove a difficult neighbour if she refused to co-operate in such things as tariff negotiations or plans for defence against the United States. Indeed in 1868 the Americans were actively bargaining with the Islanders for free trade and fishing privileges, and many suspected that the motive behind the negotiations was a desire to keep the Island out of Confederation.[1] Moreover, the provincial Legislature indicated in 1869 that it was not interested in closer political and trade relations with its Canadian neighbours, although Nova Scotia was then prepared to discuss the possibilities of such relations with the Island.[2] These factors, together with the value of the Island fisheries, prompted Sir John Macdonald to renew his efforts to bring the province into Confederation. He believed that neither Canada nor the British Government could successfully carry out any policy in regard to such matters without first preventing the Island from becoming a "rendezvous for smugglers . . . as great a nuisance to us as the Isle of Man was in days of old to England." "We must endeavour," he wrote the Governor-General, "to get Her Majesty's Government to help us as much as possible in our attempts to conciliate the Islanders."[3] The British Government, the Dominion Cabinet, the Island's Governor (William Robinson), and the unionist leaders in the province, W. H. Pope and J. H. Gray, thereupon joined hands to "conciliate the Islanders" or, as Pope more frankly called it, to "put on the screws."[4]

Appropriately enough, the Governor-General spent a summer holiday at Charlottetown in August, 1869, and he took with him some members of the federal Cabinet. The visitors discussed the prospects of union with the provincial Government and some

[1]After the visit of Representative Benjamin Butler in 1868 (*supra,* p. 95) the Island Government requested the British authorities, unsuccessfully, to arrange a reciprocity agreement between the province and the United States regardless of the wishes of Canada. *Assembly Journals,* 1869, p. 124. Meanwhile some American politicians made it apparent that they were interested in preventing further consolidation of the British provinces rather than genuine free trade, and the Islanders soon saw that they could not make a satisfactory bargain. *Ibid.,* p. 124; *ibid.,* 1870, p. 37; see also J. B. Brebner, *North Atlantic Triangle* (New Haven, 1945), p. 186.
[2]*Assembly Journals,* 1869, Appendix H.
[3]Macdonald to Governor-General, Dec. 8, 1869, P.A.C., Macdonald Letterbooks, vol. 516, p. 670.
[4]Pope to Macdonald, Sept. 18, 1870, *ibid.,* vol. 119, p. 123.

CONFEDERATION 129

prominent citizens, and upon their return to Ottawa a set of proposals was approved by Council on December 17 and sent to the Island for consideration.[1]

The Dominion offered the usual grants-in-aid and debt allowance received by the other provinces, efficient steam service between the Island and the mainland, and assistance in obtaining compensation for the loss of Crown lands and legislation permitting the purchase of the proprietors' estates.[2] The Island Government turned down these proposals because they did not include an adequate solution of the land question.[3] It was pointed out that the responsibility for the issue belonged to the British authorities and not to the Canadian Government, and that the Island would compromise her independence if she accepted aid from the Dominion. Union would have to depend, not on relations resembling a bargain between "candidates and a bribed constituency," but upon "the free and unbiased consent and approval of the contracting parties."[4] This refusal annoyed both the federal and the Imperial authorities. Macdonald spoke of his colleagues being "humbugged,"[5] while the Colonial Secretary hastened to inform the members of the Island Government that they would "not act wisely if they allow themselves to be diverted from the practical consideration of their own real interests, for the sake of keeping alive a claim against the Imperial Government which it is quite certain will never be acknowledged."[6] The refusal of the terms was, as the Canadians surmised, only an excuse, for the real factor in the situation was

[1] When the Governor-General returned to Ottawa, he wrote the Colonial Secretary in London asking that a despatch be sent to himself and suggested the the wording include the hope that the Dominion "will deal liberally as well as justly with the Island" and that the Island Government "will receive favourably such propositions . . . as it is the policy of the Imperial Government that the whole of the British North American colonies should be united under one government." The unionists on the Island wanted such a document for use at the next election. Lord Granville obliged and sent a despatch in those terms. Young to Granville, Aug. 13, 1869, P.A.C. (P.E.I.), G 21, no. 25 B.
[2] Report of a Committee of the Privy Council, Dec. 14, 1869, *Assembly Journals* (P.E.I.), 1870, Appendix F.
[3] Minute of Council (P.E.I.), Jan. 7, 1870, *ibid.*
[4] Memorandum of Council to Lieutenant-Governor, Feb. 4, 1870, *ibid.* See also *P.E.I. Legislative Council Debates*, 1870, p. 10; and R. P. Haythorne in *ibid.*, 1873, p. 24.
[5] Macdonald to Sir John Rose, Dec. 13, 1872, P.A.C., Macdonald Letterbooks, vol. 522, p. 321.
[6] Granville to Administrator, March 7, 1870, *Assembly Journals*, 1870, Appendix F.

the absence of some compelling emergency which would cause the Islanders to sink their doubts in favour of union.

Meanwhile the Imperial Government was applying appropriate pressure as the opportunity arose. The despatches of successive Secretaries of State frequently suggested the mother country's wish that the Island would join with the other provinces. The Government was told that it would have to pay the Governor's salary after the end of Dundas's term, and the threat aroused a storm of protest in the Legislature, which considered it "a Confederate screw unfairly put upon us."[1] The Colonial Secretary also asked the local Government to pay the expenses of troops stationed on the Island, but this request was refused, as had been a similar one on a previous occasion,[2] on the ground that the negligence of the mother country in respect to the land question was responsible for the presence of the troops in the first place.[3] When the Legislature passed an act in 1867 authorizing the Government to raise a loan for the public service, the Secretary of State objected to it because "the account of the general position of the Island is far from encouraging."[4] Suggested remedies for the land problem were postponed by the Colonial Secretary in the hope that Confederation might bring a solution.[5]

Joseph Howe once said that he found the Governors "acting like partisans" in Confederation negotiations. This was as true of Robinson of Prince Edward Island as it was of Gordon of New Brunswick. The interference was encouraged in both cases by the Imperial and Dominion Governments.[6] Robinson was an active crusader in the cause of union despite the fact that he was the Queen's representative in a province which was supposed to enjoy responsible government, and wherein, on his own admission, "nine tenths of the people are opposed to Confederation on almost any terms." "I have lost no opportunity," he wrote Kimberley, "of

---

[1] Cardwell to Dundas, Feb. 18, 1865, *ibid.*, 1865, Appendix Y; *Assembly Debates*, 1869, pp. 118-19.
[2] *Supra*, p. 119.
[3] *Assembly Journals*, 1867, Appendix K; *ibid.*, 1868, Appendix Z.
[4] *Ibid.*, Appendix A.   [5] *Supra*, p. 119.
[6] See also G. E. Wilson, "New Brunswick's Entrance into Confederation," *Canadian Historical Review*, March, 1928, p. 4.

CONFEDERATION 131

endeavouring to win over by legitimate argument the most prominent men of the anti-confederate party."¹ In the same despatch he intimated that the better terms of 1869 should be presented again together with the offer of a railroad. It would be best, he said, to wait until the Government got involved in building a railroad and then reopen negotiations.² Later Robinson informed Lord Kimberley of his Government's railway building policy and advised him that he had assented to it with great pleasure because he knew it would bring financial embarrassment which would be the first step toward Confederation.³ In his relations with his Ministers he enhanced his own place in the negotiations to such an extent that J. C. Pope had to remind him of the position of the Crown under responsible government.⁴ "I shall always look back with pride," the Governor said, when the Island's entry was assured, "to the share which it has been my good fortune to take in bringing about this beneficial and long wished for result."⁵ The Imperial Government agreed and rewarded him with the C.M.G.

All these efforts, however, accomplished little and the Islanders remained unconvinced. The unionists grew impatient. "Immediate profit or loss," wrote one, "is the only thing that will move them."⁶ "Their pockets are far more sensitive than their understanding," wrote another, as he recommended that Canada place a duty on Island produce, and that the Imperial Government be asked to force the province to join.⁷ Macdonald was annoyed and determined to leave the Island leaders alone until they came to him.⁸ Observers at the Colonial Office could "only hope that Time will show the P.E. [sic] people how much confederation would be for

---

¹Robinson to Kimberley, March 24, 1871, P.A.C. (P.E.I.), G 54, p. 296.
²Robinson sent a copy of this despatch to the Governor-General. Even the officials at the Colonial Office were somewhat shocked at the Governor's advice and thought his sending a copy to Lord Lisgar "a little irregular, though perhaps it will not under the circumstances be remarked on." *Ibid.*
³Robinson to Kimberley, April 17, 1871, *ibid.*, p. 309.
⁴*Supra*, pp. 87-8.
⁵Robinson to Kimberley, May 29, 1873, P.A.C. (P.E.I.), G 55, p. 29.
⁶J. H. Gray to Macdonald, Jan. 13, 1871, P.A.C., Macdonald Letterbooks, vol. 119, p. 129.
⁷W. H. Pope to Macdonald, Sept. 18, 1870, *ibid.*, p. 123.
⁸Macdonald to Rose, Dec. 13, 1872, *ibid.*, vol. 522, p. 321.

their interest."[1] The Island Government meanwhile could see no advantage in making the change, and it was determined to proceed with "prudent precaution," especially since Nova Scotia, Newfoundland, and the Red River were not yet convinced of the merits of union.[2] Yet, Lord Kimberley wrote privately, "this little community cannot permanently stand alone, and both we and Canada can afford to wait."[3]

Events in the province, however, were combining to provide the compelling emergency which forced its people to change their minds. The outlook for trade was not good, for the British and Canadians were cool and there was no sign of reciprocity with the United States. Some Islanders began to feel the loneliness of independence from neighbourhood circles and thought union might be inevitable. Others thought, wrongly, of course, that the province might as well join for she was under the jurisdiction of the Canadian Governor-General in any case.[4] The influence of Canadian commerce prompted the province to adopt the decimal system of currency in 1871. More significantly, railway troubles joined with the controversies over land and religion in the period 1870-3 to make of local politics a tangle of complications for which union might suggest a solution.[5]

The elections of 1870 returned a group of factions. The old parties were broken and in their place were unionists, anti-unionists, Catholics, Protestants, and railroad advocates from both the Conservative and the Liberal ranks. A number of unsuccessful attempts were made to form a Government, and finally J. C. Pope succeeded

[1]Memorandum on Robinson to Kimberley, March 24, 1871, P.A.C. (P.E.I.), G 54, p. 296 (insertion).
[2]Memorandum of Council to Lieutenant-Governor, Feb. 4, 1870, *Assembly Journals*, 1870, Appendix F; see also *Assembly Debates*, 1870, pp. 126 ff.
[3]Note by Lord Kimberley on Robinson to Kimberley, March 24, 1871, P.A.C. (P.E.I.), G 54, p. 296 (insertion).
[4]*Assembly Debates*, 1869, p. 79.
[5]For detailed accounts of the events which accompanied the Island's entry into union see: W. M. Whitelaw, *The Maritimes and Canada before Confederation;* J. A. Maxwell, *Federal Subsidies to the Provincial Governments in Canada,* and "Prince Edward Island and Confederation," *Dalhousie Review,* Jan., 1933; D. C. Harvey, "Confederation in Prince Edward Island," *Canadian Historical Review,* June, 1933; Frank MacKinnon, "Prince Edward Island and Confederation," Charlottetown *Guardian,* July 10, 11, and 12, 1945, and "David Laird of Prince Edward Island," *Dalhousie Review,* Jan., 1947.

in getting together a coalition Cabinet after its members signed a pledge to drop the school question and the Confederation issue for four years. The association was, however, an unstable one, for each of the groups was looking to the day when it could again advocate its particular principle. The Government clutched at straws to keep its head above water, and one of these was the demand for a railroad through the length of the province. The road would be expensive and it had not been sanctioned by the people, but certain groups wanted it and they forced it upon the Cabinet as a means of salvation rather than a popular public necessity. Pope and his colleagues, who only held office by the grace of these doubtful elements, had to accept or resign. Religion and union being barred, they made the railway their politics.[1]

The railway bill was pushed through the Legislature in the session of 1871 after a stormy debate.[2] Many members thought it a trap to lure the Island into Confederation, and (as already intimated) Governor Robinson assented to it for just that reason. The chairman of the Railway Commission, who was then in the Cabinet, suffered defeat in a by-election soon afterwards. In the following year the Government was charged with corruption when a "railway ring" was uncovered, and the resulting investigation revealed attempts to bribe members of the Assembly in return for their influence in securing railway service for various districts. Though the Government was not proved guilty of the charges, it lost the confidence of the Legislature and resigned. In the general election which followed R. P. Haythorne and his friends were returned to power.

This so-called Liberal administration was, like its predecessor, an unsteady coalition. The railroad interests now demanded branch lines to the extreme ends of the province, the Government had to agree or resign, and the branches were built. Extravagance was followed by financial embarrassment.[3] The costs were higher than expected because the contractors, paid on the basis of five thousand

[1] *Assembly Debates,* 1871, pp. 35-49; *ibid.,* 1873, pp. 64 ff.; Toronto *Globe,* Nov. 3, 1876; MacKinnon, "David Laird of Prince Edward Island," pp. 407-11.
[2] 34 Vic., c. 4.
[3] See also *Reports to the Hon. The Minister of Public Works on the Prince Edward Island Railway, 1874-1875* (Ottawa, 1875).

pounds per mile, soon added to the mileage with curves and detours, and the towns and villages vied with one another in coaxing the railway to their doors.[1] The Government, moreover, had not taken sufficient financial precautions, and it found that its debentures which had been issued for the occasion could not be sold except at a loss.[2] Consequently it sought a way out of this difficulty which threatened the Island's position in the money markets, and indeed its whole economy.[3] Haythorne and his friends then thought that union might be the only good solution if they could transfer their troublesome railroad to the Dominion.

When Sir John Rose, Canada's unofficial agent in London, was approached on the question of placing the Island bonds on the London market, he replied that it might be possible if there was assurance that the Island would join Confederation.[4] Although the Government suspected that it was being coerced by Ottawa and London, it decided to approach the federal Cabinet. "No one can shut his eyes to the fact," said J. C. Pope, "that influences have been brought to bear against our paper. Baring Brothers will not take one of our bonds."[5] The Lieutenant-Governor had made no mistake when he told Kimberley that railway troubles would bring the local politicians to terms.

The Island had long called the tune in union negotiations and the Dominion had made the offers. Now that the province had run into difficulty, Sir John Macdonald was determined that the offers were to come from the other side. Rose told him of the Islanders' troubles, and he was ready for them. When the Haythorne Govern-

[1] "There had been curves made before now in the main line to suit hon. members," was the frank explanation of Hon. Peter Sinclair, Leader of the Government in the Assembly, "and he did not see that the hon. member was asking anything out of the way, to propose a curve for the benefit of his constituents." *Assembly Debates,* 1872, 2nd session, p. 380.
[2] A number of the directors of the Bank of Prince Edward Island, with which the debentures were placed, were prominent Government supporters.
[3] See R. P. Haythorne in *Legislative Council Debates,* 1873, pp. 26 ff.; and Haythorne to Editor, in Charlottetown *Patriot,* Jan. 8, 1881.
[4] Rose to Macdonald, Nov. 26, 1872, P.A.C., Macdonald Letterbooks, vol. 119, p. 133.
[5] *Assembly Debates,* April 28, 1873, p. 62. Baring Brothers, an English financial house, did considerable business for the Island and also acted as agents for the Canadian Government.

ment asked for "better terms" early in 1873 the Prime Minister would not negotiate by letter but invited a delegation to Ottawa. "As we know from experience the style of these men, we answered guardedly," he wrote Rose.[1] Haythorne and his colleague David Laird journeyed to Ottawa and secured terms which were satisfactory both to them and to the Dominion Government. Upon their return home, they dissolved the Legislature and put the new arrangement before the people.

The election which followed was typical of the province at that time. The union issue was obscured by controversies and bargaining over questions of religion and land and much argument over the responsibility for the state of the railway.[2] The Government was defeated and J. C. Pope again became Premier.

The new administration determined to seek still better terms, but it was evident that necessity promoted the negotiations. "Union with Canada," said the Premier, "will place our public securities on a par with those of the Dominion, and our public position will be better. Feeling as we all do that all side issues should give way in order that the public credit may be maintained, and if Confederation will do this, I believe that in view of all the difficulties entailed upon the country, this side of the House feels constrained to overcome their scruples against Confederation, and for the common good, seek to obtain better terms with a view to unite our destinies with those of the people of the other provinces of the Dominion."[3]

Again an Island delegation went to Ottawa, and this time Macdonald received it with pleasure because of his personal friendship with the Popes. The Dominion Government agreed that the usual arrangements made with other provinces would be applied to the Island, and, in addition, it promised the delegation that it would assume responsibility for continuous communications, make financial provision for purchasing the estates of the pro-

[1] Macdonald to Rose, Dec. 13, 1872, P.A.C., Macdonald Letterbooks, vol. 522, p. 321.
[2] *Assembly Debates*, 1873, p. 15; Toronto *Globe*, Nov. 3, 1876.
[3] *Assembly Debates*, 1873, p. 62; *Assembly Journals*, 1873, Appendix O.

prietors, and take over the railway.[1] Pope and his colleagues accepted these terms and, after returning to Charlottetown, succeeded in having them approved in the House by a vote of 28 to 2. Prince Edward Island thereupon joined Canada on July 1, 1873.

The administrative arrangements and terms of union under which the new province was thenceforth to be governed were contained in an Imperial Order-in-Council passed under authority of section 146 of the British North America Act which had provided for the admission of new provinces.[2] But Confederation did not introduce a completely new system of government on the Island. Both the Order-in-Council and the British North America Act[3] provided for the continuance of existing provincial institutions, principles, and practices, except in so far as they were changed by the Act itself.[4]

Executive and legislative powers under the new arrangement were distributed between federal and provincial authorities to provide for the responsibilities of government at the national and local levels. This involved two sets of institutions and two sets of powers. With respect to the executive, all "powers, authorities, and functions" which were hitherto vested in the Lieutenant-Governor-in-Council were divided and in part bestowed upon the Governor-General-in-Council "as far as the same continue in existence and capable of being exercised after the Union in relation to the Government of Canada,"[5] and in part left with the Lieutenant-

---

[1] Some proprietors tried at this time to get the home Government to impress the Dominion Government with the rights of property. A few even went so far as to demand an arrangement by which there could be an appeal to the Imperial Government on land issues over the heads of both the provincial and federal Governments. See R. B. Stewart to Robinson, Nov. 25, 1873, *ibid.*, 1876, Appendix E.

The Dominion Government did not expect to spend much money on the Island after union, a fact that partially explains the generous offers. "The great local works there having been now completed," said Sir Leonard Tilley in the House of Commons, "there could never be any large local expenditure in the future, and it was in consideration of this fact that the Dominion Government had granted such liberal terms." House of Commons Proceedings, May 20, 1873, "Parliamentary Debates, 1873," scrapbook in Library of Parliament, p. 200.

[2] Order of Her Majesty in Council, June 26, 1873, *The British North America Acts and Selected Statutes* (Ottawa, 1943), pp. 168-74.

[3] Section 129.

[4] The relevant sections of the British North America Act and the Order-in-Council will be found in Appendices C and D.

[5] B.N.A. Act, section 12.

Governor-in-Council, when relating to matters coming within the jurisdiction of the provincial Government.[1] Moreover a formal link between these two authorities was embodied in provisions for the federal appointment, removal, and payment of the Lieutenant-Governor and for prevention of provincial interferences with his office,[2] as well as for the federal power of disallowance of provincial legislation and of action on reserved bills.[3]

Powers were distributed between the Parliament of Canada and the provincial Legislature under sections 91 to 95 of the British North America Act. The federal Parliament was given the power under section 91 to make laws for the "Peace, Order, and good Government of Canada, in relation to all Matters not coming within the Classes of Subjects by this Act assigned exclusively to the Legislatures of the Provinces," and, "for greater Certainty, but not so as to restrict the Generality of the foregoing Terms in this Section," twenty-nine enumerated articles indicated examples of the Dominion powers. They included powers of a general nature such as the regulation of trade and commerce, the raising of money by any mode or system of taxation, the borrowing of money on the public credit, and the administration of the militia and defence, sea coast and inland fisheries, banks and banking, the criminal law, and marriage and divorce.

Provincial powers were set out in section 92. The province could amend its constitution "except as regards the Office of Lieutenant-Governor," and its powers were those, in general, of local significance, such as direct taxation within the province for provincial purposes, the borrowing of money on the credit of the province, local public works, property and civil rights in the province, and "generally all Matters of a merely local or private Nature in the Province." Section 93 gave the province the exclusive power to make laws with respect to education subject to certain provisions concerning separate schools; section 94 gave the Dominion power to provide for uniformity of laws relating to property and civil rights and court procedure in each province; and section 95 provided concurrent jurisdiction with respect to agriculture and immigration.

[1] *Ibid.*, sections 64, 65, 66. [2] *Ibid.*, sections 58, 59, 60, 92 (1).
[3] *Ibid.*, sections 56, 90.

The Act, therefore, relieved the local Legislature of a substantial portion of its existing powers. But the Legislature was not thereby subordinated to the Dominion Parliament; it became a local body dealing with local matters, but autonomous within its own sphere. The province had forsaken private business for a partnership; it had traded independence for the constitutional diversity of federalism, and, in doing so, inevitably diluted the authority of its political institutions. From this situation there inevitably arose the problems, which do not concern us here, of interpreting the boundaries of the two fields of legislative power, of adjusting the difficulties of divided jurisdiction, and of balancing the various theories of centralism and provincialism.[1]

The distribution of authority was also carried out in the other branches of government. The Dominion was to appoint the judges, except those of Probate, but the province was responsible for the administration of justice.[2] Officials who dealt with federal matters became federal civil servants, and their duties, appointment, and salaries were the responsibility of Parliament.[3] The province naturally assumed power over the "Establishment and Tenure of Provincial Offices and the Appointment and Payment of Provincial Officers."[4]

Divided jurisdiction was not new to the Island's constitution, for the province had always shared the functions of government with outside authorities. The power to appoint, pay, and remove the Governor had been exercised by the Imperial authorities.[5] Judges had previously been appointed directly from London. The power of disallowance of provincial legislation and of action on reserved bills was merely handed over from the Queen to her representative at Ottawa. Anti-unionists could point out that local interests might be submerged in those of a central power, but it was generally appreciated that, if such should be the result, it could be no worse than the sacrifice of the province's welfare to

---

[1] See *Report of the Royal Commission on Dominion-Provincial Relations* (Ottawa, 1940), Book I.
[2] *Infra,* chapter XII.   [3] B.N.A. Act, sections 130, 131, 91 (8).
[4] *Ibid.,* section 92 (4); *infra,* chapter IX.
[5] An exception was the payment of Governor Robinson from 1870-3; *supra,* p. 130.

the privileges of distant proprietors. In other words, the Island had been accustomed to outside jurisdiction and influence, and in this respect the transition to federalism made little change.

The Island's reluctance to join Confederation was assuaged somewhat by special provisions designed to meet her most acute local problems. All railways under contract and in course of construction in the province became the property of the Dominion. "Efficient Steam Service" and "continuous communications" with the mainland were assured. The federal Government undertook to provide assistance to the province to the extent of $800,000 for the purchase of the proprietors' lands. The Island's fear that it would be inadequately represented in the federal Parliament was met by allotting her four seats in the Senate and six in the House of Commons. Thus the chief local objections to union were to be solved, it was hoped, by a constitutional guarantee forming part of the bargain of 1873.[1]

The financial terms of the union were also included in the Order-in-Council. The Island's debts and liabilities, like those of the other provinces, were assumed by the Dominion. The debt allowance, which in the other provinces had been set at approximately $25 per head on the basis of the 1861 census, was fixed for the Island at $50 per head on the basis of the 1871 census, which concession was granted in view of the limited benefits which the province would receive from Dominion public works, the possibility of a new readjustment of financial arrangements with the existing provinces, as well as "the isolated and exceptional condition" of the Island. There was a special subsidy of $45,000 in consideration of the Island's lack of Crown lands, but from this amount there was to be deducted a sum equal to 5 per cent per annum on the money granted by the Dominion to the province for the purpose of buying out the landed proprietors. In return for the transfer of the taxing powers to the Dominion the Island received for the support of its Government and Legislature a grant of $30,000 and an annual grant of 80 cents per head of the population, based on the 1871 census, and subject to certain alterations. These provisions appeared

[1]The nature and subsequent history of these provisions are discussed in chapter xiv.

generous to the Island's politicians who had feared financial disaster as a result of their railroad, but there were some who regretted that the emergency had prevented a better bargain permitting more compensation for size, isolation, and lack of natural resources.

These terms were accepted on the Island for better or for worse and with mingled satisfaction and misgiving. The Dominion in turn welcomed the new province and assured it of a great future in a growing nation. "The union of Prince Edward Island with the Dominion of Canada," wrote the Governor-General, "is a most fortunate circumstance from whatever point it may be regarded whether affecting Local, Imperial, or Canadian interests."[1] When Lord Dufferin visited Charlottetown in the summer of 1873 an arch of welcome greeted him with the appropriate slogan "Long courted, won at last."

[1]Dufferin to Robinson, May 17, 1873, *Assembly Journals,* 1873, Appendix U.

PART II

PROVINCIAL GOVERNMENT

CHAPTER VII

THE LIEUTENANT-GOVERNOR

THE LIEUTENANT-GOVERNOR is the head of the provincial Government and the representative of the Crown in Prince Edward Island. His position and powers have been inherited from the early colonial Governors and changed to meet the requirements of responsible government and of a federal system. He is also an officer of the Dominion, for he is appointed for a five-year term by the Governor-General-in-Council and he may be removed by that body for cause assigned. In this capacity he is subject to the conditions and orders set forth in his Commission and Instructions and in other instructions which may from time to time be sent him. The Governor, therefore, like the Governor-General before 1926, is linked with two governments, the one which he heads and which advises him, and the other which appoints and instructs him.[1] He is not an administrator, but a dignified and impartial symbol of authority who now wields personally only a small amount of the power of his colonial predecessors and depends almost entirely upon others for advice and guidance.

In his local capacity the Governor exercises what are generally nominal functions initiated by the Premier or the Cabinet, such as selecting Ministers, and summoning, proroguing, and dissolving the Legislature, although on some very rare occasions of unusual constitutional difficulty he might exercise them on his own responsibility by invoking the "reserve" or emergency power of the Crown. He also acts as the social head of the province, a role which he performs independently of his advisers and which is a concession to the desire for decorative functions in government. In his capacity as representative of the Governor-General he is empowered by the

---

[1]For many years there was much doubt on this point, and it took several judicial decisions to clarify the Governor's role as representative of *both* the Sovereign and the Governor-General. See *Mercer* v. *Attorney-General of Ontario*, (1881) 5 S.C.R. 538, at p. 637; *Liquidators of the Maritime Bank of Canada* v. *Receiver-General of New Brunswick*, [1892] A.C. 437, at p. 443; *Bonanza Creek Gold Mining Co.* v. *The King*, [1916] A.C. 566, at pp. 580-1; Department of Justice, *Memorandum on Office of Lieutenant-Governor of a Province, Its Constitutional Character and Functions, November 1937* (Ottawa, 1946), p. 7.

British North America Act to give to bills passed by the provincial Legislature his assent in the name of the Governor-General, to withhold the Governor-General's assent,[1] or to reserve bills for the Governor-General's pleasure. The Act also orders him to send a copy of each assented bill to the Governor-General who, within one year, may disallow it.[2]

These two capacities are normally clear and understandable, yet there have been several occasions when Governors have been able to play one against the other, particularly by using, during conflicts with Ministers, the controversial powers with respect to royal assent. Consequently, while most Governors have usually been content with a purely formal and passive role in administration, there have been a sufficient number of exceptions to indicate that the office has lagged behind its London and Ottawa counterparts in its accommodation to responsible government.

Personnel

Many characteristics of the governorship are determined by the personalities of the incumbents and the method of their appointment. This is true of most institutions, but in Prince Edward Island personnel is of special significance in the governorship because of the very limited number of men available for the post. The Governor, moreover, is not so much the distinguished and detached figurehead in the small province where he is more usually regarded as a prominent citizen about whose family and business most people are well informed.[3]

Political allegiance is the most important factor influencing appointments to the governorship. Since the choice is made by the federal Government, the prospective incumbent is expected to be of the same political persuasion as the party in power at Ottawa. Of the sixteen appointments since Robinson, the last of the English

---

[1] In actual practice the Governor is considered to have given or withheld the assent on behalf of the King.
[2] B.N.A. Act, sections 55, 56, and 90.
[3] A list of the Lieutenant-Governors of Prince Edward Island since Confederation with their occupations and dates of their Commissions will be found in Appendix F.

Governors, fifteen have been made on this basis.[1] The practice has favoured stalwarts whose party service merited some substantial reward and precluded any consideration of otherwise available persons in the ranks of the Opposition, no matter how distinguished they might be.[2] As a result, some Governors have been men of outstanding ability and achievements, while others revealed an extraordinary lack of such qualifications. The quality of the Governor, therefore, depends, above everything else, upon the discernment of the Government which makes the appointment.

The local administration has considerable influence in the selection if it is of the same political persuasion as the federal Cabinet, for the Premier is often consulted as party leader in the province. The appointment is also considered by the province's representatives in the Senate and House of Commons who are of the same party as the federal Government, and if there is an Island member in the Dominion Cabinet his opinion is very important and, at times, even decisive. The Prime Minister usually has a number of recommendations and opinions from other sources, such as retired public men and local clergy, and, in the early years at least, he could not escape appropriate pressure from the candidates themselves.

Despite its disadvantages, political affiliation usually ensures some experience in government. All the Governors, except two, have served in public office; in the Legislature, in the Cabinet, or in the federal Parliament.[3] It must not be supposed, however, that long experience in public life is of itself a necessary qualification of the Governor, for His Honour is not responsible for the complexities of administration since his actions depend on the advice of his Ministers. Nevertheless several Governors have brought to their

[1] The exception, Sir Robert Hodgson, had been Chief Justice, and in the days when local party lines did not conform to federal ones, he was recommended by both parties and by the retiring Governor. Robinson to Dufferin, May 2, 1873, Public Archives of Canada, Governor-General's Correspondence, G series, vol. 20, no. 3060.

[2] See Goldwin Smith on the appointment of Lieutenant-Governors in *Canada and the Canadian Question* (London, 1891), p. 157.

[3] The two exceptions, F. R. Heartz and G. D. DeBlois, had never held public office, but they had been active in business and party circles.

office the prestige of long years in public life, and in some instances this fact has contributed much distinction and popularity to the governorship. In some cases, too, experience in high office has sharpened their interest in constitutional questions with obvious effects upon their relations with the Cabinet. Only on rare occasions, however, has a Governor of Prince Edward Island been accused of partisanship during his term of office, for most of their controversies have been with ministries of their own party. The potential danger of political partisanship in Government House, nevertheless, is always present, and the Governor has to make certain that in both his constitutional and his social duties he gives no suspicion of favouritism one way or another and keeps clear of all party proceedings.[1]

Religion is another consideration in the selection of Governors. It is a recognized custom in Prince Edward Island to alternate where possible between Protestant and Catholic in order to avoid showing any favouritism.[2] It has sometimes been exceedingly difficult to follow this custom because there may be no otherwise "available" Catholic or Protestant at the desired moment.[3] An example of such a complication was the appointment in 1884 of A. A. Macdonald, a civil servant, because the Prime Minister was unable to make a choice from among the political contenders in the Irish and Scotch Catholic groups.[4]

No Governor has received a second term in Prince Edward Island since Confederation, although reappointment has not been

---

[1] For discussions of this point see Christopher Dunkin in Province of Canada, *Parliamentary Debates on the Subject of Confederation of the British North American Provinces* (Quebec, 1865), p. 504; and R. MacGregor Dawson, "The Independence of the Lieutenant-Governor," *Dalhousie Review*, April, 1922, p. 231.

[2] See Charlottetown *Guardian* (editorial), July 23, 1924.

[3] The majority of the Governors, eleven out of seventeen, have been Protestants.

[4] Archbishop O'Brien of Halifax recommended an Irish Catholic. Premier Sullivan was considered to have opposed this because it might spoil his (Sullivan's) chances for a judgeship on the ground that there would be too many Irish Catholics in high office. At any rate the Premier wrote Ottawa recommending a Scotch Catholic. The Bishop of Charlottetown further complicated the issue by advocating the appointment of a Protestant. The story is a most interesting account of the bargaining which accompanied appointments to the governorship half a century ago. See Public Archives of Canada, Macdonald Papers, vol. 322, pp. 47-50, 54, 106, 440, and vol. 21, p. 378; Macdonald Letterbooks, vol. 28A, p. 333, and vol. 26, p. 230; Charlottetown *Patriot*, June 5, 1884.

uncommon in other provinces. The chief reason in the earlier years was the fact that when a vacancy was pending the race was open and keen with a large number of candidates in the field.[1] After 1930 the governorship ceased to be so coveted a promotion because the financial obligations had become a serious disadvantage. A Governor who performs his duties well cannot afford a second term unless he has an adequate income. Moreover it is not easy for a man and his wife to fulfil the demands of local society to suit everyone, so that, with the end of five years, reappointment has not been seriously considered.

Several Governors remained in office some months over the five-year period,[2] but only one, F. R. Heartz, was given an extra year or more to his term. This overtime is of some advantage when the Government wishes an opportunity to look around for a successor, but there is a real danger of undermining the independence of a Governor by letting him remain without actual reappointment. He cannot be removed during his term, as already mentioned, without cause assigned, but he may be dropped without reason any time during an extension, and, as a result, either the Governor or his advisers might become careless about the constitutional relations between them. The issues which occurred between Governors DeBlois and LePage and their respective ministries after the end of their terms bore lively testimony to the possible consequences of remaining in the office without enjoying its security.[3]

[1]See, for example, Charlottetown *Examiner,* May 30, 1910.
[2]The British North America Act does not provide for the automatic retirement of the Governor at the end of his term. "The Lieutenant-Governor," reads section 59, "shall hold office during the Pleasure of the Governor-General; but any Lieutenant-Governor appointed after the Commencement of the First Session of the Parliament of Canada shall not be removable within Five Years from his Appointment, except for Cause assigned. . . ."
[3]See G. D. DeBlois in *Guardian,* March 25, 1940, and *infra,* p. 155 for the details of the LePage case. For an excellent discussion on this subject see *Canada, House of Commons, Debates,* 1893, pp. 80-4, and *ibid.,* 1895, pp. 4256-72. The Opposition criticized the Dominion Government for leaving several Lieutenant-Governors in office without reappointment after the expiry of their terms and particularly emphasized the rumour that the Governor of Manitoba had been bargaining for a second term. "Why," said Sir Richard Cartwright (p. 4268), "one merely needs to state the proposition to know that such a person must of necessity forfeit his independence pro tanto when he

The most important factor in the process of appointing a Governor today is evidently the salary. The Governor of Prince Edward Island receives $8,000 a year[1] and this sum, which is reduced substantially by income tax, is far too low to enable the Governor to fulfil even the most modest of his functions without drawing on his personal income, if he has any, or on his savings. In return, he must give up his private occupation for public duty, maintain a large mansion, and pay the bills for his entertainment and the cost of his trips through the province.[2] In the majority of cases, therefore, a man pays handsomely for the privilege of residing at Government House for five years, and prospective appointees must have a purse that can stand the strain. Excellent men have turned down the offer of the post because, in the words of Goldwin Smith's friend, "they do not want to keep a hotel for five years."[3] Moreover, a Governor's administration is apt to be judged far more on the extent of his hospitality than on his constitutional behaviour. Those who have avoided the financial burden by social inactivity have limited their own popularity, and those who have met too many demands with insufficient funds have faced financial ruin as a result. Some of the early provincial Governors did not find the position expensive,[4] but as the salary remained constant and the

ceases to be an officer holding his position for a term of years during good behaviour; and the hon. gentleman knows quite well that the value of the whole of these officials depends entirely on the belief of the public, the legislature, the Ministers with whom they act, that they are impartial and independent. There can be nothing more calculated to degrade the office of Lieutenant-Governor than to allow those who hold that office to remain there at the pleasure of the Ministry of the day."

[1] It was increased from $7,000 in 1948.

[2] The problem was recently the subject of litigation in the federal Supreme and Exchequer Courts, and some hope was held out for the Governors by the latter tribunal which decided that the remuneration of a Lieutenant-Governor is not so much a salary as an indemnity to cover expenses in connection with his duties. Decision of Exchequer Court of Canada in *Carroll v. The King*, [1949] Ex.C.R. 169. See also [1948] S.C.R. 126.

[3] Goldwin Smith, *Canada and the Canadian Question*, p. 157.

[4] For instance, T. Heath Haviland asked for a second term because he was in "straightened pecuniary circumstances" after a bank failure. Haviland to Sir John Macdonald, March 29, 1884, P.A.C., Macdonald Papers, vol. 322, p. 54. D. A. MacKinnon reported that his finances were not sufficient for politics and he would like a governorship. MacKinnon to Laurier, June 3, 1904, Public Archives of Canada, Laurier Papers, file 506. On the other hand Sir Robert Hodgson was severely criticized in both the Cabinet and the Legislature for desiring to supplement his salary by retaining his pension as a former Attorney-General. 14 Vic., c. 3; *P.E.I. House of Assembly Debates*, 1875, pp.

expenses and income tax increased, the financial demands became relatively greater. Consequently the post usually attracts only men with means. It is significant that seven of the last nine Governors have been merchants, that, in a predominantly agricultural province, only one farmer has been appointed, and that, of the professional men, only one practising lawyer and one doctor would accept the position. The day for numerous applicants is now over; the question is not only who deserves the post, but also who will take it. The obvious remedy is either an expense allowance or a tax-free salary.

Governors have not always been elderly men at the end of their careers. Only three died in office,[1] while the majority of the others carried on their businesses or professions after their terms had expired. Several returned to politics. There is nothing constitutionally wrong with an ex-Governor's return to politics so long as he does not prepare for it during his term, and no significant question has been raised as to his right to do so. But the Island has not always taken kindly to such a return. Benjamin Rogers, for example, assumed the leadership of the provincial Liberal party immediately after his retirement from the governorship in June, 1915. When the provincial elections took place on September 16 the Liberals lost and Rogers suffered a personal defeat and had to give up the leadership.[2] The fact that he had returned to politics was not as significant in itself, as was the obvious objection to a man who had represented the Crown in June and led a political party in a general election less than two months later against those who had been his constitutional advisers. There is no good reason why a Governor cannot re-enter politics after the end of his term, but if he does it too soon he lays himself open to the suspicion, not necessarily well grounded, that he has maintained his political contacts and sympathies while in office. It would appear that a waiting period should occur between the time when a Governor steps down from the rarefied atmosphere surrounding the Crown and when he returns to the rough and tumble of politics.

101-8; Macdonald to Hodgson, Sept. 13, 1873, P.A.C., Macdonald Letterbooks, vol. 20, p. 655.
[1] J. S. Carvell, A. C. Macdonald, and Charles Dalton.
[2] *Examiner*, Aug. 23, Sept. 3, 17, 1915.

The Functions of the Governor

The Lieutenant-Governor of Prince Edward Island generally plays the active ceremonial and passive political roles expected of the head of the Government. On the ceremonial side the significance of his duties is severely limited by the small local environment and by the fact that he occupies a tertiary place in relation to the more spectacular positions of the King and the Governor-General. In his political role, however, the Governor has occasionally invoked certain powers which his august counterparts have long since abandoned.[1]

The activities of the Governor which are designed to appeal to human interest are a part of the decorative side of government. "A royal family sweetens politics by the seasonable addition of nice and pretty events," wrote Bagehot, "it introduces irrelevant facts into the business of government, but they are facts which speak to men's bosoms and employ their thoughts."[2] The occupants of Government House are looked upon as the first family in the province, and as such they are expected to give to local events a touch of colour and respectability.

A wide variety of duties in this category must be performed by the Governor. At the opening and closing of the Legislature he rides to the House in state with the booming of cannon, a guard of honour, and a respectful reception from local politicians. "It was a grand sight," records a distinguished observer of this ceremony in earlier days, "democracy in gold lace and feathers, but real democracy nevertheless. I just cannot get used to the governors I see these days, governors in business suits and Stetsons who treat me as a civic equal. I am spoiled in the matter of governors. I like them old, white-haired, dignified, with plumed aides beside them, and cannon firing salutes in the distance."[3] The Governor and his wife are expected to attend official ceremonies, fairs, concerts, and other gatherings; and unveil monuments, lay cornerstones, present awards, and make speeches. These ceremonies generally take place

---

[1]For the Governor's judicial functions as Chancellor and President of the Court of Divorce see *infra*, p. 261 and pp. 262-3, 264, 265.
[2]Walter Bagehot, *The English Constitution* (World's Classics), p. 35.
[3]Bishop F. C. Kelly, *The Bishop Jots It Down* (New York, 1939), p. 29.

THE LIEUTENANT-GOVERNOR 151

with appropriate decorum; and, with a liberal use of platitudes, His Honour endeavours to avoid offending even his most sensitive listeners. A notable exception was the presentation by Governor Benjamin Rogers of a trophy during which the Governor stated that he could not see the point of presenting the trophy other than to encourage a "spirit of militarism." He was heckled at the meeting and widely criticized for his frankness.[1] The Governor is honorary president of societies and campaigns of various kinds, and he is expected to donate his patronage, time, and money accordingly; and there are numerous ladies' organizations which make similar demands upon his wife. The most exacting and expensive obligation of the Governor, however, is entertainment which he must provide on official occasions such as the opening of the Legislature, special celebrations, and visits of distinguished guests.

Prince Edward Island has been a most convenient unit for these decorative functions, since it is small enough for the Governor to serve a large proportion of the population. In the bigger provinces the Governor's activities may be confined largely to the capital, but on the Island even the most remote village celebration is only a short distance from Government House, and the "invitation list" need not be restricted to one locality. On the other hand the mistakes of a Governor are more readily criticized in a small area where they can become magnified out of all proportion to their deserved significance. Politicians may forgive His Honour's constitutional indiscretions, but they, or more particularly their wives, will not forget his social ones.[2]

---

[1]*Patriot*, Sept. 4, 1912; *Examiner*, Sept. 4, 1912; *Canadian Annual Review*, 1912, p. 487.

[2]There are many examples of public issues which arose out of the Governor's social obligations: the visit of Prince Arthur of Connaught in 1869 (Hodgson to Granville, Oct. 28, 1869, Public Archives of Canada, Colonial Office Records (P.E.I.), G series, vol. 54, p. 166; Granville to Administrator, Dec. 4, 1869, *ibid.*, G 38, p. 309); visit of Lord Dufferin in 1873 (*P.E.I. Legislative Council Debates*, 1874, pp. 129-30); alleged mismanagement of the visit of the Marquis of Lorne and Princess Louise in 1879, which was discussed in the Legislature and in contemporary newspapers; the visit of the King and Queen in 1939 (*Guardian*, March 25, 1940, and *Patriot*, "Proceedings of the Legislative Assembly for April 3, 1940"). Such disputes have also occurred in much larger provinces, e.g. British Columbia (*Vancouver News Herald*, March 7, 8, 1949, and *Ottawa Citizen*, March 9, 1949).

The political relations between the Governor and the Cabinet are usually routine and formal, and generally the only significant contact between the Cabinet and the Governor is the periodic visit of the Clerk to Government House to obtain His Honour's signature on the minutes of Council. He is expected to give his consent to executive action as a matter of course, and, unlike the King, he is rarely kept informed on the details of administration.

An example of the manner in which powers that the Governor once wielded are now generally used on ministerial advice is provided by the prerogative of pardoning offenders under the law. Early Governors of Prince Edward Island once granted pardons on their own initiative, but in 1847 Governor Huntley was advised by the Secretary of State for the Colonies to consult the Executive Council and the trial judge before doing so.[1] By Confederation the Governors had come to depend on the advice of the Attorney-General alone. From time to time, however, they pardoned offenders under prohibition legislation without consultation, and by 1928 this practice had become customary. In that year a lively debate occurred in the House and the Government defended the Governor's personal initiative in this respect.[2] The matter was clarified somewhat by the Ticket of Leave Act of 1931 which permitted the release of prisoners on order of the Executive Council,[3] yet a personal order from the Governor still remained sufficient.[4] It is now customary, however, for the Governor to rely upon the advice of the Attorney-General on matters of pardon.

There are some functions of the Crown which, like those of a fire extinguisher, may be invoked on occasions of emergency despite long disuse. The Governor may intervene in the event of a very serious, extraordinary, and intolerable disregard for the constitution on the part of his Ministers for which no other satisfactory remedy is available. His participation may also be necessary if certain normal political processes are unworkable, for instance, in facilitating the selection of a Premier where there is

[1] Grey to Huntley, Aug. 26, 1847, P.A.C. (P.E.I.), G 17, p. 157; G 18, p. 1.
[2] *Guardian*, April 19, 20, 1928.   [3] 21-22 Geo. V, c. 13.
[4] See Minute of Council, July 13, 1931, Executive Council Minute Books, Legislative Building, Charlottetown, vol. XXXVI, p. 265.

no obvious choice for the office. Such instances are rare, but the importance of these functions is not diminished by disuse or by the fact that they must be invoked with extreme caution.

There have been several exceptions to the general practice of following ministerial advice, however, for not all Governors have been content to be what Goldwin Smith called "ventriloquial apparatus" of the Premier. Some have spoken and acted of their own accord and contrary to the wishes of their First Ministers; others have forced their advisers to change Cabinet policy. In a few instances Governors have been encouraged by their Ministers to exercise their old powers in a manner quite unusual in modern cabinet government.

The power of pardon, already described, also illustrates how the unexpected interference of the Governor can upset constitutional usage. In 1932 Governor Dalton released from jail a prisoner who had committed an offence under existing liquor legislation. The Government then attempted to have the offender rejailed, but the Supreme Court held that he could not be imprisoned again after such a pardon by the Crown.[1] An even more extraordinary case occurred in 1950 when Governor Bernard released a prisoner by the simple method of telephoning the Sheriff. This time the man was rejailed but subsequently released after habeas corpus proceedings in the Supreme Court. In both these instances the intervention of the Governor was neither recommended by his advisers nor justified by the circumstances involved.[2]

Most of the issues between the Governor and his advisers have concerned the withholding of assent, and the reservation of bills for the Governor-General's pleasure.[3] Despite the tendency to regard these powers as obsolete, the Governor is occasionally tempted to use them since they are specifically provided by statute, and are

[1] See P.E.I. Supreme Court Files, no. 1935, Mackie case.
[2] The Court "assumed" that the Governor's action was "not valid" in that his order was not a written one. In both the cases the release of the prisoner involved the legal question of whether it was a "voluntary" or "involuntary escape." See *Guardian*, April 28, 1950.
[3] For discussions on the Governor's powers in connection with royal assent see articles by Eugene Forsey in *Canadian Journal of Economics and Political Science*, Feb., 1938 and Feb., 1948; Frank Milligan, *ibid.*, May, 1948; J. R. Mallory, *ibid.*, Nov., 1948; and Frank MacKinnon, *ibid.*, May, 1949.

thus more easily invoked than other old powers which have gradually fallen into disuse.

Withholding of assent to bills passed by the Legislature. There have been four cases of withholding of assent in Prince Edward Island.

1. An Orange Lodge Incorporation Bill was passed in 1878 after a bitter debate and Governor Hodgson reserved it for the Governor-General's pleasure. His Excellency took no action and advised Hodgson that if a similar bill were passed again he should deal with it at once and not send it to Ottawa.[1] Such a bill was passed in 1880 and Governor Haviland withheld assent. The Premier had tried to kill the bill, and it was widely believed, therefore, that he had advised the Governor to withhold assent in an effort to prevent a religious controversy.[2]

2. Governor Murdoch MacKinnon withheld assent in 1920 to a bill transferring Government House to the Crown.[3] Relations between successive Governors and their Ministers had previously been strained from time to time by the question of who might dispose of Government House and its property. Governor Fanning had given the land in 1789 to the Governor-General to be held by him and his successors, or, in his or their absence, by the Lieutenant-Governor for the time being, and the Colonial Secretary later pointed out that it could not be transferred "during the tenure of office of any Governor without his concurrence."[4] The Governors therefore looked upon it as their private property despite a minute of the Governor-General-in-Council of June 19, 1874 which ordered that it be appropriated to the use of the provincial Government.[5] The 1920 issue was the last of a long series of disputes most of which accompanied demands by the City of Charlottetown for portions of the Government House property as a public park.

[1] *P.E.I. House of Assembly Journals,* 1880, Appendix A; *infra,* p. 156.
[2] *Patriot,* May 1, 6, 1880; *Examiner,* May 3, 1880.
[3] *Patriot,* May 25, 1920; *Examiner,* May 20, 26, July 6, 10, and Aug. 19, 1920.
[4] Kimberley to Robinson, Dec. 15, 1870, P.A.C. (P.E.I.), G 39, p. 515.
[5] *Assembly Journals,* 1875, Appendix F. Some Governors consented to give up slices of land in return for concessions from the local Government; others accused the Cabinet of coercing them by refusing or agreeing to repairs. See Robinson to Kimberley, Nov. 12, 1870, P.A.C. (P.E.I.), G 54, p. 246; *Assembly Debates,* 1891, pp. 402-8; *ibid.,* 1893, p. 293.

3. Governor MacKinnon withheld assent to a bill known as "The United Church of Canada Act" in 1924. There had been much debate and public discussion during the passage of the bill, not so much on the merits of the union between Presbyterians, Congregationalists, and Methodists, as on the manner in which the congregations and property were to be divided. The Governor pointed out in a despatch to the Secretary of State that there was no adequate provision for hearings or appeals in disputed cases. The bill provided for the inclusion of all congregations within the United Church and the withdrawal of non-concurring congregations within six months after the act came into effect.[1] The Governor thought that non-concurring congregations should be permitted to make their decisions before, rather than after the union. "Freedom in all matters of public worship," he said, "is so jealously guarded in all His Majesty's Dominions, and sweeping interference by legislation so seldom exercised, that I deemed it advisable to withhold my assent."[2]

4. Governor Bradford W. LePage withheld assent in 1945 from a bill entitled "An Act to Amend the Prohibition Act." This measure sought to modify the existing prohibition law which had long been the source of much controversy. The Governor did not consult his Ministers beforehand and gave no reason for his action, although on the previous day he had addressed a meeting of the Prince Edward Island Temperance Federation and said that he was "deeply concerned" about the bill.[3]

Reservation of bills passed by the Legislature. Ten Island bills have been reserved for the Governor-General's pleasure.

1. The Land Purchase Bill of 1874 was reserved because it "affected private rights by enforcing a compulsory sale" under forced arbitration.[4] The Governor-General agreed that it was objectionable and refused assent.[5]

[1]United Church of Canada Act, 1924, *Canada, Sessional Papers,* 1924, no. 276, p. 9, section 7.
[2]Murdoch MacKinnon to Secretary of State, April 17, 1924, *ibid.,* p. 8. The Secretary of State, in reply, regretted the Governor's action after giving a long opinion on *reservation,* which, of course, was not involved.
[3]*Guardian,* April 18, 1945; *Patriot,* April 18, 1945.
[4]Hodgson to Secretary of State, May 18, 1874, *Assembly Journals,* 1875, Appendix E.
[5]Report of Deputy Minister of Justice, Dec. 23, 1874, *ibid.,* 1876, Appendix E.

2. The Land Purchase Bill of 1875 was reserved because of the previous reservation. The Governor-General gave his assent because the "objectionable features of the previous Bill have been removed."[1]

3. A bill to give a portion of Government House farm to the City of Charlottetown, 1876, was reserved because pre-Confederation bills of this kind had been reserved for the Queen's pleasure. No objections were raised and the Governor-General gave his assent.[2]

4. The Land Purchase Act Amendment Bill of 1876 was reserved apparently because previous land bills had been reserved. The Governor-General refused assent because it was "retroactive in its effect" and because it dealt "with rights of parties now in litigation."[3]

5. The Orange Lodge Incorporation Bill of 1878 was reserved because of its controversial nature. The Governor-General advised that the Governor should not have reserved such a bill which was "of provincial concern," but took no action.[4]

6. The Church of England Disestablishment Bill of 1878 was reserved because it interfered with the prerogative of the Sovereign as temporal head of the Church. The Governor-General assented to it because it was within the legislative authority of the province and did not involve Dominion or Imperial interests.[5]

7. A Bill Respecting the Legislature, 1892, was reserved because of its controversial nature. It abolished the Legislative Council and contained an alleged gerrymander and a provision for enfranchising mortgage-holders. The local Government advised the Governor to reconsider his action and request the return of the bill from the Governor-General, but His Honour refused.[6] The Governor-General took no action, although the Minister of Justice

[1] Report of Minister of Justice, May 26, 1875, *ibid.*
[2] Department of Justice, *Memorandum on Office of Lieutenant-Governor*, p. 59.
[3] Report of Minister of Justice, July 18, 1876, *Assembly Journals*, 1877, Appendix F.
[4] *Ibid.*, 1880, Appendix A.
[5] Department of Justice, *Memorandum on Office of Lieutenant-Governor*, p. 59.
[6] Executive Council Minute Books, Legislative Building, Charlottetown, May 10, 1892, pp. 200-8.

advised that the matter was "entirely within the competence of the Legislature."¹

8. Factories in Incorporated Cities Bill, 1881.²
9. A Bill Respecting Peddlers, 1894.³
10. A Bill Respecting Government House Property, 1904.⁴

The Lieutenant-Governor's reasons for reservation were not indicated in any of these last three cases. No discussion of them appears in the press, and no mention is made of them in the correspondence in the *Journals,* in *Provincial Legislation,* or in the Department of Justice *Memorandum* of 1937.

The giving of assent to bills after assent has been withheld. Much has been said in constitutional circles about the power of provincial Lieutenant-Governors with respect to the withholding of assent and the reservation of bills. The Governor's power to *give* assent, however, has not, until 1945, been the subject of any substantial controversy, save perhaps in connection with relations between His Honour and the Cabinet. Much interest has consequently arisen from the giving of assent by the Lieutenant-Governor of Prince Edward Island to the Prohibition Act Amendment Act of 1945 which had been refused assent by his predecessor after the session of the Legislature had ended. The local Supreme Court has passed judgment on this case and has had the unique privilege of condemning a "royal assent" and declaring it, and consequently the statute itself, null and void.⁵

The facts are as follows. On April 19, 1945 Governor B. W. LePage prorogued the Legislature, and during the proceedings withheld his assent from "An Act to Amend the Prohibition Act." The appointment of a new Governor had long been overdue and a month later J. A. Bernard was appointed to succeed Mr. LePage. On September 6 the Cabinet decided to seek again the royal assent to the bill and advised His Honour to give it. The Governor signed the bill at Government House on September 28, and on the following day the *Royal Gazette* published a proclamation which indi-

¹*Assembly Journals,* 1893, Appendix A.
²*Ibid.,* 1881, p. 297; *Examiner,* April 8, 1881.
³*Assembly Journals,* 1894, p. 288; *Examiner,* May 9, 1894.
⁴*Assembly Journals,* 1904, p. 106.
⁵The judgment is published verbatim in the *Guardian,* Dec. 14, 1948.

cated that, since the act had received first, second, and third readings in the Legislature and the royal assent had been withheld, His Honour, by and with the advice of the Executive Council, did "by this proclamation give our assent to the Bill . . ." and declared that the act would come into effect on October 1 following.[1]

The controversy which followed the Governor's action arose from the absence in the British North America Act of any indication of the status of a bill which is refused assent by a Lieutenant-Governor. Is the bill dead forthwith, or is it in a state of suspension? Can royal assent be given to a bill after the House has been prorogued? The pertinent sections of the Act, sections 55, 56, 57, and 90 and the Instructions to the Governor do not give the slightest guidance to a Government which may be tempted to override a refusal of assent by some positive action other than calling the Legislature into special session.

The only previous experience of this nature on the Island was in a pre-Confederation case of 1865. The Governor withheld assent from a land purchase bill known as the John Hodges Winsloe Bill of 1865, and the Secretary of State, Edward Cardwell, replied that the bill was of no Imperial interest and that His Honour should have assented to it. The question then arose as to whether the Governor could now give the assent in view of the fact that the session in which the bill was passed had ended. Cardwell submitted it to the law officers of the Crown in London who advised that "we do not think it is necessary that the assent of the Governor to any Bill passed by" legislatures in provinces possessing representative government "should be given before the expiration of the session within which such Bill was passed." They stated that no provision had been made in any colonial constitutions for a time limit on the royal assent, and that the law and custom of the British Parliament do not apply in such cases for, with reservation provided, such a limit would be impossible. In view of this decision, the Secretary of State recommended that the Governor give the assent and not go to the trouble of having the bill re-enacted. But

[1] *Royal Gazette* (P.E.I.), vol. LXXI, no. 39, Sept. 29, 1945. The act is 9 Geo. VI, c. 26.

the Island Executive Council would not advise the Governor to give such an assent and the bill went through the Legislature the second time.[1] It was perhaps arguable in 1945 that, in the absence of an applicable provision in the British North America Act, there was still no time limit upon royal assent in the province and, therefore, no reason why the Cabinet could not submit a bill to the Governor after prorogation.

The matter was the subject of political discussion on the Island and of some academic interest elsewhere prior to 1948.[2] In that year fresh prohibition legislation was enacted and it appeared as if the issue would remain unsettled. But someone had meanwhile been arrested for unlawful possession of intoxicating liquor under the old Prohibition Act which had been amended by the act of 1945. One question in the case was whether he was guilty under the old act or whether he could be judged innocent under the less restrictive Amendment Act of 1945. This led to a unique consideration of the validity of the assent by the Supreme Court which justified the presiding judge's comment that "while the situation is not altogether academic, it may be said to partake of the theatrical."

The case came before the Supreme Court on appeal from a magistrate and was heard by Chief Justice Thane A. Campbell sitting alone. His Lordship, after examining sections 55, 56, 57, and 90 of the British North America Act, concluded that "there is no provision for re-consideration of a 'withheld' Assent." "The precision with which the British North America Act set forth the procedure for later consideration of Bills assented to or reserved seems to me to indicate an intention to cover the whole field of Royal Assent, and to exclude the possibility of a withheld Assent being later conferred by a method similar to (or, a fortiori, less

---

[1]Law officers to Edward Cardwell, April 6, 1865, P.A.C. (P.E.I.), G 34, p. 338; Cardwell to Administrator of P.E.I., Dec. 1, 1865, *ibid.,* p. 335; Cardwell to Dundas, March 24, 1866, *ibid.,* G 35, p. 155. It should be noted, by the way, that Governor Robinson, after reserving the Railway Extension Bill of 1872 for the Queen's pleasure, was prepared to give the assent if the Colonial Secretary wished, even though the session had ended. Robinson to Kimberley, July 12, 1872, *ibid.,* G 43, p. 90.

[2]See comments by K. M. Martin, *Canadian Bar Review,* vol. XXIV, 1946, p. 435, and Bora Laskin, *ibid.,* p. 625.

precise than) the methods prescribed for later proceedings on Assents granted or reserved."

The Chief Justice then went on to examine what the B.N.A. Act "contemplates" in the absence of an appropriate provision. Since sections 55 and 90 combined provide that the Governor gives assent "upon the presentation to him of the Bill" and since the Governor is a part of the Legislature, His Lordship declared that "I therefore take it that sec. 55 contemplates the 'presentation' of a Bill to the Lieutenant-Governor by the Legislative Assembly." "It would, perhaps, be stating the case too strongly," he went on, "to say that the withholding of the Sovereign's Assent is equivalent to a veto, or that it kills the bill, as conceivably the Legislature might re-present the same Bill, and it might thereupon receive Assent; but no provision being made for subsequent action on a withheld Assent, the Lieutenant-Governor would appear to be functus officii at least until the Bill is re-presented to him by the House." The Chief Justice then declared that the act of 1945 "never received the Royal Assent, and never became law," and that the Prohibition Act itself had actually continued unaffected until its repeal in 1948.

The refusal of dissolution to a ministry. The exercise of the power of the Lieutenant-Governor to dissolve the Legislature, like that of the King and the Governor-General, must be guided, in the usual circumstances, by ministerial advice. There is substantial doubt, however, as to whether the Governor is bound to grant a dissolution on certain unusual occasions which involve a serious departure from the spirit of the constitution on the part of those ordinarily responsible for the exercise of the power. There are several schools of thought on the matter and among them the Governor must pick his careful way if he is confronted by such an issue.[1]

There has been only one case of refusal of dissolution in Prince Edward Island, the Carvell-MacLeod issue of 1891. The election of 1890 returned sixteen Conservatives under Premier Neil MacLeod and fourteen Liberals; but a series of five by-elections which

[1] For a detailed discussion of dissolution see Eugene Forsey, *The Royal Power of Dissolution of Parliament in the British Commonwealth* (Oxford, 1943), p. 259.

took place during the fall and winter of 1890-1 resulted in the loss of two Conservative seats to the Liberals and the control by the latter of a majority in the House.[1] In the spring of 1891 Premier MacLeod and his Cabinet asked for a dissolution "in view of the even strength of both political parties in the Legislature," but Governor J. S. Carvell refused to grant their wish.[2] The MacLeod Government thereupon resigned and Frederick Peters, the Leader of the Opposition, formed a Government on April 22. The House met on April 23 and adjourned the same day until June 16, and the new Ministers meanwhile secured seats in a series of by-elections.[3]

The number of issues in Prince Edward Island legislation concerning reservation and refusal of assent, and disallowance as well, has not been unusually high.[4] It is sufficient, however, to raise the

[1] *Canadian Parliamentary Companion*, 1891.
[2] Executive Council Minute Books, Legislative Building, Charlottetown, April 17, 1891, pp. 59-60.
[3] Mr. Peters' strategy was in striking contrast to that of Mr. Arthur Meighen in the famous Byng-King issue of 1926. Peters secured the immediate adjournment of the House for seven weeks and filled the seats vacated by the newly appointed Ministers before facing the House. Although this meant that the session did not get under way until June 16, Peters was sure of a majority, and, unlike Mr. Meighen, could form a Cabinet constituted in the usual way. Moreover, Mr. Carvell's intervention was not made an election issue by the Conservatives as was that of Lord Byng by Mr. King in 1926.
[4] Dr. Eugene Forsey has estimated that there appear to have been 65 reservations, 27 refusals of assent, and 112 disallowances in all the provinces from 1867 to 1948. Forsey, "Disallowance of Provincial Acts, Reservation of Provincial Bills, and Refusal of Assent by Lieutenant-Governors, 1937-47," *Canadian Journal of Economics and Political Science*, Feb., 1948, pp. 94-7. Four other reservations are also recorded. *Supra*, p. 153, n. 3. While the Island has contributed substantially to the reservations and refusals, it must be noted that the Dominion has never disallowed an Island statute. However, the threat of disallowance has occasionally been used to force desired changes. The Minister of Justice, after noting what he considered to be irregular clauses in a provincial act, has generally advised the local Government of his objections and sought assurance that the measure in question would be amended in the following session. See, for example, Report of Minister of Justice, Nov. 8, 1898, on "An Act Respecting Witnesses and Evidence," *Provincial Legislation*, vol. II, pp. 762-4. The Island authorities have usually complied, although on one occasion the provincial Premier pointed out that such procedure was anomalous in view of the fact that no Government could bespeak the action of a Legislature in advance. Premier Arthur Peters to Lieutenant-Governor, June 15, 1907, *ibid.*, p. 722. With another class of acts the Dominion has doubted their validity but left them to possible contests in the courts. See, for example, *Assembly Journals*, 1883, Appendix H, "Estates of Intestates Administration Act," 1882.

question of the right of the Lieutenant-Governor to use such prerogatives in a system of responsible government.[1]

The Governor has unquestioned power in law to reserve bills or refuse assent subject to the provisions of the British North America Act and the Governor-General's Instructions.[2] As far as reservation is concerned, however, the Instructions tell the Governor nothing except to forward the bills concerned to Ottawa "fairly abstracted in the margin" and with explanatory observations. They do not give him any guidance on withholding assent.[3] Nevertheless the Instructions command the Governor to exercise his powers subject to "instructions" which may from time to time be given him by order of the Privy Council. Most Governors receive few, if any, such "instructions,"[4] but from 1873 a series of reports to the Governor-General from the Minister of Justice gave sufficient guidance, provided the Governors were aware of them. For example, a federal Minute of Council of 1882 pointed out that the Governor should reserve bills "in his capacity as a Dominion officer only, and on instructions from the Governor-General. It is only in a case of extreme necessity that a Lieutenant-Governor should without such instructions exercise his discretion as a Dominion officer in reserving a bill. In fact, with facility of communication between the Dominion and provincial governments, such a necessity can seldom if ever arise." On refusal of assent it declared, albeit

---

[1]Two cases of refusal to approve appointments are also recorded but there seems to be no material available on them. In 1886 Governor A. A. Macdonald refused his assent to the appointment of a liquor vendor, but later changed his mind "upon further enquiry in the matter." Executive Council Minute Books, Legislative Building, Charlottetown, Jan. 13 and Feb. 3, 1886, pp. 189, 190, 200. Governor Dalton refused to appoint a sheriff in 1931. *Ibid.*, Aug. 21, 1931, p. 270. Dalton left no reason, but it is likely that he refused because the appointment was recommended between the defeat of the Government at the polls and the subsequent change of administration.

[2]For a discussion of this point see the decision of the Supreme Court of Canada of 1938, *Reference re the Power of the Governor General in Council to Disallow Provincial Legislation and the Power of Reservation of a Lieutenant-Governor of a Province,* [1938] S.C.R. 71.

[3]Indeed no Instructions were sent to Lieutenant-Governors until 1892 after the approval by Governor-General-in-Council of a general form of instruction. P.C. 1574, June 16, 1892; Department of Justice, *Memorandum on Office of Lieutenant-Governor*, p. 7.

[4]Other than formal notices about events such as occasions for official court mourning.

vaguely, that "the power of veto by the crown is now admitted to be obsolete and practically non-existent."[1] Doubtless these admonitions have kept down the number of refusals and reservations, but the Governors in several provinces have sporadically revived these powers and thereby confirmed the words of a learned judge "that neither contrary practice nor disuse can repeal the positive enactment of a Statute."[2]

Any vagueness on these points could easily be dispelled by the federal Government if it gave specific guidance to the Governors in the Instructions. For the Dominion to send them a folder of "instructions" which tells them little more than how to wear the Windsor uniform, how many guns shall be fired on state occasions, and when the National Anthem is to be played, is to invite uncertainty and confusion.[3] If constitutional flexibility and conflicting views on the limits of the royal prerogative and on Dominion-provincial relations render difficult a specific enumeration of the Governor's powers,[4] at least the inclusion in the book of "instructions" of copies of official memoranda on previous experience would provide a useful guide for both him and his Ministers.[5]

From the standpoint of responsible government in the provinces constitutional practice seems to be fairly definite. The Governor is bound to give assent upon the advice of his Ministers (that is, if the Dominion does not intervene) save in the most exceptional circumstances involving a very serious departure from recognized constitutional principles on the part of the Ministers. The Cabinet alone is responsible for the acts of the Crown, and if it is to assume that responsibility it must have a free hand. But occasionally there arises what has been called "the danger of Cabinet abso-

[1]*Provincial Legislation*, vol. I, p. 78. For a more recent opinion saying substantially the same thing see *Canada, Sessional Papers*, 1924, no. 276.
[2]Lord Hatherley L.C. in *Hebbert* v. *Purchas*, (1871) L.R. 3 P.C. 605, at p. 650.
[3]Such a folder is sent to each Governor upon his appointment.
[4]For example, the Dominion might not wish to commit itself to giving instructions in all serious constitutional issues between the Governor and his Ministers.
[5]When the Governor's powers were being discussed in the Confederation debates, Christopher Dunkin emphasized their vagueness and predicted that they would encourage "the widest divergencies of constitution." Province of Canada, *Parliamentary Debates on the Subject of Confederation*, pp. 502, 525.

lutism,"[1] and, as a safeguard against this when the constitution provides no other protection, the reserve power of the Crown is maintained.

The Prince Edward Island Governors concerned with the cases previously enumerated appear to have used their powers almost always with encouragement from either their own Cabinet or the federal Government. Most of the reservation cases, the last of which was in 1904, were of little interest or importance for they did not involve disputes between the Governors and their Ministers and merely concerned doubt which had continued from the colonial period when bills with respect to Government House and the land question had always been reserved for the Queen's assent. Indeed in the first four cases, which occurred when the Liberals were in power in Ottawa and Sir John Macdonald's views on reservation were not invoked, the Governor-General took an active interest and did not discourage the Governor. The two cases of 1878 reminded the Governor that Sir John was back in power and that reservations were once more out of fashion in Ottawa. The exceptional case was that of 1892, where the bill concerned was a controversial one which passed the Legislature by a majority of only one vote. Here the Governor was apparently wrong, for the decision of the House, and the Cabinet, and previous opinions of the Governor-General-in-Council did not justify reservation; and the right to amend its own constitution was undoubtedly within the power of the province.

The four cases of withheld assent were clearly incompatible with the principles of responsible government, although in only one does the Governor appear to be entirely to blame. There seems to be no justification whatever for the Governor's interference in 1945, particularly for his neglecting to seek the advice of his Ministers. In the other three cases the Governor and the Cabinet apparently agreed that the assent should not be given. Previous experience with denominational conflict in politics seemed to justify the incident of 1880, for the Government had a 27 to 3 majority in the Legislature and both sides were obviously anxious to avoid a resig-

[1]Eugene Forsey, *The Royal Power of Dissolution of Parliament in the British Commonwealth*, p. 259.

THE LIEUTENANT-GOVERNOR 165

nation of the Cabinet and the destruction of the usual party lines which would follow. The Governor evidently had Cabinet support in 1920, for the then Attorney-General, J. J. Johnston, has informed the writer that he and his colleagues considered the Government House bill *ultra vires,* although a good political advertisement of the Government's desire for economy, and that they had agreed that His Honour should withhold assent.[1] There is much evidence that the Governor and the Premier agreed on the refusal of 1924 as well, but it is based on hearsay. A significant fact was the Government's decision to introduce in the following year a new bill which omitted the features to which the Governor had objected despite the fact that the old Governor's term had ended.[2] Apparently, therefore, political convenience was the basis of the three issues.

The obvious objections to this collaboration between Governor and Cabinet were the lack of ministerial responsibility to the Legislature, and the exposure of the Crown to criticism on political questions. If Ministers advise a Governor to withhold assent, they immediately place him in the awkward predicament of having either to follow that unusual course or to refuse their advice, and at the same time they lay themselves open to the charge of ignoring the Legislature. Sir John Macdonald took the view that Ministers must recommend for assent all bills which pass the Legislature,[3] whereas Professor A. B. Keith has said that "if the Ministers find that an enactment is mistaken they can quite properly take the responsibility of telling the Lieutenant-Governor so, and facing Parliament on the issue."[4] The fundamental fault in the first three Island cases was the fact that such advice as was given was private,

---

[1]The Governor was, of course, willing, and both he and his Ministers apparently overlooked the federal Order-in-Council of 1874. *Supra,* p. 154.
[2]See also R. A. Mackay, *The Unreformed Senate of Canada* (Oxford, 1926), pp. 151-2, with respect to the protection of minority rights by the Senate when it forced amendments to the federal Church Union Bill of 1924.
[3]Order-in-Council, August 29, 1873, quoted in Department of Justice, *Memorandum on Office of Lieutenant-Governor,* pp. 18-19.
[4]A. B. Keith, *Responsible Government in the Dominions* (Oxford, 1928), vol. I, p. 564. It should be noted that mistakes in Island legislation have been rectified in less controversial issues and before the end of the session by amendments which received royal assent at the same time as the original act. *Assembly Journals,* April 8, 1910, and April 22, 1914.

and the issues were consequently obscured. The important element of Cabinet responsibility was clearly absent if the Ministers agreed reluctantly to humour the Governor's personal views when they were convinced of the merits of the bills, or if they had piloted the bills without carefully examining their implications and then surreptitiously disowned them. They were undoubtedly wrong (*a*) if they did not resign when they felt that the Governor was unjustifiably stubborn, or (*b*) if they had made an agreement with the Governor without informing the Legislature of what actually happened to the bills instead of leaving it with the impression that the Governor alone was responsible for their demise. Such tactics may seem desirable because they avoid embarrassing issues, but unexplained refusals later become significant and awkward precedents. If the Cabinet revives the refusal on its own initiative or agrees quietly to the Governor's personal wishes, it should not be surprised if the Governor uses the power to impose his own opinions on his advisers. The LePage case can thus be regarded in a sense as an outcome of the first three.

To sum up, one or more of several factors was obvious in each of the cases of reservation, refusal of assent, and refusal of dissolution: political expediency on the part of the Cabinet, absence of adequate instructions from the Dominion, doubt as to the legality of legislation, reliance on colonial precedents, lack of solidarity and responsibility in the Cabinet, and unwarranted interference by the Governor. In no case was the Governor ignorant of constitutional procedure, for each had had a long career in the Cabinet before going to Government House; although perhaps his previous experience may have encouraged him to challenge his Ministers. Political difference, moreover, was of no significance, for in practically all the cases the Governor was dealing with his own party. With the exception of the Carvell-MacLeod issue, there was no attempt to resign on the part of the Cabinet or individual Ministers, although in the LePage case, for example, such a resignation would have provided a justifiable demonstration of Cabinet dominance and placed the Governor in a most embarrassing and dangerous position.¹ A few Governors were not without public support. It is recorded that Haviland's action "was greeted with a burst of applause from the galleries";² Carvell reserved with a benediction from the Opposition which declared that he "acted in the interest of the country";³ and LePage was assured of posterity's favour when the Temperance Federation told him that "generations to come would rise up and call him blessed."⁴ But the galleries, the Opposition, and posterity are not the constitutional advisers of the Governor, and most of the cases serve to indicate the fundamental importance of the Cabinet's responsibility in all but the most serious and exceptional circumstances.

¹The Cabinet obviously side-stepped its responsibility in the Carvell reservation case of 1892, when it did not resign but appealed to the House of Commons through one of the Island members. *Canada, House of Commons, Debates,* May 6, 1892, pp. 2238-41. The Leader of the Opposition in the Island House pointed out that the Cabinet was "at daggers drawn with the Lieutenant-Governor and should have resigned." *Assembly Debates,* 1893, p. 24.
²*Patriot,* April 29, 1880.
³*Assembly Debates,* 1893, pp. 73 and 125. The Speaker stopped the debate on Mr. Carvell's action on the ground that members of the House were "not at liberty to discuss the Lieutenant-Governor."
⁴*Guardian,* April 18, 1945; *Patriot,* April 18, 1945.

CHAPTER VIII

THE CABINET

THE CABINET or Executive Council of Prince Edward Island is the effective executive power and, as such, is responsible for the administration of public business in the province. As a direct descendant of the old colonial Council, it retains many of the traditions of centuries; as an instrument of responsible government it embodies important features of modern democracy. It has been well suited, on the whole, to the tiny administration of which it is the centre. Nevertheless, the fact that it must operate within a very small area has caused the emergence of certain special peculiarities or variations from principles which are generally accepted as essential to responsible government.[1]

The Cabinet is formed according to the usual procedure of the English type of executive. The Governor "invites" someone to become his First Minister, and entrusts to that person the task of forming a Government.[2] While His Honour's choice is technically unfettered, it is limited in practice by the necessity of naming someone who is able to secure the support of the Legislature, and the premiership, therefore, usually falls on the leader of the party having a majority in the Assembly. Although the Governor refers to the Cabinet as "my government," it is, of course, primarily responsible to the House, and no Cabinet could govern effectively without the confidence of that body. Once the Premier is selected, the remaining positions in the Cabinet are filled by those who are invited by the Premier to assume them. Such "invitations" can in theory be extended to anyone whom the leader wishes as a colleague, but in practice he is generally limited in his choice to those members of his party who have seats in the Legislature, for the

[1]One of these peculiarities, the judicial function of the Cabinet, is discussed in the section on the Divorce Court in chapter XII. See also Frank MacKinnon, "Some Peculiarities of Cabinet Government in Prince Edward Island," *Canadian Journal of Economics and Political Science*, Aug., 1949, p. 310.

[2]A list of the Premiers of Prince Edward Island since Confederation with the date of the formation of their Governments and party allegiance will be found in Appendix H.

THE CABINET 169

responsibility of the Cabinet to the popular body has dictated that its members must have seats therein. If the Premier does go outside the House for a Minister, it is recognized that the newcomer should find a seat as soon as possible. The provincial Cabinets, with one exception since Confederation, have been formed entirely from one political party. This procedure increases the possibility of co-operation and confidence, facilitates leadership, and emphasizes steady administration as well as confident opposition. The difficulties associated with coalition government, clearly illustrated by the unfortunate history of the Davies administration of 1876-9, have discouraged the union of political opponents into uncertain executives.

THE STRUCTURE OF THE CABINET

The Cabinet of Prince Edward Island is large when compared with the other institutions of government. It has consisted of nine members since 1784, and this number, which was originally specified in the Instructions to colonial Governors and later maintained by custom, is now provided by statute.[1] The Assembly is composed of only thirty members, of whom nearly one-third, therefore, are Cabinet Ministers. Where the Government's majority is small, one-half or more of its supporters are in the Cabinet. Consequently the executive occupies an unusually dominant position both in the Legislature and in the caucus, a fact which gives it a distinct advantage in controlling legislation and debate and in maintaining discipline in the party. A similar relationship can be seen between the executive and the administration. There are only approximately 300 civil servants, who are organized into eight small departments. Indeed in some departments the Minister is sometimes the only senior official, and he is able to handle many of the routine administrative details which in larger governments would fall to junior clerks. Appointments are so few in number that the Cabinet makes them all. The effective control of the Cabinet over

[1]"The Executive Council shall consist of nine members, inclusive of the Premier and heads of Public Departments of the Government." Legislative Assembly Act, 1940, 4 Geo. VI, c. 37, s. 32. It is to be noted that up to the 1920's Ministers of the Crown in the province were termed "Commissioners." For instance, the official known today as the Minister of Agriculture was formerly called the Commissioner of Agriculture.

government at all levels is assured by such intimate and informal relations.

The selection of Ministers is greatly influenced by this close relationship between the executive, the Legislature, and the administration. Forming a Cabinet is everywhere a difficult task for a Prime Minister who wishes to choose a competent and united team and at the same time meet many demands of personal ambition, sectional representation, and party strategy. The Premier of Prince Edward Island faces the usual difficulties in this regard, but his task is further complicated by the very limited panel from which he must choose the Ministers. There is no assurance that the majority of Government supporters elected to the House will be of Cabinet quality, and the Premier has often to select some mediocre or incompetent colleagues in order to fill the positions which are at his disposal.

One powerful factor which tends to keep the Cabinet large is the desire of the various regions and interest groups for representation in it. "It is necessary," wrote Governor Huntley as far back as 1843, "to select Gentlemen from different parts of the Island for this Council, or a dissatisfaction would be created in accepting seats."[1] "It would never do," said the *Examiner* upon the formation of the Farquharson Government of 1900, "to have two members from the same district in the Cabinet."[2] It is often considered that the nine-man Cabinet lends itself to an even distribution of three seats to each of the three counties.[3] Yet a Conservative Premier, W. W. Sullivan, once said that equal representation of the counties was not necessary, and his Liberal opponent Donald (later Premier) Farquharson agreed because he "was not aware that any County had ever suffered" by unequal representation.[4] A further balance between Protestant and Catholic representatives has been recognized as desirable, although not always possible. The French-Acadians, who number about one-seventh of the population of the province, have also expected representation. In an agricultural community

[1] Huntley to Stanley, Feb. 11, 1843, *P.E.I. House of Assembly Journals,* 1844, p. 49.
[2] Charlottetown *Examiner,* Dec. 18, 1900; see also Charlottetown *Guardian,* April 7, 1945.
[3] See *Guardian,* April 7, 1945.
[4] *P.E.I. House of Assembly Debates,* 1881, pp. 99, 100.

the farmers must have an adequate voice, and the city of Charlottetown has usually been represented. But with such a small Legislature and Cabinet it has been virtually impossible for the Premier to adhere strictly to any particular rule, for it is difficult enough for him to obtain nine Ministers of even moderate talent without imposing further limits on his choice.[1] He is thus forced to do the best he can under existing conditions.[2] A balancing factor in Cabinet representation is the speakership. Where particular groups have not been given recognition in Cabinet appointments, this office has been used on occasions as a means of providing for them. In some instances, however, this practice has resulted in an obviously incompetent Speaker.

Other considerations—characteristic of cabinet-forming everywhere—increase the Premier's difficulty in selecting Ministers. Members of former Cabinets of the same party allegiance generally have a prior claim to office if they are still in the House and willing to accept. Only four or five of the nine appointments carry portfolios, and the senior party leaders are usually considered to be entitled to these. The attorney-generalship has always gone to a lawyer, while the Minister of Agriculture has generally been a farmer, although the professional affiliation of Ministers does not guarantee their competence. In addition to all these factors, there is the overriding difficulty of adjusting personalities. The members of such a team should be congenial and co-operative, as well as competent, and the Premier should be assured of a group who have confidence in his leadership and in one another.

It is a recognized rule in British constitutional government that members of the executive must have seats in the Legislature, or at least must obtain them within a reasonable time after their appointment. If a Minister is not able to find a seat he is expected to resign his place in the Cabinet. This practice rests upon the principle of executive responsibility to the Legislature and through the latter to the people. It is in the Legislature that the policies and financial expenditures of the Government are examined and de-

[1] The Jones Cabinet that was formed in 1947, for example, included two Ministers from each of two districts.
[2] See also Eugene A. Forsey, "Sectional Representation in Maritime Provincial Cabinets since Confederation," *Public Affairs,* Autumn, 1942.

bated; it is there that questions are asked concerning the working of Government departments; and it is in the hurly-burly of legislative proceedings that prospective Cabinet Ministers are singled out and trained, incompetents weeded out, and reputations made and lost. Moreover, close contact between Cabinet Ministers and the people's representatives, who are expected to voice the opinions of their constituents on public questions of all kinds, is most desirable. The informed opinions of the executive are given to the Legislature, and the Ministers are subjected to scrutiny, questioning, and criticism. Although the Cabinet will to a large extent dominate and control the House, its members are never allowed to forget that they are responsible to it.

This principle has naturally been recognized in Prince Edward Island since the beginning of responsible government and early cases clearly indicated its binding nature.[1] Resignation followed defeat in a by-election in the cases of W. W. Lord in 1857, Joseph Hensley in 1858, and James Duncan in 1861. Hon. Kenneth Henderson's experience in 1866 was the most significant, for, after refusing to run the risk of a by-election, he was forced by the Premier to resign upon pain of dismissal by the Governor.[2] The exceptions in this period, particularly during Edward Palmer's experiment which excluded all office-holders from the Legislature, served to emphasize the inconveniences which resulted when the principle was not followed.[3] After Confederation there were few deviations from the practice, for Ministers usually resigned immediately after suffering defeat in by-elections. In 1886, for example, two members of the Sullivan Government, Messrs. Burns and William Campbell, resigned after defeat and their places were taken by others more fortunate at the polls.[4]

Nevertheless the large Cabinet and the small Legislature make it extremely difficult for the Premier to find seats for certain pros-

[1] See also the *Examiner*, April 14, 1900.
[2] *Supra*, p. 93.   [3] *Supra*, pp. 97-8.
[4] *Assembly Debates*, 1887, p. 6. Mr. Campbell's case is particularly significant. After being appointed Commissioner of Public Works he was defeated in a by-election in an attempt to win a seat in the Assembly. He resigned immediately, but upon pressure from his Cabinet colleagues remained in office while he contested a seat in the Legislative Council. He suffered a second defeat and his resignation was thereupon accepted.

pective Ministers. The attorney-generalship, which by statute must be held by a lawyer, has been a frequent source of trouble. A Government majority in the Legislature may on occasion include no lawyers, or one or two of mediocre calibre, and the Premier may be forced to seek an Attorney-General outside the House and then find a seat for him. On two recent occasions the Premier solved this difficulty by simply ignoring constitutional practice. In 1930 the then Attorney-General was elevated to the bench and the Premier selected T. A. Campbell to succeed him. Mr. Campbell, who had no seat in the House, was defeated in an ensuing by-election. He thereupon resigned from the Cabinet and was immediately reappointed Attorney-General by Order-in-Council with salary but without a seat either in the Cabinet or in the House.[1] In other words, since there was no lawyer in the House, the Attorney-General was reduced from Cabinet status to that of a law officer of the Crown. The official was outside all the recognized spheres of government. He could not take part in the discussions of the Cabinet unless it recognized him as a stranger at the Council board or took him into its complete confidence. Moreover neither he nor his department were placed under another Minister. He could scarcely be considered even a regular civil servant, for his position as a salaried employee was a temporary role dictated by political expediency.

Under similar circumstances another recent Attorney-General was placed in an even more astonishing position. For three and one-half years (May 8, 1944 to December 11, 1947) F. A. Large served as Attorney-General and a member of the Cabinet and during that time he was not a member of the House and made no attempt to find a seat in any of several by-elections which occurred.[2]

[1]He served in this capacity until the general election in the following year, when, in order to seek a seat, he had to resign since the election laws prohibited him from running while a salaried officer not of the Cabinet. He could, of course, have been reappointed as a Minister before the election. See Executive Council Minute Books, Legislative Building, Charlottetown, vol. XXXI, pp. 181, 210, 267; *Guardian,* May 9, 1931; *Canadian Annual Review,* 1930-1, p. 219.

[2]The reason for this departure from the usual practice was the fact that there was only one lawyer on the Government side of the House and the Premier did not see fit to appoint him. Despite this manœuvre Mr Large was removed from the attorney-generalship in 1949 and was replaced by another lawyer who had recently been elected to the House.

The occurrence of such cases is probable so long as the Public Departments Act requires that the Attorney-General must be a lawyer, and the people do not elect an available lawyer to support the Government.[1] The objection to irresponsible Ministers is obvious,[2] and, although Premiers are entitled to some sympathy for the difficulty of finding an available Attorney-General, they could meet the issue by introducing a measure to remove the legal qualification of the office and appointing a non-professional and responsible Minister.[3] Another objection to the irregular practices is the inevitable tendency to treat lightly the basic principle of the responsibility of the Cabinet. "I am criticized because I didn't find him [F. A. Large] a seat," said Premier Jones in the House, "the Opposition leader didn't say how he was to find a seat. He didn't come to me with an offer from anyone in the opposition to resign. None of our own members offered to, and I didn't ask any one. The only seat open was Fort Augustus, and we didn't suggest that he run there. There has been no other seat opened, and we haven't particularly tried to find a seat for him."[4] Comment on this extraordinary statement is unnecessary.

The lack of proportion between the large Cabinet and the small civil service is adjusted to some degree by the number of Ministers without Portfolio. The practice of appointing such Ministers has sprung from local conditions. In the days when members had to seek re-election to the House upon appointment to the Cabinet it became politically inexpedient to force many by-elections upon a Cabinet in the face of what was often a small legislative majority,

---

[1] 3 Geo. VI, c. 42, s. 5.

[2] The Cabinet as a whole was of course responsible for the actions of such a Minister. Sometimes the absentee was permitted by the House to appear briefly to give an explanation of his policies from the floor, but such an alternative only emphasized the need for his presence, not as a visitor, but as a regular member who could pilot his own legislation, defend his own estimates, and answer for his own mistakes. See *Guardian,* April 6, 1945.

[3] Non-professional acting Attorneys-General have been appointed on the Island, e.g. William Hughes on Aug. 21, 1944, and G. H. Barbour on Aug. 2, 1945. Executive Council Minute Books, Legislative Building, Charlottetown, 1944, p. 70, and 1945, p. 158. Premier Aberhart of Alberta was the Attorney-General of that province from 1937 to 1942 although he was not a lawyer.

[4] *Guardian,* March 17, 1945. See also T. A. Campbell on the same subject in *Patriot,* "Proceedings of the Legislative Assembly for April 13, 1939."

for this was always inconvenient and often fatal to the administration.[1] Many members protested that the inclusion of too many office-holders in the small House would constitute an obvious threat to the independence of the Legislature. Occasionally the Cabinet included only a few Ministers who were competent to handle a portfolio. But most significant of all was the fact that the Island did not need a full Cabinet of salaried Ministers with Portfolio to handle the affairs of a few small government departments. It thus became customary for Premiers to bestow several portfolios upon each of four or five Ministers and in this way give the Ministers sufficient work and remuneration to warrant their devoting the major portion of their time to administration.

The Ministers without Portfolio generally perform no administrative duties, receive no payment other than a sessional indemnity and travelling allowances, and confine their activities to giving advice and participating in Cabinet discussions. The extent to which their services have been used has varied. Some Premiers have ignored them and relied largely on portfolio holders; others have increased their importance by giving them special functions. Up to 1935 they had been prevented from taking offices of emolument which were not specially provided for by statute and at the same time retaining their seats in the Legislature. In that year a special act was passed which permitted them, as well as other members of the Legislature, to take certain paid positions such as purchasing agent, and Clerk of the Assembly.[2] It was felt that their work could be done more economically by members of the Legislature than by outside officials.[3] Other special duties, such as acting as chairmen of committees and piloting certain Government bills through the House, have sometimes been placed in their charge. The extent to which this is done depends largely on the wishes of the Premier, the qualifications of such Ministers, and the availability of other officials in the Cabinet and in the civil service. The salaried Ministers, therefore, form an inner Cabinet which handles the main portion of executive duties and which seems more appro-

[1]*Supra*, pp. 96-8.   [2]26 Geo. V, c. 4.
[3]*Canadian Annual Review*, 1935-6, p. 464.

priate in the small government than a full Cabinet of portfolio holders.[1]

This inner Cabinet received statutory recognition and special powers when it was constituted the Treasury Board for the province. The Legislative Assembly Act of 1940 provided that four members of the Cabinet were to form the Treasury Board with the Provincial Treasurer as chairman and the Deputy Provincial Treasurer as secretary.[2] It became customary to confine membership in this body to Ministers with Portfolio, a practice which was recognized by a statute in 1947 which stated that the Board "shall consist of the Premier and heads of Public Departments of the Government."[3] The functions of the Treasury Board are to "act as a committee of the Executive Council on all matters relating to finance, revenue, contracts, and expenditure of public moneys which are referred to it by the Council, or to which the Board thinks it necessary to call the attention of the Council," and to "make regulations for the administration of the Public Service, subject to the approval of the Lieutenant-Governor-in-Council." While the status and functions of the Treasury Board are similar on paper to those of its namesake in the federal government, actually they are not of comparable significance in view of the small civil service and the restricted financial duties. They provide, however, a convenient justification for dispensing with the services of the whole Cabinet.[4]

There are now nine portfolios in the Prince Edward Island Cabinet: those of President of the Executive Council, Attorney- and Advocate-General, Provincial Secretary, Provincial Treasurer, and those of the Ministers of Agriculture, Education, Health and Welfare, Public Works and Highways, and Industry and National Resources.[5] The shuffling of Cabinet posts is specially provided for in

[1] Premier Jones included only one Minister without portfolio when he reorganized his Cabinet in October, 1949. This instance is exceptional.
[2] 4 Geo. VI, c. 37.   [3] 11 Geo. VI, c. 25.
[4] All the provinces in Canada have Treasury Boards with the exception of Nova Scotia, Manitoba, and British Columbia. Nova Scotia had one from 1923 to 1926, but it was abolished in the latter year; Revised Statutes of Nova Scotia, 1923, c. 12 and *ibid.*, 1926, c. 1. Some consideration has been given to the setting-up of such a board in Manitoba, but no final decision has been made. The writer acknowledges the kind assistance of the Provincial Secretaries of the provinces in providing this information and other comparisons which follow.
[5] See 8 Geo. VI, c. 17; 11 Geo. VI, c. 30.

THE CABINET 177

the Public Departments Act which permits Ministers to hold several portfolios and requires the Premier to preside over the department of any Minister who dies or resigns until a new Minister is appointed. The Act also enables the Lieutenant-Governor-in-Council to transfer any powers from one Minister to another, or from one department to another, and to combine any two or more departments under one Minister and deputy minister, provided the Assembly is notified within fifteen days of the change or fifteen days after the commencement of the next session.[1] This arrangement enables the Premier to change readily the duties of his colleagues to meet their abilities and the needs of the departments, although in some instances these abilities and needs are so variable that the administration suffers from too much change, from the mistakes of incompetent or inexperienced Ministers, or from too much centralization in the hands of one busy Minister. The Premier keeps several portfolios for himself; he is nearly always President of the Executive Council, and, if he is a lawyer, he generally takes the attorney-generalship.[2]

Ministerial salaries were for many years fixed by statute. In 1879, for example, Ministers with Portfolio received $1,300 per annum, while in 1894 their salaries were fixed at $1,200.[3] In 1912 the Premier or President of the Executive Council was for the first time assigned a salary, then set at $1,500 per annum.[4] The Public Departments Act of 1939 repealed these statutes and provided that thenceforth salaries of Ministers and all other public servants were to be paid as fixed by the Lieutenant-Governor-in-Council subject to the annual legislative appropriations.[5] The determination of salaries was therefore upon a more flexible basis than formerly, and they could be adjusted to conform to the duties involved.[6] However, the assignment of salaries to particular portfolios was open to the

[1]3 Geo. VI, c. 42.
[2]Premier Jones was in the unusual position of holding six portfolios in the summer of 1949.
[3]42 Vic., c. 5; 57 Vic., c. 17. [4]2 Geo. V, c. 6. [5]3 Geo. VI, c. 42.
[6]The salaries of the members of the Cabinet in 1940 were as follows: Premier $1,000, President of the Council $500, Attorney-General $2,000, Provincial Secretary $500, Provincial Treasurer $500, Minister of Public Works and Highways $2,000, Minister of Agriculture $2,000, Minister of Health $500, and Minister of Education $1,000. *Assembly Journals*, 1940, p. 165.

objection that it led to inequality of remuneration among Ministers and to the shuffling of several portfolios among a few Ministers in order to provide them with an acceptable total remuneration. The system was consequently changed by Cabinet action in 1945 so as to provide salaries of $4,500 to the Premier and $3,000 to all other Ministers with Portfolio regardless of the number of offices held by them.[1] Evidently the financial inducement was not sufficient, and the salaries were raised in 1949. The Premier now receives $6,000, the Attorney-General $4,500, the Ministers of Public Works and Health and Welfare $4,000, the Minister of Agriculture $3,500, and the other Ministers with Portfolio $3,000. Ministers without Portfolio, as previously indicated, have never received remuneration, although they are given a *per diem* allowance, now $10 per day, and travelling expenses (if they reside outside Charlottetown) when in the capital on Cabinet business, together with such payments as they earn for certain duties which they are permitted to perform by statute.

Frequent change of personnel is a prominent characteristic of the Prince Edward Island Cabinet. The province has had no less than twenty-two ministries and twenty Premiers since Confederation, with an average life per ministry of three and a half years. Only two Premiers, J. H. Bell and J. D. Stewart, have led their party from opposition to power and remained with it until its defeat.[2]

Premiers who make careers of public office have consequently been non-existent in the province. The position is not a glittering prize like the leadership in the Dominion Government or in the larger provinces, nor does it present scope for activities of so great a magnitude. The salary is small, and opportunities for political fame and advancement are limited. Nor is the post sufficiently onerous to compel its occupant to retire from his professional pursuits, with the result that he will not look upon it as a career in itself, but rather as a fascinating part-time job or as a stepping-stone to something more permanent. Constant changes in administration have been the result.

[1] See *Guardian*, April 20, 1945.
[2] Of the remainder only two, Arthur Peters and W. M. Lea, died in office. Mr. Stewart also died in office during his second administration.

THE CABINET

The large number of official rewards which are available for local politicians has contributed to this situation. Of these, judgeships account for the resignation of most Premiers. Of the twenty Premiers thirteen were lawyers; six of these resigned the premiership to mount the bench and three others found their way there after defeat. There have been only three Chief Justices since 1889, and they were all appointed directly from the premiership, while for some years the Supreme Court consisted entirely of ex-Premiers.

Offices other than judgeships have not had the same attraction for the Premiers. Neither the governorship of the province nor federal senatorships have enticed Premiers from office, and in only two instances has a Premier resigned to run for the House of Commons.[1] Premiers have frequently entered the Dominion Cabinet from other provinces, but none has done so from the Island.[2] The reasons for this phenomenon are probably that the lawyers prefer to await judicial appointments which carry salaries that are very high for the province, that the governorship cannot compete with other attractions because of its expense, and that federal politics usually require the virtual curtailment of professional activities. Nevertheless, these offices have taken a heavy toll of other provincial Cabinet Ministers. The fact that the Island Government has usually been of the same party allegiance as that of the Dominion has facilitated the translation of local Ministers to the governorship, to the judiciary, and to Parliament.

Cabinet Procedure

Prince Edward Island's most original contribution to cabinet government is the procedure of its Executive Council, for in some respects the province has had long experience with procedure which has been adopted only recently elsewhere. Since Cabinet meetings are secret, little is known of what goes on behind the closed doors of the council room, although from time to time certain practices have been revealed. One point is clear: Cabinet procedure varies from one Government to another, and depends largely on the

[1] J. C. Pope and Donald Farquharson; one other, Louis Davies, became a member of the federal House after his defeat.
[2] J. C. Pope and Louis Davies reached it, but not directly from the local Government.

views and personalities of the Ministers, particularly the Premier. The rules are what the Cabinet itself decides upon.

Cabinet meetings were infrequent until recent years. As colonial administration changed to provincial government, the duties of the local executive were substantially reduced, and the number of its meetings declined accordingly. Two or three meetings a week were held when the Legislature was sitting, but at other times the Cabinet might be called only once in two months unless urgent business arose. The frequency depended largely on the wishes of the Premier. If he were inclined to make and carry out decisions without submitting them to the Cabinet, or allow other Ministers to do so, the need for meetings was obviously less than in the case of a Premier who adhered more strictly to the principle of Cabinet collaboration. The Premier was not inclined to call too frequently upon the services of Ministers without Portfolio who were unpaid, for they had their personal affairs to look after and they could not be expected to be in constant attendance at the capital. This situation resulted in a tendency on the part of successive Premiers to rely upon consultation with the Ministers with Portfolio who spent a considerable portion of their time at the legislative buildings, and to dispense with frequent meetings of the whole Cabinet. It was customary in the 1930's to hold meetings on an average of once in three weeks. At present the Cabinet meets once a week except during the session when more frequent meetings are necessary.[1]

It has not been the practice to draw up an agenda prior to meetings. Rather the custom has developed of introducing business by motion, dealing with it by discussion, and disposing of it by a vote. It appears that earlier Cabinets followed the more general practice of discussion and agreement based on argument and compromise rather than a dependence on a show of hands. This practice varied with circumstances and with the skill of the Premier at manipulating the opinions of his colleagues. When an agreement was impossible a vote was occasionally called and the decision

[1]The number of meetings is not large in comparison with other provinces. The Cabinets meet once a week in Quebec, Ontario, Manitoba, and Alberta, twice weekly in Saskatchewan and British Columbia, twice monthly in New Brunswick, and once a month in Nova Scotia. In all cases they meet oftener during the session of the Legislature or in emergency.

of the majority was usually followed. It is reported that on one occasion voting went so far as a secret ballot, an extraordinary procedure in a group working on the principles of mutual confidence and co-operation. These deviations developed, not so much on matters of policy, as on the most fruitful source of ministerial disagreement, the disposal of patronage. Custom feeds upon itself, and it became easy to avoid the trouble of reaching agreement by resorting to a vote and relying on the opinion of the majority so recorded. Accompanying this trend was the introduction of business by formal motions of particular Ministers. In other words, the Cabinet gradually adopted a form of legislative procedure, which has been particularly evident in the last twenty years.

In the absence of official pronouncements it is impossible to assess with accuracy the effects of this procedure upon the deliberations of the Cabinet. There is strong evidence, however, that it has helped to break down ministerial solidarity by emphasizing majority and minority rather than mutual compromise and agreement. There have been too many public revelations of serious disputes among Ministers in recent years to leave an impression that Cabinet solidarity is always a dominant principle in Island government. Ministers will disagree, and often with vehemence—nine men cannot be unanimous on everything—but their co-operation will not be facilitated by a system which encourages division rather than team-work.[1]

The chairmanship of Cabinet meetings is the *ex-officio* function of the President of the Executive Council. Since this portfolio has been held by the Premier in almost all administrations, the leader has usually presided at Cabinet meetings. This position enables him to direct the deliberations of his colleagues, to soften differences here, to encourage agreement there, to exercise his authority and emphasize his leadership, and in general to play the captain of a co-ordinated team. "Much of the authority of the Cabinet," says a British writer, "has insensibly passed over to that of the Premier, as the powers of a Board of any kind tend to be con-

[1]The general practice in the Dominion and in the other provinces is for decisions to be reached after discussion and compromise. Votes or shows of hands are apparently rare, although it is understood that in Manitoba a vote is occasionally taken. In England voting in Cabinet is exceptional.

centrated in the Chairman, especially if his colleagues are much below him in ability and reputation."[1] The administration of Thane A. Campbell, however, was exceptional in this respect, for he gave the presidency of the Council to another Minister in 1936 and in 1940.[2] This practice would not work in ordinary circumstances which recognize the authority and leadership of the Premier over his Cabinet, but in an administration which emphasizes the procedure of motions, voting, and majority decisions, the Premier might sometimes be more effective in introducing business and voting if he gave the chairmanship to someone else. Again there is the resemblance to the Legislature with the President as a kind of Speaker, and the Premier leading a majority from a seat at the board, and again there are obvious objections from the standpoint of Cabinet solidarity. At the present time the older and more general practice prevails, with the Premier presiding over the meetings of the Government of which he is the head.[3]

Until comparatively recent times British and Canadian Cabinets functioned without agenda or minutes as a concession to informality and secrecy. During the First World War the British Cabinet set up a secretariat and a system of agenda and minutes to facilitate the conduct of its business, and a similar development has taken place in Canada since 1940.[4] Prince Edward Island, however, has always had a secretary of the Cabinet in the person of the Clerk of the Executive Council who attends all meetings, and from the first meeting of the first Government of the province in 1770 an excellent set of minutes has been maintained. This long-established procedure is unique in Canada, for in no other provincial Cabinet

[1] Sir Sidney Low, *The Governance of England* (London, 1918), p. 158, quoted and discussed in R. MacGregor Dawson, *The Government of Canada* (Toronto, 1947), p. 226.

[2] These precedents, although unusual in modern times, were not unique with the Island. There were nineteen cases in the federal Cabinet from 1867 to 1921; indeed in Macdonald's day it was the general rule for the President of the Council to be someone other than the Prime Minister. There were cases in the other provinces too. In New Brunswick, for instance, Hon. L. P. D. Tilley was President in Hon. J. B. M. Baxter's Government from 1925 to 1931.

[3] The general practice in the other provinces is for the Premier to preside over his own Cabinet; at the present time the Premier of New Brunswick is the only one who has given the presidency of the Council to another Minister.

[4] See A. D. P. Heeney, "Cabinet Government in Canada," *Canadian Journal of Economics and Political Science*, Aug., 1946, p. 292.

are official minutes of this kind kept, and, on the whole, it has worked extremely well in providing an authoritative record of Cabinet transactions.[1]

An interesting feature of these minutes is their approval by the Lieutenant-Governor. His Honour's signature is, of course, necessary to give legal effect to such minutes of Council as are executive regulations; but approval of the entire record of a Cabinet meeting is a peculiar survival of the days when the Governor presided at the Council board and a formal expression of the fact that even today the official title of the Island's Cabinet is "The Committee of the Executive Council." Until the early 1870's the Executive Council met as a whole with the Governor in the chair. In the decade which followed Confederation it developed the practice of meeting occasionally in committee without the Governor, and the minutes of this "Committee of the Executive Council" were submitted to the Governor for approval after each meeting. This occasional practice became a habit in the 1880's and after 1887 the Council met only in committee, and the Governor did not attend.[2] The Governor's approval of all minutes has, nevertheless, been retained. Consequently, executive orders which elsewhere are called "minutes of Council" are on the Island "extracts from the minutes of Council." Actually, however, with the exception of the Governor's signing the minutes, the committee position has no effect upon the powers and functions of the Cabinet.

That no clerk was admitted to meetings of most Executive Councils without being a member thereof followed from the rule of secrecy. In the early colonial period on the Island the position of clerk was attached to the office of the Colonial Secretary who sat in the Council. He was therefore a ministerial secretary and a member in his own right. The appearance of a non-member at meetings of the Island's Executive Council was the result of the stubborn pride of the first ministerial clerk. Thomas DesBrisay had held what was then the insignificant office of Lieutenant-Governor

[1]The complete set of minutes from 1770 to the present time is preserved in the Legislative Building, Charlottetown.
[2]For a similar development in British Columbia see the paper by W. N. Sage in *Essays in Canadian History,* ed. R. Flenley (Toronto, 1939), p. 178.

under the governorship of Walter Patterson. He was both incompetent and troublesome, and when the head of the Island's administration was reduced from a Governor to a Lieutenant-Governor DesBrisay was deprived of his post. But he also held the positions of Secretary and Registrar and Clerk of the Executive Council and only his large family saved him from losing them. He continued, therefore, to hold a seat in the Council for many years; but he refused to act as a clerk where he had once presided during one of Patterson's absences, and he was permitted to bring in an outsider, Charles Stewart, to perform the duties of clerk. DesBrisay thus continued as a regular member, retained the office of clerk, and drew the salary out of which he was supposed to pay Stewart ten pounds annually. Stewart's position nevertheless became so well recognized that when DesBrisay attempted to avoid paying him in 1802, both the local Government and the Colonial Office forced him to do so.[1]

This arrangement continued for thirty years before DesBrisay's death; and the presence of an outside clerk as well as a ministerial clerk became so firmly established that it continued. The Colonial Secretary of the province was always Clerk of the Executive Council or Chief Clerk of the Executive Council—the titles were used interchangeably—but he was aided by a civil servant who acted as clerk or assistant clerk at Council meetings along with his regular duties as Assistant Colonial Secretary. This arrangement was finally changed by the Public Departments Act of 1876 which established the portfolio of "Provincial Secretary and Treasurer" and the civil service office of "Assistant Provincial Secretary and Clerk of the Executive Council."[2] The clerkship thereupon ceased to be ministerial, and from then on remained in the hands of the deputy.[3] The present holder of the clerkship is the Deputy Provincial Secretary.

[1] Fanning to Lord Hobart, Sept. 27, 1802, Public Archives of Canada, Colonial Office Records (P.E.I.), A series, vol. 17-1, p. 72.
[2] 39 Vic., c. 10; *Assembly Debates,* 1876, p. 128.
[3] From 1876 to the present there have been some alterations in the title of the holder. For instance in 1879 it was "Provincial Auditor and Clerk of the Executive Council," 42 Vic., c. 5; in 1904 "Assistant Provincial Secretary-Treasurer and Clerk of the Executive Council," 4 Ed. VII, c. 8; in 1928, "Deputy Provincial Secretary-Treasurer and Clerk of the Executive Council," 18 Geo. V, c. 17.

The status of the clerk has not, however, remained stationary. The Public Service Act of 1904 and its amending act of 1928 stated that he was to hold office during good behaviour and was to be removable only for cause by the Lieutenant-Governor on the Address of the Assembly[1]—a provision which made the clerkship a protected and a permanent office. This was changed by the Public Departments Act Amendment Act of 1944, which provided that "notwithstanding the provision of the Public Service Act, the Clerk of the Executive Council shall hold office during pleasure of the Executive Council."[2] The position of the clerk has thus been made uncertain and he can never be sure of his permanency. The advantage to the Cabinet is that it is now in a position to choose and change the official who shares so intimately in its work.

The Clerk of the Executive Council is in a very real sense the secretary of the Cabinet. He sits in on all Cabinet meetings, writes the minutes, and performs other functions, such as correspondence and research, which may be assigned him by the Ministers. He does not partake in discussion or decisions, although his advice may be asked. He takes no oath of office, but he is expected, as an observer of executive deliberations, to keep the strictest secrecy and political independence. His special charge is the minute book, which contains the formal record of decisions and certain results of discussions as well as the so-called "minutes of Council" or executive regulations. It does not include the details of discussion or record votes. The clerk prepares the minutes after each Cabinet meeting, has them read and signed by the Premier, and takes them to the Governor for his signature.[3] The convenience of such an arrangement in the orderly conduct of Cabinet business has been amply proved. A record is thereby kept which can be referred to in cases of doubt; routine duties, such as summoning Ministers to meetings, handling correspondence, and informing departments of Cabinet decisions concerning them, can be performed by the clerk; and Ministers, particularly the Premier, are left free of such details.

The chief disadvantage of such an arrangement is the possibility of political sympathy and even party activity on the part

---

[1] 4 Ed. VII, c. 8; 18 Geo. V, c. 17. [2] 8 Geo. VI, c. 22.
[3] Other Ministers may or may not see the minutes before they are approved.

of the clerk, for an official in such a confidential position should be removed from even the remotest suspicion of partisanship if he is to enjoy the complete confidence of the Premier and other Ministers. This danger was emphasized in 1943 when the Premier went to the bench, and the then secretary to the Cabinet became a candidate for the leadership of the Government. He was not successful; and since the new Premier could scarcely have retained him as confidential secretary of the Cabinet of which he failed to achieve the leadership, he was removed to another office. With this exception, however, Cabinet secretaries seem to have kept out of politics and maintained the confidence of their superiors even after successive changes of government.

Prince Edward Island's long experience with this procedure is unique in the provinces. Manitoba, however, has very recently adopted a similar practice, and its Government now appoints a Clerk who attends Cabinet meetings and makes notes but apparently does not keep a set of formal minutes. In each of the other provinces one of two practices prevails. In Ontario and British Columbia the Provincial Secretary acts as a ministerial secretary. The other provinces have no Cabinet secretary whatever and the routine functions are usually performed by a Clerk of the Executive Council who is a civil servant and who does not sit in at the meetings.

Cabinet Solidarity and Responsibility

Executive unity or solidarity is everywhere recognized as one of the central principles of Cabinet government. Team-work among Ministers demands it and confident leadership of parliament and party are completely dependent upon it. "Parliamentary government," wrote A. Lawrence Lowell, "in its present highly developed form requires a very strong cohesion among the members of the majority in the House of Commons, and, therefore, absolute harmony, or the appearance of harmony, among their leaders. It is necessary to present a united front to the opposition, for if the trumpet give an uncertain sound, who shall prepare himself for the battle?"[1]

[1] A. Lawrence Lowell, *The Government of England* (New York, 1912), vol. I, pp. 63-4.

The trumpet has given many uncertain sounds in Prince Edward Island in the past decade. Confidence, co-operation, and collective leadership have been severely used by various Ministers, and the most personal Cabinet difficulties have been aired openly before the Legislature and the public. Executive troubles have been so unusual that it would seem that no administration could stand the strain. Yet it is an extraordinary feature of recent Island politics that the Governments which have permitted executive disagreements in public have yet been able to maintain a commanding position, not only in the Legislature, but also at the polls. This casual attitude to constitutional principle on the part of the Cabinet and the people is, however, a phenomenon of very recent times. Cabinet solidarity was observed faithfully, with rare exceptions, down to the 1930's, and even in such exceptional cases the results of executive indiscretion were disastrous to the administration.

The first of these early cases, which concerned the Davies administration of 1876-9, illustrated not only the dangers of Cabinet dissension, but also the weaknesses of the Island's only coalition Government. After the question of denominational schools split both political parties in the early 1870's, Protestants from both sides formed a coalition Government in 1876 under Louis Davies, while the Roman Catholic Liberals and Conservatives joined forces in the Opposition under W. W. Sullivan. The coalition, composed of five Conservatives and four Liberals under a Liberal Premier, was a temporary arrangement, and, like all coalitions, it began to weaken when the main cause for its formation was removed with the inauguration of free schools. The members of the Cabinet began to look once more to their old allegiances and to grow restive in their temporary alliance. Two Ministers opposed a Government resolution to abolish the Legislative Council in 1878,[1] another openly criticized the Cabinet's policy with respect to the settlement of the land question,[2] and in the federal election of 1878 both sides in the

[1] *Assembly Debates,* 1878, pp. 286, 305.
[2] He called the Land Purchase Act "the most radical attack upon the rights of property that in modern days has emanated from any legislative body within the British Empire . . . class legislation of the most hurtful and pernicious kind." G. W. DeBlois to Lord Dufferin, May 12, 1874, *Canada, Sessional Papers,* 1874, no. 61, p. 16. The Opposition rightly criticized him for remaining in the Cabinet while holding such views, but he made the unorthodox reply that it was impossible for every member of the Government to agree with everything it did. *Assembly Debates,* 1877, pp. 12, 25-6.

coalition campaigned for their respective friends. Some Ministers even went so far as to make important expenditures without either appropriations or the authorization of their colleagues.[1] Finally four Ministers resigned in the fall of 1878 after indicating that there was nothing to hold the Government together, and that party loyalties had clashed at the Council board.[2] The bolters thereupon joined the Opposition and assisted in defeating the Government by a vote of want of confidence. This desertion aroused so much ill feeling that hardly a session went by until the turn of the century which did not include an argument over the responsibility for it.

Two Cabinet disagreements occurred during the Sullivan administration. After the Cabinet secured the passage in the Assembly of a bill to abolish the Legislative Council in 1879, the Government Leader in the upper house introduced the bill with the astonishing remark that he disliked it and supported it only because he was a member of the Government. The Opposition rewarded his frankness with the suggestion that he resign from the Cabinet.[3] In the following year the Premier and his colleagues divided on the Orange Lodge Incorporation Bill and were rescued from this embarrassment by the Lieutenant-Governor who withheld the assent.[4]

It was forty years before another Cabinet disagreement occurred, this time in the form of a series of disputes between Premier John H. Bell and his Attorney-General, J. J. Johnston. Mr. Johnston advocated the appointment of an extra judge to the Supreme Court, and in 1922, without the knowledge or consent of Premier Bell or the Island Cabinet, proceeded to Ottawa to sound out the opinion of the federal Government. Shortly after his return from Ottawa he introduced in the Legislature a bill authorizing the appointment of the extra Supreme Court judge and the reduction of the number of county court judges to two. The Attorney-General stated that the bill was "A government measure, introduced by the government, by the unanimous instruction of the

---

[1] *Ibid.*, 1879, pp. 29, 99-100; *ibid.*, 1888, pp. 255, 258.
[2] *Ibid.*, 1879, pp. 10, 13, 23 ff.; see also G. W. DeBlois to Editor of the *Examiner* in the Charlottetown *Patriot*, March 15, 1879.
[3] *P.E.I. Legislative Council Debates*, 1879, pp. 62 ff.
[4] *Supra*, pp. 154, 164-5.

Liberal party of this province."¹ But during the debate on second reading of the bill, Premier Bell attacked it as "exceedingly dangerous legislation."² The Attorney-General then rose to a point of order to ask the Speaker if the Premier was in order for criticizing a Government bill. Mr. Bell retorted that the bill was different from what he understood it was going to be, and the two Ministers engaged in a spectacular argument amid much applause from the Opposition. It was evident that Mr. Bell and Mr. Johnston thoroughly disliked each other, and the wonder is that they were content to remain as colleagues.³ The resulting intrigue and suspicion gradually weakened the Bell Government and helped to bring about its defeat in 1923.

An issue of 1930, which did not affect the Government but which ruined the career of a Minister, indicated that a member of the Cabinet should openly oppose his colleagues only upon the most serious provocation. In August of that year W. Bruce Butler, Minister without Portfolio, resigned from the Lea Government "because," he said, "I cannot conscientiously support an administration that has flouted every principle of democracy,"⁴ and because he felt that the Premier was doing too much without consulting his colleagues. Mr. Lea thereupon retorted that Butler was frustrated because he had not been appointed Minister of Agriculture.⁵ Mr. Butler crossed the floor of the House and joined the

[1] Report of proceedings in the Assembly, *Patriot,* April 26, 1922.
[2] *Ibid.,* May 8, 1922.
[3] "My position in the Bell government," wrote Mr. Johnston, "became a continuous and ever increasing humiliation, principally owing to the fact that I was only the nominal Attorney-General of the Province, and the nominal head of my department. Mr. Bell claimed and usurped the sole right of managing my department, whilst I received a small salary to do the actual work in the Administration of Justice. His interference became intolerable as my work had to be first submitted to him and approved of. . . . In many cases my functions and duties imposed on me a personal discretion and responsibility which Mr. Bell took from me in violation of my constitutional rights and powers. In other words the office of Attorney-General became a mere appendage to his office as Premier." J. J. Johnston to John Sinclair, Sept. 8, 1924. A certified copy of this letter was given by Mr. Johnston to the Charlottetown *Guardian* in 1930. In this letter Mr. Bell also indicated that the Lieutenant-Governor had threatened Mr. Bell with dismissal for ignoring the wish of the majority of the Cabinet in not withdrawing an unauthorized expression of censure against Mr. Johnston in the minutes of Council. No other evidence of this episode has been found.
[4] *Guardian,* Aug. 19, 1930.
[5] *Patriot,* Aug. 19, 1930; *Guardian,* Aug. 20, 1930.

Conservatives in opposition. Evidently the latter did not give him an encouraging welcome, for a few months later he returned to the Liberal fold but not to the Cabinet.[1]

The present precarious position of the principle of solidarity had its beginnings in the election of 1935 which returned thirty Liberals to the thirty-seat House. The absence of any Opposition members created a unique and unfortunate situation, for parliamentary government is designed to operate under an active exchange of conflicting opinions and to assist in the training of an alternative government. Basic habits, however, are not always eliminated readily. The opposition principle in the Legislature had become so well established that the one-party group soon developed an opposition within itself.[2] The House was little more than a Liberal caucus with the Speaker in the chair, and the debating habits of caucus were readily transferred to it. In fact, the Government caucus often met in the chamber with the Premier presiding, and when the time came for the House to meet, the Speaker would take the Premier's place and the House would attempt to give formal expression to what its personnel had already discussed in caucus. The proceedings, therefore, were often dull. In the session of 1936, for example, the "debate" on the address in reply to the Speech from the Throne consisted only of speeches from the mover, the seconder, and the Premier, and the budget "debate" was a solo effort on the part of the Provincial Secretary-Treasurer. During the first year the proceedings were uneventful and there were few divisions, but by the second and third sessions a number of the more restive members had begun to assume the duties of an unofficial opposition. "We lack an opposition party," said J. Walter Jones, then a private member, and later Premier, "and it is the duty of members of this House not to save criticism of their own executive."[3] Two members made some embarrassing comparisons between the party's election platform and its policies while in office,

---

[1]*Guardian*, July 11, 1931.
[2]"We had plenty of opponents in our own party," said Hon. J. P. McIntyre, who was then in the Cabinet, "and I think some of our own party members gave us more trouble than we would have had if there had been a half dozen Conservatives in the House." *Canada, Senate Debates,* Feb. 20, 1951, quoted in *Guardian,* Feb. 28, 1951.
[3]*Patriot*, "Proceedings of the Legislative Assembly for March 31, 1939."

another attacked the Government for mismanagement and extravagance, and even the Minister of Agriculture warned of the serious financial position of the province.[1] These criticisms did not lead to any serious splits within the party, and they were, on the whole, lightly regarded, for the Legislature needed something upon which to debate and the Government did not have to worry about majorities or Opposition tactics. This easy informality, however, continued into the following decade when the Liberal party received huge majorities in the three subsequent elections, and it provided the background for the laxities in Cabinet and party discipline which occurred in the 1940's. It is not without significance, moreover, that the dissenters in the 1930's became Cabinet Ministers in the following decade.

Cabinet solidarity was repeatedly disregarded during the premiership of J. Walter Jones. The most persistent offender was Hon. J. A. Campbell, a Minister without Portfolio, who missed few opportunities to criticize the Cabinet from the floor of the House. During debate on a land assessment bill in 1945, which was sponsored by the Provincial Secretary-Treasurer, Mr. Campbell asked the meaning of the bill, inquired what the Government's intentions were with respect to its operation, and proceeded to protest its introduction.[2] The same Minister has handed down for posterity what must surely be some of the most extraordinary public statements in the recent history of Cabinet government. During the discussion of the estimates of the Minister of Agriculture in the session of 1945 he spoke to his own colleagues in a manner which would do credit to the most conscientious of Opposition Leaders. "When you fellows get an honest man," he said, "you chuck him out of office, and when you get a crook you hold on to him." "You will never get anywhere in an office with your feet stuck on a table," he told

[1]*Canadian Annual Review*, 1935-6, p. 464; *ibid.*, 1937-8, p. 293.
[2]*Guardian*, April 17, 1945. There has been no Hansard in Prince Edward Island since 1893, and newspaper accounts must be relied upon for details of the proceedings in the Assembly. Both Charlottetown newspapers are quoted from here. Many of the references are from accounts of the proceedings reported in the *Guardian* by Mr. Frank Walker, that paper's Associate Editor and legislative reporter. It is the general opinion among Island public men, Liberal and Conservative alike, that Mr. Walker's reports are accurate, fair, and reliable accounts of the proceedings, and they are frequently referred to as an unofficial Hansard on the floor of the House itself. The writer uses them with complete confidence.

the Minister of Agriculture. "You get $2000 travelling expenses and you should do something, my friends." These remarks not unnaturally produced rounds of Opposition applause. On another occasion he complimented the Leader of the Opposition for "supporting legislation that is in the interests of the people of this country," and paid his respects to his Cabinet colleagues by asking: "But do you fellows exert yourselves? You don't, and you are open to criticism now, and you have to take it as far as I am concerned."[1] What the Minister appeared to forget was, not only that he was openly undermining his own Government, but that he himself was jointly responsible for the weaknesses he criticized so long as he remained in the Cabinet. These episodes also revealed an unusually forgiving tendency on the part of the Premier who permitted such criticism and refrained from calling for the offender's resignation.

Nor was Mr. Campbell the only dissenting Minister. In the same administration a dispute occurred in the House between the Premier and a Minister over the correctness of certain official statistics;[2] contrary announcements were given by the Premier and one of his colleagues on the date of a pending election;[3] a Minister denied responsibility for statements in the public accounts on the ground that his officials had been to blame;[4] a "hint" was offered by the Premier to his Ministers on the floor of the House that he would "do something to check the tendency of departments to run wild on their estimates";[5] and two Ministers were dropped from the Cabinet after what one of them called a "Comedy of Errors."[6]

The presence of so many Ministers without Portfolio in the Cabinet has greatly affected the principle of solidarity. Such a Minister, although a junior member of the Cabinet, is, nevertheless, an integral part of the executive. He shares, or at least should share, in the determination of policy and have access to all executive plans and decisions, for he, along with his colleagues, bears the respon-

---

[1]*Ibid.*, April 21, 1945.   [2]*Ibid.*, April 11, 1945.
[3]Toronto *Globe and Mail*, Oct. 28, 1947.
[4]*Guardian*, March 30, 1946.   [5]*Ibid.*, March 18, 1948.
[6]The two men, W. F. Alan Stewart and William Hughes, discussed freely some of the causes of their downfall and frequently challenged the Premier in subsequent sessions of the House. See, for example, *ibid.*, March 21, 22, 28, 30, 1950.

sibility for them and must defend them so long as he is a member of the Government. Yet a number of Ministers without Portfolio have complained of not being consulted by their colleagues on significant Cabinet decisions or of being ignored because of their less prominent status. One resigned in 1930 and accused the Premier of running the Government without consulting his colleagues.[1] Another confessed to the House that, although Minister without Portfolio, he was not aware of certain policies of his own Government.[2] The distinction between members with and without portfolio, if carried to such an extent, not only reduces the importance of Ministers without Portfolio but also seriously undermines Cabinet confidence and co-operation. As Keith says, "it is of course natural that issues should be discussed between members of the Cabinet without necessarily referring them to the Cabinet as a whole,"[3] but such discussion should be conducted with careful consideration for the views and responsibility of the Ministers who are not consulted.

The most spectacular Cabinet dissension occurred during the passage through the House of the Prohibition Bill of 1945. The Hon. Horace Wright, a Minister without Portfolio, piloted the bill, which he understood to be a Government measure, only to find that the Premier and several other Ministers supported an amendment which entirely changed the intent of the bill. Wright was opposed to this move, of which he had received no warning, and he refused to sponsor the bill any further. "I want to say," he told the House, "that as a member of this government I consider that I could not follow a man who would act in the underhanded way that the Premier has done this afternoon, and right here on the floor of this House I resign from the government of which he is leader."[4] The other Ministers joined Mr. Wright in opposing the bill although they did not resign from the Cabinet. Even Mr.

[1]*Ibid.,* Aug. 19, 1930.
[2]Said Hon. J. A. Campbell in the Legislature in 1946: "So far as I am concerned being a member of this Government, I am not conversant with the proposals that are being offered by the federal Government. You can think of that what you like. . . . As a member of the Government I don't know a darn thing about it." *Ibid.,* Feb. 29, 1946.
[3]A. B. Keith, *The Constitution of England from Queen Victoria to George VI* (London, 1940), vol. I, p. 189.
[4]*Guardian,* April 12, 1945.

Wright, after the apparently irrevocable denunciation of his leader, decided to remain a Minister because, he said, some of his constituents protested his leaving the Cabinet. The Premier did not recognize the "resignation" because it was not what he called a formal one.[1] This unusual reconciliation was not complete, however, for Wright continued to criticize his Government's action in the House and thereby earned the obvious retort from the Opposition Leader: "Why don't you resign again?"[2] An extraordinary sequel to the issue was the fact that the Cabinet avoided the normal consequences of such a glaring weakness within its ranks, for it remained intact and won an overwhelming triumph at the subsequent general election. This success, of course, did not vindicate the Cabinet's tactics, but it seems to indicate that the Islanders relish in their politics a few constitutional gymnastics, perhaps even a Machiavellian touch.

The peculiar features of Cabinet government in Prince Edward Island are largely the result of the unique political environment. Politicians are much closer to the people and more affected by local problems than are those associated with larger governments; and, as a result, they carry on the public affairs of the province with a comparatively high degree of informality. Although the Island has respected her privilege of self-government, she has always faced the problem of adjusting an elaborate constitutional system to the intimacies of local politics. Consequently, the rules and practices of government which are rigidly followed elsewhere have often been taken with a minimum of seriousness. Indeed this informality has frequently been carried so far as to be obviously detrimental to the good government of the province. Many Island politicians have apparently held so much of the confidence of their colleagues and of the public that they could say with the American Congressman: "What's the Constitution among friends?"

[1]*Ibid.*, April 16, 18, 1945.
[2]*Ibid.*, April 5, 1947.

CHAPTER IX

THE ADMINISTRATION

THE CIVIL SERVICE of Prince Edward Island, like similar bodies elsewhere, performs the detailed administrative and clerical tasks that are assigned to it by the executive, which appoints and directs it. It is a small body of approximately three hundred persons whose numbers, functions, and professional status have developed only in recent years with the sharp increase in the activities of government which followed depression and war.

In the Island's earliest years as a British colony the civil service was not separate from the executive and Legislature, for government employees, who then were sent out from England, performed most of the administrative functions and sat in the Executive and Legislative Councils as well. After responsible government was established the elected representatives took over the principal jobs and the appointed officials thereupon retired into the background. Further changes took place at Confederation, for numerous local employees became federal officials with the transfer of their functions to the central Government. When new provincial offices were created during this period, expansion in the service was often avoided by giving several appointments to one individual, a practice which continued to be a feature of the Island's administration.[1] There was comparatively little for the civil service to do in the early years, as the need for technical experts and assistants in a tiny agricultural province was small. Indeed at times there was hardly enough to keep nine Cabinet Ministers busy, and the latter were generally able to dispose of most of the important matters themselves.

While limited functions retarded the growth of the civil service, political patronage prevented its efficiency. A few officials of independent views held their posts over a period of years and, because of exceptional ability, they were indispensable in times of rapidly changing Cabinets, but the great majority were political appointees

[1]See the two Civil Service Acts of the 1870's: 39 Vic., c. 10; 42 Vic., c. 5. See also *P.E.I. House of Assembly Debates,* 1876, pp. 97 ff., and *P.E.I. House of Assembly Journals,* 1879, 2nd session, p. 83.

who retained their party sympathies while in office and who were replaced by newcomers with each change of Government.[1] Any public officer could be removed "at the discretion" of the authority which appointed him.[2] "With every change of Government," said a Cabinet Minister in 1876, "public officials have been dismissed, and fresh, untrained men have been put in their places. The consequence is that the duties have not been properly performed."[3] Those who were able to hold on to their jobs had low salaries, few opportunities for advancement, and no guarantee of a pension. Some of these remained long after their duties disappeared. "It was difficult to make any retrenchment in the civil service," complained one member of the Assembly, "many of the officials had spent many years in the offices, and we had no machinery for pensioning them off. In some instances it was necessary to wait until a place was made vacant by the death of the official before an office would be dispensed with."[4] The result of these two extremes of change and permanency was instability and inefficiency in the service and a lack of opportunities for careers in administration.

The first three decades of the twentieth century brought little change. There was a slight increase in the number of important tasks assigned to the civil servants as the activities of government widened in scope and Ministers came to rely more and more upon experienced advisers. The turnover in personnel at all levels was high, since opportunities for an attractive career were still few, and they depended largely on party patronage. Elaborate regulations with respect to appointment, promotion, and tenure were considered unnecessary, for the Government was never embarrassed by, nor did it need, a large number of applicants of ability and ambition.

A major change began in the 1930's. The increase in the responsibilities of government, particularly in the field of social services, the development of scientific agriculture, and recurrent negotiations in Dominion-provincial affairs led the Cabinet to depend upon the

[1] A prominent exception was Arthur Newbery, who retired in 1925 as Assistant Provincial Secretary and Clerk of the Executive Council after fifty-one years in the service.
[2] 41 Vic., c. 22.
[3] Hon. W. W. Sullivan in *Assembly Debates*, 1876, p. 97.
[4] *Ibid.*, April 17, 1878, p. 334.

research and advice of permanent public officials of several kinds. Deputy ministers, agricultural inspectors, engineers, research men, and others became more necessary and the selection of qualified persons and the provision for them of careers rather than mere jobs became for the first time an important feature of government. The small province still did not require a large number of officials, but their quality and status had necessarily to be improved.

The civil service is the largest branch of the provincial Government from the point of numbers. At January 31, 1950 there were 336 permanent civil servants in the public departments, the size of which varied from 165 (Health and Welfare) to 3 (the Provincial Secretary's office). There were also 77 employed in the provincial Sanitarium and the Temperance Commission, who were not regular civil servants although they did pay into the Superannuation Fund.[1] In addition to these, there were an undetermined number of part-time employees, some, such as road supervisors, with purely seasonal duties, and others, such as crown prosecutors, whose services were required only periodically. An attempt was made in the Public Service Act to provide for gradation in rank among public servants, when thirty-eight "permanent public service positions" were set out, but gradation in the service is not indicated by even that small classification, for some officials hold several of these posts simultaneously. The Deputy Provincial Secretary, for instance, is (1951) Clerk of the Executive Council, Succession Duty Officer, Superintendent of Insurance, and deputy administrator of several acts as well. Broadly speaking, the entire service can be divided into four general classes: (1) the deputy ministers, of whom there are eight; (2) a small group of a dozen or so officials whose duties include advisory and research functions; (3) professional employees such as doctors, nurses, and engineers,[2] and (4) clerks and stenographers. The variations in salary and responsibility within each of these classes are, on the whole, extremely small.

[1] These figures are provided through the courtesy of the Deputy Provincial Treasurer.
[2] School teachers are not civil servants, but employees of the school districts where they teach; see *infra,* pp. 284-5. School inspectors are provincial civil servants.

The procedure for appointment, promotion, removal, and payment of civil servants in Prince Edward Island is without parallel in the other provinces. Appointments at all levels are made directly by the Cabinet. There is no civil service commission, no set procedure for admission, and there are no examinations.[1] Salaries are not fixed for each position, but are set either by Order-in-Council or by estimate according to what the Government, at the moment of hiring, is willing to pay to have a job done or to obtain the services of a particular person. There are only a few classifications in each department and no effective system of gradation above the clerical level or of in-service training. All civil service posts on the Island have thus continued to be the patronage of the Government of the day, and, although a prospective appointee's abilities are generally considered, his being politically acceptable to the Cabinet has been fully as important a qualification.

Security of tenure was provided by the Public Service Act of 1937[2] but the method of safeguarding it is most unusual. The old system of dismissal "at the discretion" of the Cabinet was dropped, and it was provided that henceforth no permanent public servant[3] could be dismissed except for incompetence, neglect of duties, disclosure of official secrets, "breach of confidence," political partisanship,[4] "or other misconduct," and then only after thirty days' notice "except in cases of gross misconduct." Anyone who considered his dismissal unjust could appeal to the Queens County Court for hearing by a judge, and, if the appeal were sustained, the judge might order reinstatement. If a person is dropped from the service because of the abolition or changing of his position, or because he is displaced by the appointment of a private secretary to a Minister, the Cabinet must place his name on a "waiting list," and when vacancies arise those on this list must receive priority according to the length of employment. The Act further provided that if anyone on the waiting list considered that he had been overlooked when

---

[1] Stenographers are exceptional in that they receive a purely mechanical test.
[2] 1 Geo. VI, c. 28.
[3] The Clerk of the Executive Council is an exception to the rule. *Supra*, p. 185.
[4] Political partisanship is defined as "partisan work" in federal, provincial, or municipal elections or dealing with party funds.

vacancies arose, he could appeal to the county court judge, who, after a hearing, might order his appointment. An amendment in 1949 provided for appeal to the Supreme Court rather than to the county court. This procedure has greatly increased the political independence and security of tenure of civil servants, but it has yet to stand the test of changes of Government, and it is open to the objection that it gives the courts a function which they should not really be asked to perform. More serious, however, is the fact that the regulations evidently do not *prevent* political partisanship among civil servants. Although the term is specifically defined in the Public Service Act as "partisan work" in federal, provincial, or municipal elections or dealing with party funds, the Government took it lightly enough in 1950 to permit a civil servant to stand for nomination as a federal candidate in a party convention and still retain his position in the service.[1] Such precedents, which have long been prohibited elsewhere, undermine the purpose of the Public Service Act as well as the independence and professional integrity of the civil service.

The Island's civil service administration is unique in Canada, for in no other province are civil servants appointed by the Executive Council without recommendation from a civil service commission (excepting deputy ministers and certain other senior employees), and in none is recourse to the courts provided in case of dismissal or unfair consideration when on a waiting list.[2] The other provinces, moreover, have classified positions and, in most cases, they have assigned specified salary ranges to these positions according to the responsibilities involved. The Island procedure is the result of the small size of the civil service, the power of party patronage, and the scarcity of remunerative positions and suitable available applicants. Doubtless it has been considered a convenient

---

[1] The official was Director of Physical Fitness and of the Travel Bureau. See also the criticism of the Superintendent of Old Age Pensions for alleged participation in federal elections. Charlottetown *Guardian*, April 20, 1945. See also *supra,* p. 186.

[2] Appeals in the other provinces are made either to a civil service commission or to a board of review. In Alberta persons dismissed may appeal to a Joint Council composed of three Cabinet Ministers, three representatives of the Civil Service Association, and the secretary of the latter. In Newfoundland cases of dismissal are reviewed by the Lieutenant-Governor-in-Council.

method of selecting personnel according to the funds available and duties involved, particularly where a person is to hold several positions at once. Although some excellent civil servants have been appointed, experience everywhere has, nevertheless, only too clearly revealed that political patronage and haphazard classification and remuneration are poor stimulants to professional competence, a lesson which the Island has been slow to realize.

The salaries of civil servants have risen sharply in recent years, but even yet they are not large. As a result, government positions rarely attract persons from other professions or from outside the province. A half-dozen directors of technical branches of the service receive $5,000 or more. The deputy ministers, whose duties in small departments are much less extensive than those of their counterparts in larger governments, receive from $3,500 to $5,500, and a few technical employees with special duties fall within the same range. Some deputies receive less than the technical personnel in the same departments. A few persons receive from $2,500 to $3,500, but the overwhelming majority receive less than $2,000. The superannuation has been no more generous. Indeed there was no retirement plan prior to 1945, and superannuation allowances were granted by special statutes, usually in amounts of $500 per annum or less depending upon the length of service.[1] The Public Service Superannuation Act of 1945 provided for retiring allowances on a contributory basis for employees with at least ten years' service.[2]

Civil service reform has been an important and encouraging feature of the government of Prince Edward Island in recent years,[3] but it is still very slow. It will continue to be slow as long as the recruitment of civil servants is seriously affected by political patronage, inadequate organization, and low salaries. Party considerations or the whims of a Minister or his friends and constituents are no substitute for the modern methods of recruiting, paying, and

[1] See, for example, 1 Geo. VI, cc. 31, 32.
[2] 9 Geo. VI, c. 31.
[3] The rapid development and comparative efficiency of the Department of Health and Welfare clearly indicate what can be done in this respect. The effects of outside standards and practices are obvious in this department which receives much financial aid from the Dominion Government.

promoting of government employees adopted elsewhere. Another hindrance to reform is the custom of limiting government appointments to Islanders. This weakness is most serious, for it restricts the choice of civil servants to a very few, and it bars the Island service to the growing number of Canadians in other provinces who have the training suitable for government administration and to the rich variety of experiences and ideas which a few recruits from outside could provide.[1] This exclusiveness is one of the chief reasons why so many of the generally accepted practices of modern government followed elsewhere are thus far unknown or unsuccessful in Prince Edward Island. Moreover, political patronage and the lack of organization in the service frequently discourage the ablest Islanders. The provincial Government has often lamented the exodus of trained Islanders to other provinces; its own service could be one of the most attractive alternatives to them. Finally, an important advantage of an efficient civil service on the Island would be that it could compensate to a certain extent for many of the characteristics of cabinet government. Where most Ministers can devote only a limited portion of their time to Government business, and where the Premier's choice of colleagues is often severely restricted, so much depends on able officials who have the ability, the training, and the *esprit de corps* to cope successfully with the complicated problems of modern government.

There are eight small departments in the public service of the Island: Justice, Public Works, Agriculture, Industry and Natural Resources, Health and Welfare, Education, and those of the Provincial Secretary and of the Provincial Treasurer.

The Department of the Provincial Treasurer followed the Colonial Treasurer of early years, a minor official who did not sit in the Executive Council and who received no salary save a small percentage of the revenue collected. Financial matters were handled by the Cabinet as a whole until after Confederation, and, as one Premier explained, "there was a great deal of time lost in examining

[1] For example, in all the government offices there is not a single person with a background of special training and experience in economics, political science, history, or public administration.

small accounts which should not come before the Council at all but should be examined in the office of the Finance Minister."[1] This inconvenient procedure proved disastrous during the embarrassments of the railway era, and, consequently, in 1876 the offices of Colonial Treasurer and Colonial Secretary were united into that of a Provincial Secretary and Treasurer with Cabinet rank.[2] This department remained small since its responsibilities were never onerous, and for many years it was headed by the Premier. It consists at present of a Minister, a deputy minister, and some thirty-eight other persons and it deals with matters connected with the raising and spending of public money such as taxing, borrowing, auditing, preparing the budget, and co-ordinating the financial affairs of all branches of the Government.[3]

The Department of the Provincial Secretary followed the old Colonial Secretary who, although a member of the Executive Council, was little more than an assistant to the Governor.[4] This branch is extremely small and, as mentioned above, it was for many years joined with the Treasury Department under one Minister. Now it has a separate Minister, a deputy, and one or two stenographers. Its chief function is the administration of certain acts such as the Companies Act, Marriage Act, Highway Traffic Act, Trade Union Act, Cooperative Associations Act, Credit Union Act, and the Security Frauds Prevention Act. Since the Deputy Provincial Secretary is also Clerk of the Executive Council, he is responsible for carrying out a variety of duties assigned by that body such as the care of Cabinet minutes and matters of protocol.

The Department of Justice consists of approximately fifteen persons, including largely prothonotaries, sheriffs, and stenographers. The functions of this group have, until recently, been very limited; indeed it has scarcely been looked upon as a "department" at times, for the attorney-generalship is generally held by the Premier, and a deputy minister was appointed for the first time in 1950. The amount of court work is small in comparison with that in other

[1]Hon. J. C. Pope in *Assembly Debates,* 1872, 2nd session, p. 102.
[2]39 Vic., c. 10.
[3]See also 60 Vic., c. 1; and "An Act Respecting the Treasury Department," 11 Geo. VI, c. 40.
[4]Huntley to Grey, May 9, 1847, Public Archives of Canada, Colonial Office Records (P.E.I.), G series, vol. 48, p. 414.

provinces, and, until the appointment of a deputy minister, it was handled by the Attorney-General himself or by certain practising lawyers who were hired as part-time crown attorneys on a salary and fee basis. The Attorney-General is supposed to be legal adviser to the Cabinet, but even this function is limited in the case of some Ministers whose qualifications are overshadowed by other lawyers in the Cabinet or in the civil service.[1]

The Department of Education is headed by a Minister, and it includes a deputy minister and some thirty civil servants. In cooperation with local boards of trustees in the school districts it is responsible for the supervision of the school system. To the Minister is responsible the Principal of Prince of Wales College, which institution is owned and operated by the provincial Government.

There is also a Council of Education which is composed of the Minister of Education, who is chairman, and ten other members including the Deputy Minister and the Secretary of Education, the principals of the local colleges, and representatives of the Federation of Agriculture, the Canadian Legion, the Teachers' Federation, and the Women's Institutes.[2] The old Board of Education, which had both advisory and administrative functions, was replaced by this Council which took over the advisory functions, while the Department of Education assumed the administration. The Council was designed to enable teachers and representative citizens to assist the Department in serving the educational needs of the community. Actually it is of little significance, for it rarely meets more than once a year,[3] and it has not been able to wield any effective influence.

The Department of Agriculture has always been a senior branch of the Government since it deals with the main industry of the province. It was established in 1897 after the old office of Commissioner of Crown and Public Lands was abolished when the land question was settled and immigration and land grants had ceased.[4] For

---

[1]At one time there was another legal officer in the Cabinet, the Solicitor-General. He was never an important Minister and the portfolio was abolished in 1876. 39 Vic., c. 10. See also Ready to Sir G. Murray, August 28, 1828, P.A.C. (P.E.I.), A 45, p. 349; Fitzroy to G. W. Hope, Oct. 29, 1841, *ibid.*, G 13, p. 457.

[2]9 Geo. VI, c. 11.

[3]The law requires that it meet at least three times a year.

[4]60 Vic., c. 1; *Assembly Journals*, 1897, pp. 97-8. Although the act was passed in 1897, its terms were not made effective until 1901.

twenty years thereafter the department was generally combined with the office of Provincial Secretary-Treasurer under one Minister, but the present practice is to keep it separate. It has required few civil servants; there are usually only about twenty, including a deputy minister, three county agricultural representatives, a dairy superintendent, and a pathologist. These officials co-operate closely with the Dominion Department of Agriculture which maintains a large experimental station and research laboratory near Charlottetown. Indeed their number and duties are proportionately few because of the convenient federal facilities.

The Department of Public Works was established in 1876. Its predecessor was the Board of Works which was set up in 1869 and which was composed of the Colonial Secretary, the Commissioner of Public Lands, and three others appointed by the Lieutenant-Governor-in-Council. The Board supervised the erection of buildings, construction of roads, letting of public contracts, and the performance of statute labour, and it was assisted by superintendents of works in each of the three counties. A statute specially provided that the acceptance of places on the Board by members of the Legislature would not render their seats vacant, a provision which, along with the many opportunities for patronage, exposed the Board to much criticism.[1] The Board was consequently abolished in 1876 and its functions placed under the charge of a Commissioner of Public Works whose position in the Cabinet assured more direct executive responsibility for public works.[2]

The Department of Public Works is responsible mainly for the public construction of roads and bridges. Most minor projects of this kind are carried out by departmental engineers and workmen, but the major enterprises are now handled by private companies under contract with the Government. The department also supervises all public buildings and property. The Minister is assisted by a deputy minister[3] and approximately fifty engineers, foremen, accountants, and stenographers.

[1] See 32 Vic., c. 3; 35-36 Vic., c. 19; *Assembly Debates*, 1869, p. 74; *Assembly Journals*, 1869, p. 25.
[2] 39 Vic., c. 10; *Assembly Debates*, 1876, p. 227.
[3] Before September, 1950 there were two deputy ministers of Public Works, one an engineer who dealt with technical matters, and the other an accountant in charge of administration.

The Department of Health and Welfare has been growing steadily with the increase of provincial and federal Government activity in social services. Its present complement of 54 civil servants headed by a Minister and his deputy, and 111 employees of the Falconwood and Beech Grove hospitals is responsible for the administration of community health projects, child and family welfare, old age and blind pensions, vital statistics, sanitary engineering, mental hygiene, and laboratory research, and in all these enterprises there is a close liaison with federal officials. The bulk of the staff consists of health officers, nurses, technicians, and their assistants.

This is the largest department and it is divided into two branches—health and welfare. The health branch in turn is divided into ten divisions, each with its own director and staff, which handle specific phases of public health such as tuberculosis control, mental health, and laboratory research. The department spends approximately two-fifths of the total provincial revenue and it has been able to pay to its directors of divisions the highest salaries in the public service.[1] The reasons for this comparative opulence are, of course, the fact that the Dominion Government provides over one-third of the amount of its revenue through grants for health and old age and blind pensions, and the inability to secure the services of experts without paying for them.

The Department of Industry and Natural Resources consists of a Minister and deputy minister and divisions of trade, town planning, transportation, fisheries, and electrical inspection, each under a director. It is a small department of about a dozen persons which deals with matters from which its divisions derive their names and provides financial grants for such things as industrial development, fish and game conservation, and skunk bounties.[2]

Boards of different varieties have been of some significance in provincial administration, but the Island has not had any notable success with them. The government departments have generally handled most of the important matters, and, where they have shared functions with boards, political interference and overlapping juris-

[1] The Director of Laboratories, for example, receives $7,175 per annum.
[2] This department took the place of the Department of Reconstruction which functioned from 1944 to 1947. See also 8 Geo. VI, c. 17 and 11 Geo. VI, c. 30.

diction have often precluded co-operation and efficiency. As far back as 1876 there were three boards, a Board of Education, a Board of Trustees for the Lunatic Asylum, and a Board of Works. The last two failed from the start, largely because of political interference. The Board of Works, as already mentioned, became the Department of Public Works, and the duties of the Asylum Board were taken over by the Department of Health and Welfare. It took years for the Board of Education to overcome the disrupting influence of the school question and then it was displaced by a less active body, the Council of Education. "It has been happily said that 'Boards' are screens," said the *Examiner* in 1876, "what the Board does is the act of nobody; and nobody can be made to answer for it."[1] This situation prevailed generally until recent years when unhappy experience with overlapping jurisdiction and political expediency have suggested a greater official awareness of the value and functions of boards in public administration and of the need for freeing them from political and bureaucratic interference. For instance, two commissions of inquiry were appointed in little more than a year, one in 1950 to investigate alleged political patronage in the Fishermen's Loan Board, and the other in 1951 to examine charges of corruption and inefficiency in the Prince Edward Island Industrial Corporation. Thus far the principles and practices of public administration have received very little attention in the government service of the Island.

In 1950 there were five administrative boards: the Temperance Commission, the Public Utilities Commission, the Sanitarium Commission, the Board of Pensions Commissioners, and the Fishermen's Loan Board.

The Temperance Commission, consisting of three private citizens of whom only the chairman serves full time, has inherited a stormy tradition. A succession of such boards has handled the controversial administration of the liquor trade with most unhappy results, for almost any policy which they adopted was bound to arouse public criticism and political interference. The most extraordinary experiment was a board of six clergymen which endeav-

---

[1]Charlottetown *Examiner,* Jan. 10, 1876. Under modern methods, of course, a board can be made responsible to a Minister with precautions against undue political and bureaucratic interference.

oured for a short time to supervise what was to them the singularly inappropriate function of buying and selling liquor. The Attorney-General's office took over the task for a time, but was glad to drop it and avoid the many charges of political manipulation. The present commission, which has a staff of approximately twenty employees, has power to buy and sell liquor and control its distribution through vendor stores and make regulations for the carrying-out of the Temperance Act.[1] Although the Commission is vested with wide powers, statute has provided for strict responsibility to the Minister of Public Works with respect to administration and to the Attorney-General with respect to enforcement. It must report annually to the Cabinet and the Assembly, and its decisions are subject to appeal by aggrieved parties to the county courts. The Commission is too new, however, to have yet given adequate indication that it can escape the weaknesses of its predecessors.

The Public Utilities Commission is empowered by its appointing statute to "have general supervision of all public utilities and shall make all necessary examinations and enquiries and keep itself informed as to the compliance by public utilities with the provisions of this Act and shall have the right to obtain from any public utility all information necessary to enable the Commission to fulfill its duties."[2] This body is composed of a chairman, who may be a Supreme Court or county court judge, and two other members, all of whom are appointed by the Lieutenant-Governor-in-Council, and it may appoint such additional staff as it deems necessary for the carrying-out of its functions. It has wide powers of regulation for the provision of adequate services and the setting of rates and tolls and, upon its own initiative or complaint from aggrieved parties, of hearing and investigation.[3] No mention is made in the statute of tenure or of responsibility, although the Commission must submit an annual financial statement to the Provincial Secretary. Its decisions are not necessarily final, however, for appeals may lie to the Supreme Court *in banco*. A unique feature of the Commis-

[1]See 12 Geo. VI, c. 37.
[2]12 Geo. VI, c. 32. See also 4 Geo. VI, c. 53; 10 Geo. VI, c. 28; 11 Geo. VI, c. 33.
[3]See, for example, the Electric Power and Telephone Act, 12 Geo. VI, c. 14; the Petroleum Products Act, 12 Geo. VI, c. 27; and the Public Vehicle Act, 12 Geo. VI, c. 33.

sion is the fact that the salaries and expenses of its staff must be borne by the public utilities and other bodies which come under its control, and the Commission itself decides the proportion which each must pay.

The Sanitarium Commission, which employs some eighty persons, is composed of seven private citizens. This body, which is responsible to the Minister of Health and Welfare, actually does little but determine policy, and leaves administration largely to the Medical Superintendent of the Sanitarium.[1]

The Board of Pensions Commissioners consists of three persons appointed by the Lieutenant-Governor-in-Council to consider and decide upon applications for old age pensions under regulations laid down by the Government, and administered by the Minister of Public Welfare. Appeals from this Board may be taken to a special board of review which may be appointed by the Government to examine special cases.[2]

The Fishermen's Loan Board, which is responsible to the Minister of Industry and Natural Resources, consists of seven members —a paid chairman and six unpaid private citizens.[3] Its function is to hear requests from fishermen for loans for such gear and equipment as boats and engines, and from stores and associations for loans to provide fishermen with such things as nets and traps.[4]

In 1949 the province established a Crown company called the Prince Edward Island Industrial Corporation to direct certain publicly owned business enterprises such as a cold storage plant and a boat service running between the Island and Newfoundland.[5] The Corporation is managed by a Board of Directors consisting entirely of deputy ministers, whose activities must be approved by a Minister who is entrusted by the Government with the responsibility. It is difficult to understand how such an organization can keep free of inefficiency and political interference; its success will depend on how well five deputy ministers can deal with the prin-

[1]19 Geo. V, c. 1; 23 Geo. V, c. 26.
[2]4 Geo. VI, c. 44.   [3]1 Geo. VI, c. 7.
[4]See *Regulations made under Fishermen's Loan Board Act* (Charlottetown, 1949). See also *supra,* p. 206, n. 2.
[5]13 Geo. VI, c. 21.

ciples and practices of business enterprise and resist any unwarranted intrusion by their superiors or by party supporters.[1] It is significant that in 1951 the Government announced its intention of selling the boat service two years after inaugurating it, and, as mentioned above, a commission of inquiry was appointed to investigate charges of corruption and inefficiency.[2]

In addition to these administrative bodies, there are several departmental advisory boards such as the Council of Education, already described, the Provincial Health Planning Commission to advise the Minister of Health and Welfare, and the Public Service Superannuation Board which assists the Provincial Treasurer. Some of these boards have remained dormant from their creation, very few have performed a useful and continuous function; their effectiveness has depended largely upon the administrative ability of the Minister concerned.

To sum up, it would appear that, although the government of Prince Edward Island must be kept small, there are splendid opportunities for public service which could be put to good advantage. The old easy-going methods of administration of the last century are now inadequate and expensive in a province which is difficult to govern and which must be concerned with Dominion-provincial relations as well as with complicated local problems. Effective recruitment and organization of the personnel of government departments and boards, careful study of administrative methods and public finance, together with modern provisions for responsibility to the Legislature and reasonable protection against both political interference and bureaucracy are now absolutely essential to the conduct of the public business of the province, and to participation in national affairs.

[1] See *Guardian*, March 23, 1950 for a debate in the Legislature on this subject. The anomalous position of these officials was clearly revealed during the discussions. They could not defend themselves, nor could their interests and activities be separated from those of their Ministers.
[2] See *Guardian*, March 16, 29, 31, 1951; *supra*, p. 206, n. 2.

CHAPTER X

THE LEGISLATURE

THE LEGISLATURE of Prince Edward Island is composed of the Lieutenant-Governor and the Legislative Assembly. His Honour's functions in this connection consist of giving royal assent to legislation, receiving resignations of members, and fulfilling other duties provided by tradition and statute. These, however, are largely formal, and are exercised on the advice of the Cabinet. The effective, practical part of the Legislature is the House itself. Its function is the same as that of similar bodies elsewhere—to enable the representatives of the people to make the laws by which the province is governed, to express ideas and opinions upon public business, and to praise and criticize the actions of the executive. Yet in its structure and character the House, like the Island's other institutions of government, reflects certain peculiarities which result from the size of the province and the habits and attitudes of its people.

THE ESTABLISHMENT OF THE LEGISLATURE

The Legislative Assembly is a peculiar combination of two houses in one. The events leading to its formation in 1893 were not unrelated to the forces which have determined the history of second chambers elsewhere. While the result was different in form, if not in fact, from that in other places, the same considerations were present—effectiveness of representative government, rivalry between two houses, and expense.[1] As previous chapters have indicated, the position of the Island's Legislative Council was altered to meet the developments of the thirty years before Confederation.[2] The coming of responsible government, the jealous regard for its powers on the part of the Assembly, rivalry between the two houses, and the concentration of the executive in the lower house, had all

---

[1] Some other provinces in Canada have faced the same problem. New Brunswick did away with her second chamber in 1892 and Manitoba in 1876, while Nova Scotia did not abolish hers until 1928. Ontario, British Columbia, Alberta, and Saskatchewan never had upper houses. Only Quebec has retained to the present day what is still called the Legislative Council.

[2] *Supra*, pp. 36, 62-6.

THE LEGISLATURE

affected the position of the upper chamber. In 1862 it was made elective, but differences of opinion still prevailed with respect to the influence it should have in comparison with the Assembly.[1] After Confederation the necessity for change was more apparent, and the maintenance of the old forms became more difficult. A political system consisting of a Lieutenant-Governor, Cabinet, and a two-house Legislature in addition to six members and four senators in the federal Parliament suggested over-government for so small a province, although the lack of an effective system of county and municipal institutions supplied a partial justification.

The question of union had scarcely been settled when suggestions for the alteration of the Legislature were renewed. Two factors prompted them, the desire to reduce the size of the machinery of government, and the embarrassment caused by Liberal control of the Assembly and Conservative control of the Legislative Council. On April 11, 1874 a resolution was introduced in the Assembly to the effect that the duties of the Legislature had so much decreased with union that a second chamber was no longer necessary; and the further suggestion was made that the number of members in the lower house could with advantage be reduced by one-third. It was pointed out that the abolition of the Legislative Council would result in a saving of $8,000 a year to the taxpayers. The mover of the resolution expressed the opinion that the Opposition majority in the Legislative Council "merely echoed the sentiments of their party in the House of Assembly," and that "the people did not want echoes." Several members even went so far as to suggest that, with power of disallowance given to the Dominion, there would be no need of a second chamber to exercise revising functions.[2] The Government, however, took the view that, since the province had scarcely entered Confederation, it was too soon to act on the matter, and the resolution got only as far as the committee stage.

By 1878 it became apparent that public opinion favoured the abolition of the Legislative Council, but that there were many views

---

[1]*Supra*, pp. 100-4.
[2]*P.E.I. House of Assembly Journals*, 1874, p. 60; *P.E.I. House of Assembly Debates*, April 11, 1874, pp. 348-9, 473; Charlottetown *Examiner*, Nov. 15, 1875.

on when and how such a reform could be carried out. The chief disagreement concerned the privileges of the property owners and the need for some check on the lower house. The Sullivan Government attempted to solve the problem in 1879 when it introduced a bill which provided for the abolition of the Legislative Council and included, as a compensation to property holders, a provision for stiffening the residence requirements for voters and the property qualifications of members of the Assembly.[1] The bill passed the Assembly, but it did not survive the scrutiny of the chamber it sought to abolish, and a year later a similar bill met the same fate.[2] On the latter occasion it was suggested that the Legislative Council, as well as the Assembly, was useful as a training ground for the Dominion Parliament, an argument which was prompted by the fact that in those days most of the federal representatives from the Island had already served in the local Legislature.[3] Nevertheless, even the members of the Legislative Council admitted that some reform was necessary, and in 1879 and again in 1880 they countered the Government's proposals with bills of their own which provided that the change should be carried out by reducing each branch of the Legislature by one-half, and forming one house of twenty-two members, fifteen elected by the existing Assembly franchise and seven by the existing Legislative Council franchise. This plan, which was also advocated by the Opposition in the lower house, was steadily opposed by the Government.[4]

By 1881, however, Premier Sullivan was ready to compromise with the Councillors for the sake of reform. "It is entirely beyond the means of this Province," he declared, "to maintain all the legislative machinery we possessed on entering the Confederation for

---

[1] *Assembly Journals*, 1879, p. 45.
[2] Hon. Joseph Wightman, Leader of the Government in that house and a member of the Cabinet, expressed his dislike of it and called it "a hasty measure got up during the late election campaign, by political agitators." Hon. Alexander Laird, the Opposition Leader, thought that "the one house system was too much like despotism," and he wanted to know "who authorized one branch of the Legislature to lay violent hands on the other branch. Such an act would be an outrage on parliamentary government." *P.E.I. Legislative Council Debates*, 1879, pp. 62 ff.
[3] *Ibid.*, 1880, pp. 53-4.
[4] See remarks by W. W. Sullivan, *Assembly Debates*, 1881, pp. 44-5 on negotiations with the Council; and the Opposition proposals in *ibid.*, 1879, p. 138.

the performance of the paltry little public business which has been left to the Provincial Legislature to transact."[1] One of his colleagues quoted the Toronto *Globe*'s criticism of the provinces for "travestying on every little colonial platform the grand stagery of the British House of Lords."[2] During the session of 1881 the Government introduced a bill which embodied the plan which the Legislative Council had previously made.[3] A new house with a four-year maximum term was to be established which would consist of twenty-two members, fifteen elected on the existing lower house franchise, and seven on the existing upper house franchise. It was also proposed that the Executive Council would be reduced to a maximum of five members, for, said Sullivan, too many men in the executive "would give the Government too much control of the majority in the Legislature."[4] The Assembly, as well as the Legislative Council, was now prepared to recognize the alleged virtues of property holders and it even approved a property qualification for members amounting to a minimum of $600.[5] "It is one of the safeguards of the Bill," said the Premier, "that the man sent to make the laws shall himself have some status and interest in the country."[6] "The best guarantee the electors could have," said Hon. Donald Ferguson, "was that the representative should have property. A man who could not accumulate $600 worth of property in this Province is hardly the man to represent a district in the Legislature. His inability to do this is a very good evidence that he is lacking in brains or something else."[7]

These were the opinions of the legislative reformers; and those who opposed a change held even more extreme views on the rights and virtues of property. "The abolition of the Council under present circumstances," said the *Patriot*, "would place the Island completely under the control of the lowest and most corrupt class of franchise voters."[8] The main factor behind this attitude was the predominance of the rural areas where most of the inhabitants owned or rented small farms or fishing establishments. It is inter-

[1]*Ibid.*, 1881, p. 45.   [2]Hon. Donald Ferguson in *ibid.*, p. 197.
[3]*Assembly Journals*, 1881, p. 29.
[4]*Assembly Debates*, 1881, p. 99.
[5]*Ibid.*, p. 87.   [6]*Ibid.*, p. 98.   [7]*Ibid.*, p. 97.
[8]Charlottetown *Patriot*, Sept. 7, 1882.

esting to compare this situation with that in an earlier period when the landowner was in the minority and when the influence of the proprietors in the conduct of public business was everywhere denounced. The changing of the titles to the land simply resulted in the new owners demanding the same "rights of property" that had been the sacred privilege of their predecessors.

The bill of 1881 and a similar one of 1882, which differed from its predecessor only in a provision that the Executive Council was to consist of seven members, were blocked by the Legislative Council. Moreover in the elections of 1884 it became clear to the Government that the people were not yet ready for a change.[1] Two years later, however, the Government tried the 1881 bill again, but without success.[2] This time the upper house countered with a new proposal to the effect that in future the Assembly, instead of meeting annually, should have only one session every two years although special sessions might be called by the Governor "upon the requisition of a majority of all the Members of the two branches of the Legislature." This plan, said its sponsors, would "reduce the cost of legislation to the lowest possible limit, and at the same time preserve the political rights and privileges of all classes."[3] Such a suggestion was unacceptable to the Assembly.[4]

Two decades of bickering were brought to an end in 1892 by a compromise between the two chambers.[5] A bill was passed by both houses which provided for the abolition of both houses and the creation of a new Legislative Assembly.[6] When the bill was presented for assent, Governor Carvell was not sure of its constitutionality and reserved it for the Governor-General's pleasure. As the matter was a local one involving the amending of the provincial constitution, no action was taken in Ottawa,[7] and when a similar bill was passed in 1893 it received royal assent.[8]

[1] See Premier Sullivan in *Assembly Debates*, 1884, p. 123.
[2] *Ibid.*, 1886, pp. 541 ff.
[3] Proceedings of the Legislative Council, May 14, 1886, *Assembly Journals*, 1886, p. 186.
[4] See also W. W. Sullivan in *Assembly Debates*, 1886, pp. 205-6.
[5] It is significant to note that of the 664 bills passed by the Assembly in the years 1873 to 1893, inclusive, 56 were rejected by the Legislative Council.
[6] The proposal contained no mention of the Executive Council. *Assembly Journals*, 1892, pp. 21-2
[7] *Supra*, pp. 156-7.
[8] 56 Vic., c. 1; *Assembly Debates*, 1893, pp. 131 ff.

THE LEGISLATURE

REPRESENTATION

The Legislature Act of 1893 created a Legislative Assembly of thirty members, one half elected on the old Legislative Council franchise, and the other on the franchise which had prevailed for the old House of Assembly. There were fifteen electoral districts, five in each county, and each returned two members, one called a "councillor" and the other an "assemblyman." These constituencies have remained practically unchanged since. Each is organized on the basis of a group of townships, the old "lots" of proprietorship days, except in the Third, Fourth, and Fifth Districts of Kings where, in addition, certain roads and lines are specified as boundaries. Inasmuch as they are all agricultural districts, some with towns and some without, they vary in population. The rural constituencies in Queens average about 7,000 persons; Charlottetown comprises 14,000; and the constituencies in Prince and Kings average 7,000 and 4,000 respectively. No explicit provision is made for regular redistribution, but it can, of course, be accomplished by amending the Election Act. The structure of constituencies has never been a significant problem in the Island.[1]

The qualifications of members of both classes were simple: they should be male British subjects of twenty-one years of age or over. Certain officials were declared ineligible to sit, viz., members of the House of Commons, and Crown employees, whether federal or provincial, except the Provincial Secretary-Treasurer, the Commissioner of Public Lands, the Attorney-General, and the Commissioner of Public Works if they were elected while holding their office.[2] Government contractors and clergymen were also excluded.

The qualifications of voters for the councillors provided that they must be male British subjects, twenty-one years of age, possessing real estate, freehold or leasehold, to the value of $325.

The qualifications of voters for the assemblymen provided that they also should be male British subjects of twenty-one years of age. Such a voter had to be the owner or occupier of estate of a yearly value of at least $6, *or* one who had performed certain statutory labour requirements and had resided in the province for one year, *or* one who in Charlottetown or Summerside had paid poll tax

[1] 12 Geo. V, cc. 5, 27. [2] See *supra*, pp. 96-9.

and had one year's residence, *or* one who was the owner or occupier of at least eight acres on Cardigan Point. In other words the qualifications were merely nominal, and were just sufficient to exclude transients from voting.[1]

The "rights of property," which had so long been a feature of the Island's politics, were maintained in the franchise. The Act of 1893 permitted the property holder to cast two votes in his constituency, one for the councillor and one for the assemblyman, while the voter who did not hold property had one vote for the assemblyman. This arrangement has remained unchanged to the present.[2] Furthermore, plural voting, which had been forbidden in 1861,[3] and revived in 1866,[4] was permitted in the case of property holders if they held property in several different constituencies. Actually this privilege was limited by the small number of polls which such an owner could visit on election day.[5]

These arrangements were part of a compromise without which the desired reduction of the legislative machinery would perhaps have been impossible, and they were a natural result of what was an amalgamation of two houses rather than the abolition of one. Actually they are of little significance to the members, for there are the same qualifications for them in both categories. During the campaign the councillor has fewer and more accessible constituents since only the property holders vote for him. Once members are elected, however, all distinction between them vanishes as far as their status and functions in the Legislature are concerned. Some doubts were expressed in 1893 about the possible implications of this arrangement. The Leader of the Opposition feared that "the councillor elected by the property holders will have all the arrogance of a king, and the result will be jealousy and sectionalism,"[6] but such misgivings have proved groundless. From the standpoint of electioneering, the arrangement was in one sense a distinct advantage for some years, for the two-member constituency enabled

---

[1] See also 53 Vic., c. 1; and 56 Vic., c. 1.
[2] 21-22 Geo. V, c. 5.   [3] 24 Vic., c. 34.   [4] 29 Vic., c. 10.
[5] In 1866 and again in 1878 (41 Vic., c. 20) it was provided that a voter could qualify in more than one district in any election, and he might thereupon cast all his votes at one poll. This arrangement was not included in the statutes of 1890 and 1893.
[6] *Assembly Debates*, 1893, p. 135.

the parties to present candidates of different backgrounds. The parties were thus given an opportunity to avoid the awkward consequences which might follow a contest between farmer and lawyer or Catholic and Protestant; this was by no means an unimportant advantage when some of the most controversial political issues were concerned with land and religion.

Although the peculiar structure of the Assembly has remained unchanged since 1893 the franchise has been altered periodically. The principal statutes which set forth the present franchise are the Election Acts of 1922 and 1926 and the Legislative Assembly Act of 1940. These measures provided that voters for councillors were to be male or female British subjects, over twenty-one years of age, not subject to legal incapacity, provided that "such voter or her husband or his wife" owned real estate, freehold or leasehold, to the value of $325, and had been in possession of it for at least six months prior to the election. Voters for assemblymen were to be male or female British subjects over twenty-one years of age, not subject to legal incapacity, who came under one of two of the following categories: (1) resident of the province for at least twelve months, and of the electoral district two months, before the writ of election; (2) owner, occupant, or possessor for at least six months of freehold property of $100.[1] Prior to 1931 clergymen could vote for assemblymen only, but in that year both franchises were extended to clergymen residing in the province who were engaged in pastoral work and had charge of a parish in the district where they claimed to vote.[2] Similar extensions were made in 1919 to persons who had served in the Canadian Expeditionary Force,[3] and in 1946 to persons who had served overseas in the Second World War.[4]

Successive election acts did not give the franchise to women. The Opposition advocated the adoption of woman suffrage during the negotiations of 1892,[5] but the proposal gained few supporters either then or in the ensuing thirty years. In the early 1920's a number of petitions from women's groups were presented to the

[1] 12 Geo. V, c. 5; 16 Geo. V, c. 1.
[2] 21-22 Geo. V, c. 5.   [3] 9-10 Geo. V, c. 12.   [4] 10 Geo. VI, c. 10.
[5] *Assembly Debates*, 1892, pp. 141-2.

Legislature asking for the extension of the franchise to women in provincial elections.¹ By this time women had been given the vote in all the other provinces except Quebec, and the change on the Island was inevitable. The Election Act of 1922 extended the franchise to women and applied to them the same voting qualifications that prevailed for men.²

The major change in the electoral process was the introduction of the secret ballot. Open voting was used for many years despite a number of attempts to introduce the ballot. Indeed one of these efforts was made shortly after the achievement of responsible government.³ The Registration and Electors and Ballot Act was passed in 1877 by the Davies administration in the midst of the violent contests over land, liquor, religion, and union which made the exercise of the franchise at the polls an adventure as well as a duty. The Act provided for the secret ballot and made necessary provision for voters' lists and polling procedure.⁴ Within a few months, however, there was widespread criticism of the expense involved and of alleged manipulation of the electoral machinery, and, although the statute was amended in 1878 to provide for annual revision of the lists by county court judges,⁵ it remained unpopular. Finally the Act was repealed by the Sullivan Government in 1879 on the grounds of expense and irregularity, and open voting was re-established.⁶ Various suggestions for reform were made after the turn of the century, but it was not until 1913 that the secret ballot arrived to stay.⁷

The old practice of restricting the number of office-holders in the Legislature was continued by the Legislature Act of 1893 and carried on thereafter for forty years.⁸ The Island had hardly joined Confederation when a great new intermingling of provincial and federal politics took place. The first Dominion members and sena-

¹See *Assembly Journals*, 1922, p. 82; *ibid.*, 1923, p. 35.
²12 Geo. V, c. 5; see also Catherine Lyle Cleverdon, *The Woman Suffrage Movement in Canada* (Toronto, 1950), pp. 198-208.
³*Assembly Journals*, 1854, p. 130.
⁴40 Vic., c. 20.   ⁵41 Vic., c. 14.   ⁶42 Vic., c. 2.
⁷3 Geo. V, c. 2; *Examiner*, April 8, 14, 1913. Vote by ballot had by then been adopted successfully in civic elections in Souris (1910), in Charlottetown (1911), and in Georgetown (1912).
⁸*Supra*, pp. 96-9.

tors were recruited largely from the local Legislature. Between the sessions of 1873 and 1874 seven members of the Assembly resigned to contest the Island's six seats in the House of Commons, including Speaker Perry, Premier J. C. Pope, and Opposition Leader David Laird.[1] In the same period R. P. Haythorne, Liberal leader in the Legislative Council, resigned upon his appointment to the Senate, but Colonial Secretary T. H. Haviland retained both his provincial portfolio and a senatorship. In 1874 the Assembly passed a bill which provided that no members of Parliament or salaried officials of the Dominion could sit in the local Legislature,[2] but this bill did not pass in the upper house. Meanwhile several members of both houses took salaried offices from the Dominion Government.[3]

The Independence of the General Assembly Act of 1876 finally excluded from the Legislature all senators, members of the House of Commons,[4] persons holding offices of emolument under the Dominion or the province, and, with certain exceptions, persons who "directly or indirectly" held any contract or agreement, or became surety for same, with respect to the provincial public service. But it was provided that the Colonial Secretary, the Attorney-General, the Solicitor-General, and the Commissioner of Public Works could sit if they were elected while holding office. Moreover a member of the Executive Council could resign his portfolio and within one month accept another without vacating his seat in the House.[5] Successive statutes contained similar provisions which changed with the titles of Ministers and the addition or abolition of offices.[6] This procedure, which had been common to all the British governments since the Act of Settlement of 1701, was finally

[1] *Assembly Journals,* 1874, pp. 1, 2.
[2] *Assembly Debates,* 1874, pp. 5, 224-5.
[3] *Examiner,* Feb. 28, 1876.
[4] Members of the provincial Legislature were already excluded from the House of Commons by federal statute. See R. MacGregor Dawson, *The Government of Canada* (Toronto, 1947), p. 387, n. 2.
[5] 39 Vic., c. 2; *Assembly Debates,* 1876, pp. 43-50.
[6] By the Election Act of 1913 and its amendment of 1916, 3 Geo. V, c. 2 and 6 Geo. V, c. 1, the officers who could hold seats after re-election were the Premier and President of the Executive Council, the Provincial Secretary-Treasurer, the Commissioner of Agriculture, the Attorney-General, and the Commissioner of Public Works.

ended on the Island in 1932, one year after similar action in the Dominion,[1] and members of the Assembly are no longer required to run in by-elections when appointed to the Cabinet. Except where otherwise provided by statute, officials other than Cabinet Ministers are still excluded from the Legislature.[2] It is to be noted, however, that where new portfolios are created by statute, or old ones changed, it is still customary to make special provision that the incumbent is eligible to sit in the Legislature.[3]

For some years arrangements for separating local and federal politics also appeared in the franchise. Political conditions in the 1890's made the Liberals especially sensitive on this point, for Premier Arthur Peters and his colleagues noted with dismay the large number of Conservatives who held Dominion posts within the province. The railway men, Peters said, "vote solid Tory every time."[4] In the election of 1891, he told the Assembly, he went to the Bedford station to send a telegram but could not get in because Dominion railway officials had set up a bar room in the station to treat their political friends heading for the nearby polling place.[5] Peters accordingly secured the passage of an act in 1893 which provided that no person could vote who had, within a period of thirty days before election day, been an employee of the Dominion Government, except postmasters in receipt of less than $100 a year, or employees hired temporarily by the day.[6] "The Dominion Government and the Local Government," said the Premier, "shall be absolutely separate one from the other; . . . the Dominion Government, with powers at Ottawa, shall not be able in any way, directly or indirectly, to affect the elections here."[7] This exclusion of Dominion employees was dropped in the election acts of 1922 and 1926, after independence had begun to replace political partisanship in the civil service.

[1]22 Geo. V, c. 3; H. McD. Clokie, *Canadian Government and Politics* (Toronto, 1944), pp. 128-9; Eugene Forsey, *The Royal Power of Dissolution of Parliament in the British Commonwealth* (Oxford, 1943), Appendix D.
[2]Exceptions are the Clerk and law clerk of the Assembly, and the members of the Fishermen's Loan Board, all of whom have occasionally sat in the House. 26 Geo. V, c. 4; 1 Geo. VI, c. 12; 3 Geo. VI, c. 42.
[3]E.g. the Ministers of Education and Public Health, 26 Geo. V, c. 4, and the Minister of Reconstruction, 8 Geo. VI, c. 17.
[4]*Assembly Debates*, 1893, p. 260.   [5]*Ibid.*, p. 261.
[6]56 Vic., c. 2.   [7]*Assembly Debates*, 1893, p. 258.

THE LEGISLATURE   221

One extraordinary restriction on outside influence is, however, still effective. In earlier times politicians from other provinces could exert much pressure upon local politics in well-organized election manœuvres. Sir John Macdonald, for example, participated in the provincial election of 1886 by sending a circular letter among prominent citizens in support of the Sullivan Government to which he was favourable.[1] Visiting campaigners were particularly voluble in matters concerning prohibition and the school question, and such outside participation was considered unduly disturbing in a small province. The Election Act of 1922 accordingly declared that "any person, not being a voter, who resides outside this Province and who, to secure the election of any candidate, canvasses for votes or in any way endeavours to induce voters to vote for any candidate at an election, or to refrain from voting, is guilty of an offence," and penalties are provided for infractions.[2] The way such a regulation can be enforced has not yet been indicated by any charges, although it is reported that several visiting clergymen who campaigned during the prohibition plebiscite of 1948 were silenced by the Premier when he reminded them that they were breaking the law.

The provincial election machinery in each district is under the direction of a returning officer selected for each election and appointed by the Lieutenant-Governor-in-Council. To him the Provincial Secretary sends the writs for the election and from him come the official returns of the result. He is expected not only to supervise the vote, but also to maintain peace and good order during the contest and give a casting vote in case of a tie. He and his assistants must follow an elaborate set of rules contained in the Election Act of 1922 for the conduct of elections.[3]

The candidate for election must be nominated before the returning officer's court, which is held in the county court house on nomination day not more than two weeks prior to the election. He must be proposed and seconded as candidate for councillor or assemblyman by two or more electors of the electoral district who are qualified to vote for him and his name must be duly registered. A

[1]*Patriot*, July 1, 1886.   [2]12 Geo. V, c. 5.   [3]12 Geo. V, c. 5.

candidate does not have to be a resident of the constituency which he contests and non-resident candidates are common. He must pay a deposit of $200 which is returnable to him if he is elected or obtains a number of votes totalling more than half the number cast for the winning candidate. This deposit, which was raised from $10 to $50 in 1946[1] and to $200 in 1948,[2] is designed to discourage "wildcat" candidates whose chances are much less than their desire for publicity. It serves also to emphasize a major defeat, when post-election results advertise that a candidate "lost his deposit." Both the candidate and his agent must submit sworn statements that the former is qualified under the Act. If only one candidate comes forward he is declared by the returning officer to be elected by acclamation. A candidate may subsequently withdraw but he will forfeit his deposit. His death between nomination and election day will necessitate the postponement of the election until a new proclamation and nomination day are arranged.[3]

Disputed elections occur from time to time no matter how elaborate the procedure. Perhaps a close vote will be questioned on the basis of improper counting or the rejection of certain spoilt ballots, or perhaps the entire election proceedings in a district may be disputed on the ground that statutory regulations had not been followed. A recount must be requested within four days of the count itself before a county court judge. The judge, if satisfied that there is some doubt, will arrange a recount in the presence of the candidates or their agents and the election officials, and attempt to ascertain the result of the poll as well as fix costs for the hearing. If the county court judge fails to comply with this procedure, an aggrieved party may make application to a judge of the Supreme Court for an order commanding the county court judge to comply. A hearing is necessary at this stage as well.

Controverted elections involve much more serious disputes, for they concern irregularities or practices of a corrupt nature. Hearing such issues was originally a privilege of Parliament itself, and the colonial legislatures enjoyed it as well. Controverted elections cases, although few in number, were troublesome in Prince Edward Is-

---

[1] 10 Geo. VI, c. 10.   [2] 12 Geo. VI, c. 13.   [3] 12 Geo. V, c. 5, ss. 39-64.

land, particularly in the middle of the nineteenth century when legislative majorities were often slim, corruption was common, and elections were fought with the bitterness which accompanied the major issues of the day. The cases were then tried by a committee of the whole house concerned, with the persons interested absent, the membership in both houses being sufficiently small to make this feasible. Some attempt was made to conduct the proceedings on a fair basis by examining evidence, hearing witnesses, and making a decision along judicial lines, but party feeling was always present and usually dominant. Moreover a complicated controversy would take up much of the time of the members and delay the normal legislative proceedings.[1] The Legislative Council consequently sought to transfer the jurisdiction over these cases to the Supreme Court in 1862. The Assembly, however, would not agree, on the ground that such a step would lower public estimation of the judges by involving them in politics and that "it would be interfering with the privileges of Parliament."[2] The British and Canadian Parliaments transferred such jurisdiction to the courts in 1868 and 1873 respectively, and in 1874 the Island Legislature was prepared to make a similar change. Again the upper house took the lead. This time the Assembly agreed, and an act was passed to give jurisdiction to the Supreme Court and to provide more rigid machinery for the prevention of corrupt practices.[3]

The change proved beneficial, for it freed the Legislature from a difficult duty and led to a more satisfactory handling of specific cases. But the old Assembly was not entirely wrong in its forebodings of 1862, for an unusual dispute in 1901 led to one of the spectacular battles in the Island's constitutional history, which not only concerned party strategy, but also led to an open feud between the Supreme Court and the Legislature. Mr. Justice E. J. Hodgson presided over proceedings involving a controverted election in the Fourth District of Kings in which A. F. Bruce, a Liberal candidate

[1] See 7 Vic., c. 23 as amended by 11 Vic., c. 17.
[2] *Assembly Journals*, 1862, p. 162.
[3] 37 Vic., c. 21; see also *Legislative Council Debates*, 1874, p. 25. Successive statutes of 1890, 1910, 1911, and 1940 amended the original procedure along the lines of similar Dominion acts: 53 Vic., c. 3; 10 Ed. VII, c. 3; 1 Geo. V, c. 2; 4 Geo. VI, c. 15.

and Government supporter, had been declared elected and Murdoch MacKinnon, the Opposition candidate, declared defeated. There had been suspicion of corrupt practice. Hodgson reversed the decision of the returning officer by declaring MacKinnon elected and indicated that several persons whom he named were guilty of corrupt practice and therefore disqualified as electors. At that time the Government was supported by a slim majority of one, and it prevented the new member of the Opposition from taking his seat until the House had had time to examine the judge's report. On a Government motion the report was sent back to Mr. Justice Hodgson for amendment on the ground that disqualification of electors was not part of his duty. The judge defended his report and refused to amend it. His reply to the Speaker is classic:

> There is another difficulty in the matter arising from the different conceptions which the Legislative Assembly and I take of the duties of a Judge. My conviction is that as a Judge I should never in any circumstances receive suggestions regarding a matter pending before me unless in the presence of the parties, and, if possible of their counsel, not even when these suggestions come to me from so august a body as the Legislative Assembly of Prince Edward Island—a body for which, when exercising its Legislative duties I entertain a profound respect; but when that Legislature goes beyond its proper functions, claims the right to direct and command me when and how to frame and amend my judgments and reform my decrees, my answer is that I shall never be a party to such a humiliation of the Judiciary. I emphatically decline to do the bidding of your honorable House and I feel certain that, to reasonable people, when considering the matter apart from the necessities of political expediencies, the wonder will be, not that I refused, but that I was ever asked to do such a thing.[1]

In the resulting debate in the House, Premier Peters declared that the judge had disqualified and degraded citizens who had been guilty of nothing more than treating friends to liquor, that the men in question were not guilty of corrupt practice, and that he would not permit them to be recorded as such on the rolls of the House. "Mr. Justice Hodgson," he said, "has to remember, that though he is high, the Legislature of this Province stands higher, paramount

[1] *Examiner,* March 18, 1902.

and higher, much higher."¹ He then announced that the judge's report would not be adopted, but that the new member would be given his seat by special statute. Opposition Leader Mathieson retorted that such legislation would be a whitewashing act passed to shield the political friends of the Government from the consequences of their irregularities. Since neither the Government nor the judge would yield, the new member was admitted by the extraordinary device of passing a special statute to permit him to take his seat.²

At the present time controverted elections are dealt with under the provincial Controverted Elections Act of 1940.³ Disputes are heard by one Supreme Court judge from whom an appeal lies to the Supreme Court *in banco*, and penalties are provided for candidates and other persons who are found guilty under the Act.⁴

In earlier times members could not resign, for the English rule in this regard applied to the colonies in the absence of statutory provision to the contrary.⁵ In 1856 it was provided that a member could resign by notification to the Speaker in a letter duly certified by a notary public.⁶ A member may now resign during the session

¹*Ibid.*
²2 Ed. VII, c. 1; see also *Assembly Journals*, 1902, pp. 6-18; *Examiner*, March 13, 18, 1902; and *Canadian Annual Review*, 1902, p. 64.
³4 Geo. VI, c. 15.
⁴See also 12 Geo. V, c. 5, s. 206. For an example of such proceedings see the trial concerning the election of Hon. James H. Cummiskey in 3rd Queens in 1905. *Examiner*, Oct. 25, 27, 31, Nov. 4, 23, 1905; and *Patriot* of the same dates.
⁵A member of the British House of Commons cannot resign, although actually he may forfeit his seat instead, by taking a nominal office of emolument under the Crown, such as the Stewardship of the Chiltern Hundreds, and then resigning it. See F. A. Ogg, *English Government and Politics* (New York, 1936), p. 305.
⁶19 Vic., c. 21. This arrangement did not include procedure by which the Speaker himself could resign. The omission was not noticed until 1873 when Speaker Stanislaus F. Perry resigned from the Assembly on his being elected to the House of Commons. He did so by notifying the Lieutenant-Governor, and the question later arose as to whether the Speaker could resign and consequently as to whether he could take a seat in the federal Parliament. If Perry could not resign, a new Speaker could not be elected in his absence, while he would be incurring penalties for illegally sitting in the House of Commons. The Government's law officers advised that the statute made no provision for such a resignation, and, therefore, the Speaker came under the English practice and could not resign. No act had yet been passed barring federal members from the local house, so he could not forfeit his seat. The difficulty was settled by the Assembly which, when it met in 1874, declared Perry's seat vacant and thereupon elected a new Speaker. The Dominion Parliament cleared Perry's status by passing a special act for his protection which voided any penalties which might be applied to him. *Assembly Journals*, 1874, Appendix A; "Parliamentary Debates, 1873," scrapbook in Library of Parliament, pp. 9, 71.

simply by giving notice from his place in the House, or he may address and have delivered to the Speaker a declaration of intent to resign made before two witnesses. In the period between the election and the commencement of the first session, when a Speaker has not yet been elected, such a declaration is made to any two members of the Assembly and the same procedure applies in other instances where there is no Speaker, or where the member wishing to resign is himself the Speaker. A member must, of course, forfeit his seat if he takes an office of emolument under the Crown or a contract with the Crown, for which no special provision is made by statute.[1] In all cases the recipients of such declarations must notify the Lieutenant-Governor, who in turn must, within a week, issue a writ for an election to fill the vacant seat.[2]

The required notice to the Governor is very important, for delay in submitting such notice "forthwith," as statute puts it, may keep a seat vacant indefinitely. A case in point arose in 1900. When the session opened that year the Farquharson Government and the Opposition had the same number of supporters in the House, and the Government retained power only by the casting vote of the Speaker. One member, Mr. Wise, wishing to test the opinion of his constituents on his change from the Liberal to the Conservative party, had previously submitted his resignation on condition that it be sent to the Governor immediately so that the writ for a by-election could be issued forthwith. The resignation was not sent to the Governor and the writ was not issued, a significant omission at a time when the parties were even in the House. Wise, pleading the condition, took his seat, and the question arose as to whether he was still a member. It was debated so fiercely that the Speaker ordered his expulsion, the Sergeant-at-Arms attempted to remove him, complete disorder led to an uproar and an exchange of blows in the House, and Mr. Wise had to be locked in the Speaker's room

---

[1]See, for example, the case of Dougald Currie, *Examiner,* April 14, 1904, *Assembly Journals,* 1904, pp. 24-6 and of H. J. Palmer, *Examiner,* May 29, 1904, and *Canadian Annual Review,* 1904, p. 333.

[2]12 Geo V, c. 5, ss. 20-6; 4 Geo. VI, c. 37, ss. 28-31. See also *Assembly Debates,* 1887, p. 57. An act of 1887 for the first time provided for resignations between an election and the first session of the House.

under guard until the House rose.¹ There is still no time limit within which a resignation must be submitted to the Governor for issuance of a writ, so that the choice of the date for a by-election rests with the Speaker or, actually, with the Government itself.

Statute also provides that a member automatically vacates his seat if he is absent without the leave of the Assembly for one whole session and the first day of the following session.² This provision was used to advantage by Frederick Peters who had left the province in 1897, was absent in British Columbia during the session of 1898, but returned to sit for the first day of the session of 1899 simply to hold his seat and prevent a by-election at a time when party strength was almost even in the House. It should be noted in this connection that there is no residence qualification for members, and nothing to prevent a member from leaving the Island and returning periodically to sit in the House.³

The indemnities of members of the Assembly are commensurate with their functions. Prior to Confederation the Speaker of the House and the President of the Legislative Council each received $300 per annum, while other members of both houses received $100 and travelling expenses.⁴ In 1873 these payments were raised to $500 and $200 respectively. It was not until the 1920's that frequent demands for increases resulted in an indemnity of $400 per annum with an extra $200 for the Speaker and an extra $600 for the Leader of the Opposition.⁵ The present remuneration for members is $700 indemnity and $300 expense allowance, for the Leader of the Opposition $1,500 indemnity and $500 expense allowance, and for the Speaker $1,100 indemnity and $500 expense allowance.⁶ While this scale of remuneration is small, it is based on a session of

¹*Examiner,* May 10, 16, 1900. A spectacular dispute concerning Premier Farquharson and Messrs. Wise and Pineau over the alleged bribing of Pineau while a member of the Opposition was one of the highlights of the session of 1900.
²4 Geo. VI, c. 37, s. 27.
³For instance Professor Alexander MacPhail, a resident of Kingston, Ont. sat in the Island House for several years. He had a summer home in the province.
⁴See *Assembly Journals,* 1872, 2nd session, p. 143.
⁵In 1920 the sessional allowance was set at $500, 10-11 Geo. V, c. 7; in 1924 it was cut to $400, 14 Geo. V, c. 15.
⁶11 Geo. VI, c. 25; 14 Geo. VI, c. 17.

only a few weeks' duration and the fact that, as a rule, membership in the House will make comparatively little encroachment on the members' regular earning power.

The term of the Legislature, which was set at four years in 1893, was increased in 1932 to five years;[1] but the House rarely sits the full period. The date of dissolution and that of the subsequent general election will largely be dictated by the political situation. A Government will endeavour to choose the right moment to dissolve so as to fight the election at a time and on issues which it believes will be most favourable. It will therefore not willingly permit the term to run too close to the statutory limit. Thus after a term of from three and a half to four years the members begin to show signs of warming up for a contest and the Premier scans the political weather bulletins with keen interest. Dissolution may also take place if the Government is defeated in the House itself when a series of by-elections turns a small majority into a minority, or when a vote of want of confidence is passed.[2] On such occasions a Premier may himself secure a dissolution from the Governor and try to reinforce his power in an election, or he may resign in favour of the Leader of the Opposition, who, after attaining power, may advise the dissolution.[3] In other words the term of the Legislature depends not merely on the five-year allotment of time, but as well upon the functioning of the House itself, relations within the Cabinet and the political parties, and the prevailing political circumstances in the country as a whole.

The House must meet at least once each year and no more than twelve months may intervene between sessions.[4] The session usually takes place in the early spring and runs for approximately six weeks. Its length varies very little from year to year and depends on the amount of business to be done and the nature of the discussions which take place upon it. Debate may be prolonged when controversial issues, such as prohibition or Dominion-provincial relations, are featured, or when the Government majority is small and

[1] 22 Geo. V, c. 3.
[2] E.g., the Davies Government resigned in 1879 after a vote of want of confidence.
[3] E.g., the resignation of Neil MacLeod in 1889.
[4] 4 Geo. VI, c. 37, s. 10.

THE LEGISLATURE 229

the Opposition alert and critical. On the other hand the session is likely to be short if the Government majority is very great or if there is little business to be done. The extreme example was the session of 1912, when, because of a 28-2 Conservative majority, 54 bills were passed with little discussion and without a single division.[1] A second session is occasionally held in the same year to deal with an emergency. In August, 1916, for instance, a special two-day session was held to vote revenue for war purposes; in September, 1935 the House met for one day to provide for exceptional expenditures; in September, 1950 a one-day session was held to discuss the effect of the railway strike on Prince Edward Island.

PROCEDURE

The procedure of the Legislature has been developed in such a way as to make the general features of parliamentary democracy appropriate to the limited amount of public business in the small province. It has followed British and Canadian precedents in a general way, but many practices which are accepted elsewhere have proved unsuitable and have required substantial alteration, while others have been retained for the sake of tradition although their usefulness is obviously limited.

The legislative chamber itself is little more than a large board room in size, and the debates among its thirty members are easily heard. The Speaker sits at one end on a throne which also serves for the Governor when he attends. The Clerk and his assistants sit in front of the Speaker. In most chambers the Government supporters sit to the right of the chair and the Opposition to the left. In the Island House this arrangement is reversed.[2] A gallery for visitors extends around three sides of the House, while on the fourth, behind the chair, portraits of former Speakers look benignly down upon the deliberations. The entire setting is appropriately

[1]*Examiner,* May 2, 1912.
[2]Several reasons have been put forward as to how such an arrangement began. The most plausible rests on the fact that the Clerk's office and the old legislative library were placed on the left side next to the chamber when the building was constructed and these rooms provided facilities for smoking and chatting. Early Governments therefore found it more convenient to sit on the left, which is also the sunny side, and their successors never changed even after the library was moved from the building.

arranged to fit the proceedings of this small daughter of the Mother of Parliaments.

The House has the usual array of officials who have duties which are similar to those in other legislatures. However, the short session and the limited business render these duties comparatively light and require the services of only part-time officers who need not have extensive experience. Indeed the junior posts are often held by civil servants and even by members.

The Speaker is chosen according to the traditional customs of the British Parliament. After an election and prior to the opening of the first session of a new Legislature, the Government selects a nominee for the speakership. When the members assemble the Clerk is in the chair. A commissioner in the person of a judge of the Supreme Court is present, and, upon the presentation to him by the Clerk of the returning officer's election returns, he swears in the members. The Clerk then reads a letter from the Governor's private secretary indicating that His Honour will open the House at 3 o'clock. Two members on the Government side, not necessarily Ministers, move and second a motion that a certain member take the chair as Speaker. The person they name is the Government's previously chosen nominee, and he is accepted without a vote. The Clerk then declares him elected, and the Premier and another Minister take him from his place and conduct him to the chair. In earlier times the election of the presiding officer was always contested, each side nominating a candidate.[1] As time went on the Opposition ceased to present a candidate, for in most cases the Government's nominee was assured of the post, and a battle over the election was not always the most cordial overture to what was supposed to be a dignified and independent tenure of office. The new Speaker takes the chair amid applause from both sides, and in a few dignified and humble words thanks the House for the high honour it has conferred upon him. In case of the death or resignation of the Speaker a successor is elected in the same manner.[2]

[1] In one such instance, in 1859, the House failed to elect a Speaker in the face of a slim Government majority and it had to be dissolved. *Supra*, p. 97.
[2] 12 Geo. V, c. 5, s. 2 (3).

There are no recognized rules in the Government's choice of a Speaker. The incumbent does not remain from term to term, as in England, nor does the position rotate among certain groups, as do the speakerships between French-speaking and English-speaking personnel in the Dominion Parliament. There is no tendency to regard him as automatically returnable in his constituency; the Speaker has been defeated on several occasions, 1935 and 1947 being cases in point. The Premier may perhaps assign the post to one who has just missed being appointed to the Cabinet, or to a representative of an interest group that craves, but does not get, recognition in the selection of Ministers. The speakership is not recognized as a stepping stone to Cabinet office and few Speakers have attained official prominence beyond their terms in the chair.[1] It has not been considered necessary for the appointee to have a great knowledge of rules of procedure, for such rules as are recognized are not elaborate. He should, of course, learn as much as he can about procedure after his appointment, otherwise his limitations will have a serious effect on the Assembly's proceedings.

The House must also select a deputy Speaker to preside in the absence of the Speaker. He also is nominated by the Government and approved by the members.[2] Before 1904 there was no such officer, but a statute provided that when the Speaker was absent the House could select a "temporary" Speaker.[3] In that year the House was empowered to appoint a deputy Speaker "at any time,"[4] but the occasions for using the services of such an official were not frequent, and often the appointment was permitted to lapse. But in 1931 the House, while in committee, was put in an awkward position when the Speaker was suddenly taken ill and had to leave the chamber. There was no deputy Speaker, the House could not come out of committee, nor could a new Speaker be elected unless the old one died or resigned. The Speaker, unable to leave his bed, had to resign the next day in order that the proceedings could continue.[5]

[1]There are, of course, exceptions. The Speaker was appointed to the Cabinet in 1949.
[2]12 Geo. V, c. 5, s. 2 (5); 4 Geo. VI, c. 37, s. 6.
[3]56 Vic., c. 1.   [4]4 Ed. VII, c. 1; also 12 Geo. V, c. 5.
[5]*Patriot*, "Proceedings of the Legislative Assembly for April 15, 1931"; *Canadian Annual Review*, 1930-1, p. 221.

Since then a deputy Speaker has been regularly chosen and there is a further provision that in the absence of both the Speaker and the deputy Speaker the House may elect an acting Speaker.[1] The House also appoints a Sergeant-at-Arms, law clerk, messengers, and door keepers at the beginning of each session. The Government's nominees are now accepted as a matter of form, although in former times lively debates occasionally featured the filling of these posts.[2] The Clerk of the House and assistant clerks are the only officials whom the House itself does not appoint. They are named by the Governor-in-Council, during pleasure, "either as permanent or temporary clerk or clerks."[3] It has already been noted that members of the House have at times served as Clerk or law clerk with salary and have been allowed to retain their seats.[4]

The position of the Speaker is one of great dignity and authority.[5] His chief duties are to preside over the deliberations of the House, maintain order, and give a casting vote. He is supposed to be an impartial chairman during sittings although he may participate in party activities outside the chamber. The Speaker may be called upon to give a ruling on a question of procedure, and his decision is final unless it is overruled upon appeal to the House. In this respect the Island Assembly conforms to the practice prevailing elsewhere.[5] An unusual feature of the Assembly is the absence of a mace, the traditional symbol of Mr. Speaker's authority. There is

[1] 4 Geo. VI, c. 37, s. 8.
[2] Even the choice of a chaplain was sometimes keenly contested. In 1863, for instance, the choice was between two clergymen, Messrs. Sutherland and Jenkins, and the former won the post. When Mr. Jenkins' son, Dr. John T. Jenkins, met two of his fellow members next day he accused them of voting against his father and assaulted one of them. A fight resulted, and the offending doctor was committed to the custody of the Sergeant-at-Arms until he apologized. *Assembly Journals*, 1863, pp. 10-32. There is now no chaplain in the House. [3] 12 Geo. V, c. 5. [4] 26 Geo. V, c. 4. *Supra*, p. 175.
[5] On one occasion Donald Farquharson, supported by Frederick Peters, criticized certain election proceedings by noting that there were 44 Paddy McQuaids on one of the voters' lists. Speaker Patrick Blake objected to this remark as a reflection on the name and an insinuation that it is only the Paddies that will "readily multiply their votes." Peters apologized but gave solemn assurance that he had no intention "of insulting Mr. Speaker or any others of his nationality." *Assembly Debates*, 1890, pp. 270-2. See also Mr. Speaker Cullen and Hon. J. A. Campbell, *Guardian*, Feb. 29, 1946.
[6] Upon one unique occasion, however, Mr. Speaker went far beyond the customary limits and gave at the request of the House a judicial decision upon the constitutionality of legislation. In 1921 the House was discussing the vesting of titles to certain church lands, and decided that since the matter was a

no Speaker's procession. At 3 o'clock Mr. Speaker in a robe and black silk topper, not a tri-cornered hat, comes from his chamber behind the chair; if the members are ready, he opens the day's proceedings, if not, he waits until an opportune moment.[1] His taking or leaving the chair alone indicate sittings of the House or of committee.

After the House has chosen its Speaker the session is ready to be opened by the Lieutenant-Governor who arrives in state accompanied by his aides-de-camp. Upon completing the usual inspection of the guard of honour, the Governor enters the building and, preceded by the Sergeant-at-Arms, who acts as Usher of the Black Rod on such occasions—this unusual combination of offices probably occurred with the abolition of the two-chamber system—bangs the floor three times. An official inside opens the door and is told that His Honour the Lieutenant-Governor seeks admission. When the door swings open the Governor proceeds to the chair which had been vacated by the Speaker a short time before.[2] The Governor, unlike the King and the Governor-General, is not accompanied by his wife on such occasions. His Honour reads the Speech from the Throne, which is always prepared in advance by the Government, and in which he gives a brief summary of some of the activities and proposals of "my government," reminds the members of the harvests the province has enjoyed in the past year and

constitutional question it should be referred to the Speaker for his advice. Mr. Speaker, C. G. Duffy, obliged with an elaborate opinion upon the Legislature's jurisdiction under the British North America Act and a decision that "any Act passed by this House vesting this land is absolute and there is no authority to override it." Decision of the Speaker on the rights of the Legislature in re "An Act to Incorporate the Trustees of the Canoe Cove Presbyterian Church in connection with the Church of Scotland," *Assembly Journals*, 1920, pp. 65-6. Such a decision by the Speaker is exceptional if not unprecedented, for, says Beauchesne, "The Speaker will not give a decision upon a constitutional question nor decide a question of law, though the same may be raised on a point of order or privilege"; A. Beauchesne, *Parliamentary Rules and Forms* (Ottawa, 1943), section 116, p. 56. When a similar case arose in the House of Commons in 1903, the Speaker refused to give a decision. *Canada, House of Commons, Journals*, vol. XXXVIII, 1903, pp. 577-8.

[1]The spectacle of Mr. Speaker waiting patiently in the chair until the members, particularly Cabinet Ministers, choose to take their seats has certainly not been conducive to the maintenance of his authority or of the dignity of the House. Some Speakers prefer to wait in the Speaker's chamber until the Sergeant-at-Arms advises that a quorum is present.

[2]While awaiting the Governor's arrival, the House on one occasion killed time by discussing means of depriving His Honour of his official residence.

of some of the world's current events, and invokes divine guidance upon their deliberations during the session.[1] After completing the task His Honour leaves the chamber and rejoins his parade for the return to Government House, while the Speaker takes the chair once more and the House commences the session's business. A similar ceremony occurs at the end of each session when the Governor may give royal assent to legislation and prorogues the House.

This procedure is followed at the opening of each session. If a new House is meeting for the first time, an additional formality occurs before the reading of the Speech from the Throne. The Speaker-elect addresses the Governor informing him of his selection as Speaker, seeking his Honour's approval thereof, and requesting on behalf of the House "all their ancient and accustomed rights and privileges; especially freedom from arrest, freedom of speech in debate, access to your Honour when they think the public service requires it, and that the most favorable construction be put upon all their proceedings." These His Honour grants without demur, "in as full and ample a manner as they have at any time heretofore been granted and allowed."

These privileges, which have already been described in detail in a previous chapter,[2] were carried on from session to session by custom and statute, and, although their limitations are often vague, the authority of the Island Legislature to invoke them has apparently never been seriously challenged by the Dominion Government.[3] The collective privileges of the House which enable it to regulate its own procedure, maintain order and decorum, and commit persons for contempt, and the individual privileges of members giving them freedom of speech and immunity from arrest in civil causes, have generally been respected and periodically enforced. For instance, committing members to the custody of the Sergeant-at-Arms for contempt and reprimanding outsiders at the bar for disrespect were common in the early years. In at least two instances

[1] On one occasion Governor Dalton, then aged and infirm, took the chair, but requested his private secretary to read the speech.
[2] *Supra*, pp. 43-51.
[3] Local statutes giving privileges to the Legislature existed long before Confederation, and the Dominion Government has not disallowed any Island statutes giving privileges although it has done so in the newer provinces. See Dawson, *The Government of Canada,* pp. 397-404.

the House has censured the press for taking liberties with its dignity,[1] and it has also removed one of its own officials for drunkenness in the chamber.[2] Until 1913 privileges were based on "ancient usage and the laws of the land," and they were never clearly enumerated, but in that year the Legislative Assembly Privileges Act was passed which provided that the House, its committees, and its members were to have the same privileges, immunities, and powers as the House of Commons of Canada and its committees and members.[3] By section 18, as amended, of the British North America Act, the privileges of the Canadian House must not exceed those of the British House of Commons, and, because of the provincial act, this limitation is made effective for the Island Assembly as well.[4]

The procedure of the Legislature is simple and informal. The fact that there are only thirty members itself dictates simplicity and renders elaborate procedure both unnecessary and cumbersome. The small parliamentary club greatly magnifies the importance of personal characteristics and relationships. The members usually know one another well and this intimacy facilitates co-operation even among political rivals. It is not unusual for members on either side to be relatives, close friends, or law partners, and on at least one occasion a Leader of the Opposition has been closer to the ear of a Premier than some of the latter's own colleagues. The atmosphere of informality which has resulted from such connections has always been a feature of the Island's Legislature. On occasion, however, the same characteristic may lead to unusual rivalry and bitterness, as was exemplified in the days of the land question and religious issues when the personal relations among members frequently dominated the proceedings.

The significance of procedure depends greatly upon the political division of the members. A sweeping victory at the polls will make the House little more than a formal gathering of the Government caucus, while, on the other hand, a close vote at a general election

[1] *Assembly Journals*, 1863, p. 98; *ibid.*, 1921, pp. 70-1.
[2] *Examiner*, April 25, 1904.
[3] 3 Geo. V, c. 1; see also 4 Geo. VI, c. 37, ss. 36-48.
[4] This limitation can, of course, be altered by the Dominion through constitutional amendment, and by the province by a change in the local statute.

may divide the personnel almost equally with the result that each member may be a legislative majority in himself, and by-elections almost as significant as a general one. Such extremes in strength or weakness on either side are common in a small parliament and the whole character of the proceedings is altered accordingly. Much of the informality of recent years is partially explained by the fact that governmental majorities have been consistently large and oppositions weak and ineffective.

Another major factor tending to keep the legislative machinery simple is the tremendous power of the executive in relation to the House. As an earlier chapter has indicated, the Cabinet is almost one-third the size of the House, a fact which magnifies its control over the proceedings. A similar situation exists in the Government caucus. Each party has its caucus, composed of all its members in the House, which discusses much of the business of the Legislature in great detail before it reaches the floor. In a larger parliament the executive is a small minority in caucus, and leading and conciliating the caucus is one of its vital tasks. On the Island a nine-man Cabinet is a large part, if not a majority, of a Government caucus of fifteen or more, and the Ministers may readily control its proceedings, provided, however, that this advantage is not upset by disregard for Cabinet solidarity. The principle of Cabinet responsibility to the Legislature is much affected by this situation. The familiar practice by which Ministers must defend and explain their policies and actions on the floor of the House and by which the Opposition may criticize and present alternatives is given full scope in the Island's Assembly. Moreover the private members have the usual opportunities of expressing their wishes. But the procedure, as compared with that in a large legislature, can be readily controlled by a dominant Cabinet. The significance of debate is lessened proportionally, and the passage of government bills facilitated accordingly.

The short session and the professional activities of the members also effect the procedure of the Legislature. The sessional indemnity and the amount of public business have not been sufficient to prompt the members to prolong their absence from their occupations by unnecessarily lengthening the session. Many members live in Charlottetown and the others are at most only a few hours distant from their homes. Consequently they are able to regard their legislative duties as a part-time occupation to be performed with appropriate despatch. Moreover in such a small province all members, including the Ministers, are unusually close to the people, and, therefore, the time of the House which elsewhere is devoted to the expression of public opinion is substantially reduced.

The formalities of legislation are virtually the same as those which prevail in similar chambers elsewhere.[1] The debate on the address in reply to the Speech from the Throne and the budget debate are the main forensic extravaganzas of the session wherein all members from the Premier and Opposition Leader down express a miscellany of ideas, suggestions, comments, praise, and criticisms upon a variety of topics. Bills proceed through the House in the usual stages, the first reading or introduction, the second reading or discussion of the principle, the committee stage or examination of details, the third reading where the bill is passed, and finally assent by the Lieutenant-Governor. In the vast majority of cases, this procedure is all that is required. Nor does it vary to any significant degree in respect to public, private, or financial bills, save that the last must be introduced by a Minister of the Crown.[2] However, there is often an extraordinary informality and elasticity in the process, of which the passage of the Prohibition Act of 1945 is an example.[3] Where Ministers have criticized the departmental estimates of their colleagues, condemned their own Government for extravagance, introduced Government bills and changed them entirely in one stage or other, and sponsored a number of other equally unusual practices, it is impossible to say that there is any definite, formal set of recognized rules, other than the above skeleton procedure. Once again, the important contributory causes are the small House, the brief session, and the very modest legislative programme.

The same may be said to an even greater degree for the rules of order and decorum.[4] The control of a thirty-man House is generally a much simpler matter than that of a large chamber, and, despite

---

[1] See *Rules of the Legislature of Prince Edward Island* (Charlottetown, n.d.).   [2] *Ibid.*, rule 40.   [3] *Supra*, p. 193.
[4] "We have in this House rules and regulations," a Minister is reported as saying in 1951, "but they are being broken indiscriminately." *Patriot*, March 30, 1951.

the rules, a high degree of informality is inevitable. The House and the Speaker have thus been exceptionally forgiving in some instances which elsewhere would probably have raised serious objections. There is no Hansard in the Island Legislature and its *Journals* give a very inadequate outline of its debates. Members, therefore, need not fear the publication of irregular banter in an official record.[1] A great deal depends upon the Speaker. A firm chairman can usually maintain strict order, while a weak one often finds control slipping out of his hands.

This casual attitude to rules can easily be changed by resorting to rule 65 which states that "in all unprovided cases the rules, usage and forms of the House of Commons of the Dominion of Canada as in force at the time shall be followed." Indeed the House may even invent some procedure of its own which, unusual as it may be, can be applied to some extraordinary circumstance. A case in point was the "naming" of Opposition Leader J. H. Bell in 1916 for saying that the Government had falsified certain accounts. Premier Mathieson moved that the offender be named and the House agreed by a vote. The Speaker then named Mr. Bell for "having used unparliamentary language." That was all; Mr. Bell remained in his seat and the debate resumed.[2] This use of what is elsewhere the most powerful disciplinary weapon of the Speaker as a Government tactic for gently chastising a member[3] indicates clearly how the local Legislature has made and interpreted its rules to suit its own particular needs or to compensate for lack of knowledge of proper procedure.[4]

The significance of committees of the House is another example of traditional parliamentary practice which has not proved effective.

Legislative standing committees are usually appointed, in theory at least, for special discussion on specified topics or for the per-

[1]There was an official Hansard as well as a *Journal* for both the House of Assembly and Legislative Council up to 1893 when the one-house system was adopted. Since then the *Journal* is the sole official record. Both the *Guardian* and the *Patriot* report the proceedings, and for this service the Legislature now votes $250 each session to each newspaper.
[2]*Assembly Journals*, May 2, 1916, pp. 95-6.
[3]In the Canadian House of Commons, for example, the Speaker names a member only after the most extreme provocation. The member is then escorted from the House by the Sergeant-at-Arms, and the House determines an appropriate punishment.
[4]See *Patriot,* March 30, 1951, for examples.

formance of certain supervisory functions, in order to take some load off the main body to expedite business. There are approximately a dozen standing committees: Agriculture, Public Accounts, Standing Rules and Orders, Private Bills, Printing and Binding the Journals, Legislative Library, Engrossing Bills, Revising the Journals, Contingent Accounts, Fox Industry and Fisheries, and Public Health. All of these are empowered "to examine and inquire into all such matters and things as may be referred to them by the House, and to report from time to time their observations and opinions thereon, with power to send for persons, papers and records."[1] Some have seven members and a quorum of four, while others usually have five members and a quorum of three. The majority in each committee is of Government members, and some include one or two Ministers. The Opposition is represented on each according to its strength in the House.

Actually these committees do virtually nothing. They rarely meet, and generally no effective work is either assigned to them or expected from them. In recent years the committees on Contingent Accounts, Public Accounts, and Private Bills are the only ones which have functioned at all. The first of these meets once or twice a session to deal with sundry items in connection with House expenses. The public accounts committee, although it meets each session, has become an anomaly in a Legislature which itself is quite able to examine the small expenditures involved. The private bills committee meets once each session, examines the private bills—there are usually very few—and recommends the fees to be charged. For all essential purposes the standing committee system in the Island Legislature is an anachronism, although at the beginning of each new term the House faithfully sets up the committees as a concession to tradition.

The chief reason why the need for such committees is not great is the fact that the House is itself the size of a committee. Most matters are readily discussed by the Committee of the Whole, which is the House sitting with a private member in the chair. In this capacity the members discuss any matters which have been referred to them by the House such as the estimates of particular

[1] *Assembly Journals,* 1940, p. 18.

departments and other financial matters, special subjects brought forward by petition, or the examination of bills which have received first and second reading. In dealing with special matters with respect to legislation or petitions, the House in committee may hear and interrogate petitioners and witnesses at the bar. There is no attempt to distinguish, as at Ottawa, between committee of ways and means and committee of supply, nor is the elaborate financial procedure of the House of Commons followed at Charlottetown, for the small House and the limited budget make these quite unnecessary. Much of the most effective work of the House is done in Committee of the Whole. Consequently there is not much left by way of effective discussion and action for the standing committees after the House and the House in Committee of the Whole, not to speak of the Cabinet, the government departments, and the party caucus, have already sifted the wheat from the chaff.

The same is true of special committees. A special temporary committee may be appointed to report upon some particular topic or problem, but these are now very rare. Their functions of investigation, just like the supervisory functions of standing committees, could hardly be extensive when the House sits for only six weeks in the year. Moreover the same reasons which prevent members from devoting too much time to debates discourage them from seeking extensive committee work—the small indemnity, the demands of their professions, and the limited amount of public business. There are no doubt many local problems which could be investigated by such bodies if more time and remuneration were available. Yet the possibilities in this respect can perhaps be more readily met by fuller use of civil servants and Ministers without Portfolio. After all the traditional purpose of committees is to perform efficiently such functions as the parent body is too large to handle and for which there is no other effective machinery. The theory of legislative committees on Prince Edward Island, however, meets the basic fact that the parent body is itself small and other parts of the government can be readily used.

The small size of the Prince Edward Island Legislature need not impair its dignity, nor does the simple procedure necessarily reflect upon its efficiency. Informal debate and flexible rules, taken in conjunction with the small membership and the limited functions, may contribute greatly to the acceleration of business. Like any other legislature, it reflects the qualities of its members, and the latter are sufficiently diversified to provide a share of both respectability and mischief, of ability and incompetence, and of common sense and nonsense.

CHAPTER XI

POLITICAL PARTIES

THE POLITICS of Prince Edward Island, like those of most other provinces in the Dominion, have been motivated by the rivalry of "Liberal" and "Conservative" parties. The general structure and functions of these groups have been fashioned after those of others elsewhere, but many of their characteristics reflect the unique peculiarities of their local setting.

Previous chapters have described the beginnings of political parties, and at this point their early history need only be summarized briefly. The first political factions appeared on the Island during the struggles between the colonial Governors and their relatives and rivals, and from the very beginning the relations between landlords and tenants classified the early colonists into opposing groups. But they were factions, and not organized political parties in the modern sense. They sprang up and faded away as the personnel of government changed or as passing issues were settled. It was constitutional reform that gave direction to the development of organized political parties. The demand for, and resistance to, changes in government fostered reform and conservative elements. The reformers sought the solution of the land question, the transfer of effective power from the Governor to the Council and from both to the Assembly, and, finally, responsible government. The conservatives were in two groups. Some resisted change in favour of the status quo or enjoyed power which they were determined to keep—the political diehards and their followers and many influential landowners and their agents. Others were moderate conservatives, or conservative reformers, who wanted gradual change and unhurried progress, and who emphasized institutional maturity before reform. The 1830's saw the consequent rise of the "Conservative" and "Liberal" groups which, in the long struggles of these and following years, had opportunity to develop from factions to organized parties. While constitutional change prompted their rise, they, in turn, were necessary to its success.

The achievement of responsible government brought the Liberals to office in 1851 and placed the Conservatives in opposition. The former enjoyed for a time the prestige of their victory; the latter gradually became accustomed to the new situation and conscious of their part in making it work thenceforth. But this development had scarcely got under way when disrupting forces appeared to shatter the nice distribution of public men between two coherent parties. The land system produced much ill feeling and at times threatened the very foundations of law and order. The problem of denominational schools involved the Protestants and Roman Catholics in a bitter feud which took years to settle and which moderation and common sense could readily have avoided. "Old party lines are broken," said Louis Davies, "old party ties have been severed. It is now a question not of men, not of party, but of principle."[1] The Catholic hierarchy took the same view: "No matter what ties may bind a man, or a party, they ought to be broken, if necessary, to obtain the right we seek."[2] While politics effervesced with these issues, the question of federal union classified still further the politicians and the voters.[3] It is not surprising, then, that during the two decades, the 1860's and the 1870's, in which these problems were most significant, public men changed their political allegiance and personal loyalties with the many demands made upon them, Governments were weak and short-lived, and the two political parties became unsteady and unnatural coalitions of crusading interests motivated by temporary expediencies rather than political comradeship. After this stormy period had passed the Conservatives and Liberals began all over again their development along party rather than factional lines.

The break-up of the coalition Government in 1879[4] marked the beginning of the modern period in Island politics. The issues of land, religion, and union had abated, and party strategy replaced factional intrigue. The electorate was composed of many elements,

---

[1] Charlottetown *Patriot*, July 29, 1876.
[2] Pastoral letter from Archbishops and Bishops of the Ecclesiastical Province of Halifax to the Clergy and Laity, *Patriot*, Feb. 28, 1874.
[3] For details of the Confederation issue, see chapter vi.
[4] *Supra*, pp. 187-8.

and the parties now adjusted themselves so as to reflect as many of them as possible. The change saw the rise to power of the Conservative party under W. W. Sullivan, a former Liberal Minister of the Crown, and the leader of the Catholic group in the school issue. His group of colleagues, which in Opposition had consisted entirely of Catholics, now included a large number of Protestants who broke away from the Davies fold in the dying days of the coalition. Thus the Conservatives once more combined different elements under one party, and, largely because of this fact, they won an overwhelming victory at the polls in 1879. The Liberals were disorganized for the time being, for their leader had led the coalition and they were blamed for its troubles, and the Catholics were not as quick to change to the Liberal side as Protestants to the Conservative. Consequently it took the Liberals twelve years to secure the reins of office.

Participation in federal politics also strengthened the local parties. New alliances and broader questions attracted the Island's public men and drew their attention from local contentious issues. Henceforth the bitter personal and group conflict was gradually displaced by less disrupting, but more important controversies over trade, communications, and finance.

The Conservatives had a head start on their opponents in the formation of federal alliances. Prior to union Sir John Macdonald had made a number of close friends among Island Conservatives, the Popes and Colonel John H. Gray in particular, and when the Dominion Government was negotiating with the province between 1867 and 1873 he turned these friendships to political advantage. The Liberals under Haythorne and Laird had little or no contact with their namesakes at Ottawa. When in power they had to deal with Macdonald, and they did not react kindly to the criticism of the federal Liberals that the "better terms" to the Island were too favourable. Consequently in 1873 the Ottawa Conservatives were preparing to welcome to their party both Conservatives and Liberals from the Island. They were sure of the local Conservatives, and Macdonald was advised by Sir Robert Hodgson, then Administrator, and Sir Charles Tupper, who had visited Charlottetown, that the Liberals would join him as well.[1]

The "Pacific Scandal," which placed Macdonald in difficulty in consequence of his western railway negotiations, helped to provoke the Island Liberals into supporting their federal namesakes. This issue enhanced the significance of the arrival of six new Island members in the House of Commons in 1873. Macdonald's majority was slim and uncertain, and the Government's fall was a distinct possibility. No one knew whom the new members would support. The Islanders' views were vital and "for some weeks," said Sir Richard Cartwright, "they held the balance of power, and the situation was really dramatic."[2] David Laird, who led four of the six, announced that, while they had no party affiliation, they would support the Opposition on the scandal issue. This announcement contributed to the change of Government which brought Alexander Mackenzie to power with David Laird as his Minister of the Interior and the support of six Island Liberals in the House of Commons after the election of 1874. These circumstances suddenly linked the local and federal Liberals, to the accompaniment of accusations of bribery and corruption from their opponents.[3]

Strategic association was not, nevertheless, an effective substitute for old friendships. Island Liberals took their time before becoming wedded to the federal party.[4] While David Laird was a Minister of the Crown at Ottawa, his own paper, the *Patriot*, declared that "we Islanders owe no fealty to Macdonald, and we are not bound by strong party ties to Mackenzie. Both these leaders are to us almost abstractions, and we are in a position to judge them by their acts as statesmen, independent of personal considerations."[5]

[1]Hodgson to Macdonald, Sept. 26, 1873, Public Archives of Canada, Macdonald Papers, vol. 119, p. 179; Sir Charles Tupper, *Recollections of Sixty Years in Canada* (London, 1914), p. 163.
[2]Sir Richard Cartwright, *Reminiscences* (Toronto, 1912), p. 117; see also Sir George W. Ross, *Getting into Parliament and After* (Toronto, 1913), p. 70.
[3]For the details of this subject see Frank MacKinnon, "David Laird of Prince Edward Island," *Dalhousie Review*, Jan., 1947, pp. 412-13.
[4]For similar trends in other provinces see Escott M. Reid, "The Rise of National Parties in Canada," *Papers and Proceedings of the Canadian Political Science Association*, 1932, p. 187.
[5]*Patriot*, Oct. 14, 1876.

Some Conservatives felt the same way. Attorney-General F. D. Brecken complained in 1874 that local politics "were too much mixed up with Dominion politics,"[1] and Hon. Samuel Prowse, a member of the Sullivan Government, declared as late as 1882 that he was "wedded to no party."[2] But with the development of local interest in national issues, particularly in tariffs, the Island's parties soon allied themselves permanently with their federal associates. The Conservatives also gained the advantage at this point. Macdonald entered upon a long lease of power in 1878 and Sullivan likewise in the following year. The Island sent five Conservatives to Ottawa in 1878 and Macdonald rewarded it by including J. C. Pope in his Cabinet and encouraging cordial personal relations with Sullivan. The Liberals, on the other hand, did not maintain their initial advantage in federal activities. Laird left the Cabinet in 1876 to take the governorship of the Northwest Territories, and most of his Island colleagues were defeated two years later. It was not until Louis Davies became a firm friend of Laurier in the 1880's and Minister of Fisheries in 1896 that the local Liberal organization became closely allied with the federal.

Once these initial contacts were made, the provincial parties maintained a close liaison with the larger groups. This relationship was aided by the fact that change of Government in the Island followed similar trends in the Dominion. When Macdonald was in power the Island was always Conservative; while Laurier was in office it remained Liberal.[3] Borden had scarcely become Prime Minister when the Island ended twenty years of Liberal rule and returned John Mathieson and the Conservatives. During Bennett's term the Island had two Conservative Governments. In 1935, when Mackenzie King took over, the province celebrated by returning an all-Liberal Legislature; it remained predominantly Liberal during Mr. King's long years of office. This situation was in direct contrast to that in Ontario, for instance, which since Confederation has

[1]*P.E.I. House of Assembly Debates*, 1874, p. 40.
[2]*Ibid.*, 1882, p. 241. It should be noted, too, that Sir John Macdonald made a special effort to find a postmastership for Brecken and a senatorship for Prowse.
[3]During the Laurier era the local Liberals invariably held their elections one month after federal contests.

generally returned Governments hostile to those of the Dominion. Although this remarkable record seems to indicate how well the Island's political barometer recorded national change, it did not, nevertheless, as the final chapter will indicate, ensure favourable consideration of the province's claims for economic concessions and representation in the federal Cabinet.

Sir John Willison once made the famous remark that "no man in Canada has been more inconsistent than the man who has faithfully followed either political party for a generation." By this he meant that the parties have not followed a consistent course in their platforms and actions over a long period of time. There is much truth in this view as far as Dominion politics are concerned, and parties in Prince Edward Island have proved no exception. Both the Liberals and Conservatives have followed opposite courses at different times, and there is no indication whatever that, in the long run, the Conservatives have been any more conservative than the Liberals, or the Liberals any more liberal than their opponents.

This inconsistency has been evident in every period. The Conservative party was a Protestant stronghold in the 1860's and a solid Catholic group a decade later, while the Liberals reversed the process. The Conservatives introduced the original Prohibition Act in the face of strong Liberal opposition, yet one of their leaders lived to declare it *ultra vires* from the bench and another supported its drastic alteration in 1945. The Liberals welcomed all prohibitionists in 1927, but within two decades a Liberal administration introduced government control. The *coup d'état* of 1945 was possible because both parties so forgot the past that the prohibitionists had nowhere to turn except to the Lieutenant-Governor. No major reform has been the exclusive prerogative of either party, and both have from time to time been firm in their opposition to change. Their consistency has largely been confined to loyalty to a name. This is not an unnatural phenomenon, however, for parties change from generation to generation to adjust themselves to trends in an ever varying public opinion; the events and circumstances with which they deal do not remain stationary; and their whole nature must change with the personnel of which they are composed.

Island politics do not encourage variations in party types. The population is largely rural; agriculture is predominant, and commercial enterprise is closely allied to it. There is no "big business," and industrial labour exists in very small numbers. Consequently the interests of the people do not vary to any appreciable extent from one part of the province to another. Both political groups have reflected this lack of variation, and, because of it, the alteration of power in the province has in most cases emphasized changes in personnel rather than in party character.[1]

These factors have discouraged the advent of third parties. A labour party would be out of place. Farmers' groups are unnecessary, for the agricultural interests have a firm hold on both major parties. The farmers organized in 1919, not to form a party, but to encourage farmer candidates in rural ridings, but such efforts have not been necessary since, for agriculture is always sure of a legislative majority regardless of what party is in power. A Conservative, J. A. Dewar, managed to sit as a lone Independent from 1919 to 1923, but the few others who ran as such have received little support. J. Walter Jones and Horace Wright ran as Progressives in 1921, without success. The Cooperative Commonwealth Federation sponsored candidates in 1943 and 1947; however, this group was unable to organize an effective party in the province, and all its candidates in both contests lost their deposits.

This consistency has also been reflected in long terms of office. It takes a good deal to defeat a Government in a settled environment where the parties conform to the same general attitudes. The rapid changes of Government in the period of instability before Confederation gave way to the relative tranquillity which has prevailed since 1879. The voters have rarely been restless, and unless they were upset by some major issue, such as prohibition, Oppositions have found it difficult to convince them that the time for a change was at hand. The Government, for example, changed only once from 1879 to 1911, and one party has dominated the House with overwhelming majorities since 1935. Even rapid change of leadership

[1] Political consistency is most evident in Prince County, which has been Liberal for generations.

has not been detrimental to governmental fortunes, for although the Liberals had six leaders in the twenty years after 1891, they held power continuously during that time. The Liberals have had the advantage from the standpoint of years in office; from 1873 to 1951 they held power for 44 years, to 31 for the Conservatives and 3 for the Davies coalition.

The characteristics of party politics on the Island are partially explained by the dominance of political patronage in such a small province. The same factors which bring the Cabinet, the Legislature, and the party so close to the people encourage the relentless pressure of influential individuals and powerful groups. In many ways this pressure facilitates the democratic process, but in others it results in unwise decisions, political appointments, and patronage of the worst type. The "pork barrel" is, of course, an institution of some importance in most governments, but in Prince Edward Island, Ministers and other party leaders require more than the usual amount of political courage to keep it in its place.

Party Organization

Organization is a major factor in party politics on the Island. The limited size and population of the constituencies render it comparatively easy for candidates and party officials to know the voters and their sympathies, to build up an effective machinery, and, more important, to keep in close contact with that machinery. Moreover, Islanders generally see and know more of their candidates than do voters elsewhere. This contact is vital in the winning of elections in the small constituencies, and it can be said that, almost invariably, the quality of a candidate or the attractiveness of a platform will not bring victory without organization and leadership. Yet size and population have revealed the disadvantages of over-organization, for too many officers, associations, and committees can be a serious handicap to effective campaigning. Each party has poll, district, and county organizations, while the Progressive Conservatives have a provincial organization as well. Many characteristics are common to both parties and to the various areas, but there is a substantial variety in practice resulting from local outlooks and experience. In both cases the same organization is used for purposes of provincial and federal elections.[1]

The Poll Organization

The basic unit of the party machine, and its closest contact with the voters and their needs, is the poll organization. Its functions at election time are to organize party workers, scrutinize the voters' lists and ascertain the affiliations of the names thereon, canvass the sympathizers, woo the doubtfuls and the less ardent opponents, arrange transportation for those who are likely to cast their votes in the right direction, escort the candidates through the district, designate scrutineers, and, in the case of the party in power, arrange for the location and staffing of the poll. Between elections it must maintain a watchful eye on local problems, keep in touch with the sitting member and the party chieftains, give advice on the distribution of patronage, and, in general, keep alive the interests of the party's local membership. It is expected, moreover, to send representatives to party meetings and conventions, share in the operation of the larger groups, and carry to the local area the policies of the higher levels of the party machine.

There are 214 polls in Prince Edward Island, 66 in Prince County, 94 in Queens, and 54 in Kings.[2] Of these only 30 are urban polls, 25 being in Charlottetown and 5 in Summerside. The number of voters in the urban polls is somewhat higher than the average for all polls. In each case there is a poll committee composed of a chairman[3] and a number of members varying from five to twenty, including a secretary, who are selected at an advertised annual meeting of party supporters in the poll.[4] There are no membership fees or qualifications save friendship to the party. In view of the unique franchise, many polls have representatives of property and franchise voters on the committee. The general structure is the

[1]The writer acknowledges gratefully the co-operation of local officials and federal members and senators in both parties who provided information from which material for this section was selected.
[2]The following description applies to both parties except where indicated.
[3]The poll chairman goes by different names, sometimes being called poll convener or poll director.
[4]The number of the committee will depend on party strength in the poll. The Progressive Conservative constitution stipulates from five to eight members. The Liberal practice is more flexible.

same for all polls, with the exception of Summerside where, in the case of the Liberal party, there is one committee and one convener for the five polls with each poll represented on the committee.

There is a wide variety of practice among the poll organizations. A few meet regularly and discuss political questions or plan strategy; others function only for the period prior to an election and remain dormant at other times; and still others are continuously weak. The difference arises from the quality of the poll chairman and committeemen, the degree of enthusiasm for the candidate, the amount of attention received by the district from the party, the number of party supporters in the area, and the prospects of victory or defeat. Actually the poll organization is highly informal. Few hold "annual meetings" annually and most of them retain the same chairman and committeemen from year to year. As long as the control of willing workers is reasonably effective there will be little change in personnel and a minimum of formality. The polls are independent one of another, except in Summerside, as noted above, but there is, with some exceptions, a high degree of co-operation among them in participation in the parent organization. Effective co-ordination is also fostered by the candidates and organizers through frequent visits to poll meetings and correspondence with poll officials. On a rare occasion the party hierarchy may interfere if trouble arises, but usually the local governization is left to look after its special interests in the manner best suited to local circumstances.

The District Organization

There are fifteen districts or constituencies for provincial election purposes, five in each of the three counties, with an organization in each. The district organization in Queens and Kings is formed at an advertised annual meeting of party supporters in the district. There are no poll delegates as such at an annual meeting as distinct from a convention. The meeting in Queens will select a president, vice-president, and secretary and two representatives[1] to the county association. In Kings there is a district president only and he is selected by the county organization. While these bodies are designed

[1]Three in the case of Charlottetown and Royalty, the Fifth District.

to serve in both provincial and federal elections, their usefulness is more evident in the case of the former, since they provide the official convention machinery of the provincial candidates. There are no district organizations as such in Prince County, in view of the peculiar division of the county machinery noted below.

The annual meeting in the district is of little significance in actual practice. When held, it confines itself to selecting officers, which is a routine procedure save where some intra-party rivalry has sprung up, passing resolutions of confidence in party leaders, and discussing current issues if there are any of interest to discuss. The annual meeting generally lapses, however, until just before a provincial election when it is combined with a district convention for the selection of candidates for the local house.

The district organization is thus of little consequence except in arranging the district convention and, in Queens, selecting the officers of the county organization. The reason for the lack of emphasis on this body seems to be the absence of any real need for it, other than in the selection of district candidates, in view of the work of the poll and county machinery and the inconvenience of over-organization in a small area.

The County Organization

The most effective work is done by the county organizations of which there are four, two in Prince and one each in Queens and Kings.

The Progressive Conservative county organizations are much alike. Membership includes party supporters eligible to vote at either federal or provincial elections. The county executive in Prince and Kings is composed of ten members, two from each of the district organizations; in Queens there are eleven, for the Charlottetown district sends three representatives. The annual meeting selects a president, vice-president, and secretary-treasurer, and an executive committee, all from the district representatives. The district representatives are the official links between the county and district organizations, and they act as conveners, and usually as presidents and secretaries, of the district machine.

The Liberal county organizations are different. Membership in the Queens County Liberal Association is open to all Liberal electors in the county. Its affairs are managed by a central committee of eleven members composed of two representatives from each of the four rural districts and three from Charlottetown and Royalty, all selected at district annual meetings. From this central committee are elected at the county annual meeting a president, vice-president, and secretary. The annual meeting, although not always "annual," is generally held with some degree of regularity. In Kings County the membership comprises the Liberal supporters in the county. There is no central committee. A president, vice-president, secretary, and five district presidents form the executive, and they are elected at an "annual" meeting which actually meets only as a convention prior to elections.

The organization in Prince County in both parties is unique, and may be illustrated by the Liberal practice which has been extremely successful in holding the county for many decades. There are no district organizations, but there are two county groups, the West Prince, comprising the First and Second Districts, and the East Prince, which includes the Third, Fourth, and Fifth Districts. District meetings and conventions are called by the president of the East or West organization as the case may be. There is a sharp division as far as county business is concerned. East Prince has a president, a secretary, and three vice-presidents, one from each of the three districts, while West Prince has a president, a secretary, and five vice-presidents selected on a regional rather than district basis. These officers are elected at respective annual meetings which, with occasional lapses, do meet annually. This situation has lingered from the days when the Island had six members in the House of Commons and Prince County was divided into two federal constituencies, East and West. The machinery of other days had become so well established that it was left virtually unchanged.

The chief value of the county organization is manifest in federal politics where the counties are the constituencies. Its efforts are directed principally toward the needs of federal candidates just as those of the district machine are more significant in provincial contests. This distinction appears to have been a useful factor in the division of authority and responsibility between the two groups.

The Provincial Organization

The Progressive Conservatives have a provincial organization; the Liberals do not. The Progressive Conservative officers are chosen from the county association; the president of the Queens association is generally president of the provincial body, while the presidents from Prince and Kings become vice-presidents. A secretary is chosen by the executive. There is supposed to be an annual meeting, but it is usually held only prior to an election. The Liberal party, on the other hand, has never favoured a provincial organization. Many Liberals hold that a provincial organization is unnecessary in such a small province if the poll and county units are effective. More significant than this, however, is the fact that in Prince County there has been for many years a suspicion that party control would be lodged in Charlottetown if a provincial body were formed. The Liberals, consequently, have left the county groups to look after the affairs of their own areas, and have made no formal attempt to co-ordinate the party efforts of the three divisions. There does not seem to be any evidence of serious inconvenience in this plan; on the contrary it seems to have worked well in view of the Liberal electoral successes in the province in recent years.

There have been some special organizations in the form of women's and young people's groups, but their value has been limited by the fear of over-organization and by the fact that such groups have not been representative of the province as a whole. Women's associations in both parties have not been effective, particularly in the rural areas. The few women who can spare the time from their home and social duties for party activities generally participate in the main party units; the vast majority prefer to exert their influence through the ballot box and their husbands. Urban women's groups are active to a limited degree in Charlottetown and Summerside, but their efforts are largely blended with those of the parent organization. Young people's groups have not flourished on the Island. For some years there was a Twentieth Century Liberal Club, but it disintegrated. In 1900 the young Conservatives organized a Tupper Club prior to a visit from Sir Charles Tupper; but it too did not last. In recent years there has been a Young Progressive Conservative Association for the province, the membership and efforts of which have been largely confined to Charlottetown and are of negligible influence. The main reason for the failure of these groups appears to be the fact that a young person is either too young to be of much assistance in politics or old enough to share in the work of the parent body.

Conventions

As noted above, it is the convention that serves as the main rally for party supporters. Here the candidates for provincial and federal elections are chosen, and here the leaders expound the virtues of their cause and make elaborately worded, but not too definite, pronouncements on the party's attitude on contemporary public questions. Resolutions of loyalty and confidence come from the floor and reports on party activities reveal the successes of various committees amid expressions of thanks and much applause. Behind the scenes and in out-of-the-way corners little groups exchange views on strategy and opinions on personalities. The next day the party press will impart some of the enthusiasm to the public at large.

The real business of the convention, however, is the selection of candidates. Provincial candidates are chosen for both parties at district conventions which are held some weeks before a provincial election. Such a convention is called by the district president who will be its chairman. He notifies the poll chairmen, and asks each to call a poll meeting to select five delegates. On many occasions there is no contest, and after five persons are nominated, the delegation is complete; on others rivalry among supporters of prospective candidates may result in a ballot. Occasionally there are attempts to "pack" the poll committee or poll delegation in the interests of rival candidates for nomination, and such interference is often successful.[1] Some polls include a women's representative on the delegation,

[1] For some years the Kings County Liberal Association followed the practice of holding all such poll meetings on the one night in order to prevent the packing of delegations by roving organizers during a disagreement between rival factions within the party. This procedure was abolished in 1947.

and many polls seek to name representatives of both property and franchise voters. Actually the delegates are selected in most cases from the members of the poll committee without much formality. When they go to the convention the poll delegates may sometimes be pledged as a body to support a particular candidate; more often they vote according to their individual inclination. At a well-attended district convention there will be approximately one hundred delegates, all bearing official credentials signed by their respective poll chairmen. While the conventions are invariably open to all party supporters in the district—indeed a few opponents sometimes come to heckle—only accredited delegates may vote and speak, usually from special seats in one section of the hall.

The convention procedure varies considerably and is often highly informal. In some districts the names of those from whom the two candidates must be selected are submitted from the floor; in others they are presented by a nominating committee. In many instances where there has been general satisfaction with the sitting members, no additional names will be submitted and acclamations will end the proceedings. Where the honour is contested, separate votes are taken for councillor and assemblyman and the procedure is the same in both cases. If there are more than two candidates, the one receiving the lowest number of votes on each ballot is dropped until a winner obtains a majority of votes. The losers will then move that the selection be made unanimous, although on a rare occasion a loser has declined to take his defeat so graciously.[1] In some instances the contestants are in attendance and speak before and after the balloting; in others they remain at home, all the while expecting the call to hurry to the convention to accept, but not wishing to appear too anxious for the prize.

The county convention, summoned to select candidates for federal elections, is carried on in much the same way. The call is sent to the poll organizations by the county president, and five dele-

[1] The Liberal convention of Queens County which met in 1901 to select a successor to Sir Louis Davies was badly split by the refusal of rival forces to back the party nominee. The constitution of the Queens County Liberal Association now requires (article 8) that "before proceeding to ballot, each Candidate and delegate shall pledge himself that he will cheerfully support the regular Nominee of the Convention, and adopt all lawful means to secure his triumphant election."

gates are sent from each. Two special features must be noted. Queens is a two-member constituency, and the task of selecting the candidates is, consequently, more interesting. Anywhere from four to eight or nine persons may be in the running, and, after a number of elimination ballots, the two highest are selected. In Prince County the candidate is chosen at a joint convention of the East and West organizations. The two presidents call the convention; sometimes the two act as joint chairmen; occasionally the senior one presides.

With one exception, conventions have not selected the party leaders in Prince Edward Island. This task has been performed by a caucus of the party's members in the Assembly who meet to discuss the matter. Perhaps the retiring leader will suggest his successor and the mantle will fall on him without difficulty. The caucus may, however, divide and vote on two or more candidates.[1] The choice of the caucus has generally been given some form of recognition at subsequent meetings or conventions either by ratification or resolution of confidence, but, although some selections have not been too popular with the rank and file of party members, party support has generally been given without demur.

The selection of leaders by caucus has been followed largely as a matter of convenience in a small province. In many instances a new leader has been the crown prince of the previous administration whose obvious availability rendered a convention unnecessary. The number of possible successors to the leadership in either party has not usually been so large as to make the choice difficult. The premiership usually becomes vacant suddenly through death or elevation to the bench, and quick selection by caucus has been found more satisfactory than the protracted procedure of calling a convention. Certainly the caucus-chosen leader has never been repudiated by the party, although on one or two occasions there was every indication that the leader was forced upon it from above. The matter of changing the leader of the Opposition party is more complicated. If the Opposition group in the House were composed

[1]On one occasion, the selection of Benjamin Rogers as Liberal leader in 1915, the leadership was given to someone without a seat in the House, and in only one case, that of J. Walter Jones, has the leadership of the Government party been won by a member outside the Cabinet.

of only four or five members, it could scarcely be expected to choose a leader. In such a situation the Progressive Conservatives selected a new leader in 1950 at a party convention.

While the numerous details of the machinery described above are impressive on paper, there is, in fact, a high degree of flexibility and informality about their actual operation. This is almost inevitable in a tiny province with a small population where an elaborate mechanism of poll, district, county, provincial, women's, and young people's organizations, each taking itself too seriously, would be too unwieldy and rigid for effective action. Many party workers, consequently, have appreciated the dangers of over-organization, and have stressed certain effective parts of the machine and allowed others to lapse. For instance, the annual meeting, as already indicated, has generally been ignored, for it takes a widespread enthusiasm and an aroused opinion on current events to bring an interested number of representatives together in the tranquil period between elections when the nomination of candidates is not an issue. A lukewarm and unrepresentative annual meeting is poor strategy, and where there is a satisfactory executive it has often proved better to retain the executive, allow the annual meeting to lapse, and accumulate the business and fanfare for a rousing, well-timed convention. The best work is actually done by the executive, volunteer workers, and the candidates themselves. Where the constituencies are so few in number and small in size and population, the task of getting to know the voters and their political sympathies is not difficult. Such personal contact is far more effective than an over-sized machine. Letters and flowers in case of death, illness, marriage, births or other such occasions, for example, will bring more votes to a candidate than the resolutions of confidence of an annual meeting. Expressions of opinion made to the candidate over the farmer's gate, at the church social, or on the village street corner and enthusiastically received by him, are often more valuable than the hurried debate of a formal party gathering. The significance of these factors will depend very largely, of course, on the personalities concerned. In general it may be said that organization is indispensable, but that it must be accompanied by the subtle and informal tactics without which it is useless.

CHAPTER XII

THE JUDICIARY

THE EARLY ADMINISTRATION of justice on Prince Edward Island, which was described in chapter II, was affected at every point by the problem of developing an adequate system of courts in a tiny colony and by the quality and political activity of the judges. These factors became less evident after Confederation, but their influence remained in many of the characteristics of the provincial judiciary.

Responsibility for the administration of justice was divided in 1873 along the same lines as in the other provinces. The British North America Act gave the province jurisdiction over "the Administration of Justice in the Province including the Constitution, Maintenance and Organization of Provincial Courts, both of Civil and of Criminal Jurisdiction, and including Procedure in Civil Matters in those Courts."[1] The Dominion, on the other hand, was given the power to appoint superior and county court judges in the province, except judges of probate.[2] The Dominion Parliament became responsible for the salaries, allowances, and pensions of superior and county court judges[3] and of admiralty judges in certain cases.[4] The Dominion also had the power to provide a general court of appeal for Canada and "any additional Courts for the better administration of the Laws of Canada," a provision which led to the establishment of the Supreme Court of Canada and the Exchequer Court of Canada in 1875, to which appeals lie in certain cases from the provincial courts. Federal authority also extended to the criminal law, except for the constitution of courts of criminal jurisdiction.[5] The province thus establishes, organizes, and maintains the provincial courts, while the Dominion appoints and pays the judges. The existing court system of Prince Edward Island was retained after union; indeed the province set up and manned a system of county courts only two weeks before she entered Confederation.

[1]B.N.A. Act, section 92 (14).
[2]*Ibid.*, section 96.
[3]Except those of probate.
[4]B.N.A. Act, section 100.
[5]*Ibid.*, section 91 (27).

In addition to the provincial and federal courts, there was, until 1949, the Judicial Committee of the Privy Council in London to which appeals lay in non-criminal matters from the Supreme Court of Canada or direct from the courts of last resort in the province. In practice, however, such appeals were limited by the Committee itself to cases "of gravity involving matters of public interest, or some important questions of law, or affecting property of considerable amount, or where the case is otherwise of some public importance of a very substantial character."[1] Appeals to the Privy Council were abolished in 1949, and the Supreme Court of Canada is now the final authority.

The judicial system of Prince Edward Island consists of a Supreme Court, with which are associated the Court of Appeal, the Court of Appeal in Equity, the Court of Criminal Appeal, the Court of Bankruptcy, and two Courts of Chancery; a Court of Divorce; a Court of Probate; county courts; magistrates' courts; and coroners' courts. There is also a Court of Admiralty, but its functions are dormant since admiralty cases have not arisen for many years. There is still a Judge of Admiralty, who was usually a judge in earlier years, but who was for some time a practising lawyer receiving a special fee of $800 a year, and who since 1948 has been the Judge of Probate.

The Supreme Court

The Supreme Court is composed of a Chief Justice and three other judges, although the fourth seat has never been filled.[2] Its judges are appointed by the Dominion Government; they hold office during good behaviour and are removable only by the Governor-General on address of the Senate and House of Commons if a serious charge has been laid by responsible persons and substantiated after careful investigation.[3] The Chief Justice is paid $13,333.33 annually and the other judges $12,000.

[1]Lord FitzGerald in *Prince* v. *Gagnon,* (1882) 8 App. Cas. 103.
[2]4 Geo. VI, c. 35; and 5 Geo. VI, c. 16.
[3]B.N.A. Act, section 99; for detailed discussion on the appointment and tenure of judges, see chapter on the judiciary in R. MacGregor Dawson, *The Principle of Official Independence.*

THE JUDICIARY 261

The jurisdiction of the Supreme Court is not specifically set out in any one statute, but is determined by a wide variety of local acts, by custom, and by the will of the Court itself. The Judicature Act describes it as a court of common law having also an equitable jurisdiction and possessing original and appellate jurisdiction in civil and criminal cases.[1] Actually its original jurisdiction is limited to civil cases where the amount in question is more than $32 and to criminal cases upon indictment in court by grand jury; in other words, to the more serious and important cases. Special original and appellate jurisdiction is given from time to time by provincial and Dominion statutes, e.g. trial of election cases, and appeals under the Public Utilities Act.[2] The Supreme Court acts also as the Court of Appeal and the Court of Criminal Appeal and in those capacities it sits *in banco* without the trial judge.

The Court also has equity jurisdiction and two of its judges are judges of the Court of Chancery. The Governor, as previously stated, originally presided over this court as Chancellor, and he was assisted in this capacity by a Master.[3] In 1848 a Master of the Rolls for the Court of Chancery, who was also to be an Assistant Judge of the Supreme Court, was appointed to exercise all jurisdiction in equity, but appeals could be made from his decisions to the Chancellor himself, and the latter had to sign certain chancery decrees and other documents.[4] In 1869 a Vice Chancellor was appointed, also an Assistant Judge of the Supreme Court, to have co-ordinate jurisdiction with the Master of the Rolls. These two judges effectively relieved the Chancellor of his judicial responsibility, and appeals to him had ceased by Confederation; even his signature was not required after 1879.[5] The Governor is still legally the Chancellor, but his intervention in chancery matters is highly improbable.

The Chancery Act now provides for a Court of Chancery, consisting of the "Rolls Court" and the "Court of the Vice Chancellor." Actually there is no difference between the two judges, except in name, and they have the same powers in respect to Island cases as the Master of the Rolls had in England in 1848 in respect to Eng-

[1] 4 Geo. VI, c. 35. [2] *Supra*, pp. 207, 225. [3] *Supra*, pp. 27-8.
[4] 11 Vic., c. 6. [5] 42 Vic., c. 9.

lish cases save as altered by provincial statute.¹ Cases come before one judge by bill of complaint, petition, and prayer, as distinct from writs before the Supreme Court, and they usually involve such matters as trusts, mortgages, estates, cases in lunacy, and adoption where equity is required. Appeals in chancery may be lodged to the "Court of Appeal in Equity" consisting of the Chief Justice of the Supreme Court and the judge who did not sit on the original hearing. Appeals are normally the only instances where the Chief Justice acts in Chancery, although he may do so in special cases upon request of one of the chancery judges.

The Supreme Court has the power to hear, *in banco*, "any matters" which the Lieutenant-Governor-in-Council "thinks fit" to refer to it, and to give its opinion thereon.² Although this vague provision would apparently permit the reference of almost any question to the Court, it is intended to enable the Government to secure judicial opinions on jurisdiction or on the constitutionality of provincial legislation, without awaiting litigation arising in the normal manner.³

THE COURT OF DIVORCE

The most extraordinary contribution of Prince Edward Island to modern government is probably the role of the Cabinet as a court of law. The normal development of colonial government in the nineteenth century resulted in the separation of judicial duties from those of the executive, and their transference to systems of national and local courts. Prince Edward Island was no exception, but in 1945 it reverted to the early colonial practice and constituted the Governor and his Cabinet a Court of Divorce for the province.

A Divorce Court was established on the Island in 1835 after a husband had sought relief from the Assembly as the only body to which he had recourse.⁴ It consisted of the Lieutenant-Governor, or

[1]4 Geo. VI, c. 11; see also Chancery Act of 1910, 10 Ed. VII, c. 8.
[2]5 Geo. VI, c. 16.
[3]For example, in 1950 the provincial Government referred to the Supreme Court the question of the legality of legislation transferring jurisdiction on divorce from the Divorce Court to the Supreme Court.
[4]*P.E.I. House of Assembly Journals*, 1833, pp. 67, 68, 73, 91. A previous bill, passed in 1833, did not receive the King's assent because it included a provision that the offender in an action could not remarry during the lifetime of

THE JUDICIARY   263

other administrator of the government, and His Majesty's Council. The Governor was named President of the Court, but "whereas the arduous affairs of Government may render it impossible" for His Honour "at all times to preside in person," he was empowered to appoint the Chief Justice of the Supreme Court "to preside in his place and stead." The Chief Justice, as well as the other judges of the Supreme Court, was, in 1835, a member of the Council and therefore a logical deputy.

The Court had little to do during its first years, for few cases came before it. Only one divorce action achieved prominence in Island jurisprudence, by virtue of the fact that the husband concerned, although wealthy, preferred to remain in prison for life rather than pay the alimony ordered by the Court.[1] By the twentieth century the Court had remained unused for many decades and had almost been forgotten.[2] Meanwhile the Dominion Parliament, which under section 91 of the British North America Act had jurisdiction over divorce, made provision in other provinces for divorce machinery within their systems of civil courts. Quebec was unprovided for, and Prince Edward Island had only the old unused Court of 1835. In these two provinces, therefore, recourse lay to the federal Parliament which, through the divorce committee of the Senate, heard cases brought before it and dealt with them by special private bills.[3]

his or her former spouse. Report of Attorney-General Hodgson, April 27, 1833, Public Archives of Canada, Colonial Office Records (P.E.I.), A series, vol. 50, p. 159; *ibid.,* A 52, p. 289. The second bill (1835) repealed the first and omitted the undesired clause. 5 Wm. IV, c. 10; *Assembly Journals,* 1835, p. 36.

[1]*Capell* v. *Capell* cited in John A. (later Chief Justice) Mathieson, "Bench and Bar," in *Past and Present in Prince Edward Island,* ed. D. A. MacKinnon and A. B. Warburton (Charlottetown, 1905), p. 140.

[2]See *Royal Gazette* (P.E.I.), extra, vol. LXXI, no. 51, Dec. 22, 1945.

[3]One attempt was made to change the procedure on the Island. On April 8, 1920 a bill was introduced in the Senate by Hon. W. B. Ross which provided for the creation of a divorce court in Ontario and for the transfer of divorce jurisdiction in Prince Edward Island from the Governor-in-Council to the Supreme Court. *Canada, Senate Debates,* 1920, pp. 137, 165 ff. Senator Murphy (P.E.I.) said that there was no need for such a measure, and that the existing Divorce Court was "perfectly capable of doing the work." He indicated that a divorce case had come up during the Mathieson administration, when the Government refused to reconstitute the Divorce Court and the case had to go to Parliament. *Ibid.,* p. 171. Senator John McLean (P.E.I.), who favoured the bill, and who had been a member of the Mathieson Government, noted that, when the case had occurred, the Government refused to reopen the Court because it felt that the man who petitioned for the divorce did

The Divorce Court was carried by law down to the modern provincial Cabinet by the change of 1838 which divided the old Council into the Executive and Legislative Councils and gave to the Executive Council all the powers of the old Council, save legislative powers, and by the British North America Act, 1867, and the Order-in-Council of 1873 which admitted the province into the union, both of which, except where otherwise provided, left intact the old courts and existing executive powers. The Divorce Court today has, therefore, exactly the same legal status and construction as it had in 1835.

More effective divorce machinery was considered necessary by the provincial Government in 1945 because of the number of war veterans seeking relief from unfortunate marriages. The Government thereupon introduced into the Legislature a resolution which provided for petitioning the federal Parliament to apply the English law of divorce to the Island and grant the necessary jurisdiction to the provincial Supreme Court. This resolution was defeated 14-11.[1] Upon the advice of the Cabinet the Governor then resurrected the old Divorce Court by proclamation and thus placed himself and the Cabinet upon the bench. His Honour, as a Roman Catholic, could scarcely preside, and he appointed the Chief Justice to act in his stead.[2]

The procedure of the Divorce Court was carefully planned to meet some of the difficulties of associating judicial and political personnel. Three sets of rules of practice and procedure were applicable in the Court, general rules and special rules of the Court itself, and, in other respects not specified by these or by statute, the

not deserve one, but rather it was the wife who deserved it. This comment is significant in view of the fact that, when it made such a decision, the Cabinet really assumed a quasi-judicial if not a judicial function. The bill passed in the Senate, but only went as far as first reading in the House of Commons. When the provincial Legislature was informed of this proposal, it passed unanimously a resolution to the effect that the province had not requested such a change which, if made, would "destroy the stability of the home and encourage the dissolution of the marriage tie," and that no change should be made until the province asked for it. Charlottetown *Examiner,* April 29, 1920; *Assembly Journals,* April 27, 1920.

[1]*Ibid.,* 1945, pp. 97-8; Charlottetown *Guardian,* April 13, 1945. The Government was obviously not at all disturbed by the defeat of its own measure.

[2]Executive Council Minute Books, Legislative Building, Charlottetown, Sept. 6, 1945, p. 185; *Royal Gazette,* extra, vol. LXXI, no. 51, Dec. 22, 1945.

rules of the Supreme Court in civil actions.¹ The Chief Justice was to make rulings on questions of evidence and points of law, while the Council could either make findings of fact or render verdicts upon the evidence by majority vote or request the Chief Justice to do so. Finally the Council was to "advise and recommend the judgement at which the Court should arrive." By this process the knowledge and experience of the Chief Justice were relied upon in technical matters, while the opinion of the majority of the Council prevailed in the final judgment.

Such a tribunal was contrary to all modern concepts of judicial independence, attitudes, and qualifications. It marked a resort to powers of the Governor which could make him an active functionary in the judicial sphere. It placed on the bench a group of Cabinet Ministers which at first included only one lawyer and which had little time or training for dealing with the complicated mechanism of divorce law.² Moreover its revival was essentially an expedient to override a decision of the Legislature of 1945 by an enactment of the Legislature which existed 110 years before. Its temporary composition raised some interesting questions. What would happen if both the Governor and the Chief Justice were Roman Catholics and refused to sit; or if the Governor were a Protestant but not a lawyer, and he presided? With respect to cabinet responsibility, are Ministers responsible to the Assembly for their judgments on the bench? Is there any possibility under the circumstances of political influence being brought to bear upon what is essentially a judicial function? These questions indicated that the Court was both a political and a judicial anomaly.

A new procedure was thereupon adopted in March, 1949 when the Legislature passed an act to amend the old Divorce Court Act by giving the Supreme Court concurrent jurisdiction in divorce. It was provided that the Divorce Court or the Chief Justice in Chambers may order that any divorce action be transferred to the Supreme Court providing that this transfer is not opposed "by any

[1] For the Court's rules of practice and procedure, see *Royal Gazette*, extra, vol. LXXI, no. 51, Dec. 22, 1945, Schedules B and C.
[2] See the Government's statement on the Court's personnel in *Guardian*, April 12, 1947.

party to the proceedings or by the King's Proctor." It is too early to assess the operation of this extraordinary procedure, and as yet it is not clear if any objection will be taken to it on grounds of legality in view of the Dominion's jurisdiction over marriage and divorce. If the arrangement is successful, the Cabinet will no doubt retire from the judicial field; if it is not, the Island will enjoy an unusual combination of two divorce courts between which litigants may take their choice.

The Probate Court

The Judge of Probate is appointed by the province, and is removable only by "impeachment."[1] Until 1947 he was remunerated through fees, but in that year he was assigned a salary of $7500, and the fees thenceforth went to the provincial treasury.[2] The Court has jurisdiction over the probate of wills and the administration of estates of deceased persons. A unique feature of this court is a provision that if the judge is not able to act either because of personal interest in a case or because of absence from his court, the Lieutenant-Governor may "specially appoint some other person in his stead"; the qualifications and status of this other person are not indicated. A peculiar section of the Judicature Act provides that by proclamation of the Governor-in-Council the Probate Court can be made a part of the Supreme Court, although with its own judge and its own distinct procedure. Such a proclamation has not yet been made.[3]

The County Courts

Three county courts, composed of one judge each, were established in 1873 to relieve the Supreme Court of minor cases and to replace the "Courts of Commissioners for the Recovery of Small Debts" which were composed of laymen whose precarious tenure of office depended upon political favour.[4] The judges are appointed by the Dominion, and hold office during good behaviour, but they

---

[1] 3 Geo. VI, c. 41. When and how the judge is to be impeached are not indicated although careful provision is made to safeguard the independence of other judges.
[2] 11 Geo. VI, c. 29.   [3] See 4 Geo. VI, c. 35, s. 11.
[4] 36 Vic., c. 3; see also *Assembly Journals,* 1873, p. 151.

THE JUDICIARY

must retire at seventy-five. They are removable only by federal Order-in-Council if a sufficiently serious charge can be substantiated before a commission of inquiry.[1] They are paid $6,666.66 per annum together with any extra grants for special duties. These courts are essentially civil courts which try cases where the sum involved does not exceed $500, but they also have the power to try certain criminal cases where the accused is given the power to elect.[2] They also have many powers specifically assigned to them by federal and provincial statutes, e.g. hearing appeals under the Election Act.[3]

Magistrates' Courts

There is a stipendiary magistrate for each county, for Charlottetown, and for Summerside. They have preliminary jurisdiction over all criminal cases, except those initiated in a higher court upon indictment by a grand jury, and over certain quasi-criminal cases, e.g. those which arise under the Highways Traffic Act, over petty misdemeanours, such as juvenile delinquency, and over any special matters for which trial before a magistrate is provided by federal or provincial statute. The magistrates are not judges, but practising lawyers appointed at pleasure upon a part-time basis at $1,000 a year by the provincial Government. They try many of their cases in their own offices, seated at their desks, at a time which fits into business hours, with the parties, witnesses, and police gathered informally—a procedure which lacks much of the dignity of judicial proceedings. The more serious cases, however, are tried in a court-room.

Appointment

The chief qualification for appointment to the bench is a political career. In fact all judges appointed to the courts of Prince Edward Island since Confederation have either held public office or given substantial service to a political party. The choice is generally made after the Prime Minister and Minister of Justice have considered the recommendations of the Dominion Cabinet Minister

---

[1]For a discussion of the position of judges generally, see R. MacGregor Dawson, *The Government of Canada* (Toronto, 1947), pp. 472-91.
[2]1 Geo. VI, c. 6.   [3]*Supra*, pp. 222-5.

from the province (if there is one), the Island senators and members of the House of Commons who are Government supporters, and the provincial Premier and Attorney-General if they are of the same party complexion as the federal Government. Traditionally the Premier and Attorney-General, if lawyers and on the right side of politics, have prior claim to a vacancy. As early as 1851 the Secretary of State for the Colonies recommended that, while appointments should be made chiefly on the basis of merit, "preference is fairly due to the Chief Law Adviser of the existing government" if there be a "reasonable equality" among the candidates.[1] A year later Robert Hodgson, who had been Attorney-General for many years, became the first local lawyer to be appointed to the bench; when the third judgeship was created in 1869 it went to Premier Hensley; and since then there has been a steady procession of Premiers and Attorneys-General to the Supreme Court.[2] Since Prince Edward Island's Government has always been of the same party allegiance as the federal, and Premiers and Attorneys-General apparently more than anxious for judgeships, other candidates have rarely reached the Supreme Court. Party service of a humbler character has generally been required for a county court judgeship. Experience in legal practice is sometimes considered, but unfortunately it has occasionally been overlooked in a display of political qualifications. The Island has been fortunate in the calibre of many of its Supreme Court judges, but political appointment has sometimes resulted in the elevation of men whose legal qualifications were much more modest than their ambitions. This last point is even more applicable to the county courts, for here mediocrity has more often displaced ability.

Religion is another factor in the selection of judges, for, like Cabinet portfolios, judgeships have been assigned with a view to satisfying the claims of Catholic and Protestant candidates whereever possible.[3] There is no definite rule other than this general understanding, however, since there are so few seats on the bench and political availability is so important.

[1]Grey to Bannerman, Jan. 31, 1851, P.A.C. (P.E.I.), G 20, pp. 38-9.
[2]See also *supra*, p. 179.
[3]See, for example, Premier Sullivan and the chief justiceship, *supra*, p. 146, n. 4.

The Island's senior judgeships tend to be relatively much more attractive financially and socially than those of other provinces, and for this reason the best politically available lawyers do not hesitate to seek them. The salaries are enormous as salaries go in the province, and private practice and hard work can rarely yield as attractive a remuneration. Judicial duties are not arduous; judges do not have to go far from home when on circuit, and they are not called upon to serve on boards and royal commissions in a province where there have been no labour conciliation boards and few commissions of inquiry.[1]

Promotion of judges has been virtually unknown in Prince Edward Island. With the exception of Edward Palmer, who became Chief Justice in 1874, no county court judge has been elevated to the Supreme Court. No puisne judge of the Supreme Court has been appointed Chief Justice. This practice of bringing in new men to preside over older and more experienced judges has often been criticized, yet it has gone a long way to prevent the unseemly political manœuvring of judges with an eye to promotion which often occurred in earlier years. In the Palmer case, for example, Justice J. H. Peters was looking for the promotion as well, and much bitterness resulted among the supporters of the respective claimants which disrupted the work of both county courts and Supreme Court.[2]

The political appointment of judges resulted in early years in much partisanship on the bench. Both Peters and Palmer were accused of using party contacts to obtain promotion. There was much seeking of patronage among the judges in connection with the revision of electoral lists. Although Sir John Macdonald thought Judge George Alley "exceedingly crochitty" and easily slighted, he appointed him revising officer to placate the moderate Grits whose support he was trying to win, despite the determined opposition of one of Alley's judicial brethren.[3] Alley's political interests were the

[1] Exceptions were Chief Justice J. A. Mathieson who sat on the White Commission in 1935 and Judge S. DesRoches who acted as a Commissioner to inquire into certain activities of the Fishermen's Loan Board in 1950.
[2] *Examiner,* Aug. 3, 1874; Charlottetown *Patriot,* Aug. 6, 1874.
[3] J. T. Jenkins to Macdonald, Public Archives of Canada, Macdonald Papers, vol. 10, p. 141; Macdonald to Jenkins, Sept. 18, 1885, *ibid.;* E. J. Hodgson to Macdonald, July 15, 1885, *ibid.*

subject of much debate in the Legislature where the Government accused him of campaigning in elections and lobbying in the House, and some Opposition members expressed the view that judges had a perfect right to participate in politics.[1] In 1886 Judge O. M. Reddin raised a similar controversy by his extraordinary theory that, since he was appointed by the Dominion, judicial independence was expected only in federal elections and he could do what he liked in provincial contests.[2] The trial of land purchase appeals[3] and of controverted election cases[4] also exposed the judges to much political criticism. Only one judge, however, A. B. Warburton, resigned to enter politics.[5] In recent years there has been very little public indication of political partisanship on the bench, for most judges have scrupulously recognized the independence of their position, and the controversial extra-judicial activities of former days have largely disappeared.

The number of judges on the Island has always been a subject of controversy. The establishment in a small community of a judiciary sufficient to meet the local needs for legal remedies and with enough work and influence to attract competent judges and keep them out of politics was a serious problem before Confederation. After 1873 the size of the judicial system invited comparison with those of other provinces with consequent suggestions for retrenchment. In 1939 Prince Edward Island had one Supreme Court judge for every 30,000 of its population, as compared with one for every 63,000 in the Maritimes as a whole, one for every 74,000 in the Prairie Provinces, and one for every 177,000 in Ontario.[6] Some have considered the province too small for elaborate courts of its own, since there are no large industries or concentrations of wealth, and comparatively few disputes of any magnitude either in private or in government business, and this view has sometimes led to specu-

[1]*P.E.I. House of Assembly Debates*, 1889, pp. 215 ff.
[2]*Patriot*, July 29, Aug. 5, 1886; *Examiner*, Aug. 6, 1886.
[3]*Assembly Debates*, 1874, pp. 405-12.
[4]*Assembly Journals*, 1906, pp. 5, 7; *supra*, pp. 222-5.
[5]Mr. Warburton was appointed county court judge for Kings in 1898. He resigned in 1904 to run, unsuccessfully, for the House of Commons, was elected in 1908, defeated in 1911, and later returned to the bench as Judge of Probate in 1920. See also *Patriot*, July 7, 1920.
[6]*Report of the Royal Commission on Dominion-Provincial Relations* (Ottawa, 1940), Book II, p. 170.

THE JUDICIARY

lation on the desirability of placing the Island under the jurisdiction of mainland courts. On the other hand there have been many proposals for increasing the number of judges, resulting from special difficulties in the local courts. Some of these have called for a substantial reshuffling of duties among the judges to provide more efficient service. As a result of the opposing viewpoints, suggested changes have been prevented and the judicial structure has remained the same since Confederation. The overriding principle seems to be that the importance of the judicial process on the Island does not rest entirely on the size of the population or the number and variety of cases, but also on the satisfaction of legitimate needs for judicial remedies with fairness and despatch.

The association of Island judges with the other provinces failed in the first and only trial, when strong objection was taken to the administration of Chief Justice Archibald in the 1820's.[1] The inconvenience of arranging court sittings to suit the schedule of an outside judge and local pride in a separate judiciary prevented further experiments of this kind, although the plan was suggested occasionally as an answer to local demands for additional judges. The most substantial suggestion for retrenchment was that of a Maritime court of appeal, which had some prominence in the 1930's. The Rowell-Sirois Commission reported in favour of such a court which would hold successive sittings in the provincial capitals at a considerable saving in expense and gain in efficiency.[2] Most Island lawyers have opposed this scheme in view of the differences in the laws of the three provinces, the inevitable reduction of patronage, the loss of local prestige associated with a separate judiciary, and, more important, doubt as to whether any saving in either expense or effort would result from exchanging a local court which is close to the area it serves for a distant one which would require travelling judges and lawyers and extra expense, delay, and inconvenience for litigants.

More effort has been made to increase than to decrease the number of judges. Until 1922 the Supreme Court was provided with three judges; after that date the Judicature Act, as amended,

[1]*Supra*, pp. 58-9.
[2]*Report on Dominion-Provincial Relations*, Book II, pp. 170-1.

declared that it was to be composed of a Chief Justice and three other judges, "provided that nothing herein contained shall be construed to require that the full Court be composed of four or any fixed number of Judges."[1] Difficulties with a three-man court provoked this change in statute. When a judge is unable to sit through illness or personal interest in a case, or when the trial judge is unable to sit on appeal, there are only two judges to make a decision, and, if they disagree, there is no decision. In such a small province cases in which one or other of the judges are interested to some extent are not improbable.[2] Moreover, the influence of an incompetent judge is much overweighted on a three-man court.

The province provided an extra seat on the bench in 1922 and the Attorney-General negotiated with the Dominion Government for the appointment of a fourth judge. The Dominion, however, was not convinced that the extra judge was necessary. Indeed even the provincial authorities did not agree on the matter, and a Cabinet crisis resulted.[3] Consequently the fourth judge was never appointed although the position was retained in the statute books. In 1947 an unsuccessful attempt was made in the Legislature to have a bill passed which would reduce the number of county court judges to two if the Dominion would appoint an extra judge to the Supreme Court. It was suggested that there were too many county court judges. "I remember talking to the late Judge Stewart," the Minister of Public Works told the House, "and he said there was not enough County Court work in the Province for one judge, and that he could do it all and part of the Supreme Court work too, and not be overworked."[4] Proposals were made to reduce the number of county court judges to one for the whole Island, or to divide the province into two county jurisdictions with one judge each. The practical obstacles to the change seem to have been the

[1] 4 Geo. VI, c. 35, s. 11 (c).
[2] A unique statute of 1856 provided that, where all the judges were interested in a case, the Lieutenant-Governor might issue, by and with the advice of the Executive Council, a special commission "to a fit and proper person, being a barrister of not less than five years' standing either at the bar of this Island, or of England, or of any of the British Colonies" to preside at court, and such a person was to be considered for the time being a judge with all the powers thereof and was to be paid £3 a day. 21 Vic., c. 13.
[3] The details of this issue are discussed *supra*, pp. 188-9.
[4] Hon. George Barbour in *Guardian*, April 5, 1947.

difficulty in adjusting two judgeships to three counties, and a controversial clause which permitted the Attorney-General to determine the circuits.[1] There was also no assurance that the Dominion would appoint the fourth judge to the Supreme Court, even if the local authorities agreed to reduce the number of county court judges.[2] The uncertainty seems to have dictated the postponement of a decision on the matter until the death or retirement of one of the sitting county court judges might facilitate a change.

[1] It is significant that this bill was a Government measure, and although it was introduced into a House in which the Government had a large majority, it was withdrawn.
[2] *Guardian*, April 5, 10, 1947.

CHAPTER XIII

LOCAL GOVERNMENT

JURISDICTION over municipal institutions in Canada is vested in the provincial legislatures by the British North America Act,[1] and local governments, consequently, are subordinate jurisdictions dependent upon provincial statutes for their creation, structure, and powers.[2] Actually, however, this relationship is accompanied by a substantial amount of regional democracy, for municipalities are not mere branches of the provincial administration but units of local self-government responsible directly to the citizens who elect them.

The administration of local communities in Prince Edward Island is a relatively simple process involving the affairs of one small city and seven towns which together comprise only 23 per cent of the total population of the province. There are no rural municipal authorities such as counties[3] and townships, and the predominantly rural population is thus dependent upon the provincial government for the conduct of the greater portion of its local business. Indeed the existence of a provincial government in such a small area makes an elaborate municipal administration unnecessary, while the simplicity of local units in turn lays greater emphasis on the need for an effective provincial organization.

The history of municipal government on the Island has been uneventful, for there have been no great issues of municipal reform and no significant struggles for local democracy. Before Confederation the communities, with the exception of Charlottetown, were straggling villages with no distinct systems of administration of their own. Local improvements of any magnitude, such as the building of streets, were largely the responsibility of the provincial government, while the simpler tasks, such as clearing and lighting the streets and manning the fire brigades, were dealt with by voluntary

---

[1]Section 92 (8).
[2]See J. A. Corry, *Democratic Government and Politics* (Toronto, 1946), chap. XIV, and H. C. Goldenberg, *Municipal Finance in Canada*, a study prepared for the Rowell-Sirois Commission (Ottawa, 1939).
[3]The three counties are geographic divisions only.

action of the citizens themselves. Regulation by provincial statute was largely confined to such rudimentary functions as preventing the running at large of animals, ordering the disposal of rubbish, and requiring the erection of fences. Charities and social services were left to the good offices of local organizations and individuals, although the Legislature rendered some small assistance by means of grants to those seeking its co-operation by petition.

THE CITY OF CHARLOTTETOWN

The first municipal administration on the Island was formed on August 17, 1855 when civic elections were held under the City of Charlottetown Incorporation Act of that year.[1] It was composed of a Mayor, elected at large, and ten "Common Councilmen," two for each of five wards, all elected for two years by the open vote of male property owners and tenants. The Council was to set up committees from among its members to perform special tasks subject to the control of Council, and appoint a Clerk, Treasurer, City Marshal, assessors, constables, and other clerks. This administration was empowered to make by-laws for the "good rule, peace, welfare, and government" of the city, which would include such local functions as police protection, fire control, lighting, and the regulation of markets and amusement houses. The Mayor was given no individual powers; he was to share those of the Council as a whole.

The provincial Government retained control over many of the Council's actions. All by-laws had to be sent to the Lieutenant-Governor-in-Council who, within three months, might disallow any of them. By-laws repugnant to "the laws of the land" were to be null and void, and no by-laws imposing tolls on articles brought into the city or limiting the sale thereon were to be valid until sanctioned by the Legislature. The appointment of a recorder or of a legal adviser to the Council had to be approved by the Cabinet. Control over finance was particularly rigid. The Council could "raise money by assessment" up to a sum of £1,000 annually; if it wanted more by assessment it had to apply to the Governor for leave, and such leave could be given up to an extra £250 only.

[1] 18 Vic., c. 34; see also *P.E.I. Magazine,* vol. IV, p. 22.

The issue of debentures was to be permitted only by special provincial statutes.[1]

The City Council was at first too large for the small number and limited significance of its functions, and there was much inefficiency. It was difficult to secure the services of competent personnel, for the trouble and expense of running elections for short terms of office and limited power and influence deterred most prominent citizens from entering municipal politics. "Everyone admits," said the *Patriot* in 1879, "that we, as citizens, are badly governed; and everyone says that a better class of men ought to be placed in the City Council, yet when the election comes no one acts upon his convictions, but allows the Corporation to jolt along in the old ruts."[2] The civic employees were apparently not drawn from the most respectable citizens. "There is scarcely one of them," said Mr. (later Justice) E. J. Hodgson of the policemen, "that has not either been in gaol for beating his wife or suspended for drunkenness."[3] Some improvement in the Council resulted from the increased number of its meetings after 1880,[4] and the reduction in its composition from ten to eight Councillors in 1891.[5] It was not until the city grew in size and population, however, that municipal politics could boast of some interest and efficiency and the machinery set up in 1855 became appropriate for the amount of business involved.

The qualifications for voting and holding office favour the property holders and business interests.[6] The Mayor and Councillors must have a small freehold or leasehold property in the city. Those who vote must be residents of at least one year's standing and British subjects of twenty-one years of age, and they must possess a small amount of freehold or leasehold property and pay a poll tax. Persons holding office or contract with the City, licensed teachers, clergymen, and members of the Legislature may not be

[1]See, for example, 46 Vic., c. 23.
[2]Charlottetown *Patriot,* July 26, 1879.
[3]*Ibid.,* Feb. 6, 1876.
[4]Regular meetings were held monthly rather than quarterly after 1880; 43 Vic., c. 15.
[5]55 Vic., c. 10. Efforts to abolish the ward system were unsuccessful. Charlottetown *Examiner* and *Patriot,* Feb. 14, 1901.
[6]See 12 Geo. VI, c. 43.

elected to the Council, although they may vote if otherwise qualified. Plural voting is permitted if a voter can qualify in more than one ward.

The work of the City Council is, comparatively speaking, not onerous and the amount of time spent by its members on official business depends on the individuals themselves. Civic politics are regarded as a duty of citizenship and little more than a part-time hobby. Remuneration is no attraction, for the Councillors are unpaid, and the Mayor receives only $325 per annum. Mayors have rarely had second terms, although Councillors generally seek re-election until they have a turn as Mayor.[1] Council posts are not generally regarded as stepping stones to provincial politics; indeed there is a sharp division between the two spheres as far as political machinery and influence are concerned. The City Council has to deal with the provincial Government whatever party is in power, and, consequently, the intrusion of party considerations into municipal politics has not been regarded as desirable.

The procedure of the City Council as outlined in the by-laws is much like that of the Legislative Assembly. The Mayor, who is chairman at all meetings, is supposed to preserve order and decorum, decide questions of procedure, and give a casting vote if there should be a tie; indeed he is expressly forbidden to take part in any debate unless to preserve order or give reasons for his casting vote. Actually, however, it is impossible for the Mayor, as the chief executive of the city, to maintain the position of the speaker in a legislature when circumstances compel him to discuss matters or defend actions for which he is responsible. Consequently, the Mayor generally participates in the debates of Council, the by-laws notwithstanding.[2] Discussions and decisions are carried out by motion and voting, and provision is made for an agenda and minutes under the supervision of the Clerk. It is also provided that "the law of parliamentary procedure shall be followed" where Council rules are not applicable, but most Councils carry on their business with

[1] Only 2 out of 21 Mayors since 1904 have had second terms. Previous to that date longer terms were the rule. Nevertheless, the Mayor was elected for a third term in 1950.
[2] See, for example, Charlottetown *Guardian*, Jan. 28, 31, 1950.

a lively informality which is more suitable for a nine-man group than for a legislature.

The administrative functions of the City Council are directed by its standing committees of which there are eight: finance, street, public property, market, police, fire, light and power, and tender. These committees are appointed by the Council from among its members and each Councillor is chairman of one committee. After policy is decided by the Council as a whole the appropriate committee becomes responsible for carrying out the details and instructing the city officials. Co-ordination among committees is facilitated by the fact that most members serve on several of them at once. Special committees may also be appointed to deal with questions of a more temporary nature.

There is also a Commission of Sewers and Water Supply consisting of three members who are elected at large along with the Council and who are paid $133.33 per annum. They are completely independent of the City Council except that their bond issues must be approved by it. This commission has its own office and staff of engineers and inspectors to administer the entire water system of the city.

The City officials are appointed by the Council with the exception of the stipendiary magistrate, who, although paid by the City, is appointed by the Lieutenant-Governor-in-Council. The City Clerk, who is called the "general accountant," is actually an administrator who is responsible to the Council as a whole. The recorder, assessors, chief of police, rate collectors, city surveyors, and other officers are responsible to the appropriate standing committee which directs their activities and reports thereon to the Council.[1]

About four-fifths of the City's revenue is secured from assessment on real property and personal property (autos, furniture, etc.) and from poll taxes.[2] The remainder is obtained from: (1) licences

[1]For example, the Police Committee of the Council controls and manages the police and prescribes and regulates their duties; a Police Commission, consisting of the Mayor as chairman, the chairman of the Police Committee, and a magistrate, have power to discipline, suspend, or discharge, and establish qualifications for officers; yet the power of appointment, subject to qualifications set by the Commission, is vested in the Council. 12 Geo. VI, c. 43, s. 135.

[2]Source: Financial Statements of the City of Charlottetown for year ending December 31, 1949.

on auctioneers, meat dealers, restaurants, etc., 1 per cent; (2) sundry taxes (on dogs and bicycles), rents (on city property), and police court fines, 3 per cent; (3) revenue from Commission of Sewers and Water Supply, 5 per cent; and (4) grants from the provincial Government for fire protection and the local library, for the vacating of the income tax fields under Dominion-provincial agreements, and for social and other municipal services, all of which amount to about 14 per cent of the total. This revenue is not large, but it has been sufficient to meet the city's needs in view of the number of local services which, as mentioned below, are taken over by the provincial Government.

Towns

The administration of towns before incorporation was generally informal and often disorganized, for a wide variety of committees and individuals dealt with minor local matters while the more important problems were attended to by the provincial Government. The first town to be incorporated was Summerside, which in 1877 received an administration modelled on that of Charlottetown.[1] The other towns, all of which remained unincorporated until after the turn of the century, received temporary governments to serve until they were big enough to seek charters. The government took the form of a "Board of Assessors" composed of five or six elected assessors of whom one was chairman. In all cases the by-laws and business transactions of these boards were subject to the supervision of the Lieutenant-Governor-in-Council.[2]

The procedure by which towns were to seek incorporation was set out in a statute entitled "An Act for the better government of certain rising Towns and Villages in this Island."[3] This act provided that residents in any town desiring incorporation could petition the Lieutenant-Governor-in-Council. The Governor was then to instruct a Justice of the Peace to lay out boundaries and call a meeting of all British male inhabitants over twenty-one years of age. If two-thirds[4]

[1] 40 Vic., c. 15.
[2] For examples of this type of organization, see 47 Vic., c. 16, 48 Vic., c. 7, and 62 Vic., c. 27.
[3] 33 Vic., c. 20.
[4] This figure was changed to "a majority" in 1874. 37 Vic., c. 19.

of the resident householders favoured incorporation, the Justice of the Peace was to advise the Governor and receive from him instructions to hold an election of three or more "Wardens" who were to administer the area until an act of incorporation was passed. Provision was made for the election of these wardens (one of whom was to be chairman), for local administration, and for the supervision of the provincial Government. This procedure was not used after 1919, and it was abolished in 1950. In the latter year a "Village Service Act" was passed which provided that a village might decide (by a poll of ratepayers) to place certain of its affairs under three "Village Commissioners" appointed by the Lieutenant-Governor-in-Council.[1] These commissioners could direct certain municipal services such as the construction of sidewalks and sewers, the provision of fire and police protection, and the like. They could make by-laws but these must be approved by a Minister. Communities which are not large enough for incorporation may thus secure small administrations of their own.

The machinery set up in the various towns as they became incorporated was not elaborate, nor did it differ to any great degree from place to place.[2] In all cases provision was made for a Town Council consisting of a Mayor and six Councillors. In some instances this body was elected annually, but eventually the term was everywhere extended to two years.[3] There was always a small property qualification of $500 for members, but nowhere was a salary provided for either the Mayor or his colleagues. No one could sit on any of the Councils while holding office or contract under it, and in all cases school-teachers, judges, magistrates, and sheriffs were disqualified. A special statute provided that no person holding the post of Mayor or Councillor in any municipality could sit in the provincial Legislature.[4] A property qualification for voters was included, and it varied from $100 to $400. The Mayor and Coun-

[1]14 Geo. VI, c. 30.
[2]See Souris, 10 Ed. VII, c. 21; Georgetown, 2 Geo. V, c. 29; Alberton, 3 Geo. V, c. 27; Kensington, 4 Geo. V, c. 14; Montague, 7 Geo. V, c. 17; Borden, 9-10 Geo. V, c. 23.
[3]It was customary at first to have annual elections and two-year terms, with one half the members retiring each year. This procedure proved too cumbersome and unnecessary, and it was changed to provide that all retire together every second year.
[4]4 Ed. VII, c. 2.

cillors have always been elected at large except in Summerside and Montague where the Councillors are elected by wards. The Councillors are divided into committees in the larger towns to deal with specific matters such as assessment, streets, property, and fire. Provision is made in all cases for the appointment of a Clerk, Treasurer, collectors, and other such officers, generally on a part-time basis.

The municipal administration in the towns is actually much simpler than it appears on paper. There is much indifference in the selection of the Town Councils and in the manner in which they carry out their duties. The interest in town politics is so small that there has been little competition for the post of Mayor or Councillor. Georgetown was a striking example of this in 1921 when no one was nominated for any of its civic offices, and a special statute had to be passed to continue the existing incumbents for another term.[1] Such difficulties were subsequently provided for by special rules which permit officers to continue until their successors are elected. Consequently the Mayors and Councillors of most towns remain in office from term to term until they wish to be relieved of their duties.

Municipal problems on the Island do not differ greatly from town to town, and the structure and functions of the local administrations have consequently tended to assume a standard pattern over the years. This trend has been recognized by the passing of the Town Act of 1948 which has guaranteed a separate government to each town, but has provided the same institutions and powers for all except Summerside.[2] The Act is administered by any Minister of the Crown who happens for the time being to be charged by the Governor-in-Council with the responsibility. It provides for each town a Mayor and six Councillors who are elected for two years or until their successors are appointed. The occasional difficulty of finding persons to take office is covered by a unique clause which permits the Minister to fill vacancies with his own appointees, whether otherwise qualified or not. In all other respects the powers and functions set out are substantially the same as those granted to Charlottetown and Summerside.

[1] 11 Geo. V, c. 16.
[2] "An Act to Provide Uniform Legislation for the Towns of Prince Edward Island," 12 Geo. VI, c. 39.

The functions of the Town Councils include management of town property, regulation of local businesses and amusements, prevention of fires and public nuisance, control of animals, and direction of municipal improvements. The streets are usually little more than side roads with asphalt, cinder, or plank sidewalks, and the small sums devoted to their upkeep come from either local funds or special assistance given by the provincial Government. Since the main street usually forms part of a public highway, the province generally provides for its upkeep. Water supply and sanitation systems for the towns are not elaborate, and most of the operations in this sphere are in private hands. The fire brigade in all municipalities, including Charlottetown, consists of volunteers. A policeman or two is generally sufficient for the local constabulary, or perhaps a town will depend entirely on the services of the Royal Canadian Mounted Police in the vicinity, for which the provincial Government pays the federal Government $1,000 per man. The funds available to the town from municipal taxes are small. They are derived from real and personal property taxes, poll taxes, and special taxes and licence fees on horses, trucks, taxis, etc. But the rural surroundings and the absence of concentrations of industrial and personal wealth restrict the income available to the towns, and force the local Councils to appeal frequently to the provincial Government for assistance.

Provincial-Municipal Relations

The relations between the provincial and local governments are dominated by the fact that the Island is small enough to permit the ready administration of many local services by the central government and by the inability of the towns to bear the cost of elaborate facilities of their own. The Cabinet and Legislature are close to the people for whose affairs they are responsible, and the local districts are well represented in both. Moreover, the interests of the two spheres of administration are often so similar that it is difficult to distinguish them. Municipal affairs consequently depend on the relations between the Government and the towns to a much greater extent than in the other provinces and their significance is affected accordingly.

Many of the newer functions, particularly the social services, for which the municipalities would normally have been responsible, have been retained by the Province because of local inability to pay for them and because it has not been financially or administratively desirable to maintain in each small area the required institutions, staff, and equipment. The Department of Health and Welfare and other such bodies have thus assumed the appropriate responsibilities for the whole province, and left to the towns only those functions which can most readily be performed by local Councils with limited resources. Even where the Province could have given special grants for municipal enterprises, it has often preferred to spend the money and direct the enterprises itself. There are instances where the towns might prefer to settle some of their own problems, but these are often left unsolved because the Province does not choose to assume the burden. This inaction is only too frequently caused by the fact that the provincial Government is itself generally short of funds, and it cannot divert too large a proportion of its revenues to municipal purposes because the urban population comprises less than a quarter of the total. Moreover local administration is further limited by the enforcement of regulations with respect to standards, inspection, and other forms of control by the provincial authorities.

The relations between the City of Charlottetown and the provincial Government are somewhat different from those arising between the latter and other municipal authorities, although in degree rather than substance. Inasmuch as the Legislature and Cabinet consist largely of men from the small towns and rural areas, the official attitude to civic needs has a strong rural bias. Direct representation of the city in the Cabinet has often been advocated, but has not always been given. The Mayor has had to serve as the main link with the Government, and his effectiveness in this respect has generally depended almost entirely upon his personal relations with the Premier.

The provincial Government has assumed the task of co-ordinating the various bodies which share the responsibility for community services. Broadly speaking these services are performed by the municipalities, the provincial Government, private agencies, and joint enterprises. In addition the Dominion has provided funds for certain special services which are largely handled by the Province. The municipalities deal with fire prevention, police protection, sanitation, building inspection and the erection of community halls, rinks, and other buildings. The provincial Government maintains hospitals for the insane and for those afflicted with tuberculosis, a home for the poor, public health clinics, research laboratories, a town planning office, and other such institutions which can readily serve the entire province. It may also supplement municipal efforts where they are inadequate, e.g. in providing extra police protection or sanitation facilities. The private agencies such as the hospitals, orphanages, free dispensaries, churches, and the Red Cross Society carry (with some assistance from the Government) a large share of poor relief, children's aid, and the various forms of home service. Some services, such as garbage disposal, which are performed by many municipalities elsewhere, must be arranged and paid for by the individual citizens themselves. The Dominion and provincial Governments and private organizations share the expense of the facilities for crippled children, control of tuberculosis, cancer, and other diseases, and general public health.

Joint enterprises nearly always take the form of a pooling of financial resources with the administration in the hands of one body. The schools, however, are administered and financed jointly by the local areas and the provincial Government. The province is divided into school districts each with its own elected board of trustees. The Minister of Education is responsible for the supervision of schools, the licensing of teachers, and the maintenance of the standards of instruction. The trustees manage the school property and funds and employ the teachers. Teachers' salaries are paid partly from the provincial treasury and partly by district assessment; all other items of fixed or current expenditures are the responsibility of the district. The province sets minimum salaries for each class of teachers and in the rural areas provides approximately five-sixths of the amount so specified. It also pays a "supplement" amounting to one-half any amount raised by the district by local assessment over and above the minimum salary required of the district. The Boards of Trustees in Charlottetown and Summerside are composed of representatives of both the Province and the local Council.[1]

Another type of joint enterprise is the local board of health created by the Public Health Act. The board is composed in each municipality of the Mayor and Councillors, and in rural districts (known as "health units") of five residents appointed by the provincial Government. These bodies are empowered to make public health regulations of a local nature under the supervision and instruction of the Lieutenant-Governor-in-Council.[2] The system has been in existence only a short time, and it is too early to assess the efficiency of the boards or the effectiveness of their co-operation with the provincial Department of Health and Welfare.

The close association between province and municipalities has not altered the broad principle of local self-government (although it has to a degree affected the practical operation of that principle), for the Province has interfered as little as possible in the passage of municipal by-laws of a purely local nature. The towns, as already indicated, were required originally to submit their regulations to the Lieutenant-Governor-in-Council who had the power to veto them. This review caused much delay, and, as Premier Sullivan told the Legislature, many resented the fact that the Cabinet "constituted a court of appeal" from the Town Council.[3] The practice was dropped in Charlottetown in 1880 and in Summerside in 1887, and it has never been enforced in the other towns.[4] Nevertheless, the general restriction which prohibited the municipalities from passing by-laws repugnant to provincial statutes was maintained, and any venture on their part into activities unprovided for in their charters has still to be approved by special legislation. There is little danger,

[1] See 10-11 Geo. V, c. 6; 4 Geo. VI, c. 1; 9 Geo. VI, c. 11; 11 Geo. VI, c. 32.
[2] 10 Geo. VI, c. 26 as amended by 13 Geo. VI, c. 18.
[3] *P.E.I. House of Assembly Debates*, 1887, p. 118.
[4] As already noted, village by-laws must be approved by the Minister responsible for the administration of the Village Service Act.

however, of their trespassing on provincial jurisdiction; indeed their prosperity depends on encouraging the Province to increase its interest in municipal affairs. Consequently, what there is of local administration is still largely autonomous but subject to provincial oversight; and interdependence, particularly in new fields, is likely to increase with as yet unpredictable effects on local self-government.

CHAPTER XIV

THE PROVINCE AND THE DOMINION

THE RELATIONS between Prince Edward Island and the federal Government are dominated by the small size and population of the province. These characteristics, so evident at Confederation, have since raised many questions as to the role in a large nation of a tiny island which could boast a total population no bigger than a medium-size city in another province. The Island, moreover, is not strategically placed in the union, but is situated at one end of the continent and at least nine miles from the coast of its nearest neighbour. It is not on the main lines of commerce, and Northumberland Strait keeps it isolated, particularly during the winter months. It has few bargaining assets, either economic or political; it does not produce anything which is not available in quantity elsewhere, although it boasts high quality in agricultural products and fish. Transportation costs make it difficult for the province to compete with producers elsewhere in the goods which it can export. Politically, the number of votes contributed by the Island is very small, and its members of Parliament have rarely played major roles at Ottawa.

Size, however, is not everything in public affairs. Regardless of the extent of its influence and material wealth, the Island is a province and a partner in Confederation with rights and responsibilities of its own. Nature has seen fit to give it its location and characteristics which in turn have led to a separate government and a distinctive public life; like Rhode Island and Tasmania, it must make the best of what it has in a large and complicated federal system. The Island therefore presents a special problem in Dominion-provincial relations, that of recognizing its peculiar difficulties and privileges, yet giving it a place in national affairs commensurate with its size and influence.

Why should such a small province have a government all its own for so few people? The answer, which has been suggested in earlier pages, is contained in the traditional belief of its public men that the province is too distinct in both location and outlook to flourish under the possibly careless attentions of a distant government in another province. Maritime union has sometimes been suggested as a logical arrangement for the three eastern provinces, but the official attitude of the Island has never been favourable to such a plan. When the Government of Nova Scotia invited the Island in 1877 to appoint delegates to a conference to discuss Maritime union, the Island Cabinet declined.[1] The *Examiner* occasionally commented favourably on Maritime union during the adjustments which followed Confederation,[2] but such observations became comparatively rare after 1880. "So far as this province is concerned," said the *Patriot* in 1885, "any attempt to adopt such a scheme would be snuffed out, and the political party that would entertain such a proposition for a moment would, and ought to be, looked upon ever after with suspicion."[3] There was some sporadic discussion on the subject as late as 1905 after the Island's representation in the House of Commons was reduced, but it did not arouse widespread public interest.[4] At this time a friend of Laurier asked the Prime Minister if Maritime union would not be a solution to many problems. "I doubt if any change will ever take place in the condition of things in the Maritime Provinces," replied Sir Wilfrid. "You could no more induce Nova Scotia, New Brunswick and Prince Edward Island to drop their identity than you could get Rhode Island, Connecticut and New Hampshire to join together. Such communities are particularly tenacious of their autonomy. It is a respectable sentiment and one which must be recognized."[5] This exclusiveness did not, however, prevent joint action of the Island and its neighbours on matters of mutual concern. As one Premier emphasized in 1937, the Island would oppose any plan of

[1]For correspondence see *P.E.I. House of Assembly Journals*, 1878, Appendix M.
[2]Charlottetown *Examiner*, April 13, May 11, 18, Sept. 21, 28, 1874.
[3]Charlottetown *Patriot*, June 5, 1885.
[4]See *Examiner*, May 15, 1905.
[5]Laurier to A. E. Burke, Nov. 30, 1906, Public Archives of Canada, Laurier Papers, no. 3581. See also *Canada, House of Commons, Debates,* May 26, 1912, p. 6147.

Maritime union, but it would co-operate with Nova Scotia and New Brunswick on common problems.[1]

This attitude was once reflected in the Island's sad reminiscences of the times when she stood alone. "We as a people," said the *Patriot* solemnly in 1879, "have certainly no cause to rejoice on Dominion Day."[2] Black crêpe adorned the entrance of the Provincial Building on July 1, 1880. "Crape on the door of our Provincial Building," mourned the *Patriot*, "represents the feeling of sorrow for their lost independence entertained by a very large majority of the inhabitants of this Province. Nine Prince Edward Islanders out of ten feel that . . . it was a calamity that ever Prince Edward Island entered the Dominion."[3] The reason for this outlook at that time was the province's exclusion from the advantages of the main federal efforts of the day—interprovincial trade, western expansion, railway building, and Macdonald's tariff policies. These efforts prompted a long and complicated series of complaints with respect to the Island's share in national affairs, the accusation that the terms of union had not been honoured by the Dominion, and a demand for more representation and influence in the federal Government. After the turn of the century the old regret that the province had joined the union passed away, but the special Island problems have remained as part of the complications of Dominion-provincial relations. These involved such issues as representation at Ottawa, the solution of the land question, communications with the mainland, and financial assistance.

REPRESENTATION IN PARLIAMENT

Provincial influence in federal affairs is not solely a matter of relations between the local and federal Governments, but also of participation by provincial representatives in the Dominion Parliament and Cabinet. Prince Edward Island's experience in this respect

---

[1] Thane A. Campbell, *Canadian Annual Review*, 1937-8, p. 289. For a detailed discussion on the merits and disadvantages of Maritime union see George G. Melvin, "Maritime Union," *University Magazine*, Oct., 1909, p. 436; also C. R. Fay, "Problems of the Maritime Provinces," *Dalhousie Review*, Jan., 1925, p. 438.
[2] *Patriot*, July 3, 1879. [3] *Ibid.*, July 3, 1880.

raises the delicate and controversial question of just how much recognition a small province should have at Ottawa.

Representation in the Senate and the Supreme Court of Canada has not raised any serious problems. In 1867 the Maritimes were given a bloc of twenty-four senatorships, and in 1873 four of these went by previous arrangement to the Island. The province is therefore very much over-represented in the Senate from the standpoint of population,[1] and, like the other small provinces of Canada and the small states of the United States, it benefits from the theory that the upper chamber should represent regions rather than population. While appointments to the Supreme Court of Canada have been federalized to a limited extent, there has been no suggestion that the Island has any steady claim to a seat on that tribunal or a regular turn in the succession of appointments, and it has been content to receive its share with the other Maritime provinces. Only Sir Louis Davies has represented the province on the Court, but the fact that he sat from 1901 to 1924 and became Chief Justice of Canada gave his province the feeling that it had made a substantial contribution to the federal judiciary.

The main issues with respect to Island representation at Ottawa involve the House of Commons and the federal Cabinet. Prince Edward Island was originally assigned six seats in the House of Commons on the basis of its population in 1873. These were distributed two to each of the three counties, and each county thereupon became a two-member constituency. This representation could not be maintained, however, in view of the steadily decreasing population of the Island. Consequently, and in accordance with section 51 of the British North America Act which provided for readjustment of representation after each census, the Island suffered a series of reductions in its number of members of Parliament.[2] In 1892 the number was reduced to five,[3] in 1904 to four,[4] and in 1911 the province became entitled to only three members.

[1]The population per senator in Prince Edward Island is approximately 23,800, in Nova Scotia 57,800, in New Brunswick 45,800; and in the other provinces it varies from 122,000 in Manitoba to 158,000 in Ontario.
[2]The Island arrangement differed from that of British Columbia which provided that the number of members in that province could be "increased" under the provisions of the B.N.A. Act but apparently not decreased. Order-in-Council admitting British Columbia into the union, *The British North America Acts and Selected Statutes* (Ottawa, 1943), p. 163.
[3]55-56 Vic., c. 11.   [4]3 Ed. VII, c. 60.

The provincial Legislature and Cabinet made strong representations to the federal Government after the census of 1901, claiming that the spirit of federation and consideration for the rights of a small province dictated that the original number of members should remain untouched. A reduction, they said, was a breach of the "compact" made by the Island delegates at Quebec, and might lead in time to the province having no members at all.[1] In 1903 Premier Arthur Peters carried on a series of unsuccessful negotiations on the subject with the Laurier Government in Ottawa.[2] New Brunswick meanwhile was suffering from the same complaint, and the two provinces joined in an appeal to the courts.[3]

Before the Supreme Court of Canada Mr. (later Sir) Allen Aylesworth, chief counsel for the two provinces, based the issue on the theory that the original representation had been part of a binding contract, and therefore, could not be reduced:

Our position is that under the terms of that compact and agreement, Prince Edward Island was given six members in the House of Commons and that that representation was then fixed for the Island,— not as a matter of right, not as a matter of giving representation by population in accordance with the provisions of the British North America Act itself, but because of the peculiarly isolated position of the Province, and because unless there had been an arrangement of that sort it would, as the delegates to the Conference from the Island stated, have been quite impossible to have carried in the Island the terms of Union. . . . it was a term of the Union that the Representation of the Island should be six members at least, and it was never contemplated that that number should at a future time be reduced.[4]

The Supreme Court disagreed, and reminded the Island that the Order-in-Council which admitted it in 1873 provided that its representation was "to be readjusted, from time to time, under the provisions of the British North America Act, 1867." The judgment

[1] See resolutions of the Assembly, in *Assembly Journals*, 1902, p. 93; *ibid.*, 1903, p. 32; *Canada, House of Commons, Debates*, April 14, 1903, pp. 1269-82. The reference to the Quebec Conference was quite irrelevant (*a*) because there was no "compact" made there, and (*b*) because the Island dissociated itself from the Quebec terms.
[2] *Examiner*, June 3, 1903; *Patriot*, Feb. 17, 1903.
[3] See *Canadian Annual Review*, 1904, p. 354.
[4] Public Archives of Canada, *Representation Case to Supreme Court of Canada: Report of Proceedings* (Charlottetown, 1903), p. 3.

also pointed out that the other provinces had just as much right to say they would not have joined unless their terms were more favourable.[1] The two provinces thereupon appealed in 1904 to the Judicial Committee of the Privy Council which upheld the judgment of the Supreme Court upon substantially the same grounds.[2]

During the decade which followed these decisions, the Island exerted constant political pressure upon the Dominion Government in an attempt to bolster its falling representation.[3] When A. B. Aylesworth became Minister of Justice in 1905, the Islanders thought their chance had now come, but, to their chagrin, he opposed the provincial views which he had championed before the courts a few years before.[4] The province suggested an amendment to the British North America Act which would provide that "each Province of the Dominion of Canada should have as a minimum representation in the House of Commons, the representation it had on becoming a Province of the Dominion."[5] Premier Haszard's Government announced that it would fight for this principle to the point of "rebellion," and its leader carried on negotiations with other provincial governments in an effort to secure nation-wide support for the claim.[6]

The matter was not settled until Premier J. A. Mathieson met with the Borden Government in Ottawa in January, 1914 and demanded that the original representation be restored as a permanent minimum. Sir Robert Borden suggested a compromise to the effect that no province should have fewer members in the House of Commons than it had in the Senate. This arrangement would give the Island a permanent minimum representation of at least four members. Mathieson agreed, and the plan was later embodied in the 1915 amendment to the British North America Act.[7] This guarantee

[1]*Ibid.*, pp. 60-1. Sir Louis Davies, who had long championed the Island's case in Parliament, was then on the Court and he agreed with the judgment.
[2]*Attorney-General for Prince Edward Island* v. *Attorney-General for Canada* and *Attorney-General for New Brunswick* v. *Attorney-General for Canada*, [1905] A.C. 37.
[3]See address from the Assembly to the Governor-General, *Assembly Journals*, 1905, pp. 64-5; *Examiner*, April 24, 26, 1905.
[4]*Ibid.*, Feb. 7, 9, 1907.
[5]*Assembly Journals*, 1910, p. 117; see also *Examiner*, April 8, 1910.
[6]*Canadian Annual Review*, 1910, p. 474.
[7]5-6 Geo. V, c. 45.

was preserved in the British North America Act of 1946 which instituted a new arrangement for the readjustment of representation in the House of Commons.[1] Prince Edward Island is therefore now represented by four members of Parliament. The three counties form three federal constituencies, Prince and Kings having one member each, and Queens two members.

REPRESENTATION IN THE CABINET

The federalization of the national Cabinet has long been an outstanding principle in Canadian politics. The Cabinet must provide representation for many of the different regions and interest groups of the Dominion in order that none of the significant sections of public opinion should be overlooked in the formulation of high policy. One aspect of this principle requires that, where possible, each province should have a representative in the Cabinet.[2]

The Island has not fared well in this respect since Confederation.[3] There are two reasons. On the one hand the demands upon a Prime Minister for Cabinet posts are innumerable, and it has usually been difficult for him to assign one of the cherished seats to such a small area. Secondly, the province returns so few members that a capable prospective Minister is not always among them. There has very rarely been an Island member who could effectively demand such a promotion because of his prominence in the party structure, or because he commanded great personal prestige in national, as distinct from purely local, affairs.[4]

In the seventy-eight years since the Island entered Confederation, she has been represented in the federal Cabinet by local politicians for a total of only twenty-three years, despite many assurances from Prime Ministers that she was entitled to a seat. On three occasions, however, the Island has provided a convenient con-

[1]10 Geo. VI, c. 63.
[2]See Norman McLeod Rogers, "Federal Influences on the Canadian Cabinet," *Canadian Bar Review*, Feb., 1933.
[3]Contrast R. MacGregor Dawson, *The Government of Canada* (Toronto, 1947), pp. 212-13.
[4]For instance, an examination of the proceedings in Parliament clearly indicates that Prince Edward Island members rarely concern themselves with anything but Island matters. A prominent exception, Sir Louis Davies, participated effectively in federal affairs of all kinds, and was in many ways a national figure.

stituency for Cabinet Ministers from other provinces who for one reason or another were in need of a seat.[1] Technically speaking, these visiting Ministers were considered Island representatives in the Cabinet, but their interests were only remotely associated with the province. Precedent, therefore, has not established a rule that the province must have a seat, despite Professor Norman Rogers's prediction that the practice would likely be followed of giving her a seat without portfolio.[2] The omission has been remedied somewhat since 1943, for, with the exception of two years, the Island has been represented in Ottawa by a parliamentary assistant.

The most significant statement on this problem was made in 1902 by Sir Wilfrid Laurier. Sir Louis Davies had gone to the bench, and the Island Liberals were clamouring for the appointment to the Cabinet of Donald Farquharson who had resigned the premiership to contest the seat vacated by Davies. Laurier had previously welcomed provincial Premiers to the Cabinet, but he did not elevate Farquharson when the latter won the seat, although there was a Cabinet vacancy at the time.[3] When the local Government demanded the post for Farquharson[4] Laurier replied that representation of the Island was secondary to personal qualifications, and that he had given the seat to a member from the West:

> This policy is dictated by general reasons resulting largely from the fact of the more rapid development of that section of the country. Such a rule is not, however, absolutely invariable, and a man may arise in any locality, East or West, of such power as to command his own place. Sir Louis Davies was a man of that character. Without any disparagement to any of the members that were elected in 1900 in Prince Edward Island, no one would claim to occupy such a place as he did. As to Mr. Farquharson, I do not know him yet sufficiently to form an

---

[1] W. L. Mackenzie King sought temporary shelter in the security of the Liberal stronghold in Prince County from 1919 to 1921; J. L. Ralston represented Prince from 1940 until his retirement in 1945; and Charles A. Dunning represented one of the Queens County constituencies from December, 1935 until July, 1939.

[2] "Federal Influences on the Canadian Cabinet," p. 115.

[3] Farquharson won a by-election on January 11, 1902, and R. R. Dobell, Minister without Portfolio, had died just four days before.

[4] Premier Arthur Peters to Laurier, Jan. 16, 1902, P.A.C., Laurier Papers, file 3096½.

opinion, but he will have an opportunity very soon to take his place in the House of Commons and to achieve for himself the position he may be entitled [to] therein.¹

Laurier thus emphasized the main factor with respect to Island representation in the Cabinet. Since Prime Ministers usually consider her too small to command a seat as a matter of right, her federal members, in order to qualify, must include someone who is sufficiently capable "to achieve for himself the position."

A Cabinet Minister in Canada is recognized as having a special duty toward the province which he represents. He plays a leading role in the relations between the provincial and federal Governments, and between the federal and local party machines. Within the Cabinet he is a ready source of information on official, party, and public opinion in the province, and he is an effective agent for impressing executive views and desires upon his constituents. He is sufficiently familiar with local personalities to wield substantial influence in the making of federal appointments and in planning federal public works.² When Prince Edward Island has had a representative in the Cabinet, he has proved no exception to the rule. When one has been lacking, she has been forced to seek some other arrangement.

This influence is best illustrated in the making of appointments. When a vacancy occurs in Government House, on the provincial bench, or among the Island's senators, it has been the practice for the federal Government to obtain the opinion of the Cabinet Minister from the province.³ He in turn frequently consults with any other provincial representatives in Parliament that are supporting the Government, and with the provincial Government as well if it belongs to the same party. He will endeavour to secure a candidate acceptable to all of these, but in case of disagreement his opinion

¹Laurier to Peters, Jan. 20, 1902, *ibid.* The opportunity did not come to Mr. Farquharson, for he was in indifferent health and died a few months later.
²See Dawson, *The Government of Canada,* pp. 214-15.
³Sir Louis Davies handled federal appointments in the Island to such an extent that Premier Farquharson complained to the Prime Minister that Davies was wielding too much patronage, and that the local party organization should have more of it. Farquharson to Laurier, June 13, 1901, P.A.C., Laurier Papers, file 2256.

will generally be the deciding factor. Thus an Island Minister in recent years was known to insist on a doubtful senatorial appointment despite the strong objections of the local Government and the party organization. In judicial appointments, however, the opinion of the local Government is usually supposed to carry more weight where the Premier or the Attorney-General is available for the post, and, of course, the Minister of Justice will have substantial influence in the final decision. In the case of the lieutenant-governorship, as already mentioned, both federal representatives and the provincial Government are usually consulted, if they are of the same party as the Dominion Government. Other factors, such as the personal relations between Prime Minister and Premier, are also important, but it is generally the Minister who takes the initiative and sponsors the recommendations. Where there is no Minister from the Island in the Cabinet, the Prime Minister will generally handle appointments himself after consultation with his federal supporters, the provincial Government (if belonging to his party), and even, at times, with the local party organizations.

The Land Question

The land question, as chapter v has indicated, was always a contentious issue between the Island and the mother country in the colonial period, and, when the province entered Confederation, it became a continuing problem of Dominion-provincial relations. The Dominion agreed to assist the Island in the purchase of the proprietary holdings, and the Order-in-Council which united the province with Canada included a special clause to this effect: "As the Government of Prince Edward Island holds no lands from the Crown, and consequently enjoys no revenue from that source for the construction and maintenance of local works, the Dominion Government shall pay by half-yearly instalments, in advance, to the Government of Prince Edward Island, forty-five thousand dollars per annum, less interest at five per centum per annum, upon any sum not exceeding eight hundred thousand dollars which the Dominion Government may advance to the Prince Edward Island Government for the purchase of lands now held by large proprietors." Thus after years of ineffective appeals to the Imperial Government, the Island obtained the desired financial aid which, it was hoped, would finally settle the issue.

One of the first acts of the provincial Government after the union was to draw up a plan of compulsory arbitration to dispossess the proprietors.[1] This plan was embodied in the Land Purchase Act of 1874, which provided for the appointment of a commission of three members to set a value upon the estates, and arranged for an appeal in contested cases to the local Supreme Court. The proprietors immediately branded the bill as "communist," an "outrage on law and justice," "subversive to the rights of property," "most ruinous to the proprietors," "class legislation of the most hurtful and pernicious kind," and "a dangerous precedent to establish as a mode of allaying popular agitation." The outcry was such that the Lieutenant-Governor reserved the bill for the Governor-General's pleasure, and the federal Government advised that assent be refused because the act did not provide for sufficiently impartial arbitration.[2] A new measure was thereupon passed in the following year. It was substantially the same in principle as its predecessor, but it altered the procedure of the commission in such a way as to ensure an adequate hearing to all parties.[3] The Governor again reserved the bill; but this time the Governor-General's signature was duly inscribed and the bill became law.[4] There was a great rejoicing in the province, and the Government proceeded to carry out its plan.

The commission held periodic sittings during the fall of 1875. Counsel and witnesses were heard in each case, and various compensations were fixed. Before final settlement could be made, however, one of the proprietors appealed to the local Supreme Court, and, on technical grounds, the Court unanimously set aside the award in her case. Doubt was thus thrown upon the whole proceedings, the tenants were once more aroused, and popular agitation

[1]*P.E.I. House of Assembly Debates*, 1874, p. 211.
[2]The correspondence is in *Assembly Journals*, 1875, Appendix E. See also *Assembly Debates*, 1874, pp. 260-4, and *Patriot*, Jan. 21, Feb. 11, 1875.
[3]*Assembly Journals*, 1875, p. 34; *ibid.*, 1876, Appendix E.
[4]See Public Archives of Canada, Governor-General's File, G series, vol. 21, no. 63.

was renewed. After some hesitation, the Government instituted an appeal to the Supreme Court of Canada. The Court unanimously upheld the Land Purchase Act and stressed the importance, not merely of landlord rights, but also of tenant rights and of the development of the province.[1]

This judgment ended the century-old land question as far as the proprietary system was concerned. The commissioners met again and concluded the necessary arrangements. The purchase prices were paid forthwith and the land was transferred to the provincial Government, which later sold it to the tenants.[2] In view of the long and turbulent history of the issue, it is not surprising that in 1887, on the occasion of renewed friction between England and Ireland over the latter's land question, the Island Assembly passed a resolution expressing the deep sympathy for Ireland of a people that knew from bitter experience what such trouble involved.[3]

This solution of the land question would not have been possible without the financial assistance of the Dominion Government, and in that respect the Island was especially fortunate in its Confederation bargain. But what both the Dominion and the province appeared too easily to forget was that the real responsibility for the solution of the issue lay with the Imperial Government which had so long neglected it, and that the Dominion was merely assisting the province to assume the burden. The Dominion did its best under the circumstances, but it did not pay the necessary expenses; it only provided a loan of up to a total of $800,000, and received in turn interest at 5 per cent per annum on the latter amount.[4] The province then neglected to pay back the loan as the tenants purchased the lands, despite the fact that it received some $600,000 from the

---

[1] "The recital in the Statute," wrote the Chief Justice, "that it was desirable to convert the leasehold tenures into freehold estates, indicated that it was a matter affecting the public interest. This Statute ought, therefore, to be viewed, not as ordinary legislation, but as the settling of an important question of great moment to the community, and in principle like the abolition of seigneurial tenure in Lower Canada and the settling of the land question in Ireland." *Kelly* v. *Sullivan*, (1876) 1 S.C.R. 3.

[2] The last estate to be bought out under the act of 1875, the W. Sidney Smith property, was purchased in 1895. Even at that late date the proprietors unsuccessfully petitioned the Governor-General to disallow the act as "subversive to the rights of property." *Assembly Journals*, 1896, Appendix D.

[3] *Ibid.*, 1887, p. 133.

[4] The loan actually amounted to $782,402.33.

sale. Consequently it still pays the interest which is deducted from the subsidy allowed in lieu of public lands.[1]

This arrangement was nevertheless satisfactory to the province until the 1920's when the local Government, seeking more revenue, asked for an additional subsidy in lieu of land. A comparison with the land subsidies given to the western provinces apparently prompted this request, and at the hearings before the Duncan Commission in 1926 and the White Commission in 1935 the Island claimed redress for this discrimination. The western provinces, it was pointed out, received substantial land subsidies without deductions, whereas the Island had actually received comparatively little. Neither of these Commissions made any specific recommendations on the land claim other than to note that it was belated and that any difficulty associated with it had already been taken into account in other ways.[2] The Island Government repeated its case before the Rowell-Sirois Commission, and this time asked the cancellation of the entire loan.[3] But the commission took the same view as the Duncan and White Commissions and could "see no sound reason for reopening the matter."[4] It pointed out, however, that the claim would in effect be settled under its general proposals which included a recommendation that the Dominion should assume all of the provincial debt.[5]

At the present time this residue of the land question still remains a problem of Dominion-provincial relations. One hundred and eighty years after the original grants were made to the proprietors, the final cost has yet to be paid of "the association of rights in the soil with rights of government."

[1]The $45,000 subsidy is accordingly reduced to $6,000. It is, of course, not paid while the Dominion-provincial agreement of 1947 is in force; see *infra*, pp. 312-13.
[2]"Memorial of Claim of P.E.I. for an Increase in Its Subsidy in Lieu of Public Lands," *Assembly Journals*, 1930, Appendix I; *Report of the Royal Commission on Maritime Claims* (Ottawa, 1926), pp. 18-19; *Report of the Royal Commission on Financial Arrangements between the Dominion and the Maritime Provinces* (Ottawa, 1935), pp. 17-18; *Attorney-General's Brief for the Province of Prince Edward Island for Readjustment of Financial Arrangements* (Charlottetown, 1934).
[3]*The Case of Prince Edward Island: A Submission to the Royal Commission on Dominion-Provincial Relations* (Charlottetown), pp. 9-10, 53-4.
[4]*Report of the Royal Commission on Dominion-Provincial Relations* (Ottawa, 1940), Book II, pp. 265-6.
[5]See also *ibid.*, pp. 87-8.

COMMUNICATIONS

The communications question has resulted from an alleged non-fulfilment of the terms of union. The federal Government agreed in 1873 to provide for "efficient steam service for the conveyance of mails and passengers, to be established and maintained between the Island and the mainland of the Dominion, Winter and Summer, thus placing the Island in continuous communication with the Intercolonial Railway and the railway system of the Dominion."[1] The Island's politicians had urged in 1873 that this provision was an essential condition of Confederation and that the province would not join without such an arrangement, for it could not prosper as part of Canada unless its links with the other provinces were strengthened.[2]

For many years communications were neither "continuous" nor "efficient." The service was provided by a succession of obsolete steamers which were slow in summer and virtually powerless in winter.[3] A constant flow of correspondence circulated between Charlottetown and Ottawa. The local Government and Legislature protested that the economy of the province suffered from lack of connections with mainland commerce; and they accused the Dominion of ignoring the Island while undertaking vast public works in the west.[4] The federal Government was of the opinion that it had done all that was possible in view of the difficult physical conditions of the Northumberland Strait, and that "both contracting parties to the union" understood the difficulties. The Dominion reminded the Island that it contributed little to the national revenues, and rebuked it for comparing the steam service with "a great national work," the Canadian Pacific Railway.[5] The Island's reply was that

[1] Order-in-Council, June 26, 1873, admitting Prince Edward Island into the union. *The British North America Acts and Selected Statutes*, p. 171.
[2] *Supra*, chapter VI.
[3] For a detailed discussion of the communications issue, see Frank MacKinnon, "Communications between Prince Edward Island and the Mainland," Charlottetown *Guardian*, Dec. 13, 14, 1948, and *Dalhousie Review*, July, 1949.
[4] *Assembly Journals*, 1881, pp. 250-2; *ibid.*, 1883, p. 11 and Appendix H; *ibid.*, 1884, pp. 282-8 and Appendix H; *ibid.*, 1885, pp. 38-44 and Appendices A and L. *Assembly Debates*, 1885, pp. 96 ff. *Canada, House of Commons, Debates*, Feb. 19, 1883, pp. 43-52.
[5] Report of a Committee of the Privy Council of Canada, Nov. 7, 1885, *Assembly Journals*, 1886, Appendix L. See also *Canada, Sessional Papers*, 1886, no. 76.

its steam service, though not an undertaking of such magnitude as a transcontinental railway, was nevertheless a national obligation similar to, and no less binding than, the railway part of the Confederation bargain with British Columbia.

Premier Sullivan appealed to the Queen in 1886 over the head of the federal Government, and a conference subsequently took place in London between Sullivan, Sir Charles Tupper, and the Colonial Secretary, Lord Granville. After much discussion, Granville wrote the Governor-General and suggested that "it would reflect great credit on the Dominion" if adequate rail communications or a metallic subway could be provided for Prince Edward Island.[1] The immediate results of this Imperial venture in Dominion-provincial relations were the assignment of two new ships to the service, an addition to the provincial subsidy, and a survey of the floor of the Strait for subway purposes. The subway was an attractive possibility, but a British engineer reported in 1886 that, even if the sea bed were suitable, the project would cost over two million pounds sterling.[2] Sir John Macdonald safely avoided committing himself by promising "favourable consideration."[3] By 1901, however, the scheme was abandoned because of the cost of construction and upkeep and the unsuitable condition of the sea bed.[4]

The prolonged negotiations between the Sullivan and Macdonald Governments were followed by similar discussions between the Laurier Cabinet and the local Liberals. The latter, who had promised "better terms" on the hustings, sought payment for "damages" resulting from inadequate communication facilities or reference of the issue to an independent commission. Laurier, aware of the significance of arbitration in Dominion-provincial relations, preferred "careful consideration," and, after much discussion, ap-

---

[1] See *Assembly Journals*, 1886, Appendix L. *Canada, Sessional Papers*, 1886, no. 76; Public Archives of Canada, Colonial Office Records (P.E.I.), G series, vol. 21, p. 128; *Assembly Debates*, 1886, pp. 258-67; *Patriot*, Jan. 20, 21, Feb. 3, 5, March 8, 20, 1886.

[2] Douglas Fox to W. W. Sullivan, April 7, 1886, P.A.C. (P.E.I.), G 21, no. 128.

[3] See Macdonald to G. W. Howlan, Jan. 28, 1887, *Assembly Debates*, 1887, p. 12, and Feb. 6, 1891, Public Archives of Canada, Macdonald Letterbooks, vol. 27, p. 435; *Canada, House of Commons, Debates*, 1891, pp. 158-72.

[4] *Ibid.*, 1901, p. 4675.

proved the purchase of another boat.¹ Finally a "full settlement" of all existing communications claims was reached in 1901 in the form of an additional annual subsidy of $30,000.²

This settlement proved temporary, however, and from 1901 to 1911 correspondence and resolutions continued in even greater volume. Not only did high freight rates provide additional complaints, but the federal Government's railway building programme in the west prompted requests for additional favours to the Island.³ The tunnel scheme was revived but again abandoned as impracticable.⁴ Meanwhile R. L. Borden, the Leader of the Opposition, gave a hostage to fortune when he visited the Island in 1903 and 1908, promised his support, and expressed his view that the tunnel could have been built "out of one year of Liberal stealings."⁵

Fresh negotiations commenced in 1911 when Borden took office in Ottawa and Mathieson in Charlottetown. The result was a contract for a new ferry and terminals which, after some delay during the war years, were put into operation in 1918.⁶ This service was still not satisfactory, for it was not until 1927 that the railway gauge on the Island was changed to permit train traffic from the mainland to points on the Island. Meanwhile a significant forecast of things to come was voiced by the critics and particularly by Mr. Mackenzie King, who asked what would happen if an accident occurred to the one boat.⁷ The Duncan Commission declared that "the ferry boat service is unsatisfactory" and urged the establishment of a "regular and complete service."⁸ The tunnel scheme was revived once more, but the estimated cost of $40,000,000 killed any

¹*Canada, Sessional Papers*, 1897, no. 56; *ibid.*, 1898, no. 104; *Assembly Journals*, 1898, Appendix N.
²*Canada, House of Commons, Debates*, May 8, 1901, pp. 4675-88; *Examiner*, May 9, July 20, 1905; *Patriot*, May 9, 1901; *Morang's Annual Register*, 1901, p. 474; 1 Ed. VII (P.E.I.), c. 3.
³*Assembly Journals*, 1903, pp. 116-17; *ibid.*, 1905, pp. 34-9; *ibid.*, 1906, p. 145; *ibid.*, 1907, p. 141; *ibid.*, 1910, p. 69; *Canadian Annual Review*, 1905, p. 341; *ibid.*, 1907, p. 628; *ibid.*, 1909, p. 475; *Canada, House of Commons, Debates*, Jan. 28, 1907, p. 2147.
⁴*Ibid.*, Nov. 22, 1909, pp. 277 ff.; Jan. 23, 1911, pp. 2176 ff.
⁵*Examiner*, Dec. 2, 1903; Oct. 21, 1908.
⁶*Canadian Annual Review*, 1912, p. 484; Borden to A. A. MacLean, Dec. 28, 1911, quoted in *Assembly Journals*, 1924, p. 30.
⁷*Canada, House of Commons, Debates*, April 23, 1920, p. 1601; May 6, 1920, p. 2103.
⁸*Report of the Royal Commission on Maritime Claims*, pp. 27-8.

enthusiasm for it.[1] The old ferry was then inspected and judged inadequate, and in 1931 it was replaced by a new and larger one.

The communications issue then lay dormant for ten years, only to arise again in 1941 when the S.S. *Charlottetown* hit a reef and sank when on the way to dry dock in Saint John. The Island demanded a new steamer, but the federal Government emphasized that it could not find a vessel of any kind during the war and that the Island would have to get along with the old boat which had been abandoned ten years before.[2] After six years of negotiations, a new vessel was assigned to the service in 1947.[3]

The problem is not yet settled, however, for the question of whether the service is "efficient" and "continuous" is still raised, and the varied answers are important features of the present relations between the province and the Dominion. The *Abegweit* is judged by some experts to be the finest ship of her kind in the world, and her regular crossings, winter and summer, fulfil many of the dreams of the Confederation statesmen. Yet the service is slow and the boat is so crowded during the tourist and exporting season that travellers and cargo have often to wait many hours for service.[4] The most serious objection is the cost of transporting automobiles and trucks across the Strait. Some regard the service as a part of the national highway system, an interprovincial link, the use of which should be free of charges. "Ferries," said Premier Jones at the Dominion-provincial conference of 1945, "should be a national highway under the terms upon which we entered Confederation."[5] The Canadian National Railways operates the steamer for the federal Government, and this arrangement, it is alleged, precludes fair competition from trucks and buses in freight and passenger traffic. "We feel," said the

[1]*Canada, House of Commons, Debates,* 1929, p. 3078.
[2]In a rare case of Cabinet disagreement on the floor of the House of Commons, the Minister of Transport said the service was adequate and the Minister of National Defence said it was not. *Ibid.,* April 2, 1943, pp. 1823, 1826.
[3]Meanwhile a private company, the Northumberland Ferries Limited, organized a service between Cariboo, near Pictou, and Wood Islands, at the eastern end of the Island, which received a small federal subsidy.
[4]Some improvement was made in the summer of 1950 when the old boat, the S.S. *Prince Edward Island* was pressed into service along with the *Abegweit.* The continuance of such an arrangement during the summer months was recommended by the Royal Commission on Transportation in 1951.
[5]*Guardian,* Dec. 19, 1945.

304 GOVERNMENT OF PRINCE EDWARD ISLAND

Duncan Commission, "that, by reason of its association with railway accounts, this service does not get the attention it should receive."[1] "We as a railroad," wrote the Vice-President of the C.N.R. to an Island Premier, "cannot afford to overlook the fact that in reality every automobile we handle on the ferry is in competition with our own rail route."[2] Since the ferry tolls on trucks and their cargo are fixed charges on the transport of produce and livestock across a short distance, they seriously hamper the participation of Island industry in mainland commerce.[3] Therefore, the province contends, the service should not be the responsibility of the C.N.R., but a public utility in the hands of a government department, administered free of charge as a federal compensation for geography, and designed as an interprovincial connection which would be both "efficient" and "continuous" in terms of the Island's needs in the Canadian economy of today.[4]

FINANCE

The share of the smallest province in national finance is very limited, but financial arrangements with the federal Government have for many years been of major concern to the Island. This is not the place to examine in detail the economic history of the province, but a review of the significant features of its financial position will reveal in large measure the nature of its relations with the federal Government.

There are comparatively few sources of public revenue on Prince Edward Island, for the economy is largely rural and it is dominated almost entirely by agriculture. There are no large concentrations of industrial activity, property, or capital; there are no public lands and few large personal incomes; and consequently there is a very restricted field for either personal or corporate taxation. The urban

[1] *Report of the Royal Commission on Maritime Claims*, p. 28.
[2] Quoted in *Guardian*, Dec. 19, 1945.
[3] The Island, of course, benefits from the 20 per cent reduction in freight rates to the Maritimes suggested by the Duncan Commission and included in the Maritime Freight Rates Act of 1927.
[4] See also Prince Edward Island brief to Royal Commission on Transportation, Charlottetown, July, 1949. The connection between the ferry service and the C.N.R. was criticized severely during the railway strike of 1950 when the service was suspended.

centres are small and municipal administration is limited; the costs and revenues associated with urban development are proportionately much less than in other provinces. As a result the total per capita revenue from provincial sources in 1937 was only one-third of the average for all the provinces, while the total per capita expenditure was less than half the average for all the provinces.[1] "These circumstances suggest," writes one authority, "that a review of Prince Edward Island's financial position ought to be mainly concerned with its special features, and less with comparisons between it and other provinces."[2]

Special arrangements had to be made at Confederation (as noted in chapter VI) to compensate for this weakness of local public finance. The purchase of the landed estates, the provision of communications with the mainland, and the building of the railway were so costly that the Dominion had to provide the funds necessary for the first and assume responsibility for the other two as part of the bargain of 1873. The fact that the province's taxable capacity was low and that it could not benefit from the great federal public works expenditures on railways and canals in central and western Canada put it at a further disadvantage and provided partial justification for raising the Island's debt allowance from $25 to $50 per capita.[3] The conditions which brought about these financial concessions continued to exist after Confederation, and, as a result, the Island has been forced to rely much more heavily upon federal grants for its provincial revenues than have the other provinces. This dependence is illustrated by the following table which includes

[1] *Report of the Royal Commission on Dominion-Provincial Relations*, Book I, pp. 219-20. See also Stewart Bates, *Financial History of Canadian Governments*, pp. 91-103, and Wilfrid Eggleston and C. T. Kraft, *Dominion-Provincial Subsidies and Grants*, pp. 69-87. The two last are special studies prepared for the Rowell-Sirois Commission.

[2] Bates, *Financial History of Canadian Governments*, pp. 91-2.

[3] Other reasons for this change were the sharp increase in the local debt from $3 to $41 per capita in nine years, largely because of the railway, and the fact that, with the debt allowance which had been permitted the other provinces, the Island would have had to pay $60,000 a year interest on the debt, which to her would have been an enormous charge. The new arrangement entitled her to $43,000 a year *from* the Dominion. See Eggleston and Kraft, *Dominion-Provincial Subsidies and Grants*, pp. 14-15, and J. A. Maxwell, *Federal Subsidies to the Provincial Governments in Canada* (Cambridge, Mass., 1937), pp. 47-9.

the percentage of provincial revenues from federal sources in 1874 and 1937.[1]

	1874	1937
Ontario	47	1
Quebec	48	2
Nova Scotia	81	10
New Brunswick	92	11
Manitoba	88	7
British Columbia	62	3
Prince Edward Island	75	32
Saskatchewan		15
Alberta		5

The Rowell-Sirois Report states the situation clearly: "The manifest inability of a small agricultural economy, possessing no taxable surplus, to raise revenues and to finance services on the same scale as in the rest of Canada was recognized from the first in the special debt allowance and subsidy in lieu of land, provided when Prince Edward Island entered Confederation. Much of Prince Edward Island's financial history since then has been one of subsidy claims and adjustments, and special increases . . . maintained the subsidy as much the most important source of revenue."[2]

The character of the financial negotiations between Charlottetown and Ottawa since 1873 has clearly illustrated this reliance on federal grants. The province thought it had made a satisfactory financial bargain with the Dominion at Confederation, but within four years its Government faced declining revenues and the consequent need for increased taxation. Nevertheless when the Davies coalition instituted a poll tax and a real property tax in 1877,[3] the resulting criticism contributed in no small measure to the downfall of the Government. Subsequent administrations consequently refused to endanger their fortunes by seeking revenue from the small taxable wealth in the province and therefore looked to the Do-

[1] *Report of the Royal Commission on Dominion-Provincial Relations*, Book I, tables 87-103, and D. G. Creighton, *British North America at Confederation*, p. 94. By 1950 the Island's percentage had reached 64 per cent. *Infra*, pp. 313-14.
[2] *Report of the Royal Commission on Dominion-Provincial Relations*, Book I, pp. 219-20.
[3] 40 Vic., c. 2.

minion for funds. The Islanders emphasized that they were suffering from the Dominion's commercial policies, and, although they were helping to pay for a policy of national expansion, they were deriving no benefits from it. "However much the National Policy may promote the interests of the Dominion as a whole," wrote J. C. Pope when a member of Macdonald's Cabinet, "we cannot shut our eyes to the fact that so far as the Island individually is concerned it means largely increased taxation with no corresponding advantages. They have no manufactures of any importance, and must necessarily import many of their manufactured articles from Montreal and Ontario, and for their English goods they have to pay in the way of duties 50 per cent more than formerly."[1] These arguments resulted in some minor concessions in the form of refunds in expenditures for penitentiaries and piers, amounting to nearly $100,000, and an extra annual subsidy of $20,000.[2]

Successive Island Governments sought an increase in revenue by demanding a share of the Halifax Fishery award. Under the Treaty of Washington, 1871, fishing privileges in the waters of Canada, Prince Edward Island, and Newfoundland, were given to American fishermen in return for a sum which was later to be determined by arbitration. The Island, which would have preferred a trade agreement to a money payment, consented to the arrangement upon pressure from the British Government, and passed the necessary legislation in 1872. In 1877 an arbitration commission met in Halifax and awarded five and a half million dollars, of which one million went to Newfoundland and the rest to Canada. Although the Island had joined the Dominion on July 1, 1873, she demanded a share of the sum given to Canada because she had entered the bargain as an independent province. R. P. Haythorne and David Laird sought to have this share included in the terms of union, but the Dominion Government would not agree.[3] Successive attempts of the provincial Government and the Island's representatives at Ottawa and an appeal to the Queen met the same fate. The

[1]Pope to Macdonald, April 26, 1880, Public Archives of Canada, Macdonald Papers, vol. 255, p. 168.
[2]Maxwell, *Federal Subsidies to the Provincial Governments in Canada*, pp. 73-6.
[3]R. P. Haythorne to Editor of the *Patriot, Patriot,* April 1, 1880.

Island had been part of Canada while the treaty was in effect, and Dominion responsibilities under the treaty overshadowed any provincial claims.[1]

Except for the gains in communications, the province received nothing from 1887 to 1911 save an upward revision in its allowance for the costs of government from $30,000 to $100,000 in 1907. Demands for further financial concessions nevertheless continued without abatement.[2] "As far as the claims by the local government are concerned," said W. S. Fielding, the Minister of Finance, in 1905, "I must do these gentlemen the justice of saying that they are claiming everything in sight. . . . If everything is not arranged as they wish it it will not be from any want of claiming on their part."[3]

Fielding's successor, Sir Thomas White, shared the sympathy of the Borden Cabinet for the Island's demands of 1911. The economic position of the province was serious, and her population, which in 1871 had been 94,000, and in 1891, 109,000, dropped to only 73,000 in 1911, despite the great increase in the population of the Dominion as a whole. This situation, the province asserted, was the result of the disadvantages of federalism over which it had no control, and the failure of the Dominion to live up to its obligations. In a long memorandum to the federal Government, Premier Mathieson criticized the "sell outs" of former years, and demanded "damages" for Dominion neglect. He pointed out that federal revenue from the Island was greater by one-third than the total of Dominion obligations to the Island, including subsidies; that other provinces had received huge grants from the federal Government for economic expansion, whereas the Island had received no such encouragement; and that the Dominion controlled the com-

[1]*Assembly Journals,* 1871, Appendix K; *ibid.,* 1879, p. 200 and Appendix M; *ibid.,* 1880, p. 257; *ibid.,* 1881, Appendix M; *ibid.,* 1883, Appendix H; *Canada, House of Commons, Debates,* April 2, 1884, pp. 1273-81; *Canada, Sessional Papers,* 1879, no. 73 d; *Patriot,* Jan. 30, 1879; *Assembly Journals,* 1921, p. 41. The attitude of the British Government, which supported the Dominion view, is contained in Kimberley to Marquis of Lorne, Dec. 18, 1880, *Assembly Journals,* 1881, Appendix M. The subject has also been included in numerous Island briefs to the federal Government.

[2]See resolutions passed by the Assembly in 1903 and 1906; *ibid.,* 1903, pp. 47-51; *ibid.,* 1906, p. 79; *Examiner,* June 1, 1905.

[3]*Canada, House of Commons, Debates,* May 26, 1905, p. 6644.

merce of the province through the tariff while hindering it with inadequate communication facilities.[1] This presentation gained a sympathetic, indeed enthusiastic, welcome at Ottawa, and a provision for an increased annual subsidy of $100,000 received the support of both Government and Opposition: "In looking over this case of Prince Edward Island," said Sir Thomas White, "I have become enthusiastic about it, and I say that Prince Edward Island from the date of union has been hardly treated, and I believe that her dwindling population is, to a very large extent, due to the fact that she has been deprived of the subsidies to which she was justly and reasonably entitled from the Dominion since Confederation. I hope to show to the satisfaction of the House that this grant is not only justified, but abundantly justified. I hope that a new era will dawn for the Province of Prince Edward Island when it gets this enlarged subsidy."[2] Sir Wilfrid Laurier, whose own Minister of Finance had not been at all receptive to the claims a few years before, agreed with the grant on grounds of equity: "The one reason only which has impressed me—and it is not a constitutional reason, it is not a legal reason, it is simply a reason of equity—is the fact that Prince Edward Island has not profited by Confederation. For some years past it has been largely losing its population by reason of its connection with Canada, and it is going backward instead of forward. Its trade has been diverted from its natural channel—perhaps I should not call it the natural channel but a channel of trade which has been created—and in the process of many years the trade of the Island has suffered."[3] The province and the Dominion agreed for once, and their financial relations rested quietly for the next decade.

Financial negotiations in the 1920's concerned the demand for land subsidies, and a share in a general revision of subsidies in the Maritimes. The sharp drop in the prices of foxes and potatoes seriously disrupted the agricultural industry of the province during this period, and the Government sought some means of compensat-

[1] "Report of P. E. I. Government Delegation to the Government of Canada to Present Claims for Further Subsidy," Feb. 17, 1912, *Assembly Journals,* 1912, Appendix C.
[2] *Canada, House of Commons, Debates,* March 26, 1912, pp. 6114 ff.
[3] *Ibid.*

ing for the subsequent decline in agricultural income.[1] The province benefited to the extent of an additional annual subsidy of $275,000 recommended by the White Commission, but again the increase was sufficient for only a decade.

During the 1930's Prince Edward Island was faced with a growing discrepancy between her limited funds and resources and the high costs of the new services which the Government was called upon to provide. Recent developments in health and welfare, education, and public works were provincial responsibilities, but the Island, along with other poorer provinces, found herself without the funds or the civil service personnel to administer them effectively. The local Government then had to renew its demands on the Dominion, for its own resources would not permit increased indebtedness and the necessary enlargement and improvement of the public service.

The Island Government stressed the gravity of its situation before the Rowell-Sirois Commission in 1938 and emphasized that it could never keep up with the other provinces in the provision of public services unless special assistance was given to the Island on the basis of fiscal need. The old arguments about unique local problems and the disadvantages suffered because of national economic policies were raised once more. "Our people have been obliged," said the Premier in his presentation to the Commission, "to look on while other Provinces, more fortunately situated, or perhaps with a lesser degree of carefulness, have implemented many services equally necessary here, but which we felt we were unable to afford. We have seen other Provinces forge ahead of us in public welfare work, in health measures, in education. Their public servants have been adequately paid and their public works greatly improved. This is not possible in Prince Edward Island, unless what appears to us to be undue carelessness is exhibited toward future expenditures. This carelessness we have sought to avoid."[2] The Commission it-

[1]The agricultural income for the province dropped from $9.8 million in 1927 to $2.3 million in 1932. S. A. Saunders, *The Economic History of the Maritime Provinces,* p. 53; this is a study prepared for the Rowell-Sirois Commission.

[2]*The Case of Prince Edward Island: A Submission to the Royal Commission on Dominion-Provincial Relations,* p. 2.

self acknowledged the truth of this statement, and pointed out that, while the Island's expenditures were administered economically and its credit and outlook for financial stability were good, "there is little prospect under the present system of the Island Government being able to raise sufficient taxation from the sources open to them to bring the standards of governmental services to real equality with those in the rest of the country."[1]

The Commission recommended that the existing relations between the federal and provincial Governments be adjusted by an exchange of responsibilities and taxing powers and by a system of Dominion grants to the provinces on the basis of fiscal need. The provinces would give up personal income and corporation taxes, succession duties, and existing subsidies. The Dominion would be responsible for all the provincial debt, and the employable unemployed, and it would pay the poorer provinces a "national adjustment grant" based on fiscal need, provide emergency grants for any province which suffered from unusually serious economic conditions, and pay to each province a sum of 10 per cent of the net revenue received from mining and oil companies within the province.

Although the report of the Commission was not adopted, many of its suggestions were implemented during the war. The provinces transferred to the Dominion temporary jurisdiction over income taxes, corporation taxes, and taxes on securities in return for an annual sum less deductions for any such taxes collected by the province or municipalities during the term of the agreement.[2] Before the end of the war the Dominion also moved into the succession duties field, took over unemployment insurance by constitutional amendment, and commenced to pay family allowances.

The necessity for the continuation in peace-time of a form of Dominion-provincial co-operation which would provide some federal control of the nation's economic problems and at the same time preserve a substantial measure of provincial autonomy was the theme of the conferences of provincial Premiers which commenced

[1] *Report of the Royal Commission on Dominion-Provincial Relations,* Book I, p. 221.
[2] Prince Edward Island was to receive $701,943.96 less the deductions; 6 Geo. VI, c. 1.

in 1945. At the Dominion-Provincial Conference on Reconstruction in that year a number of proposals were presented by the federal Government which were designed to give the Dominion increased powers and responsibilities and to replace the old subsidies with a new one based largely on population. No basis of agreement was found, and the Conference adjourned. Shortly afterwards, however, all the provinces except Ontario and Quebec made separate five-year agreements with the Dominion along the lines of the Dominion proposal.

Throughout these negotiations the Prince Edward Island Government again emphasized unique local problems and the desirability of federal assistance depending on fiscal need. It pointed out from time to time that the Island's per capita expenditure on various services did not compare unfavourably with that of other provinces[1] but that such comparisons were unfair in the case of a province with such a small population and so little revenue.[2] Premier Jones expressed grave doubts concerning the federal proposals of 1945, but his Government later entered into a modified agreement which, although it was on a per capita basis, was satisfactory for the time being from the standpoint of fiscal need.

Under this new arrangement the province was to receive annually a payment of $2,100,000 ($15 per capita plus the amount of the statutory subsidies), and this sum was to be a guaranteed minimum which could be increased with rises in the national popu-

[1] Per capita expenditures of provincial Governments on health and social welfare and on education, 1946.

	Health and social welfare	Education
Prince Edward Island	11.13	6.66
Nova Scotia	14.94	7.44
New Brunswick	12.63	5.56
Quebec	11.95	7.36
Ontario	10.90	9.65
Manitoba	10.25	5.49
Saskatchewan	19.06	8.39
Alberta	12.72	7.25
British Columbia	17.80	10.87

Dominion Bureau of Statistics, Memorandum, "Financial Statistics of Provincial Governments in Canada," 1946.

[2] See Dominion-Provincial Conference, 1945, *Submissions and Plenary Conference Discussions* (Ottawa, 1946), pp. 34, 164-71, 454-76.

lation and income. In return it would give up the older subsidies which in all amounted to $657,000, and the right to levy income taxes, succession duties, and certain corporation taxes, which, over a period of years, had never yielded much more than $300,000 annually.¹ The Provincial Treasurer jubilantly informed the Island Legislature that this was the best agreement the province had made since Confederation. Some of his colleagues were not so certain; one Minister said that he was not satisfied with the plan, but that it was the best the province could do; "it isn't all we want," said another, "but it is better than anything we ever had before."² This doubt, also expressed by the Opposition on subsequent occasions, was caused by the fear of being "victims of Ottawa's failure to adhere to the principle of fiscal need."³

The results of this financial dependence upon federal aid are manifest in two important ways. In the first place, the loss of taxing power to the Island is more apparent than real. The province has generally refrained from participating in demands for greater "provincial autonomy," for, under existing circumstances, it would be impossible for the local Government to exert effectively any substantial degree of independence. Consequently, the retention of taxing powers has never been a major consideration with Island Governments, for it is much more difficult for the province to get money by taxation than to seek assistance from the Dominion. "Provincial rights" in the province, therefore, have usually meant Dominion obligations rather than local autonomy.

The second result of financial dependence is the fact that, although the Island is financially better off than before, her revenue has lost its elasticity. The entire revenue of the provincial Government is now approximately $7,500,000, of which about $1,500,000 comes from gasoline, amusement, liquor, and tobacco taxes now levied by the province, about $1,200,000 from licences, fees, and miscellaneous sources, and approximately $4,800,000, or 64 per

---

[1]The text of the agreement with the Island is contained in 11 Geo. VI (P.E.I.), c. 2; see also speech by the Provincial Treasurer in the local Legislature on March 24, 1947; *Patriot*, "Proceedings of the Legislative Assembly for March 25, 1947."

[2]*Ibid.*

[3]See Opposition Leader W. J. P. MacMillan in *Guardian*, March 17, 1950.

cent, from the Dominion treasury.[1] Moreover, approximately one-third of the entire $7,000,000 annual expenditure is now assigned to social services, an item which is rapidly increasing in urgency as time goes on. The Government, therefore, is always faced with a comparatively fixed revenue and it must give up many desirable improvements to avoid extravagance. It can never escape the fact that its services must be limited in comparison with those in other provinces, all of which are economically far better off.[2] This situation, which will be further complicated by rising costs and increased government activity, will be one of the major problems of future years in both provincial administration and the Island's relations with the Dominion.

There is no doubt that Prince Edward Island, in comparison with her sister provinces, has suffered many material disadvantages, and, consequently, has had to curtail her activities. Yet the Island has enjoyed many assets of which her people have been proud, not the least of which is a certain compensating advantage in being a province with all the privileges of her larger neighbours and with the right of administering her own affairs. Self-government imposes many obligations under the most favourable circumstances; small wonder if it proves difficult and expensive in a tiny area which for more than two centuries has always been in a position of having to justify what it has and what it wants.

The challenge which political independence has presented since 1769 requires renewed vigour and inventiveness on the part of the government and people of Prince Edward Island and fresh approaches to the role of the province in national affairs. Her political history only too clearly reveals that the comparatively small size and fundamental difficulties of her government must be counterbalanced by efficiency and initiative and that her isolation must be met by active participation in national economic,

[1] These figures are from the Government's estimates for the year ending March 31, 1952.
[2] The per capita net production in the provinces in 1946 was: Prince Edward Island $236.64; Nova Scotia $323.15; New Brunswick $337.39; Quebec $491.85; Ontario $624.34; Manitoba $451.79; Saskatchewan $472.84; Alberta $534.13; British Columbia $589.71; Yukon and Northwest Territories $274.94; total Canada $526.30. *Canada Year Book,* 1948-9, p. 1099.

political, and cultural enterprises. The obligation of Dominion-provincial relations, nevertheless, must work both ways, and the federal government should give the Island much good-will because of her size and her special problems. "The claims of Prince Edward Island," said Sir Thomas White, when Minister of Finance, "are not, in my judgment, legal. They proceed upon equitable grounds, upon grounds of fairness and justice as between this Dominion and the smallest of the provinces, the little sister, as it were, of the Confederation."[1]

[1] *Canada, House of Commons, Debates,* March 26, 1912, p. 61.

APPENDICES

A   Commission to Governor Walter Patterson, August 4, 1769

B   Instructions to Governor Walter Patterson, August 4, 1769

C   Sections of the British North America Act Affecting the Government of Prince Edward Island

D   Documents Respecting the Entrance of Prince Edward Island into Confederation

E   The Lieutenant-Governors of Prince Edward Island from 1769 to Confederation

F   The Lieutenant-Governors of Prince Edward Island since Confederation

G   The Premiers of Prince Edward Island from the Granting of Responsible Government to Confederation

H   The Premiers of Prince Edward Island since Confederation

APPENDIX A

COMMISSION TO GOVERNOR WALTER PATTERSON[1]
AUGUST 4, 1769

Walter Paterson, Esqr. Govern^r of the Island of John [sic]

George the Third by the Grace of God of Great Britain, France, and Ireland, King, Defender of the Faith, &c. To our trusty and well beloved Walter Paterson, Esquire, Greeting: Whereas, we did, by our Letters Patent bearing date the eleventh day of August, one thousand seven hundred and sixty-six, in the sixth year of our reign, constitute and appoint our trusty and well beloved William Campbell, Esquire, commonly called Lord William Campbell, to be our Captain General and Governor in Chief in and over our Province of Nova Scotia, bounded on the westward by a line drawn from Cape Sable across the entrance of the Bay of Fundy to the mouth of the River Saint Croix by the said River to its source, and by a line drawn due north from thence to the southern boundary of our colony of Quebec to the northward, by the said boundary as far as the western extremity of the Bay des Chaleurs to the eastward, by the said Bay and the Gulf of Saint Lawrence to the cape or promontory called Cape Breton in the island of that name, includ^g that island, the Island Saint Johns and all other islands within six leagues of the coast, and to the southward by the Atlantic Ocean from the said Cape to Cape Sable aforesaid, including the island of that name and all other islands within forty leagues of the coast, with all the rights, members, and appurtenances whatsoever thereunto belonging, for and during our will and pleasure as by the said recited Letters Patent, relation being thereunto had may more fully and at large appear; now know you that we have revoked and determined, and by these presents do revoke and determine, such part and so much of the said recited Letters Patent and every clause, article, and thing therein contained as relates to or mentions the Island of Saint John. And further know you that we, reposing especial trust and confidence in the prudence, courage, and

---

[1]Public Archives of Canada, Commissions and Instructions (P.E.I.), 1766-1839, M series, vol. 593, pp. 1-12. The text follows the document except for the addition of punctuation, the modernization of spelling, and the restriction of capital letters.

loyalty of you, the said Walter Paterson, of our especial grace, certain knowledge, and mere motion have thought fit to constitute and appoint, and by these presents do constitute and appoint you, the said Walter Paterson, to be Captain General and Governor in Chief, in and over our Island of Saint John and territories adjacent thereto in America, and which now are or heretofore have been dependent thereupon; and we do hereby require and command you to do and execute all things in due manner which shall belong to your said command and the trusts we have reposed in you according to the several papers and directions granted or appointed you by this present Commission, and the instructions and authorities herewith given to you or by such further powers, instruction, and authorities as shall at any time hereafter be granted or appointed you under our signet and sign manual or by our order in our Privy Council and according to such reasonable laws and statutes as shall hereafter be made and agreed upon by you with the advice and consent of the Council and Assembly of the Island under your government in such manner and form as is hereafter expressed. And our will and pleasure is that you, the said Walter Paterson, do after the publication of these our Letters Patent, and after the appointment of our council of our said Island in such manner and form as is prescribed in the Instructions which you will herewith receive, in the first place take the oaths appointed to be taken by an act passed in the first year of the reign of King George the first, entitled "An Act for the further security of His Majesty's person and government and the succession of the Crown in the heirs of the late Princess Sophia, being Protestants, and for extinguishing the hopes of the pretended Prince of Wales and his open and secret abettors." As also that you make and subscribe the declaration mentioned in an Act of Parliament in the twenty-fifth year of the reign of King Charles the Second, entitled "An Act for preventing dangers which may happen from Popish recusants," and likewise that you take the oath usually taken by Governors in other colonies for the due execution of the office and trust of our Captain General and Governor in Chief in and over our said Island and for the due and impartial administration of justice. And further that you take the oath required to be taken by Governors in the Plantations to do their utmost [that] the several laws relating to trade and the plantations be duly observed, which said oaths and declaration our Council of our said Island, or any three of the members thereof, have hereby

COMMISSION TO WALTER PATTERSON

full power and authority and are required to tender and administer to you and in your absence to our Lieutenant Governor of our said Island. All which being duly performed you shall yourself administer unto each of the members of our said Council and also to our Lieutenant Governor of our said Island the said oaths mentioned in the said Act, entitled "An Act for the further security of His Majesty's person and government and the succession of the Crown in the heirs of the late Princess Sophia, being Protestants, and for extinguishing the hopes of the pretended Prince of Wales and his open and secret abettors." As also to cause them to make and subscribe the aforementioned declaration and to administer unto them the usual oaths for the due execution of their places and trusts; and we do further give and grant unto you, the said Walter Paterson, full power and authority from time to time, and at any time hereafter, by yourself or by any other to be authorized by you in this behalf, to administer and give the oaths mentioned in the said Act for the further security of His Majesty's person and government and the succession of the Crown in the heirs of the late Princess Sophia, being Protestants, and for extinguishing the hopes of the pretended Prince of Wales and his open and secret abettors, to all and every such person and persons as you shall think fit who shall at any time or times pass into our said Island or shall be resident or abiding there; and we do hereby authorize and empower you to keep and use the Public Seal, which will be herewith delivered to you, or shall be hereafter sent to you, for sealing all things whatsoever that shall pass the Great Seal of our said Island. And we do hereby give and grant unto you, the said Walter Paterson, full power and authority, with the advice and consent of our said Council, to be appointed as aforesaid so soon as the situation and circumstances of our Island under your government will admit thereof and when and as often as need shall require, to summon and call General Assemblies of the freeholders and planters within the Island under your government in such manner as you in your discretion shall judge most proper or according to such further powers, instructions, and authorities as shall be at any time hereafter granted and appointed you under our signet and sign manual, or by our order in our Privy Council. And our will and pleasure is that the persons thereupon duly elected by the major part of the freeholders of the respective counties, parishes, or townships, and so returned, shall before their sitting take the oaths mentioned in the said Act entitled "An Act for the further security of His Majesty's person and government and the succession of the Crown in the heirs of the late Princess Sophia, being Protestants, and for extinguishing the hopes of the pretended Princes of Wales and his open and secret abettors," as also make and subscribe the afore mentioned declaration, which oaths and declaration you shall commissionate fit persons under the Public Seal of that our Island to tender and administer unto them, and until the same shall be so taken and subscribed no person shall be capable of sitting, though elected. And we do hereby declare that the persons so elected and qualified shall be called and deemed the Assembly of our said Island of Saint John, and that you, the said Walter Paterson, by and with the advice and consent of our said Council and Assembly, or the major part of them, shall have full power and authority to make, constitute, and ordain laws, statutes, and ordinances for the public peace, welfare, and good government of our said Island and of the people and inhabitants thereof, and such others as shall resort thereunto, and for the benefit of us, our heirs and successors, which said laws, statutes, and ordinances are not to be repugnant but as near as may be agreeable to the laws and statutes of our Kingdom of Great Britain, provided that all such laws, statutes, and ordinances of what nature or duration soever be within three months or sooner after the making thereof transmitted to us under our Seal of our said Island for our approbation or disallowance of the same, as also duplicates thereof by the next conveyance. And in case any or all of the said laws, statutes, and ordinances not before confirmed by us shall at any time be disallowed and not approved and so signified by us, our heirs or successors, under our or their signet or sign manual, or by order of our or their Privy Council, unto you, the said Walter Paterson, or to the Commander in Chief of the said Island for the time being, then such and so many of the said laws, statutes, and ordinances as shall be so disallowed and not approved shall from thenceforth cease, determine, and become utterly void and of none effect, any thing to the contrary thereof notwithstanding. And to the end that nothing may be passed or done by our said Council or Assembly to the prejudice of us, our heirs and successors, we will and ordain that you, the said Walter Paterson, shall have and enjoy a negative voice in the making and passing of all laws, statutes, and ordinances as aforesaid, and that you shall and may likewise, from time to time as you shall judge necessary, adjourn, prorogue, and dissolve all General Assemblies as aforesaid. And we do by these presents give and grant unto you, the said Walter Paterson, full power and authority, with the advice and consent of our said Council, to erect, constitute, and establish such and so many Courts of Judicature and Public Justice within our said Island under your government as you and they shall think fit and necessary for the hearing and determining of all causes, as well criminal as civil, according to law and equity and for awarding execution thereupon, with all reasonable and necessary powers, authorities, fees, and privileges belonging thereunto, as also to appoint and commissionate fit persons in the several parts of your government to administer the oaths mentioned in the aforesaid Act, as also to tender and administer the aforesaid declaration to such persons belonging to the said Courts as shall be obliged to take the same. And we do hereby grant unto you full power and authority to constitute and appoint judges and in cases requisite Commissioners of Oyer and Terminer Justices of the Peace, sheriffs, and other necessary officers and ministers in our said Island for the better administration of justice and putting the laws in execution, and to administer or cause to be administered unto them such oath or oaths as are usually given for the due execution and performance of offices and places and for the clearing of truth in judicial causes. And we do hereby give and grant unto you full power and authority when you shall see cause, or shall judge any offender or offenders in criminal matters or for any fines or forfeitures due unto us fit objects of our mercy, to pardon all such offenders and to remit all such offences, fines, and forfeitures, treason and wilful murder only excepted, in which cases you shall likewise have power upon extraordinary occasions to grant reprieves to the offenders until and to the intent our royal pleasure may be known therein. We do by these presents authorize and impower you to collate any person or persons to any churches, chapels, or other ecclesiastical benefices within our said Island as often as any of them shall happen to be void. And we do hereby give and grant unto you, the said Walter Paterson, by yourself or by your captains and commanders by you to be authorized, full power and authority to levy, arm, muster, and employ all persons whatsoever residing within our said Island, and as occasions shall serve to march from one place to another or to embark them for the resisting and withstanding of all enemies, pirates, and rebels, both at land and sea, and to transport such forces to any of our plantations in America if necessity shall require for defence of the same against the invasion or attempts of any of our enemies, and to execute martial law in time of invasion or other times when by law it may be executed. And to do and execute all and every other thing or things which to our Captain General or Governor in Chief doth or ought of right to belong. And we do hereby give and grant unto you full power and authority, by and with the advice and consent of our said Council, to erect, raise, and build in our said Island such and so many forts and platforms, castles, cities, boroughs, towns, and fortifications as you, by the advice aforesaid, shall judge necessary, and the same or any of them to fortify and furnish with ordinance, ammunition, and all sorts of arms fit and necessary for the security and defence of our said Island, and by the advice aforesaid the same again, or any part thereof, to demolish or dismantle as may be most convenient. And for as much as divers mutinies and disorders may happen by persons shipped and employed at sea during the time of war, and to the end that such as shall be shipped and employed at sea during the time of war may be better governed and ordered, we do hereby give and grant unto you, the said Walter Paterson, full power and authority to constitute captains, lieutenants, masters of ships, and other commanders and officers, and to grant to such captains, lieutenants, masters of ships, and other commanders and officers to execute the law martial during the time of war according to the directions of an Act passed in the twenty-second year of the reign of our late royal grandfather, entitled "An Act for amending, explaining, and reducing into one Act of Parliament the laws relating to the government of His Majesty's ships, vessels, and forces by sea," and to use such proceedings, authorities, punishments, and executions upon any offender or offenders who shall be mutinous, seditious, disorderly, or any way unruly, either at sea or during the time of their abode or residence in any of the ports, harbours, or bays of our said Island as the cause shall be found to require according to martial law and the said directions during the time of war as aforesaid; provided that nothing herein contained shall be construed to the enabling you or any by your authority to hold plea or have any jurisdiction of any offence, cause, matter, or thing committed or done upon the high sea or within any of the havens, rivers, or creeks of our said Island under your government by any captain, commander, lieutenant, master, officer, seaman, soldier, or person whatsoever, who shall be in our actual service and pay in or on board any of our ships of war or other vessels acting by immediate commission or warrant from our Com-

COMMISSION TO WALTER PATTERSON 325

missioners for executing the office of our High Admiral, or from our High Admiral of Great Britain for the time being under the Seal of our Admiralty, but that such captain, commander, lieutenant, master, officer, seaman, soldier, or other person so offending shall be left to be proceeded against and tried as their offences shall require either by commission under our Great Seal of Great Britain as the statute of the twenty-eighth of Henry the eighth directs, or by commission from our said Commissioners for executing the office of our High Admiral of Great Britain for the time being according to the afore mentioned Act, entitled "An Act for amending, explaining, and reducing into one Act of Parliament the laws relating to the government of His Majesty's ships, vessels, and forces by sea," and not otherwise; provided, nevertheless, that all disorders and misdemeanours committed on shore by any captain, commander, lieutenant, master, officer, seaman, soldier, or other person whatsoever belonging to any of our ships of war or other vessels acting by immediate commission or warrant from our said Commissioners for [executing] the office of our High Admiral, or from our High Admiral of Great Britain for the time being under the Seal of our Admiralty, may be tried and punished according to the laws of the place where any such disorders, offences, and misdemeanours shall be committed on shore notwithstanding such offender being [sic] in our actual service, and born in our pay on board any such our ships of war or other vessels acting by immediate commission or warrant from our said Commissioners or executing the office of High Admiral or our High Admiral of Great Britain for the time being as aforesaid, so as He shall not receive any protection for the avoiding of justice for such offences committed on shore from any pretence of his being employed in our service at sea. And our further will and pleasure is that all public money raised or which shall be raised by any Act hereafter to be made within our said Island be issued out from warrant from you by and with the advice and consent of the Council and disposed of by you for the support of the government and not otherwise. And we likewise give and grant unto you full power and authority, by and with the advice and consent of our said Council, to settle and agree with the inhabitants of our said Island for such lands, tenements, and hereditaments as now are or hereafter shall be in our power to dispose of, and them to grant to any person or persons upon such terms and under such moderate quit rents, services, and acknowledgments to be thereupon reserved unto us as you, with the advice aforesaid, shall think fit; which said grants are to pass and be sealed by our Public Seal of our said Island, and being entered upon record by such officer or officers as shall be appointed thereunto shall be good and effectual in law against us, our heirs and successors. And we do hereby give you, the said Walter Paterson, full power and authority to order and appoint fairs, marts, and markets, as also such and so many ports, harbours, bays, havens, and other places for the convenience and security of shipping and for the better loading and unloading of goods and merchandise in such and so many places as by and with the advice and consent of our said Council shall be thought fit and necessary. And we do hereby require and command all officers and ministers, civil and military, and all other inhabitants of our said Island to be obedient, aiding, and assisting unto you, the said Walter Paterson, in the execution of this our Commission and of the powers and authorities herein contained, and in case of your death or absence out of our said Island to be obedient, aiding, and assisting unto such person as shall be appointed by us to be our Lieutenant Governor or Commander in Chief of our said Island, to whom we do therefore by these presents give and grant all and singular the powers and authorities herein granted to be by him executed and enjoyed during our pleasure or until your arrival within our said Island; and if upon death or absence out of our said Island there be no person upon the place commissionated or appointed by us to be our Lieutenant Governor or Commander in Chief of the said Island, our will and pleasure is that the eldest councillor who shall be at the time of your death or absence residing within our said Island shall take upon him the said administration of the government and execute our said Commission and Instructions, and the several powers and authorities therein contained, in the same manner and to all intents and purposes as other our Governor or Commander in Chief should or ought to do in case of your absence until your return, or in all cases until our further pleasure be known therein. And we do hereby declare, ordain, and appoint that you, the said Walter Paterson, shall and may hold, exercise, and enjoy the office and place of our Captain General and Governor in Chief in and over our said Island of Saint John, with all its rights, members, and appurtenances whatsoever, together with all and singular the powers and authorities hereby granted unto you for and during our will and pleasure. In witness, &c., witness ourself at Westminster the fourth day of August.

By Writ of Privy Seal

APPENDIX B

INSTRUCTIONS TO GOVERNOR WALTER PATTERSON[1]
AUGUST 4, 1769

FIRST. With these our instructions you will receive our Commission under our Great Seal of Great Britain, constituting you our Captain General and Governor in Chief in and over our Island of St. John and the territories dependent thereon in America; you are therefore to fit yourself with all convenient speed, and to repair to our said Island of St. John, and being arrived at Charlottetown within our said Island, which we do hereby appoint to be the capital of our said Government, and the chief place of your residence, you are forthwith to cause our said Commission to be read and published, in such manner and form and with such solemnity and ceremonial as is usually practised on like occasion in our other colonies in America; and you are to take upon you the execution of the place and trust we have reposed in you, and the administration of the Government, and to do and execute all things in due manner that shall belong unto your command according to the several powers and authorities of our said Commission under our Great Seal of Great Britain, and these our Instructions to you or such further powers and instructions as shall at any time hereafter be granted or appointed you under our signet and sign manual, or by our orders in our Privy Council.

2. The powers and directions contained in our said Commission to you under our Great Seal of Great Britain will fully point out to you our royal intention with regard to the form and constitution of government which is to be established within our Island of Saint John; the first object of your duty will therefore be to constitute a Council, to advise and assist you in the administration of the affairs of our said Government, which said Council is for the present to be composed of the following persons, viz., Thomas DesBrisay, Esquire, our Lieutenant Governor of our said Island, or our Lieutenant Governor of our said Island for the time being; our Chief Justice of our said Island for the time being; William Allanbey and David Higgins, Esquires; and of such and so many other persons, chosen by you from amongst the prin-

[1]Public Archives of Canada, Commissions and Instructions (P.E.I.), 1766-1839, M series, vol. 593. The text follows the document exactly except for the modernization of the spelling and punctuation and the restriction of capital letters.

cipal inhabitants and proprietors of land in our said Island, as shall make up the number of twelve; which said persons so chosen by you shall be to all intents and purposes members of our said Council until our royal will and pleasure be further known or until we shall think fit to appoint other persons in their stead. It is nevertheless our will and pleasure that the said Chief Justice shall not be capable of taking the administration of the Government upon the death, or absence of you, our Governor or Commander in Chief for the time being.

3. It is our further will and pleasure, that our said Council so to be constituted, as aforesaid, shall have and enjoy all the powers, privileges, and authority usually exercised and enjoyed by the members of our Councils in our other American colonies, subject nevertheless to the like rules, restrictions, & limitations as to their attendance, suspension, and removal as are prescribed with respect to the Councils of our other colonies by our instructions to our Governor thereof; that is to say,

That, if it shall at any time hereafter happen that there are less than seven members of our Council resident within our said Island of Saint John you shall in that case choose as many persons out of the principal inhabitants of our said Island as will make up the full number of the Council to be seven and no more; which persons so chosen and appointed by you shall be to all intents and purposes, Councillors in our said Island, till either they shall be confirmed by us, or by the nomination of others by us, under our sign manual and signet, our said Council shall have seven or more persons in it.

That you do suspend and remove any of the members of our said Council from sitting, voting, and assisting therein, if you shall find just cause for so doing, and appoint others in their stead until our pleasure shall be known; but that you do not suspend or remove any of the members of our Council, when they shall have been confirmed by us, as aforesaid, without good and sufficient cause, nor without the consent of the majority of the said Council, signified in Council after due examination of the charge against such Councillor, and his answer thereunto; and in case of suspension of any of them you are to cause your reasons for so doing, together with the charges and proofs against such person, and his answer thereunto, to be duly entered upon the Council books, and forthwith to transmit copies thereof to us by one of our principal Secretaries of State; nevertheless if it should happen that you should have reasons for suspending any of the said persons not fit to be communicated to the Council, you may in that case suspend such persons without the consent of the said Council; but you are thereupon immediately to send unto [us] by one of our principal Secretaries of State an account of your proceedings therein, together with your reasons at large for such suspension, as also your reasons at large for not communicating the same to the Council, and duplicates thereof by the next opportunity.

That if any of the members of our said Council shall hereafter absent themselves from the said Island, and continue absent above the space of six months together, without leave from you or from our Commander in Chief for the time being, first obtained under your or his hand and seal, or shall remain absent for the space of one year without our leave given them under our royal signet and sign manual, their place or places in the said Council shall immediately thereupon become void; and that if any of the members of our said Council then residing in the Island under your command shall hereafter wilfully absent themselves when duly summoned, without a just and lawful cause, and shall persist therein after admonition, you suspend the said Councillors so absenting themselves till our further pleasure be known, giving us timely notice thereof; and we do hereby will and require you that this our royal pleasure be signified to the several members of our Council aforesaid, and entered in the Council books of the Island under your government, as a standing rule.

4. That establishing such and so many Courts of Judicature as shall be found necessary for the due and impartial administration of justice, and the directing the rule of their proceedings will necessarily become an immediate and important object of consideration; it will therefore be your duty to give the fullest attention to it, to consult and advise with the person whom we have appointed to be our Chief Justice of our said Island as to the measures proper to be pursued for this purpose, governing yourself therein as far as difference of situation and circumstances will admit by what had been approved and found most advantageous in respect to such establishments in our neighbouring colony of Nova Scotia; and taking especial care that, at the same time, nothing is omitted from which our good subjects there may derive that privilege and protection which the British constitution allows them in all parts of our dominions, they be not harassed and vexed with unnecessary attendances and proceedings, or oppressed by exorbitant fees or demands; but that on the contrary justice be administered in the most speedy and effectual way, and all fees of offices

and officers of every kind settled by you with the advice of the Council upon a plan of the greatest moderation. And to the end that nothing may be done or finally established in our said Island of St. John under your government without our consent or approbation, you are by the first opportunity and with all convenient speed to transmit unto us by one of our principal Secretaries of State authentic copies of all acts—orders, grants, commissions, or other powers by virtue of which any courts, offices, jurisdictions, pleas, authorities, fees, and privileges have been settled or established for our confirmation or disallowance; and in case any or all of them shall at any time or times be disallowed or not approved then such and so many as shall be so disallowed or not approved, and so signified by us, shall cease, determine, and be no longer continued or put in practice.

You are to take care that no man's life, member, freehold, or goods be taken away or harmed in our said Island, otherwise than by established and known laws not repugnant to [but] as much as may be agreeable to the laws of this Kingdom.

6. Whereas we are above all things desirous that all our subjects may enjoy their legal rights & properties, you are to take especial care that if any person be committed for any criminal matters (unless for treason or felony plainly and especially expressed in the warrant of commitment) he have free liberty to petition by himself or otherwise the Chief Judge or any of the judges of the Common Pleas for a writ of habeas corpus, which upon such application shall be granted and served on the provost marshal, gaoler, or other officers having the custody of such prisoner, or shall be left at the gaol or place where the prisoner is confined; and the said provost marshal or other officer shall, within three days after such service (on the petitioner's paying the fees and charges, and giving security that he will not escape by the way) make return of the writ and prisoner before the judge who granted out the said writ, and there certify the true cause of the imprisonment, and the said judge shall discharge such prisoner, taking his recognizance & security for his appearance at the court where the offence is cognizable, and certify that said writ and recognizance into the court, unless such offences appear to the said judge not bailable by the laws of England.

7. And in cas[e] the said Chief Judge or any of the judges of the Common Pleas shall refuse to grant a writ of habeas corpus, on view

INSTRUCTIONS TO WALTER PATTERSON

of the copy of commitment, or upon oath made of such copy having been denied the prisoner, or any person requiring the same in his behalf, or shall delay to discharge the prisoner after the granting such writ, the said Chief Judge or other judge shall incur the forfeiture of his place.

8. You are likewise to declare our pleasure, that in case the provost marshal or other officer shall imprison any person above twelve hours, except by a mittimus setting forth the cause thereof, he be removed from his said office.

9. And upon the application of any person wrongfully committed, the said Chief Judge or any of the said judges shall issue his warrant to the provost marshal or other officer to bring the prisoner before him, who shall be discharged without bail or paying fees. And the provost marshal or other officer refusing obedience to such warrant shall be thereupon removed; and if any of the said judges denies his warrant he shall likewise incur the forfeiture of his place.

10. You shall give directions that no prisoner being set at large by an habeas corpus be recommitted for the same offence but by the court where he is bound to appear; and if any of the said judges, provost marshal, or other officer, contrary hereunto, shall recommit such person so bailed or delivered, you are to remove him from his place, and if the provost marshal, or other officer having the custody of the prisoner, neglects to return the habeas corpus, or refuses a copy of the commitment within six hours after the demand made by the prisoner or any other in his behalf, he shall likewise incur the forfeiture of his place.

11. And for the better prevention of long imprisonments, you are to appoint two Courts of Oyer and Terminer to be held yearly, viz., on the second Tuesday in December and the second Tuesday in June; and you are to recommend to the Assembly, when met, forthwith to make provision for defraying the charge of holding such courts.

12. You are to take care that all prisoners in cases of treason and felony have free liberty to petition in open court for their trials, that they be indicted at the first Court of Oyer and Terminer, unless it appear upon oath that the witnesses against them could not be produced; and that they be tried at the second Court or discharged; and the said Chief Judge or other judge, upon motion made the last day of the sessions in open court, shall discharge the prisoner accordingly;

and upon refusal of the said judge and provost marshal or other officer to do their respective duties herein, they shall be removed from their places.

13. Provided always, that no person be discharged out of prison who stands committed for debt by any decree of chancery, or any legal proceedings of any court of record.

14. And for the preventing of any exactions that may be made upon prisoners you are to declare our pleasure that no Chief Judge or other judge of our said Court of Common Pleas shall receive for himself, or clerks, for granting a writ of habeas corpus, more than two shillings and sixpence, and the like sum for taking a recognizance, and that the provost marshal or other officer shall not receive more than five shillings for every commitment, one shilling and three pence for the bond the prisoner is to sign, one shilling and three pence for every copy of a mittimus, and one shilling and three pence for every mile he bringeth back the prisoner.

15. And further, you are to cause this our royal pleasure, signified to you by the nine articles of Instructions immediately preceding this, to be made public and registered in the Council books of our said Island.

16. You are to take care that all writs be issued in our name within our said Island.

17. The forming a lower House of Assembly or House of Representatives for our said Island of Saint John is a consideration that cannot be too early taken up, and ought to be maturely weighed; for until this object is attainable the most important interests of the inhabitants will necessarily remain without that advantage and protection which can only arise out of the vigour and activity of a complete constitution. The division already made of the Island of Saint John into counties, parishes, and townships will naturally suggest to you what ought to be established in respect to the places that should elect representatives; and by a due attention to what has been found practicable and convenient in forming the like constitutions in the late established colonies of Nova Scotia and Georgia, you cannot materially err in such other regulations incident to this institution as may be necessary, until the form of it and the rules and method of proceeding can be more precisely defined by a permanent law. It will be necessary, however, in forming this essential establishment, that the greatest care should be taken that no colour or pretence is given for the assumption of any powers or privileges by the said lower House of Assembly or

House of Representatives which have not been allowed to Assemblies in our other colonies; and that their mode of passing laws, and the exercise of that negative upon those laws which we have thought fit to reserve to you, by our commission under our Great Seal, do conform to, and correspond with those regulations and restrictions which have been established in this respect in our other American colonies; that is to say,

That the style of enacting laws, statutes, and ordinances to be passed in the Island be by the Governor, Council, and Assembly, and no other.

That each different matter be provided for by a different law, without including in one and the same act such things as have no proper relation to each other.

That no clause be inserted in any act or ordinance which shall be foreign to what the title of it imports; and that no perpetual clause be part of any temporary law.

That no law or ordinance whatever be suspended, altered, continued, revived, or repealed, by general words; but that the title and date of such law or ordinance be particularly mentioned in the enacting part.

That no law or ordinance respecting private property be passed without a clause suspending its execution until our royal will and pleasure is known, nor without a saving of the rights of us, our heirs and successors, and of all bodies politic and corporate, and of all other persons except such as are mentioned in the said law or ordinance, and of those claiming by, from, and under them; and before such law or ordinance is passed proof must be made before you in Council, and entered in the Council books, that public notification was made of the party's intention to apply for such act in the several parish churches where the lands in question lie, for three Sundays at least successively, before any such law or ordinance shall be proposed. You are to transmit, and annex to the said law or ordinance, a certificate under your hand that the same passed through all the forms abovementioned.

That in all laws or ordinances for levying money or imposing fines, forfeitures, or penalties, express mention be made that the same is granted or reserved to us, our heirs and successors, for the public uses of our said Island and the support of the government thereof, as by the said law or ordinance shall be directed. And you are not to permit any clause whatsoever to be inserted in any law for levying any money, or the value of money, whereby the same shall not be made liable to be accounted for unto us here in this Kingdom and to our Commissioners of our Treasury, or our High Treasurer for the time being, and audited by our Auditor General of our plantations or his deputy.

That all such laws, statutes, and ordinances be transmitted by you within three months after their passing, or sooner if opportunity offers, to us by one of our principal Secretaries of State, that they be fairly abstracted in the margents and accompanied with very full and particular observations upon each of them; that is to say, whether the same is introductive of a new law, declaratory of a former law, or does repeal a law then before in being. And you are also to transmit in the fullest manner the reasons and occasion for enacting such laws or ordinances, together with fair copies of the Journals of the Proceedings of the Council and Assembly, which you are to require from the clerks of the said Council and Assembly.

That you do not pass or give your assent to any bill or bills in the Assembly of our said Island of an unusual or extraordinary nature and importance, wherein our prerogative or the property of our subjects may be prejudiced, or the trade and shipping of this Kingdom any ways affected, until you shall have first transmitted unto us by one of our principal Secretaries of State the draught of such a bill or bills, and shall have received our royal pleasure thereupon, unless you take care that there be a clause inserted therein, suspending and deferring the execution until our pleasure shall be known concerning the same.

That you do not give your assent to any law that shall be enacted for a less time than two years, except in cases of imminent necessity, or immediate temporary expediency. And that you do not re-enact any law, to which the assent of us or our royal predecessors has once been refused without express leave for that purpose first obtained from us, upon a full representation by you to be made to us by one of our principal Secretaries of State, of the reasons and necessity for passing such law; nor give your assent to any law for repealing any other law passed in your government, whether the same has or has not received our royal approbation, unless you take care that there be a clause inserted therein suspending and deferring the execution thereof until our royal pleasure shall be known concerning the same.

That no law for raising any imposition on wines or other strong liquors be made to continue for less than one whole year; as also that all other laws made for the support of government shall be without limitation of time except the same be for a temporary service and which shall expire and have their full effect within the time therein prefixed.

That you do not assent to [or] pass any act in our Island of St. John under your government whereby bills of credit may be struck or issued in lieu of money, either to you the Governor or to any Lieutenant Governor or Commander in Chief, or to any of the members of our Council or Assembly, or to any other person whatsoever except to us, our heirs and successors, unless there be a clause inserted in such act, declaring that the same shall not take effect until the said Act shall have been approved and confirmed by us, our heirs and successors.

That you do not upon any pretence whatsoever, on pain of our highest displeasure, give your assent to any law wherein the natives or inhabitants of the Island of Saint John under your government are put on a more advantageous footing than those of this Kingdom or whereby duties shall be laid upon British shipping or upon the product or manufactures of Great Britain upon any pretence whatsoever.

18. It is equally unnecessary and impracticable to point out to you in these our Instructions all the various and important objects to which the several constitutions, both legislative and judicial, herein before established and defined will apply; such objects will be very many in the first establishment of government and will require an exertion of the greatest activity and discretion as to the rules and principles by which the proceedings either of the Council, Assembly, or Courts of Judicature are to be governed in all cases not herein before provided for or explained. Many useful precedents may be found in the Instructions to our Governor of Nova Scotia, a copy whereof is hereunto annexed, and by which you are to regulate your conduct as far as different circumstances will admit in all cases wherein they refer to establishments of a similar nature.

19. The having a revenue competent to all the necessary services of government, both fixed and incidental, established, upon a solid and permanent foundation, is essential to every civil institution of this nature, and ought to be one of the first objects of legislation; the establishment already formed will point out what the extent of that

revenue should be and the nature of the duties and taxes to be granted to us for this purpose must depend upon circumstances that can neither be know[n] or judge[d] of here, and upon a full consideration of what has been found most beneficial in other infant colonies in the like case. It will, however, be your duty, so soon as a General Assembly is formed, to recommend this matter to the consideration of the House of Representatives and require them in our name to grant to us such revenue as may amount to all the expenses of government upon some certain estimate.

20. In the meantime, and until such revenue can be established, we have taken into our royal consideration a proposal made by the principal proprietors of lots or townships within our said Island of Saint John by which they respectively engage to take out fresh grants for their lots under the seal of our Island of Saint John, in exchange for those they have already taken out under the seal of our province of Nova Scotia upon the following terms and conditions.

That is to say,

That one moiety of the quit-rent originally reserved on such lots and to commence at the expiration of five years from the date thereof shall, by the terms of these new grants, commence and become payable to us, our heirs and successors, from and after the first day of May last past.

That the other moiety, the payment of which was to take place at the expiration of ten years, shall, by the terms of the said new grants, not commence and become payable until the expiration of twenty years from the date thereof.

21. As this proposal has in view to enable us to make provision for the support of government within our said Island until the inhabitants thereof shall be in a condition to provide for that purpose by a proper revenue arising out of the duties and taxes granted to us by act of Legislature, we have thought fit graciously to accept the same; and therefore our will and pleasure is, that you do forthwith, upon your arrival in your Government, cause the said proposals, the original whereof in writing and subscribed by the proponents will be herewith delivered to you, to be registered and entered upon record upon the Council books; and that you do forthwith proceed to pass fresh patents under the seal of our said Island for the respective lots upon the terms and conditions above mentioned, for which patents no fee

or reward whatever shall be taken either by yourself or by any other person acting under your authority.

22. The annual amount of the quitrents which will thus become due and payable to us is estimated as follows,

That is to say

Twenty-six lots at six shillings per one hundred acres,
a moiety of which is £780
Twenty-nine lots at four shillings per one hundred acres . . . 580
Eleven lots at two shillings per one hundred acres 110
Rent of town and pasture lots, uncertain . . . .

It is therefore our will and pleasure that out of the produce of our said revenue of quit-rents so to be paid, as aforesaid, you do take to yourself as Governor of our said Island the sum of five hundred pounds sterling per annum, and that you also do cause the following annual salaries to be paid out of the said revenue to the several officers hereinafter mentioned, that is to say,

To the Secretary and Register of our said Island, one hundred and fifty pounds.

To the Chief Justice of our said Island, two hundred pounds.

To the Attorney General of our said Island, one hundred pounds.

To the Clerk of the Crown & Coroner, eighty pounds.

To the Provost Marshal, fifty pounds.

To a minister of the Church of England, one hundred pounds.

And it is our further will and pleasure that the said salaries, as well to yourself as to the rest of the officers abovementioned, do commence and become payable from and after the first day of May last past, and that the same be paid quarterly by our Receiver General of our quitrents for our said Island, or his deputy, pursuant to warrants signed by you, our Governor, with the consent of our Council for our said Island, as directed by our commission under our Great Seal of Great Britain; provided, nevertheless, that it be understood, and we do hereby declare it to be our royal will and pleasure, that the foregoing appropriation of our said quit-rents to the support of the civil establishment of our said Island, as aforesaid, shall be only for a limited time, that is to say, not to exceed the space of ten years, and that in case the annual amount of said quit-rents shall fall short of the appointments above mentioned, either by a failure of consent in any number of the proprietors to the alterations proposed in the terms of their grants, or hereafter by any accident or casualty whatever, the salaries & allowances to the several officers abovementioned shall be diminished in proportion. And it is our will and pleasure that neither yourself, nor any other of our officers for our Island as aforesaid, shall be entitled to any part of the said salaries and allowances, nor shall any warrant be granted for the same, unless you or they be resident upon our said Island, excepting only when yourself or any of our said officers respectively shall be absent by leave from us under our signet and sign manual or by order in our Privy Council, in which case one full moiety of the salary and of all perquisites and emoluments whatsoever, which would otherwise become due unto you or to our said officers respectively, shall, during the time of such absence, be paid and satisfied to the person on whom the administration and execution of government or of such office, as aforesaid, shall devolve or be conferred; provided, nevertheless, and it is our royal intent and meaning, that whenever we shall think fit to require you by our especial order to repair to any other of our Governments in America for our particular service, that then & in such case you shall receive your full salary, prequisites, and emoluments, as if you were then actually resident within our said Island of Saint John, anything in these Instructions to the contrary in any wise notwithstanding.

23. And in order the more effectually to secure and enforce the payment and collection of the quit-rents due to us upon all grants of land, as aforesaid, and upon which the support of our government is to depend, it will be an essential and immediate object of your attention to consider, with the advice of our Council, of some proper law to be passed within our said Island for that purpose, in which you will conform as near as may be to what has been approved and established for that purpose in our other colonies under like circumstances.

24. The annexed copy of our order in our Privy Council on the 26th day of August, 1767, will fully inform you of the plan we have thought fit to adopt for the settlement of our said Island of Saint John, and for the distribution of lands there under all descriptions; you will therefore be particularly careful to carry the said plan into full execution, and more especially in laying out the lands we have thought fit to reserve for the towns within our said Island, taking care that all reservations whatever for public uses be made justly and exactly so as fully to answer our royal intentions therein.

25. And whereas it hath been represented unto us that there are now sundry stores, materials, and provisions belonging to us within our said Island which we have thought fit to entrust to the ca[r]e and custody of a storekeeper appointed for that purpose, with instructions to obey such directions as he shall receive from you touching the disposal and application thereof to the public service, it is therefore our will and pleasure that you do, upon your arrival in our said Island, take an account of such stores, materials, and provisions as are under the care of our storekeeper, as aforesaid; and you are to cause the said stores and materials to be applied and disposed of for the public use and benefit, in such manner as shall appear to you to be most advantageous for our service; and in case our said storekeeper shall have sold, or otherwise disposed of the provisions, or any part thereof (which being perishable would not continue long fit for [p]ublic use) in that case you are to require of our said storekeeper an account of the produce of such sale, making him such an allowance out of the sum that shall be produced therefrom as you shall think a proper reward for his trouble in this business.

26. You are to permit a liberty of conscience to all persons (except Papists) so they be contented with a quiet and peaceable enjoyment of the same, not giving offence or scandal to the Government.

27. And whereas nothing can more effectually promote the peace and happiness of our subjects there, and impress upon their minds a just sense of religion and morality th[a]n an uniform and regular observance of those rites and duties which our holy religion require[s], you will therefore have a very particular attention to this important object, and to that end you shall take [especial] care that God Almighty be devoutly and duly served throughout your Government; the Book of Common Prayer as by law established read each Sunday and holidays; and the Blessed Sacrament administered according to the rites of the Church of England.

28. You shall be careful that the churches, hereafter to be built within our said Island, be well and orderly kept, and that, besides a competent maintenance to be assigned to the minister of each orthodox church, a convenient house be built at the public charge for each minister; and you are in an especial manner to take care that one hundred acres of land for the site of a church and as a glebe for a minister of the gospel, and thirty acres for a schoolmaster, be duly reserved in a proper part

of every township, conformable to the directions and conditions annexed to our Order in Council of the 26th of August, 1767, herein before referred to.

29. You are not to prefer any minister to any ecclesiastical benefice in that our Island without a certificate from the Right Reverend Father in God the Lord Bishop of London, of his being conformable to the doctrine and discipline of the Church of England, and of a good life and conversation, and if any person preferred already to a benefice shall appear to you to give scandal, either by his doctrine or manners, you are to use the proper means for the removal of him.

30. You are to give orders forthwith that every orthodox minister within your Government be one of the vestry in his respective parish; and that no vestry be held without him, except in case of sickness, or that after notice of a vestry summoned he omit to come.

31. You are to inquire whether there be any minister within your Government who preaches and administers the Sacrament in any orthodox church or chapel without being in due orders, and to give an account thereof to the said Lord Bishop of London.

32. And to the end the ecclesiastical jurisdiction of the said Lord Bishop of London may take place in that Island so far as conveniently may be, we do think fit that you do give all countenance and encouragement to the exercise of the same, excepting only the collating to benefices, granting licences for marriages and probate of wills, which we have reserved to you our Governor and to the Commander in Chief of our said Island for the time being.

33. We do further direct that no schoolmaster be henceforth permitted to come from England and to keep school in the said Island without the licence of the said Bishop of London, that no other person now there or that shall come from other parts shall be admitted to keep school in that our said Island of Saint John without your licence first obtained.

34. And you are to take especial care that a table of marriages established by the canons of the Church of England be hung up in every orthodox church and duly observed, and you are to endeavour to get a law passed in the Assembly of that Island for the strict observation of the said table.

35. The Right Reverend Father in God Edmund, late Lord Bishop of London, having presented a petition to His late Majesty King George the First, humbly beseeching him to send instructions to the Governors

of all the several plantations in America that they cause all laws already made against blasphemy, profaneness, adultery, fornication, polygamy, incest, profanation of the Lord's Day, swearing, and drunkenness in their respective Governments to be rigorously executed, and we, thinking it highly just that all persons who shall offend in any of the particulars aforesaid should be prosecuted and punished for their said offences, it is therefore our will and pleasure that you take due care for the punishment of the aforementioned vices, and that you earnestly recommend it to the Assembly of our said Island to provide effectual laws for the restraint and punishment of all such of the aforementioned vices against which no laws are as yet provided; and also to use your endeavours to render the laws in being more [efficacious] by providing for the punishment of the aforementioned vices by presentment on oath to be made to the temporal courts by the church wardens of the several parishes at proper times of the year to be appointed for that purpose; and for the further encouragement [sic] of vice and encouragement of virtue and good living (that by such example the infidels may be invited and desire to embrace the Christian religion,) you are not to admit any person to public trusts or employments in the Island under your government whose ill fame and conversation may occasion scandal. And it is our further will and pleasure that you recommend to the Assembly to enter upon proper methods for the erecting of schools in order to the training up of youth to reading and to a necessary knowledge of the principles of religion.

36. And whereas, you will receive from our Commissioners for executing the office of High Admiral of Great Britain and of our plantations a commission of Vice Admiralty of our said Island, you are hereby required and directed carefully to put in execution the several powers thereby granted you.

37. And there having been great irregularities in the manner of granting commissions in the plantations to private ships of war, you are to govern yourself, whenever there shall be occasion, according to the commissions & instructions granted in this Kingdom, copies whereof will be herewith delivered you. But you are not to grant commissions of marque or reprizal against any prince or state, or their subjects in amity with us, to any person whatsoever without our especial command. And you are to oblige the commanders of all ships having private commissions to wear no other colours than such as are described in an Order in Council of the 7th of January, 1730, in

relation to colours to be worn by all ships and vessels except our own ships of war.

38. Whereas divers acts have from time to time been passed in several of our colonies in America, imposing a duty of powder on every vessel that enters and clears in the said colonies, which has been of great service in furnishing the magazines with powder for the defence of the said colonies in time of danger, it is our express will and pleasure, and you are hereby required and directed to recommend to the Assembly of our said Island to pass a Law for collecting of Powder Duty, and that the law for that purpose be made perpetual, that a certain time in the said Act not exceeding twelve months be allowed for giving notice thereof to the several masters of vessels trading to our said Island; and that for the more ample notification thereof a proclamation be also published in your said Government declaring that from and after the expiration of the time limited by the said Act for such notice, no commutation shall be allowed of but upon evident necessity which may some time happen, whereof you or the Commander in Chief for the time being are to be the judge, in which case the said master shall pay the full price gunpowder sells for there, and the monies so collected shall be laid out as soon as may be in the purchase of gunpowder. And you are also to transmit every six months to us by one of our principal Secretaries of State an account of the particular quantities of powder collected under the said Act in your Government, and likewise a duplicate thereof to the Master General or principal officers of our ordnance.

39. And in case of distress of any other of our plantations, you shall, upon application of the respective Governors thereof to you, assist them with what aid the condition and safety of our Island under your government can spare.

40. You are likewise, from time to time, to send unto us by one of our principal Secretaries of State as aforesaid, an account of the wants and defects of the said Island, and what are the chief products thereof; what new improvements are made therein by the industry of the inhabitants and planters; and what further improvements you conceive may be made or advantages gained by trade, and which way we may contribute thereunto.

41. If anything shall happen that may be of advantage and security [to] our said Island which is not herein or by our Commission provided for, we do hereby allow unto you, with the advice and consent

of our Council, to take order for the present therein, giving unto us by one of our principal Secretaries of State speedy notice thereof that so you may receive our ratification, if we shall approve of the same; provided always that you do not by colour of any power given you commence or declare war without our knowledge and particular commands therein, except it be against the Indians upon emergencies, wherein the consent of our Council shall be had and speedy notice thereof given unto us by one of our principal Secretaries of State as aforesaid.

42. And you are upon all occasions to send to us, by one of our principal Secretaries of State, particular account of all your proceedings and of the conditions of affairs with your Government.

43. And whereas, great prejudice may happen to our service and the security of the said Island by your absence from those parts, you are not upon any pretence whatsoever to come to Europe from your Government without having first obtained leave for so doing from us under our sign manual and signet or by our order in our Privy Council.

44. And whereas we have been pleased by our Commission to direct that in case of your death or absence from our said Island, and in case there be at that time no person upon the place commissionated or appointed by us to be our Lieutenant Governor or Commander in Chief, the eldest Councillor whose name is first placed in these Instructions to you, and who shall be at the time of your death or absence residing within our said Island, shall take upon him the administration of the government, and execute our said Commission and Instructions, and the several powers and authorities therein contained in the manner therein directed, it is nevertheless our express will and pleasure that, in such case, the said eldest Councillor or President shall forbear to pass any act or acts, but such as shall be immediately necessary for the peace and welfare of our said Island, without our particular order for that purpose, and that he shall not take upon him to dissolve the Assembly, if it should happen that there should be an Assembly then in being, nor to remove or suspend any of the members of our said Council, nor any judges, justices of the peace, or other officers, civil or military, without the advice and consent of at least seven of the Council. And our said President is to transmit to us by one of our principal Secretaries of State, by the first opportunity, the reasons for such alterations, signed by himself and our Council.

APPENDIX C

SECTIONS OF THE BRITISH NORTH AMERICA ACT AFFECTING THE GOVERNMENT OF PRINCE EDWARD ISLAND

ROYAL ASSENT.

Royal Assent to Bills, etc.   **55.** Where a Bill passed by the Houses of Parliament is presented to the Governor General for the Queen's Assent, he shall declare, according to his Discretion, but subject to the Provisions of this Act and to Her Majesty's Instructions, either that he assents thereto in the Queen's Name, or that he withholds the Queen's Assent, or that he reserves the Bill for the Signification of the Queen's Pleasure.

Disallowance by order in Council of Act assented to by Governor General.   **56.** Where the Governor General assents to a Bill in the Queen's Name, he shall by the first convenient Opportunity send an authentic Copy of the Act to one of Her Majesty's Principal Secretaries of State, and if the Queen in Council within Two Years after Receipt thereof by the Secretary of State thinks fit to disallow the Act, such Disallowance (with a Certificate of the Secretary of State of the Day on which the Act was received by him) being signified by the Governor General, by Speech or Message to each of the Houses of the Parliament or by Proclamation, shall annul the Act from and after the Day of such Signification.

Application to Legislatures of provisions respecting money votes, etc.   **90.** The following Provisions of this Act respecting the Parliament of Canada, namely,—the Provisions relating to Appropriation and Tax Bills, the Recommendation of Money Votes, the Assent to Bills, the Disallowance of Acts, and the Signification of Pleasure on Bills reserved,—shall extend and apply to the Legislatures of the several Provinces as if those Provisions were here re-enacted and made applicable in Terms to the respective Provinces and the Legislatures thereof, with the Substitution of the Lieutenant-Governor of the Province for the Governor General, of the Governor General for the Queen and for a Secretary of State, of One Year for Two Years, and of the Province for Canada.

PROVINCIAL CONSTITUTION.

Executive Power.

58. For each Province there shall be an Officer, styled the Lieutenant-Governor, appointed by the Governor General in Council by Instrument under the Great Seal of Canada. Appointment of Lieutenant-Governors of Provinces.

59. A Lieutenant-Governor shall hold Office during the Pleasure of the Governor General; but any Lieutenant-Governor appointed after the Commencement of the First Session of the Parliament of Canada shall not be removable within Five Years from his Appointment, except for Cause assigned, which shall be communicated to him in Writing within One Month after the Order for his Removal is made, and shall be communicated by Message to the Senate and to the House of Commons within One week thereafter if the Parliament is then sitting, and if not then within One Week after the Commencement of the next Session of the Parliament. Tenure of office of Lieutenant-Governor.

60. The Salaries of the Lieutenant-Governors shall be fixed and provided by the Parliament of Canada. Salaries of Lieutenant-Governors.

61. Every Lieutenant-Governor shall, before assuming the Duties of his Office, make and subscribe before the Governor General or some Person authorized by him, Oaths of Allegiance and Office similar to those taken by the Governor General. Oaths, etc., of Lieutenant-Governor.

62. The Provisions of this Act referring to the Lieutenant-Governor extend and apply to the Lieutenant-Governor for the Time being of each Province or other the Chief Executive Officer or Administrator for the Time being carrying on the Government of the Province, by whatever Title he is designated. Application of provisions referring to Lieutenant-Governor.

66. The Provisions of this Act referring to the Lieutenant-Governor in Council shall be construed as referring to the Lieutenant-Governor of the Province acting by and with the Advice of the Executive Council thereof. Application of provisions referring to Lieutenant-Governor in Council.

67. The Governor General in Council may from Time to Time appoint an Administrator to execute the Office and Functions of Lieutenant-Governor during his Absence, Illness, or other Inability. Administration in absence, etc., of Lieutenant-Governor.

GOVERNMENT OF PRINCE EDWARD ISLAND

DISTRIBUTION OF LEGISLATIVE POWERS.

Powers of the Parliament.

Legislative Authority of Parliament of Canada.

91. It shall be lawful for the Queen, by and with the Advice and Consent of the Senate and House of Commons, to make Laws for the Peace, Order, and good Government of Canada, in relation to all Matters not coming within the Classes of Subjects by this Act assigned exclusively to the Legislatures of the Provinces, and for greater Certainty, but not so as to restrict the Generality of the foregoing Terms in this Section, it is hereby declared that (notwithstanding anything in this Act) the exclusive Legislative Authority of the Parliament of Canada extends to all Matters coming within the Classes of Subjects next hereinafter enumerated; that is to say,—

1. The Public Debt and Property.
2. The Regulation of Trade and Commerce.
2A. Unemployment Insurance.*
3. The raising of Money by any Mode or System of Taxation.
4. The borrowing of Money on the Public Credit.
5. Postal Service.
6. The Census and Statistics.
7. Militia, Military and Naval Service, and Defence.
8. The fixing of and providing for the Salaries and Allowances of Civil and other Officers of the Government of Canada.
9. Beacons, Buoys, Lighthouses, and Sable Island.
10. Navigation and Shipping.
11. Quarantine and the Establishment and Maintenance of Marine Hospitals.
12. Sea Coast and Inland Fisheries.
13. Ferries between a Province and any British or Foreign Country or between Two Provinces.
14. Currency and Coinage.
15. Banking, Incorporation of Banks, and the Issue of Paper Money.
16. Savings Banks.
17. Weights and Measures.

*Section 91 was amended by inserting item 2A in 1940. This amendment was made by the British North America Act of 1940 (3-4 Geo. VI, c. 36, s.1).

18. Bills of Exchange and Promissory Notes.
19. Interest.
20. Legal Tender.
21. Bankruptcy and Insolvency.
22. Patents of Invention and Discovery.
23. Copyrights.
24. Indians and Lands reserved for the Indians.
25. Naturalization of Aliens.
26. Marriage and Divorce.
27. The Criminal Law, except the Constitution of Courts of Criminal Jurisdiction, but including the Procedure in Criminal Matters.
28. The Establishment, Maintenance, and Management of Penitentiaries.
29. Such Classes of Subjects as are expressly excepted in the Enumeration of the Classes of Subjects by this Act assigned exclusively to the Legislatures of the Provinces.

And any Matter coming within any of the Classes of Subjects enumerated in this Section shall not be deemed to come within the Class of Matters of a local or private Nature comprised in the Enumeration of the Classes of Subjects by this Act assigned exclusively to the Legislatures of the Provinces.

Exclusive Powers of Provincial Legislatures.

92. In each Province the Legislature may exclusively make Laws in relation to Matters coming within the Classes of Subjects next hereinafter enumerated; that is to say,— *Subjects of exclusive Provincial Legislation.*

1. The Amendment from Time to Time, notwithstanding anything in this Act, of the Constitution of the Province, except as regards the Office of Lieutenant-Governor.
2. Direct Taxation within the Province in order to the Raising of a Revenue for Provincial Purposes.
3. The borrowing of Money on the sole Credit of the Province.
4. The Establishment and Tenure of Provincial Offices and the Appointment and Payment of Provincial Officers.
5. The Management and Sale of the Public Lands belonging to the Province and of the Timber and Wood thereon.
6. The Establishment, Maintenance, and Management of Public and Reformatory Prisons in and for the Province.

7. The Establishment, Maintenance, and Management of Hospitals, Asylums, Charities, and Eleemosynary Institutions in and for the Province, other than Marine Hospitals.
8. Municipal Institutions in the Province.
9. Shop, Saloon, Tavern, Auctioneer, and other Licences in order to the raising of a Revenue for Provincial, Local, and Municipal Purposes.
10. Local Works and Undertakings other than such as are of the following Classes:—
    (*a*) Lines of Steam or other Ships, Railways, Canals, Telegraphs, and other Works and Undertakings connecting the Province with any other or others of the Provinces, or extending beyond the Limits of the Province:
    (*b*) Lines of Steam Ships between the Province and any British or Foreign Country:
    (*c*) Such Works as, although wholly situate within the Province, are before or after their Execution declared by the Parliament of Canada to be for the general Advantage of Canada or for the Advantage of Two or more of the Provinces.
11. The Incorporation of Companies with Provincial Objects.
12. The Solemnization of Marriage in the Province.
13. Property and Civil Rights in the Province.
14. The Administration of Justice in the Province, including the Constitution, Maintenance, and Organization of Provincial Courts, both of Civil and of Criminal Jurisdiction, and including Procedure in Civil Matters in those Courts.
15. The Imposition of Punishment by Fine, Penalty, or Imprisonment for enforcing any Law of the Province made in relation to any Matter coming within any of the Classes of Subjects enumerated in this Section.
16. Generally all Matters of a merely local or private Nature in the Province.

Education.

Legislation respecting Education. **93.** In and for each Province the Legislature may exclusively make Laws in relation to Education, subject and according to the following Provisions:—

(1) Nothing in any such Law shall prejudicially affect any Right or Privilege with respect to Denominational Schools which any Class of Persons have by Law in the Province at the Union:
(2) All the Powers, Privileges, and Duties at the Union by Law conferred and imposed in Upper Canada on the Separate Schools and School Trustees of the Queen's Roman Catholic Subjects shall be and the same are hereby extended to the Dissentient Schools of the Queen's Protestant and Roman Catholic Subjects in Quebec:
(3) Where in any Province a System of Separate or Dissentient Schools exists by Law at the Union or is thereafter established by the Legislature of the Province, an Appeal shall lie to the Governor General in Council from any Act or Decision of any Provincial Authority affecting any Right or Privilege of the Protestant or Roman Catholic Minority of the Queen's Subjects in relation to Education:
(4) In case any such Provincial Law as from Time to Time seems to the Governor General in Council requisite for the due Execution of the Provisions of this Section is not made, or in case any Decision of the Governor General in Council on any Appeal under this Section is not duly executed by the proper Provincial Authority in that Behalf, then and in every such Case, and as far only as the Circumstances of each Case require, the Parliament of Canada may make remedial Laws for the due Execution of the Provisions of this Section and of any Decision of the Governor General in Council under this Section.

Uniformity of Laws in Ontario, Nova Scotia, and New Brunswick.

94. Notwithstanding anything in this Act, the Parliament of Canada may make Provision for the Uniformity of all or any of the Laws relative to Property and Civil Rights in Ontario, Nova Scotia, and New Brunswick, and of the Procedure of all or any of the Courts in those Three Provinces, and from and after the passing of any Act in that Behalf the Power of the Parliament of Canada to make Laws in relation to any Matter comprised in Legislation for uniformity of Laws in three Provinces.

any such Act shall, notwithstanding anything in this Act, be unrestricted; but any Act of the Parliament of Canada making provision for such Uniformity shall not have effect in any Province unless and until it is adopted and enacted as Law by the Legislature thereof.

Agriculture and Immigration.

<u>Concurrent powers of Legislation respecting Agriculture, etc.</u>
95. In each Province the Legislature may make Laws in relation to Agriculture in the Province, and to Immigration into the Province; and it is hereby declared that the Parliament of Canada may from Time to Time make Laws in relation to Agriculture in all or any of the Provinces, and to Immigration into all or any of the Provinces; and any Law of the Legislature of a Province relative to Agriculture or to Immigration shall have effect in and for the Province as long and as far only as it is not repugnant to any Act of the Parliament of Canada.

JUDICATURE.

<u>Appointment of Judges.</u>
96. The Governor General shall appoint the Judges of the Superior, District, and County Courts in each Province, except those of the Courts of Probate in Nova Scotia and New Brunswick.

<u>Tenure of office of Judges of Superior Courts.</u>
99. The Judges of the Superior Courts shall hold office during good Behaviour, but shall be removable by the Governor General on Address of the Senate and House of Commons.

<u>Salaries, etc., of Judges.</u>
100. The Salaries, Allowances, and Pensions of the Judges of the Superior, District, and County Courts (except the Courts of Probate in Nova Scotia and New Brunswick), and of the Admiralty Courts in Cases where the Judges thereof are for the Time being paid by Salary, shall be fixed and provided by the Parliament of Canada.

<u>General Court of Appeal, etc.</u>
101. The Parliament of Canada may, notwithstanding anything in this Act, from Time to Time, provide for the Constitution, Maintenance, and Organization of a General Court of Appeal for Canada, and for the Establishment of any additional Courts for the better Administration of the Laws of Canada.

BRITISH NORTH AMERICA ACT 351

Arrangements of Courts and Offices at Confederation.

129. Except as otherwise provided by this Act, all Laws in force in Canada, Nova Scotia, or New Brunswick at the Union, and all Courts of Civil and Criminal Jurisdiction, and all legal Commissions, Powers, and Authorities, and all Officers, Judicial, Administrative, and Ministerial, existing therein at the Union, shall continue in Ontario, Quebec, Nova Scotia, and New Brunswick respectively, as if the Union had not been made; subject nevertheless (except with respect to such as are enacted by or exist under Acts of the Parliament of Great Britain or of the Parliament of the United Kingdom of Great Britain and Ireland,) to be repealed, abolished, or altered by the Parliament of Canada, or by the Legislature of the respective Province, according to the Authority of the Parliament or of that Legislature under this Act. _{Continuance of existing Laws, Courts, Officers, etc.}

130. Until the Parliament of Canada otherwise provides, all Officers of the several Provinces having Duties to discharge in relation to Matters other than those coming within the Classes of Subjects by this Act assigned exclusively to the Legislatures of the Provinces shall be Officers of Canada, and shall continue to discharge the Duties of their respective Offices under the same Liabilities, Responsibilities, and Penalties as if the Union had not been made. _{Transfer of officers to Canada.}

131. Until the Parliament of Canada otherwise provides, the Governor General in Council may from Time to Time appoint such Officers as the Governor General in Council deems necessary or proper for the effectual Execution of this Act. _{Appointment of new officers.}

ADMISSION OF OTHER COLONIES.

146. It shall be lawful for the Queen, by and with the Advice of Her Majesty's Most Honourable Privy Council, on Addresses from the Houses of the Parliament of Canada, and from the Houses of the respective Legislatures of the Colonies or Provinces of Newfoundland, Prince Edward Island, and British Columbia, to admit those Colonies or Provinces, or any of them, into the Union, and on Address from the Houses of the Parlia- _{Power to admit Newfoundland, etc., into the Union.}

ment of Canada to admit Rupert's Land and the Northwestern Territory, or either of them, into the Union, on such Terms and Conditions in each Case as are in the Addresses expressed and as the Queen thinks fit to approve, subject to the Provisions of this Act; and the Provisions of any Order in Council in that Behalf shall have effect as if they had been enacted by the Parliament of the United Kingdom of Great Britain and Ireland.

As to Representation of Newfoundland and Prince Edward Island in Senate.

147. In case of the Admission of Newfoundland and Prince Edward Island, or either of them, each shall be entitled to a Representation in the Senate of Canada of Four Members, and (notwithstanding anything in this Act) in case of the Admission of Newfoundland the normal Number of Senators shall be Seventy-six and their maximum Number shall be Eighty-two; but Prince Edward Island when admitted shall be deemed to be comprised in the third of the Three Divisions into which Canada is, in relation to the Constitution of the Senate, divided by this Act, and accordingly, after the Admission of Prince Edward Island, whether Newfoundland is admitted or not, the Representation of Nova Scotia and New Brunswick in the Senate shall, as Vacancies occur, be reduced from Twelve to Ten Members respectively, and the Representation of each of those Provinces shall not be increased at any Time beyond Ten, except under the Provisions of this Act for the Appointment of Three or Six additional Senators under the Direction of the Queen.

APPENDIX D

DOCUMENTS RESPECTING THE ENTRANCE OF PRINCE EDWARD ISLAND INTO CONFEDERATION

ORDER OF HER MAJESTY IN COUNCIL ADMITTING PRINCE EDWARD ISLAND INTO THE UNION

At the Court at Windsor, the 26th day of June, 1873.

PRESENT:

The QUEEN'S Most Excellent Majesty.
Lord President.   Earl of Kimberley.
Earl Granville.   Lord Chamberlain.
Mr. Gladstone.

WHEREAS by the British North America Act, 1867, provision was made for the Union of the Provinces of Canada, Nova Scotia and New Brunswick into the Dominion of Canada, and it was (amongst other things) enacted that it should be lawful for the Queen, by and with the advice of Her Majesty's Most Honourable Privy Council, on Addresses from the Houses of the Parliament of Canada, and of the Legislature of the Colony of Prince Edward Island, to admit that Colony into the said Union on such terms and conditions as should be in the Addresses expressed, and as the Queen should think fit to approve, subject to the provisions of the said Act; and it was further enacted that the provisions of any Order in Council in that behalf, should have effect as if they had been enacted by the Parliament of the United Kingdom of Great Britain and Ireland.

And whereas by Addresses from the Houses of the Parliament of Canada, and from the Legislative Council and House of Assembly of Prince Edward Island respectively, of which Addresses, copies are contained in the Schedule to this Order annexed, Her Majesty was prayed, by and with the advice of Her Most Honourable Privy Council, under the one hundred and forty-sixth section of the hereinbefore recited Act, to admit Prince Edward Island into the Dominion of Canada, on the terms and conditions set forth in the said Addresses.

And whereas Her Majesty has thought fit to approve of the said terms and conditions, it is hereby ordered and declared by Her Majesty, by and with the advice of Her Privy Council, in pursuance and exercise of the powers vested in Her Majesty, by the said Act of Parliament, that from and after the first day of July, one thousand eight hundred and seventy-three, the said Colony of Prince Edward Island shall be admitted into and become part of the Dominion of Canada, upon the terms and conditions set forth in the hereinbefore recited Addresses.

And in accordance with the terms of the said Addresses relating to the Electoral Districts for which, the time within which, and the laws and provisions under which the first election of members to serve in the House of Commons of Canada, for such Electoral Districts shall be held, it is hereby further ordered and declared that "Prince County" shall constitute one district, to be designated "Prince County District," and return two members; that "Queen's County" shall constitute one district, to be designated "Queen's County District," and return two members; that "King's County" shall constitute one district, to be designated "King's County District," and return two members; that the election of members to serve in the House of Commons of Canada, for such Electoral Districts shall be held within three calendar months from the day of the admission of the said Island into the Union or Dominion of Canada; that all laws which at the date of this Order in Council relating to the qualification of any person to be elected or sit or vote as a member of the House of Assembly of the said Island, and relating to the qualifications or disqualifications of voters, and to the oaths to be taken by voters, and to Returning Officers and Poll Clerks, and their powers and duties, and relating to Polling Divisions within the said Island, and relating to the proceedings at elections, and to the period during which such elections may be continued, and relating to the trial of controverted elections, and the proceedings incidental thereto, and relating to the vacating of seats of the members, and to the execution of new writs, in the case of any seat being vacated otherwise than by a dissolution, and to all other matters connected with or incidental to elections of members to serve in the House of Assembly of the said Island, shall apply to elections of members to serve in the House of Commons for the Electoral Districts situate in the said Island of Prince Edward.

And the Right Honourable Earl of Kimberley, one of Her Majesty's Principal Secretaries of State is to give the necessary directions herein, accordingly.

ARTHUR HELPS.

SCHEDULE.

To the Queen's Most Excellent Majesty.

Most Gracious Sovereign,

We, Your Majesty's most dutiful and loyal subjects, the Commons of the Dominion of Canada in Parliament assembled, humbly approach Your Majesty for the purpose of representing:—

That during the present Session of Parliament we have taken into consideration the subject of the admission of the Colony of Prince Edward Island into the Union or Dominion of Canada, and have resolved that it is expedient that such admission should be effected at as early a date as may be found practicable under the one hundred and forty-sixth section of the British North America Act, 1867, on the conditions hereinafter set forth, which have been agreed upon with the Delegates from the said Colony that is to say:—

That Canada shall be liable for the debts and liabilities of Prince Edward Island at the time of the Union;

That in consideration of the large expenditure authorized by the Parliament of Canada for the construction of railways and canals, and in view of the possibility of a readjustment of the financial arrangements between Canada and the several Provinces now embraced in the Dominion, as well as the isolated and exceptional condition of Prince Edward Island, that Colony shall, on entering the Union, be entitled to incur a debt equal to fifty dollars per head of its population, as shewn by the Census Returns of 1871, that is to say: four millions seven hundred and one thousand and fifty dollars;

That Prince Edward Island not having incurred debts equal to the sum mentioned in the next preceding Resolution, shall be entitled to receive, by half-yearly payments, in advance, from the General Government, interest at the rate of five per centum per annum on the difference, from time to time, between the actual amount of its indebtedness and the amount of indebtedness authorized as aforesaid, viz., four millions seven hundred and one thousand and fifty dollars;

That Prince Edward Island shall be liable to Canada for the amount (if any) by which its public debts and liabilities at the date of the Union, may exceed four millions seven hundred and one thousand and fifty dollars and shall be chargeable with interest at the rate of five per centum per annum on such excess;

That as the Government of Prince Edward Island holds no lands from the Crown, and consequently enjoys no revenue from that source for the construction and maintenance of local works, the Dominion Government shall pay by half-yearly instalments, in advance, to the Government of Prince Edward Island, forty-five thousand dollars per annum, less interest at five per centum per annum, upon any sum not exceeding eight hundred thousand dollars which the Dominion Government may advance to the Prince Edward Island Government for the purchase of lands now held by large proprietors;

That in consideration of the transfer to the Parliament of Canada of the powers of taxation, the following sums shall be paid yearly by Canada to Prince Edward Island, for the support of its Government and Legislature, that is to say, thirty thousand dollars, and an annual grant equal to eighty cents per head of its population, as shown by the Census returns of 1871, viz., 94,021, both by half-yearly payments in advance—such grant of eighty cents per head to be augmented in proportion to the increase of population of the Island as may be shown by each subsequent decennial Census, until the population amounts to four hundred thousand, at which rate such grant shall thereafter remain, it being understood that the next Census shall be taken in the year 1881;

That the Dominion Government shall assume and defray all the charges for the following services, viz.:—

The salary of the Lieutenant-Governor;

The salaries of the Judges of the Superior Court and of the District or County Courts when established;

The charges in respect of the Department of Customs;

The Postal Department;

The protection of the Fisheries;

The provision of the Militia;

The Lighthouses, Shipwrecked Crews, Quarantine and Marine Hospitals;

The Geological Survey;

The Penitentiary;

Efficient Steam Service for the conveyance of mails and passengers, to be established and maintained between the Island and the mainland of the Dominion, Winter and Summer, thus placing the Island in continuous communication with the Intercolonial Railway and the railway system of the Dominion;

The maintenance of telegraphic communication between the Island and the mainland of the Dominion;

And such other charges as may be incident to, and connected with, the services which by the British North America Act, 1867, appertain to the General Government, and as are or may be allowed to the other Provinces;

That the railways under contract and in course of construction for the Government of the Island, shall be the property of Canada;

That the new building in which are held the Law Courts, Registry Office, etc., shall be transferred to Canada, on the payment of sixty-nine thousand dollars. The purchase to include the land on which the building stands, and a suitable space of ground in addition, for yard room, etc.;

That the Steam Dredge Boat in course of construction, shall be taken by the Dominion, at a cost not exceeding twenty-two thousand dollars;

That the Steam Ferry Boat owned by the Government of the Island, and used as such, shall remain the property of the Island;

That the population of Prince Edward Island having been increased by fifteen thousand or upwards since the year 1861, the Island shall be represented in the House of Commons of Canada by six Members; the representation to be readjusted, from time to time, under the provisions of the British North America Act, 1867;

That the constitution of the Executive Authority and of the Legislature of Prince Edward Island, shall, subject to the provisions of the British North America Act, 1867, continue, as at the time of the Union, until altered under the authority of the said Act, and the House of Assembly of Prince Edward Island existing at the date of the Union shall, unless sooner dissolved, continue for the period for which it was elected;

That the provisions in the British North America Act, 1867, shall, except those parts thereof which are in terms made, or by reasonable intendment, may be held to be especially applicable to, and only to affect one and not the whole of the Provinces now composing the Dominion, and except so far as the same may be varied by these resolutions, be applicable to Prince Edward Island, in the same way and to the same extent as they apply to the other Provinces of the Dominion, and as if the Colony of Prince Edward Island had been one of the Provinces originally united by the said Act.

That the Union will take place on such a day as Her Majesty may direct by Order in Council, on Addresses to that effect from the House of Parliament of Canada and of the Legislature of the Colony of Prince Edward Island, under the one hundred and forty-sixth section of the British North America Act, 1867, and that the Electoral Districts for which, the time within which, and the laws and provisions under which, the first Election of Members to serve in the House of Commons of Canada for such Electoral Districts shall be held, shall be such as the said Houses of the Legislature of the said Colony of Prince Edward Island may specify in their said Addresses.

We, therefore, humbly pray that Your Majesty will be graciously pleased, by and with the advice of Your Majesty's Most Honourable Privy Council, under the provisions of the one hundred and forty-sixth section of the British North America Act, 1867, to admit Prince Edward Island into the Union or Dominion of Canada, on the terms and conditions hereinbefore set forth.

(Signed)   JAMES COCKBURN,
Speaker.

HOUSE OF COMMONS,
20th May, 1873.

The Queen's Most Excellent Majesty.

Most Gracious Sovereign,

We, Your Majesty's most dutiful and loyal subjects, the Senate of the Dominion of Canada in Parliament assembled, humbly approach Your Majesty for the purpose of representing:—

That on the sixteenth day of May, instant, His Excellency the Governor General transmitted for our information a copy of the minutes of a Conference between a Committee of the Privy Council of Canada and certain Delegates from the Colony of Prince Edward

Island, on the subject of the Union of the said Colony with the Dominion of Canada, and of the Resolutions adopted by them, as the basis of such Union, which are in the following words, that is to say:—

(*Here follows a statement of the conditions of Union as set forth in the Address of the House of Commons,* supra, *pages 355, 356, 357, and 358.*)

The House of Commons having in the present Session of the Parliament of the Dominion passed an Address to Your Majesty, praying that Your Majesty would be graciously pleased, by and with the advice of Your Most Honourable Privy Council, under the provisions of the one hundred and forty-sixth section of the British North America Act, 1867, to admit Prince Edward Island into the Union or Dominion of Canada, on the terms and conditions set forth in the above-mentioned Resolutions.

Wherefore, we, the Senate of Canada, fully concurring in the terms and conditions expressed in the Address of the House of Commons, humbly pray that Your Majesty will be pleased, by and with the advice of Your Most Honourable Privy Council, under the provisions of the one hundred and forty-sixth section of the British North America Act, 1867, to admit Prince Edward Island into the Dominion of Canada.

(Signed)   P. J. O. CHAUVEAU,
Speaker of the Senate.

THE SENATE, May 21, 1873.

To the Queen's Most Excellent Majesty.

Most Gracious Sovereign,

We, Your Majesty's most dutiful and loyal subjects, the Legislative Council of Prince Edward Island, in Parliament assembled, humbly approach Your Majesty, and pray that Your Majesty will be graciously pleased, by and with the advice of Your Majesty's Most Honourable Privy Council, under the provisions of the one hundred and forty-sixth section of the British North America Act, 1867, to admit Prince Edward Island into the Union or Dominion of Canada, on the terms and conditions expressed in certain Resolutions recently passed by Houses of the Parliament of Canada, and also by the Houses of the Legislature of Prince Edward Island, which said Resolutions are as follows:—

(*Here follows a statement of the conditions of Union as set forth in the Address of the House of Commons, supra.*)

That for the first election of members to be returned by this Island for the House of Commons of the Dominion of Canada, this Island shall be divided into Electoral Districts as follows:—That "Prince County" shall constitute one district and return two members; that "Queen's County" shall constitute one district, and return two members; that "King's County" shall constitute one district, and return two members; that the first election of members to serve in the House of Commons of Canada, shall take place within three calendar months after this Island shall be admitted, and become part of the Dominion of Canada; and we further humbly pray, that all laws which at the date of the Order in Council, by which the said Island of Prince Edward shall be admitted into the Dominion of Canada, relating to the qualification of any person to be elected to sit or vote as a member of the House of Assembly of the said Island, and relating to the qualifications or disqualifications of voters, and to the oaths to be taken by voters, and to returning officers and poll clerks, and their powers and duties, and relating to polling divisions within the said Island, and relating to the proceedings at elections, and to the period during which such election may be continued, and relating to the trial of controverted elections and the proceedings incident thereto, and relating to the vacating of seats of members, and to the execution of new writs, in case of any seat being vacated otherwise than by a dissolution, and all other matters connected with or incidental to elections of members to serve in the House of Assembly of the said Island, shall apply to elections of members to serve in the House of Commons for the Electoral Districts, situate in the said Island of Prince Edward.

(Signed)   DONALD MONTGOMERY,
President.

COMMITTEE ROOM, LEGISLATIVE COUNCIL,
      May 28, 1873.

To the Queen's Most Excellent Majesty.

Most Gracious Sovereign,

We, Your Majesty's most dutiful and loyal subjects, the House of Assembly of Prince Edward Island in Parliament assembled, humbly approach Your Majesty, and pray that Your Majesty will be graciously pleased, by and with the advice of Your Majesty's Most Honourable Privy Council, under the provisions of the one hundred and forty-sixth section of the British North America Act, 1867, to admit Prince Edward Island into the Union or Dominion of Canada, on the terms and conditions expressed in certain Resolutions recently passed by the Houses of the Parliament of Canada, and also by the Houses of the Legislature of Prince Edward Island, which said Resolutions are as follows: —

(*Here follows a statement of the conditions of Union as set forth in the Address of the House of Commons, supra, and the Address concludes with a paragraph identical with the last paragraph of the Address of the Legislative Council of Prince Edward Island, supra.*)

(Signed) STANISLAUS F. PERRY,
Speaker.

HOUSE OF ASSEMBLY,
   May 28, 1873.

APPENDIX E

THE LIEUTENANT-GOVERNORS OF PRINCE EDWARD ISLAND

FROM 1769 TO CONFEDERATION, WITH DATE OF APPOINTMENT

Walter Patterson	1769
(Governor, 1769; Lieutenant-Governor, 1784)	
Edmund Fanning	1786
J. F. W. DesBarres	1805
Charles Douglas Smith	1813
John Ready	1824
Aretus W. Young	1831
John Harvey	1836
Charles A. Fitzroy	1837
Henry Vere Huntley	1841
Donald Campbell	1847
Alexander Bannerman	1851
Dominick Daly	1854
George Dundas	1858
William C. F. Robinson	1870

APPENDIX F

THE LIEUTENANT-GOVERNORS OF PRINCE EDWARD ISLAND

SINCE CONFEDERATION, WITH DATE OF COMMISSION AND OCCUPATION

William Robinson	June 10, 1873	British Colonial Service
Sir Robert Hodgson	July 4, 1874	Chief Justice
T. Heath Haviland	July 10, 1879	Merchant and land agent
A. A. Macdonald	July 18, 1884	Postmaster
Jedediah S. Carvell	Sept. 2, 1889	Merchant
George W. Howlan	Feb. 21, 1894	Merchant
P. A. MacIntyre	May 23, 1899	Doctor
D. A. MacKinnon	Oct. 3, 1904	Lawyer
Benjamin Rogers	June 1, 1910	Merchant
A. C. Macdonald	June 3, 1915	Merchant
Murdoch MacKinnon	Sept. 2, 1919	Farmer
Frank R. Heartz	Sept. 8, 1924	Banker-merchant
Charles Dalton	Nov. 19, 1930	Fox breeder
George D. DeBlois	Dec. 28, 1933	Merchant
Bradford W. LePage	Sept. 11, 1939	Merchant
Joseph A. Bernard	May 18, 1945	Merchant
T. W. L. Prowse	Oct. 1, 1950	Merchant

APPENDIX G

THE PREMIERS OF PRINCE EDWARD ISLAND

FROM THE GRANTING OF RESPONSIBLE GOVERNMENT TO CONFEDERATION, WITH THE YEAR OF THE FORMATION OF THEIR GOVERNMENTS AND THEIR PARTY ALLEGIANCE

George Coles	1851	Liberal
John Holl	1854	Conservative
George Coles	1855	Liberal
Edward Palmer	1859	Conservative
John H. Gray	1863	Conservative
J. C. Pope	1865	Conservative
George Coles	1867	Liberal
Joseph Hensley	1869	Liberal
R. P. Haythorne	1869	Liberal
J. C. Pope	1870	Conservative
R. P. Haythorne	1871	Liberal
J. C. Pope	1873	Conservative

APPENDIX H

THE PREMIERS OF PRINCE EDWARD ISLAND

SINCE CONFEDERATION, WITH THE YEAR OF THE FORMATION OF THEIR GOVERNMENTS AND THEIR PARTY ALLEGIANCE

J. C. Pope	1873	Conservative
L. C. Owen	1873	Conservative
L. H. Davies	1876	Coalition
W. W. Sullivan	1879	Conservative
Neil MacLeod	1889	Conservative
Frederick Peters	1891	Liberal
A. B. Warburton	1897	Liberal
Donald Farquharson	1898	Liberal
Arthur Peters	1901	Liberal
F. L. Haszard	1908	Liberal
James Palmer	1911	Liberal
J. A. Mathieson	1911	Conservative
A. E. Arsenault	1917	Conservative
J. H. Bell	1919	Liberal
J. D. Stewart	1923	Conservative
A. C. Saunders	1927	Liberal
W. M. Lea	1930	Liberal
J. D. Stewart	1931	Conservative
W. J. P. MacMillan	1933	Conservative
W. M. Lea	1935	Liberal
Thane A. Campbell	1936	Liberal
J. Walter Jones	1943	Liberal

BIBLIOGRAPHY
OF
PRINCE EDWARD ISLAND HISTORY

BIBLIOGRAPHY OF PRINCE EDWARD ISLAND HISTORY

THERE IS NO adequate general history of Prince Edward Island. Existing material consists largely of commentaries, sketches of local community life, some accounts of the early years of settlement, and one or two studies on specialized topics. There are no collections of private papers of Island public men. Consequently, the student of the Island's past has had to resort almost entirely to the primary sources in the Public Archives of Canada, the Library of Parliament, the Charlottetown Public Library, and the local Legislative Building. Studies on Island politics and government have not heretofore been made, and the material for the second part of this book has been secured almost entirely from public documents and personal interviews.

Primary Sources

There is a wealth of material on Prince Edward Island in the Public Archives of Canada contained in the section entitled "Colonial Office Records (P.E.I.), A and G series." This collection includes all the official documents and correspondence of the colonial and early provincial periods. The Macdonald and Laurier Papers also contain much information on Island politics.

The official records of the Island Cabinet are found in the collection of "Minutes of Council" kept in the Legislative Building in Charlottetown.

There are sets of the *Journals* of the Legislative Council, the *Journals* of the Legislative Assembly, the Legislative Council *Debates,* and the *Debates* of the Legislative Assembly in both the Library of Parliament in Ottawa and the Charlottetown Public Library.

The government documents include the annual departmental reports to be found in the Legislative Building, Charlottetown, and the numerous submissions to royal commissions and the federal government which are in the local library and in the Library of Parliament.

There are many newspapers. The three most useful are the *Examiner,* the *Guardian,* and the *Patriot,* which have recorded contemporary affairs over many years. Both the Library of Parliament and the Charlottetown Public Library have excellent sets of the above three. The other newspapers are found in the Charlottetown Public Library:

The Agriculturist	1883-1890
The Island Argus	1870-1876
The Colonial Herald	1837-1844

The Constitutionalist	May, 1846 - Oct., 1846
The Daily Times	1901-1902
The Express and Commercial Advertiser	1850
Haszard's Gazette	1853-1856
The Charlottetown Herald	1866-1912
The Islander	1842-1871
The Morning News	Sept., 1843 - Dec., 1845
The Monitor	1857-1864
The Protestant	1863-1865
The People's Journal	1857-1858
The Register	1828-1831
The P.E.I. Times	1836-1838
The Palladium	1843-1845
The Pioneer (Alberton)	1876-1880
The Pioneer (Summerside)	1880
The Journal (Summerside)	1868-1890
The Progress (Summerside)	1856-1869
The Protector and Christian Witness	1857-1860
The Presbyterian	1884-1885
The Protestant Union	1885-1886
Ross's Weekly	1859-1862
The Watchman	1893-1920
P.E.I. Magazine	1900-1904
The Royal Gazette	

Secondary Sources

The Arrival of the First Scottish Catholic Emigrants in P. E. I. and After, 1772-1922 (memorial volume). Summerside: Journal Publishing Co. 1922.

BAGSTER, C. B. *The Progress and Prospects of Prince Edward Island* ("written during the leisure of a visit in 1861"). Charlottetown: Ings. 1861.

BLANCHARD, J. HENRI. *Histoire des Acadiens de l'Ile du Prince Edouard.* Moncton: L'Evangéline. 1927.

BREMNER, BENJAMIN. *An Island Scrapbook.* Charlottetown: Irwin. 1932.

────── *Memories of Long Ago* ("a series of sketches pertaining to Charlottetown in the past"). Charlottetown: Irwin. 1930.

────── *Tales of Abegweit* ("containing historical, biographical, and humorous sketches"). Charlottetown: Irwin. 1936.

CAMPBELL, DUNCAN. *History of Prince Edward Island.* Charlottetown: Bremner. 1875.

CHAMPION, HELEN JEAN. *Over on the Island* (a travel sketch). Toronto: Ryerson. 1939.

COTTON, W. L. *Chapters in Our Island Story.* Charlottetown: Irwin. 1927.

CROSKILL, W. H. *Handbook of Prince Edward Island.* Charlottetown: Haszard and Moore. 1906.

HART, G. E. *The Story of Old Abegweit.* N.p., n.d.

HARVEY, D. C. *The French Régime in Prince Edward Island.* New Haven: Yale University Press. 1926.

LEARD, GEORGE. *Historic Bedeque.* Bedeque United Church. 1948.

LIVINGSTON, W. ROSS. "Responsible Government in Prince Edward Island," *University of Iowa Studies in the Social Sciences,* vol. IX, no. 4, 1931.

McCOURT, PETER, ed. *Biographical Sketch of the Honourable Edward Whelan* (together with a compilation of his principal speeches). Charlottetown: McCourt. 1888.

MACKINNON, D. A. and WARBURTON, A. B., eds. *Past and Present in Prince Edward Island.* Charlottetown: Bowen. C. 1905.

MACMILLAN, JOHN C. *Early History of the Catholic Church in Prince Edward Island.* Quebec: L'Evénement. 1905.

MACQUEEN, MALCOLM. *Skye Pioneers and "the Island."* Winnipeg, privately printed, n.d.

MEACHAM, J. H. *Historical Atlas of Prince Edward Island.* Charlottetown: Bremner. 1880.

POLLARD, J. B. *Historical Sketch of the Eastern Regions of New France ... also Prince Edward Island: Military and Civil.* Charlottetown: Coombs. 1898.

PUTNAM, ADA MACLEOD. *The Selkirk Settlers and the Church They Built at Belfast.* Toronto: Presbyterian Publishing Co. 1939.

STEWART, JOHN. *An Account of Prince Edward Island.* London: Winchester. 1806.

WARBURTON, A. B. *A History of Prince Edward Island, 1534-1831.* Saint John: Barnes. 1923.

INDEX

INDEX

ABEGWEIT, 19
Abegweit, M.V., 303
Aberhart, William, 174n
Acadians, 3, 170
Administrator, *see* devolution of government
Admiralty, Court of, 260
　Judge of, 260
　law of, 22
Agriculture, Dept. of (P.E.I.), 203-4
　Minister of (P.E.I.), 171, 178
Alberta, 180n, 199n, 210n, 306, 312, 314n
Alberton, 280n
Alley, George, 269
amendment, constitutional, 137, 164, 214
annexation of P.E.I. to Nova Scotia, 4, 6, 17, 18, 70n, 77, 120-1
Aplin, Joseph, 39
Appeal, Courts of, 91-2, 260, 261, 262
appropriations, 70-4
Archibald, S. G. W., 57, 58-9, 68, 71, 271
arrest, freedom from, *see* privilege, parliamentary
Assembly (*see also* elections, franchise), 16, 26, 36, 40, 48, 54, 74, 86, 210-41
　chaplain of, 232n
　Clerk of, 50, 220n, 230, 232
　committees, 238-40; Committee of the Whole, 240; Committee on Elections, 50, 223
　constituencies, 215
　controverted elections and, 222-3
　councillors and assemblymen in, 215-16
　early development of, 41-53
　establishment of (1773), 14, 21; (1873), 210-14
　Executive Council and Cabinet and, 61, 62-6, 77, 88, 96-9, 161n, 169-74, 213, 218-20, 236
　federal politics and, 218-20
　franchise, *see* franchise
　lack of (1770-3), 13
　Legislative Council and, 62-6, 68, 70-4, 77, 96-9, 210-14
　length of session, 228-9, 236-7
　Lieutenant-Governor and, 44-8, 61, 68-70, 86-7, 150, 160, 210, 230, 233-4
　members, indemnities of, 227-8, 236; number of, 41, 51, 52-3, 215, 235, 237-8; resignation of, 225-7
　municipalities and, 275, 282-6
　officials of, 231-2
　opening of, 233-4
　Patterson, Walter, and, 23-4
　petitions, 50, 275
　privileges of, *see* privilege, parliamentary
　procedure in, 229-41
　provision for (1769), 9
　public funds and, 67-9
　qualification of members, 41, 51, 215, 227; of voters, 215-18
　report of proceedings, 238n
　representation, 215-29
　Speaker of, *see* Speaker
　term of, 53, 228
assent, *see* Lieutenant-Governor
Attorney-General (P.E.I.), 12, 27, 28, 39, 52, 54, 56, 97, 152, 178, 189n, 219, 268, 273, 296; Cabinet and, 98-9, 171, 173-4, 177, 203; provision for (1769), 10; suspension of, by Governor Smith, 48; two Attorneys-General in 1800, 39
　Dept. of, 202-3, 207
Attorney-General for P.E.I. v. Attorney-General for Canada, 292n
Aylesworth, Allen, 291-2

BACON, FRANCIS, 56
Bagehot, Walter, 150
Bank of P.E.I., 134n
Bankruptcy, Court of, 260
Bannerman, Sir A., 84-5, 86, 90, 94, 97, 100n, 111
Barbour, George, 174n, 272n
Baring Brothers, 134
Bates, Stewart, 305n
Bathurst, Lord, 27n, 30, 38, 46, 47, 75
Baxter, J. B. M., 182
Beauchesne, A., 48n, 233n
Bedford, 220
Beech Grove Infirmary, 206
Beer, Henry, 93-4
Belfast, election of 1846, 50n, 79
Bell, J. H., 178, 188-9, 238
Bennett, R. B., 246
Bermuda, 31n
Bernard, J. A., 153, 157-60
bills, procedure for passing, 237
Bishop of Charlottetown, 146
　of London, 10, 65
　of Nova Scotia, 24, 26, 121
Black Rod, Usher of, 233

375

Blake, Patrick, 232n
Board of Assessors, 279
    of Education, 203, 206
    of Health, 285
    of Pensions Commissioners, 208
    of School Trustees, 285
    of Trade, 4, 75n
    of Works, 204, 206
boards, 205-9
Bonanza Creek Gold Mining Co. v. The King, 143
Borden (town of), 280n
Borden, Sir Robert, 246, 292, 302, 308
Brebner, J. B., 128n
Brecken, F. D., 246
British Columbia, 151n, 176n, 180n, 183n, 186, 210, 290n, 306, 312, 314n
British Government, 4, 16, 77-8; appointment of Governors and, 29-31; assent and, 74-5, 158-9; Chief Justice and, 58; colonial finance and, 7; colonial legislation and, 75n; conditions in civil service and (1851-73), 98; Confederation and, 128-32; Crown revenues and, 69; Executive Councillors and, 66-7; external affairs (P.E.I.) and, 94-5; formation of Assembly and, 13, 42; Government House and, 154; Governor's relations with Assembly and, 47, 80; Governor's salary and, 33-4, 69-70, 86-7; Halifax Fishery Award and, 308n; land question and, 8, 77, 105-17, 129, 296-9; official despatches and, 15, 27-8, 87; pardon and, 152; Patterson-Fanning issue and, 25-7; President of the Legislative Council and, 101-4; P.E.I. communications and, 301; reduction of status of P.E.I. government (1784) and, 17-18; reform of Legislative Council and, 101-4; responsible government and, 76-85; selection of Ministers and, 94n, 97; separation of Executive and Legislative Councils and, 62-6; suspending clause and, 74
British North America Act, 124, 136; divorce and, 263; judiciary and, 259-60; Lieutenant-Governor and, 144, 147, 158-60, 159, 162; local government and, 274; representation in Parliament and, 290-3
    section (91), 137; section (92), 137; section (94), 137; section (95), 137
Bruce, A. F., 223-4

Budd, John, 16
budget, 237
Burns, Mr., 172
Butler, Benjamin, 95, 128n
Butler, W. Bruce, 189-90
Byng, Lord, 161n

CABINET (British), 181n, 182
Cabinet (Canadian), 154, 182; P.E.I. representation in, 145, 179, 267-8, 293-6
Cabinet (P.E.I.), 90, 168-94
    Assembly and, 88, 93, 96-9, 168-70, 213, 219-20, 230, 236
    change of personnel in, 178-9
    Court of Divorce and, 262-6
    early development of, *see* Council, Executive Council, Legislative Council
    formation of, 85
    government appointments and, 169
    land question and, 112-13, 115
    Legislative Council and, 96-9, 104
    Lieutenant-Governor and, 93, 144-5, 152-67, 168, 183
    meetings, 180
    Ministers, committees of the House and, 239; dismissal of, 93; election on appointment, 96-9, 161; financial bills and, 237; number of, 96; salaries of, 177-8; selection of, 94n, 96-9, 168-9, 201; without Portfolio, 98, 174-5, 178, 180, 192-3
    minutes of, 182-6
    municipal administration and, 275-6, 278, 279, 280, 281, 282-6
    number of members in, 169-71, 213, 214
    procedure, 179-86
    representation in, 170-1
    responsibility, 93, 166, 167n, 171-4, 236, 264n, 265, 273n
    secretary (Clerk) of, 152, 182-6
    solidarity, 39-40, 86, 92-3, 113, 186-94, 212n, 236, 237
    voting in meetings, 180-1
Callbeck, Philipps, 16, 88n
Campbell, Sir Colin, 64, 78, 111
    Donald, 66, 82-4
    Duncan, 5n
    J. A., 191-2, 193n, 232n
    Thane A., 159-60, 173, 174n, 289
    William, 172
    Lord William, 5, 6

INDEX 377

Canada, Government of (*see also* Cabinet (Canadian), Governor-General), 287-315; Dept. of Agriculture, 204; entry of P.E.I. into Confederation and, 128-40; financial negotiations with P.E.I., 306-15; judiciary and, 159-60, 259-68; land question and, 106, 129, 298-9; Lieutenant-Governor and, 145, 162-3; police protection and, 282; provincial legislation and, 234, *see also* disallowance; provincial politics and, 218-20; public works in P.E.I. and, 136n; social services and, 205, 284

Canada, Province of, 100, 123-4
Canadian Legion, 203
Canadian National Railways, 303-4
Canadian Pacific Railway, 300
Cape Breton, 27, 89n, 120, 122
Capell v. *Capell*, 263n
Cardwell, Edward, 158
Carleton, Sir Guy (Lord Dorchester), 8n, 16n, 19, 26, 27n
Carmichael, J. E., 46
Carnarvon, Lord, 106n
Carroll v. *The King*, 148
Cartwright, Sir Richard, 147n, 245
Carvell, J. S., 149, 160-1, 164, 166, 167
caucus, party, 190, 235, 236, 257-8
Caulfield, Rev. Mr., 13n
Champion, Helen Jean, 16n
Chancellor, 27, 261
Chancery, Court of, 27, 28, 260, 261-2
Charlottetown, 154-6; administration of, 275-9, 283; chosen as capital, 5; incorporation of, 275; poll organization in, 250; representation, in Assembly, 52, in Cabinet, 283; revenue of, 278-9, 285; secret ballot in, 218n
Charlottetown, S.S., 303
Charlottetown Conference of 1864, *see* Confederation
Chief Justice (Canada), 91n, 290
Chief Justice (P.E.I.) (*see also* judiciary, Supreme Court), 11, 12, 16, 17, 26, 27, 34, 38, 54-60, 179, 260-2, 269; as Administrator, 91-2; Divorce Court and, 262-6; extrajudicial duties of, 58; Lieutenant-Governor and, 24, 28; as President of Legislative Council, 36, 39, 58, 63, 65; provision for (1769), 10
Chiltern Hundreds, Stewardship of, 225n

Church of England, Bishop of Nova Scotia and, 121; Disestablishment Act, 156; first clergyman in P.E.I., 13
City Clerk (Charlottetown), 278
civil list, 83-4
civil service, 195-209; appointment to, 198-201; conditions in (1851-73), 98-9; development of, 195-7; political activities in, 98-9, 185-6, 199; reform of, 195-7, 198, 200-1, 209; responsibility for, 138; size of, 197; tenure, 198-9
Civil War (U.S.), 95
Clarke, Mary P., 44n, 48n
Clerk of the Crown and Coroner, 10, 16n
 of the Executive Council, 37, 182-6; *see also* Cabinet, secretary
 of the House, *see* Assembly
Cleverdon, Catherine L., 218n
Clokie, H. McD., 220n
coalition government, 93, 112-13, 132-3, 169, 187-8, 243, 306
Cockram, Thomas, 56
Coffin family, of Magdalene Islands, 121n
Colborne, Sir John, 64, 65n
Colclough, Caesar, 28, 39, 54, 55, 56
Coles, George, 84-5, 89-90, 96-9, 100, 125
Colonial Office, *see* British Government
 Secretary (P.E.I.), 98, 99, 204, 219
 Treasurer (P. E. I.), 201, 202
Commission and Instructions (*see also* Instructions), 10, 26-7, 65n; of Walter Patterson, 10, 21-2, 88, 143
Commission of Sewers and Water Supply (Charlottetown), 278, 279
commission on land question, *see* land question
Commissioner of Crown and Public Lands (P.E.I.), 203, 204
Commissioners, Cabinet members, 169n
 Courts of, for the Recovery of Small Debts, 266
 Village, 280
Committee on Good Correspondence, 102n
committees, of City Council (Charlottetown), 278
 of Legislature, *see* Assembly

378 INDEX

communications, 129, 135, 139, 300-4
compulsory voting, 42n
Confederation, 31, 32n, 87, 92, 119, 120-40; B.N.A. Act passed, 124; Charlottetown Conference, 122-4; communications and, 300-4; events leading up to, 120; land question and, 296-9; P.E.I. enters, 136; Quebec Conference, 123-4, 291n; terms of union, 136-40
Connaught, Prince Arthur of, 151n
Connecticut, 288
Conservative party, 55, 87, 93, 220; development of, 242-9; organization of, 249-58; reform of Legislative Council and, 100-4; salaried officers and, 96-9
constituencies, *see* elections
contested elections, *see* elections
Controller of Navigation Laws, 99
controverted elections, *see* elections
conventions, party, 255-8
Cooper, William, 29n, 65n, 113-15
Co-operative Commonwealth Federation, 248
coroners' courts, 260
Corry, J. A., 274n
Cotton, W. L., 87n
Council (*see also* Executive Council, Legislative Council), 16, 21, 22; appointment of first Council, 13; changed to two Councils (1773), 36; description of, 34-41; land question and, 112; Patterson-Fanning issue and, 26; powers of, 34-5; provided in constitution, 9; separation of two Councils (1838), 60, 62-6, 73
Council, City (Charlottetown), 276-8
Council of Education, 203, 206, 209
county courts (*see also* judiciary), 57, 60, 92, 259, 260, 266-7, 272
 organization (party), 252-4
courts (*see also* judiciary), 138, 198-9
Creighton, D. G., 306n
Crown attorneys, 203
 company, 208-9
criminal law, 259
Cullen, Mr. Speaker, 232n
Cummiskey, J. H., 225n
Cunard, Sir Samuel, 107, 109n
Currie, Dougald, 226n

DALTON, CHARLES, 149n, 153, 162n, 234n
Daly, Dominic, 86, 90, 97, 112
Davies, Benjamin, 94
 Louis, 112-13, 169, 179n, 187-8, 228n, 243, 246, 256n,
290, 292n, 293n, 294, 295n, 306
Dawson, R. MacG., 48n, 146n, 182n, 219n, 234n, 260n, 267n, 293n, 295n
DeBlois, G. D., 145n, 147
 G. W., 187n, 188n
debt allowance, 129, 139, 305
decimal system, adoption of, 132
departments, government, organization of, 169, 201-9
deposit (election), 222
Deputy Provincial Secretary, 184-7, 197, 202
 Treasurer, 176
 Speaker, 231
DesBarres, J. F. W., 27n, 28, 30, 31, 37, 40, 54, 55, 57, 72, 89n
DesBrisay, Thomas, 23, 37, 38, 89n, 183-4
despatches, transmission of, 28-9, 79, 80, 87
DesRoches, S., 269n
devolution of government, 10, 22, 34, 88-92
Dewar, J. A., 248
disallowance, 21, 74-5, 137, 138, 161n, 234n, 298n
dissolution, *see* Lieutenant-Governor
district organization (party), 251-2
Divorce, Court of, 168n, 260, 262-6
Dobell, R. R., 294n
Dominion Government, *see* Canada, Government of
Dominion-provincial relations, 287-315
Dorchester, Lord, *see* Carleton, Sir Guy
Doughty, A. G., 8n, 16n, 19n, 126n
Doyle, Governor, 122
drafting (of statutes), 75
Dufferin, Lord, 140, 151n
Duffy, C. G., 233n
Duncan Commission, 299, 302, 304n
Dundas, George, 31, 32, 86, 93n, 95, 122
Dunkin, Christopher, 146n, 163n
Dunning, C. A., 294n
Duport, John, 12, 14, 16, 58
Durham, Lord, 64, 105, 109n, 116-17, 120

EDUCATION, administration of, 197n, 203, 284-5
 Council of, 203, 206, 209
 Dept. of (P.E.I.), 203
 Minister of (P.E.I.), 203, 220n, 284
Eggleston, W., 305n
Egmont, Earl of, 4

INDEX 379

elections (*see also* franchise), 41-2; constituencies, 52, 53, 215; controverted, 222-5; deposits, 222; disputed, 50, 222; first, 41; municipal, 276-81; nomination, 221-2; outside influences in, 221; party organization and, 249-58; procedure of, 221-5; time of, 52
Elgin, Lord, 83
Equity, Court of, 260
escape, voluntary and involuntary, 153n
Estates of Intestates Administration Act of 1882, 161n
Examiner, 170, 206, 288
Exchequer Court of Canada, 148n, 259
Executive Council (*see also* Cabinet, Council), 58, 61-2, 77; Assembly and, 77-9, 96-9; composition of, 64-6, 77-9; election of members when appointed, 66-7, 80-1; establishment of, 36; separation from Legislative Council, 60, 62-6, 73; solidarity in, 39-40, 67n

FACTORIES IN INCORPORATED CITIES BILL (1881), 157
Falconwood Hospital, 205, 206
family compact, 37-8, 43, 54, 66, 68, 78-9, 81
Fanning, Edmund, 24-5, 30, 31, 32, 89n, 110, 112, 154
Farquharson, Donald, 170, 179n, 226, 232n, 294-5, 295n
Fay, C. R., 289n
Federation of Agriculture, 203
Ferguson, Donald, 213
Fielding, W. S., 308
finance, provincial, 304-15
fisheries, 4, 5
Fishermen's Loan Board, 206n, 208, 220n, 269n
FitzGerald, Lord, 260
Fitzroy, Sir Charles, 31, 64, 65, 73, 89, 110, 114-15, 116
Forsey, E. A., 153n, 160n, 161n, 164n, 171n, 220n
franchise (*see also* Assembly, elections), 41-3, 51-3, 156, 215-29; compulsory voting, 42n; legislative reform and, 210-14; municipal, 276-81; property franchise, 104, 112; plural voting, 216; qualifications of members of Assembly, 215, of voters for councillors and assemblymen, 215-18; secret ballot, 218; structure of constituencies, 215; woman suffrage, 217-18

Francklin, Michael, 5, 6
freedom of speech, *see* privilege, parliamentary

GEORGETOWN, 281; incorporation of, 280; secret ballot in, 218n
Gladstone, W. E., 70, 80, 82n
Glenelg, Lord, 60, 63, 64, 65, 82n, 89, 114
Globe (Toronto), 213
Goderich, Lord, 29
Goff, Fade, 36n
Goldenberg, H. C., 274n
Gordon, Governor (N.B.), 130
Government House, 33, 148, 154, 156, 157, 164, 165, 233n
Governor (*see also* Lieutenant-Governor), changed to Lieutenant-Governor, 18, 184; early difficulties of, 11-20; first, 10; provided for in constitution, 9
Governor-General, 19, 26, 64, 83, 89n, 91, 132, 233, 260; entry of P.E.I. into Confederation and, 128-9, 140; Lieutenant-Governor and, 143-4, 150, 154-7
grants-in-aid, 129
Granville, Lord, 119, 301
Gray, J. H. (N.B.), 118n
  J. H. (P.E.I.), 104, 113, 122, 125, 127, 128, 131, 244
  Robert, 37, 89n
Great Seal, 22, 27
Greene, E. B., 8, 11n, 26
Grey, Lord, 32, 67, 80-5
  Sir George, 33, 95, 117-18
Guardian, 191n, 238n

HALIFAX FISHERY AWARD, 307-8
Halliburton, Brenton, 28
Hansard, 238, 191n
Harvey, D. C., 4n, 132n
  Sir John, 30, 31, 33, 63, 64, 73, 110, 114-15, 116
Hatherley, Lord, 163n
Haviland, T. H., 38
  T. H., Jr., 148n, 154, 167, 219
Hay River meeting, 114n
Haythorne, R. P., 87, 93, 94, 99, 104, 133-5, 219, 244, 307
Health and Welfare, Dept. of (P.E.I.), 200n, 205, 283, 285,
  Minister of (P.E.I.), 178, 208, 209, 220n
Health Planning Commission, 209
health units, 285

INDEX

Heartz, F. R., 145n, 147
Hebbert v. *Purchas,* 163n
Heeney, A. D. P., 182n
Henderson, Kenneth, 93, 172
Hensley, Joseph, 95, 172, 268
Hillsborough, Earl of, 5, 6
Hodgson, E. J., 223-5, 265n, 276
   Robert, 38n, 51, 52, 91, 145n, 148n, 154, 244, 263n, 268
Holl, John, 90, 100
Holland, Samuel, 4, 59
House of Commons (British), 43, 61, 225n, 235
   (Canadian), 167, 179, 225n, 240, 260; P.E.I. representation in, 139, 145, 245, 287, 288, 290-3, 293n; privileges of, 235; rules of, 238
House of Lords, 213
Howe, Joseph, 76, 105, 118n, 130
Hughes, William, 174n, 192n
Huntley, H. V., 30, 40, 49, 73, 79, 121n, 152, 170

IMPEACHMENT OF JUDGES, 266
Imperial Government, *see* British Government
incorporation of towns, 279-80
independents, 248
Industries and Natural Resources, Dept. of (P.E.I.), 205-6
   Minister of (P.E.I.), 208
Instructions (*see also* Commission and Instructions), 10, 41, 44, 71, 80, 158, 162, 163, 166

JARVIS, Chief Justice, 57
Jenkins, J. T., 49n, 232n, 269n
Johnston, J. J., 165, 188-9
   William, 28
Jones, J. Walter, 171n, 174, 176n, 190, 191, 248, 257, 303, 312
Judicial Committee of the Privy Council, 260, 292
judiciary (*see also* Chief Justice, country courts, Supreme Court), appointment of, 138, 179, 259-60, 295-6; description of, 259-73; early development of, 56-60, 91-2; independence of, 58-60, 92, 223-5, 269-70; number of judges, 92, 188-9, 270-3
Justice, Dept. of (P.E.I.), 202-3
   Minister of (P.E.I.), 267

KEITH, A. B., 7n, 165, 193
Kelly, F. C., 150
Kelly v. *Sullivan,* 298n
Kempt, Sir James, 28, 68
Kensington, 280n
Kent, Duke of, 20, 120
Kimberley, Lord, 131, 132, 134
King, His Majesty the, 43, 150, 151n, 233
King, W. L. Mackenzie, 161n, 246, 294n, 302
Knaplund, Paul, 62n
Kraft, C. T., 305n

LABAREE, L. W., 89n
Laird, Alexander, 212n
   David, 132n, 135, 219, 244, 245, 246, 307
Land Purchase Act, 155, 156, 297-8
land question, 4, 51, 74, 75, 92, 94, 95-6, 105-19, 164, 203, 213-14; commission on, 106n, 108, 118-19; Confederation and, 129, 132, 135, 139; Governor and, 109-12, 155; settlement of, 296-9; settlers and, 106-7
Large, F. A., 173
Laskin, Bora, 159n
Laurier, Sir Wilfrid, 246, 288, 294, 301-2, 309
law, practice of, 56, 57, 269
Lea, W. M., 178, 189
Leacock, Stephen, 3
Leader of the Opposition, *see* Opposition, Leader of the
Legislative Assembly, *see* Assembly
Legislative Council (*see also* Council), abolition of, 156, 210-14; Assembly and, 62-6, 68, 70-4, 77, 86, 96-9, 102n; composition of, 64-6, 72, 73, 78-9, 102-4; controverted elections and, 223; dissolution of, 103; election of, 65, 99-104; establishment of, 36, 39; President of, 36, 39, 58, 63, 65, 90, 91, 100; representation in Cabinet and, 96-9, 104; separation from Executive Council, 60, 62-6, 73
Legislature Act (1893), 215-16
LePage, B. W., 147, 155, 157, 166, 167
Liberal party, 55, 87, 93, 149, 220; development of, 242-9; organization of, 249-58; reform of Legislative Council and, 100-4; salaried officers and, 96-9
Lieutenant-Governor (*see also* Governor), 11, 16, 17, 18, 40, 57, 98, 137, 138, 143-67, 179

INDEX 381

adjustment to responsible government, 86-92
appointment of, 29-32, 137, 143, 144-7, 295-6
Assembly and, 23-24, 43, 44-8, 53, 68, 77-81, 95n, 150, 210, 225-6, 230, 233-4
assent, giving of, 144, 152, 157-60, 234, 237; withholding of, 74-5, 144, 153, 154-5, 161n
British Government and, 28-9
Cabinet and, 93, 144-5, 152-67, 172, 183, 210
Chief Justice and, 58, 92n
in colonial period, 21-34, 183
Commission and Instructions, *see* Commission and Instructions
Confederation and, 130-1
dissolution and, 53, 55, 143, 160-1, 228
Executive Council and, 77-8, 81
first powers of, 21-22
formal and decorative functions of, 86, 143, 148, 150-1
independence of, 69-70, 147n
judicial functions of, 27-8, 261, 262-8
land question and, 109-12
Patterson and Fanning issue, 24-6
personnel, 144-9
political independence of, 146, 166
politics after retirement, 149
power of pardon, 152, 153
Premier and, 87-8, 93, 168-9
refusal to approve appointments, 162n
removal of, 137, 143
reservation of bills, 137, 138, 153, 155-7, 161n, 162-7, 214, 297
salary of, 12, 33-4, 69-70, 70n, 79, 83, 86-7, 130, 137, 138, 147, 148-9
term of office, 31-2; second term, 146-7
Lieutenant-Governor-in-Council, *see* Cabinet
Liquidators of the Maritime Bank of Canada v. Receiver-General of New Brunswick, 143
Livingston, W. R., 76n
Lord, W. W., 172
Lorne, Marquis of, 151n
Louisburg, 3
Louise, Princess, 151n
Low, Sidney, 182n
Lowell, A. L., 186

Lower Canada, 62, 64, 76, 78
"Loyal Electors," 54-5, 61
Loyalists, 54

MACARMIC, WILLIAM, 27n
Maccallum, Peter, 78
McCourt, Peter, 97n
McCready, J. E. B., 42n
Macdonald, A. A., 126n, 146, 162n
          A. C., 149n
          Sir John A., 123, 128, 129, 131, 134-5, 164, 165, 182n, 221, 244, 246, 269, 301, 307
McGee, T. D'Arcy, 125
McGowan, Peter, 39n
McIntyre, J. P., 190n
MacKay, R. A., 165n
MacKenzie, Alexander, 245
Mackie case, 153n
MacKinnon, D. A., 57, 148n, 263n
          Frank, 132n, 133n, 153n, 168n, 245n, 300n
         Murdoch, 154, 155, 224-5
McLean, John, 263n
MacLeod, Neil, 161, 166, 228n
MacMillan, W. J. P., 313n
MacPhail, Alexander, 227
McQuaid, "Paddy," 232n
Magdalene Islands, 121
magistrates' courts, 260, 267
Mallory, J. R., 153n
Manitoba, 306, 312, 314n; Cabinet meetings in, 180n, 181n; Cabinet secretary in, 186; Legislative Council of, 210n; Lieutenant-Governor of, 147n; representation in Senate, 290n; Treasury Board of, 176n
Maritime Freight Rates Act (1927), 304n
Maritime Union, 122-3, 288-9
Martin, Chester, 9n, 12n, 64n, 78n
      K. M., 159n
Massachusetts, 10
Master in Chancery, 27, 28, 261
Master of the Rolls, 91, 261-2
Mathieson, J. A., 57, 225, 238, 246, 263n, 269n, 292, 302, 308
Maxwell, J. A., 126n, 132n, 305n, 307n
mayors of municipalities, 275-86
Meighen, Arthur, 161n
Melvin, George G., 289n
members of the Legislature, *see* Assembly
Mercer v. Attorney-General of Ontario, 143

militia, 26, 114
Milligan, Frank, 153n
Minister of Justice (Canada), 296
Ministers, see Cabinet
Minto, Lord, 91n
minutes of Council, 152
molestation, see privilege, parliamentary
Monck, Lord, 122
Montague, 280n, 281
municipal government, 274-86
Murphy, Senator, 263n

NAMING, 238
"National Policy," 307
New Anglesea, 20
Newbery, Arthur, 196
New Brunswick, 17, 31, 62, 63n, 64, 68, 71, 120, 122, 124, 125, 182, 288, 306, 312, 314n; Cabinet meetings in, 180n; Legislative Council of, 210n; representation in House of Commons, 291-2, in Senate, 290n
Newcastle, Duke of, 90, 118-19
Newfoundland, 19, 57, 124, 132, 199n; boat service to, 208-9, 307
New Guernsey, 20
New Hampshire, 288
New Ireland, 19
Northumberland Ferries Ltd., 303n
Northwest Territories, 246, 314n
Nova Scotia, 62, 64, 76, 78, 119, 122, 124, 125, 126, 132, 306, 312, 314n; Cabinet meetings in, 180n; Legislative Council of, 210n; P.E.I. government and, 4, 6, 7, 17-18, 28, 54, 57, 58-9, 68, 71, 72, 89n, 105, 120-1, 128, 288-9; representation in Senate, 290n; Treasury Board of, 176n

O'BRIEN, Archbishop, 146n
Ogg, F. A., 225n
Ontario, 180n, 186, 210n, 246-7, 263n, 306, 312, 314n
Opposition, 90, 101, 167, 189, 190, 191, 229, 230, 236, 239, 313
Opposition, Leader of the, 49, 96, 167n, 191, 227, 235, 257-8
Orange Lodge, 92, 127, 154, 156, 188
Osgood, H. L., 9n

"PACIFIC SCANDAL," 245
Palmer, Edward, 81, 96, 97-9, 104, 112, 172, 269
H. J., 226
J. B., 45, 54-5

Papineau, L. J., 76
pardon, power of, 21, 152, 153
Paris, Treaty of, 4
Parliament (British), 223
(Canadian) (see also House of Commons, Senate), 138, 223, 287
parliamentary grant, 12, 43, 45, 68-9, 79, 83
privilege, see privilege, parliamentary
Parr, John, 18, 89n
parties, political, 91, 93, 242-58; beginnings of, 53-6, 242-3; conventions, 255-8; development of, 243-9; federal politics and, 244-7; leadership of, 248-9, 257-8; organization of, 249-58; responsible government and, 55-6
Patriot, 213, 238n, 245, 276, 288, 289
patronage, 37-8, 198-200, 249
Patterson, Walter, 10, 11, 12, 31, 121n; Commission and Instructions of, 10, 21-2, 88, 143; difficulties of administration, 11-20, 22-5, 41; dismissal of, 25; recall of, 24
Peddlers, Bill Respecting (1894), 157
Pensions Commissioners, Board of, 206, 208
Perry, Stanislaus, 219, 225n
Peters, Arthur, 161n, 220, 224-5, 291
Frederick, 161, 227, 232n
J. H., 269
Philipps, Colonel, 11
Physical Fitness, Director of, 199n
Pineau affair, 227n
poll organization, 250-1
Pope, J. C., 87-8, 93, 112, 127n, 131, 132-3, 135-6, 179n, 202, 219, 244, 246, 307
Joseph, 38n, 79-81, 112
W. H., 123, 127n, 128, 131n, 244
Pownal, Thomas, 10
Premier, 98-9, 178-9, 180, 268, 283, 296; as Administrator, 90; dissolution and, 228; first Premier, 85; in Legislative Council, 98, 104; Lieutenant-Governor and, 145, 168-9; salary of, 177-8; selection of, 152-3, 168; selection of Ministers and, 96, 168-70
President, of Executive Council, 177, 181-2; of Legislative Council, see Legislative Council
Prime Minister, 145, 267, 296
Prince Edward Island, communications in, 300-4; Confederation and,

120-40; disintegration of government (1775-85), 16; Dominion-provincial relations and, 287-315; early history of, 3-4; establishment of government, 9-20; federal Cabinet and, 293-6; finances of, 304-15; first government of, 5; land question, *see* land question; name of, 19-20; reduction of status (1784), 17-19; relations with neighbouring colonies, 120-1; responsible government achieved, 85; separation from Nova Scotia (1769), 6-7
Prince Edward Island, S.S., 303n
Prince Edward Island Industrial Corporation, 206n, 208-9
Prince of Wales College, 203
Prince Regent, 30n
Princetown, 51
privilege, parliamentary, 43-51, 71, 222, 234-5
Privy Council, 260, 292
Probate, Court of, 260, 266
        Judge of, 90n, 138, 260, 266
Proctor, King's, 266
Progressive Conservative party, *see* Conservative party
Progressive party, 248
prohibition, 152, 155, 206-7, 221, 247
Prohibition Act (1945), 157-60, 193-4, 237
proprietors (*see also* land question), 6-7, 8-9, 14, 16, 51-2, 68, 74, 77, 105-19, 138-9, 296-9
prorogation, 234
Protestants, public office and, 146, 170
Provincial Health Planning Commission, 209
provincial organization (party), 254-5
Provincial Secretary, 176n, 221; Dept. of, 202; as secretary to the Cabinet, 152, 184-7
Provincial Treasurer, 49, 65, 176, 209; Dept. of, 201-2
Provost Marshal (*see also* Sheriff), 10, 16, 57, 65
Prowse, Samuel, 246
Public Health Act, 285
public opinion, 42, 43, 51, 211, 237, 247, 249
Public Service Superannuation Board, 209
Public Utilities Commission, 207-8
Public Works, Dept. of (P.E.I.), 204
        Minister of (P.E.I.), 178, 207, 219

QUEBEC, 19, 263, 180n, 306, 312, 314n; Legislative Council of, 210n; woman suffrage in, 218
Queen's Printer, 49, 99
quit rents, 7, 9, 12, 13, 14, 33, 43, 105-6

RAILWAYS, Confederation and, 131, 132-4, 139
Railway Extension Bill (1872), 159n
Ralston, J. L., 294n
Ready, John, 30, 31, 39, 48, 58, 69, 71, 72
Reconstruction, Dept. of (P.E.I.), 205n
        Dominion-Provincial Conference on, 312
        Minister of (P.E.I.), 220n
Red Cross Society, 284
Reddin, O. M., 270
Red River, 132
Reference re Disallowance and Reservation, 162
Registrar of Deeds, 99
Reid, E. M., 245n
religion and politics, *see* Orange Lodge, school question
reservation of bills, *see* Lieutenant-Governor
responsible government, 51, 53, 55, 61-85, 92, 94, 94n, 95-6, 98, 100, 111, 115-16, 144, 164, 210
Rhode Island, 287, 288
Richard II, 21
Riddell, W. R., 57n
Ripon, Lord, 63n
Ritchie, J. W., 118n
Robinson, William, 86, 87-8, 128, 130-1, 133, 138, 144, 159n
Rogers, Benjamin, 149, 151, 257n
        N. McL., 293n, 294
Roman Catholics, Bishop of Quebec, 121; enfranchisement of, 53; public office and, 146, 170
Ronhell, William, 31n
Rose, Sir John, 134-5
Ross, Charles W., 245n
        W. B., 263n
Rowell-Sirois Commission, 271, 299, 306, 310-11
Roy, J. A., 105n
royal assent, *see* Lieutenant-Governor
Royal Canadian Mounted Police, 282
Royal Commission on Transportation, 303n
Russell, Lord John, 29, 70n, 77-8, 81, 115, 118

INDEX

SAGE, W. N., 183n
Saint-Jean, Ile, 19
salaries, 7, 12, 16, 33, 130; of civil servants, 198, 200-1; of judges, 7, 12, 260, 266, 267, 269; of Lieutenant-Governor, 12, 33-4, 69-70, 70n, 79, 83, 86-7, 130, 137, 138, 147, 148-9; of Ministers, 98-9, 177-8; of teachers, 284-5
Sanitarium Commission, 206, 208
Saskatchewan, 180n, 210n, 306, 312, 314n
Saunders, S. A., 310n
school question, 56, 92, 127, 132-3, 187-8, 221, 243
schools, administration of, 197, 284-5
secret ballot, 218
Selkirk, Lord, 39, 111
Senate, 260; appointments to, 295-6; divorce committee of, 263; representation in, 139, 145, 290
Sergeant-at-Arms, 41, 49, 114, 226, 232, 233, 234
Settlement, Act of, 219
Seymour, Lord William, 91n
Sheriff (*see also* Provost Marshal), 48, 50, 78, 153, 162n
Shortt, A., 8n, 16, 19n
Sinclair, Peter, 134n
Smith, C. D., 28, 30, 31, 37, 40, 44-8, 54, 55, 68, 69, 72, 75
    Goldwin, 145n, 148, 153
    Henry, 46
    Sir Sydney, 30n
    W. Sidney, 298n
social services, 205, 284
Solicitor-General, 31n, 36, 203n, 219
Souris, incorporation of, 280n; secret ballot in, 218n
Speaker, of the Assembly (*see also* privilege, parliamentary), 23, 29, 42n, 49, 65, 66, 69, 79-81, 94, 97, 114, 122, 127, 167, 225-7, 230-3, 238; appointment of, 171, 230-1; duties of, 232-4; Governor Smith and, 46; resignation of, 225; salary of, 227
Speech from the Throne, 233-4, 237
Spring-Rice, 63n
Stanley, Lord, 38, 118
Stephen, James, 29n, 31, 46, 47n, 72n, 74, 117-18
Stewart, Charles, 37, 54-5, 184
    J. D., 178
    John, 15n, 23-4, 37, 51n
    Peter, 23-4, 37, 38, 56, 58
    Mrs. Peter, 24
    R. B., 136n
    W. F. Alan, 192n
    W. S., 272

Strong, Sir Henry, 91n
subsidies, 139, 299, 306, 309
Sullivan, W. W., 146, 154, 170, 187, 188, 196n, 212-14, 244, 246, 268n, 285, 301
Summerside, 285; incorporation of, 279; poll organization in, 250; wards in, 281
Superintendent of Old Age Pensions, 199n
Supreme Court (Canada), 91n, 148n, 259, 260, 290, 291-2, 298
    (P.E.I.) *see also* judiciary, Chief Justice), 38, 39n, 199, 207-8, 297; appointments to, 179, 188-9, 267-73, 153, 159-60; controverted elections and, 223-5; description of, 260-2; early history of, 56-60; establishment of, 14, 21; judges of, 59-60n; Lieutenant-Governor and, 26, 28
Surveyor-General, 38, 89n
suspending clause, 74
Swan, Michael, 12
Sydenham, Lord, 70n, 83

TASMANIA, 287
teachers, payment and supervision of, 197, 284-5
Teachers' Federation, 203
Temperance Commission, 206-7
    Federation, 155, 167
tenant league, 107
tenants, *see* land question
term, of the Assembly, *see* Assembly
Thompson, C. P., *see* Sydenham, Lord
Thorpe, Robert, 56
Ticket of Leave Act, 152
Tilley, L. P. D., 182n
    Sir Leonard, 136
Town Act, 281
Town Major, 90, 91
towns, administration of, 279-82, 285
Townsend, William, 37
Travel Bureau, Director of, 199n
Treasury, *see* Provincial Treasurer
Treasury Board, 176
Tremlett, Thomas, 55, 57, 58
Trotter, R. G., 124n
Tupper, Sir Charles, 245, 255, 301
Tupper Club, 255
Twentieth Century Liberal Club, 254

INDEX 385

United Church of Canada Act, 155
United States, 94, 95, 97, 128, 132, 390
Upper Canada, 56, 62, 64, 76, 78

Veterans, divorce and, 264; voting privileges of, 215
Vice Chancellor, 261-2
Victoria, Queen, 20
Village Service Act, 280, 285n
voting, *see* elections, franchise

Walker, Frank, 191n
want of confidence, motion of, 188, 228
Warburton, A. B., 56n, 57n, 263n 270
  James, 66
wardens, village, 280
wards, 275; proposed abolition of, 276n
"warming pan" Ministry, 99n
Washington, Treaty of, 307-8
Wentworth, John, 39

Westminster Palace Hotel conference, 124
Whelan, Edward, 97n, 100, 123n, 125n
White, Sir Thomas, 308, 309, 315
White Commission, 269n, 299, 310
Whitelaw, W. M., 121n, 123n, 132n
Wight, Martin, 57n, 62n
Wightman, Joseph, 212n
Willison, Sir John, 247
Wilson, G. E., 130n
Winsloe Bill, 158-9
Wise, Mr., 226-7
Witness and Evidence Act, 161n
woman suffrage, 217-18
Women's Institutes, 203
Wright, George, 89n
  Horace, 193-4, 248
  Thomas, 37, 38

Young, Aretus, 37, 69, 73, 110
  Charles, 90
Young Progressive Conservative Association, 255
Yukon, 314n